HAMLET IN PURGATORY

STEPHEN GREENBLATT

Hamlet in Purgatory

PRINCETON UNIVERSITY PRESS

PRINCETON AND OXFORD

Copyright © 2001 by Princeton University Press
Published by Princeton University Press, 41 William Street,
Princeton, New Jersey 08540
In the United Kingdom: Princeton University Press, 3 Market Place,
Woodstock, Oxfordshire OX20 1SY

Library of Congress Cataloging-in-Publication Data

Greenblatt, Stephen, 1943–
Hamlet in purgatory / Stephen Greenblatt.
p. cm.
Includes bibliographical references and index.
ISBN 0-691-05873-3 (alk. paper)
1. Shakespeare, William, 1564–1616. Hamlet. 2. Purgatory in literature.
3. Christianity and literature—England—History—17th century.
4. Christianity and literature—England—History—16th century.
5. English drama (Tragedy)—Christian influences. 6. Voyages to
the otherworld in literature. 7. Ghosts in literature.
8. Tragedy. I. Title.
PR2807 .G69 2001
822.3'3—dc21   00-060667

This book has been composed in Baskerville and Caslon

Printed on acid-free paper. ∞

www.pup.princeton.edu

Printed in the United States of America

1 3 5 7 9 10 8 6 4 2

For Ramie

CONTENTS

ILLUSTRATIONS

PLATES

(following p. 52)

FIGURES

ACKNOWLEDGMENTS

As is appropriate for a book about Purgatory, I have benefited greatly from the kindness of loved ones, friends, and strangers. I have deep debts of gratitude to both institutions and individuals who have helped me bring this project to completion. An invitation to deliver the University Lectures at Princeton University provided me with the key incentive to work out my ideas, and I received helpful criticism, suggestions, and encouragement from many friends there, including Oliver Arnold, Lawrence Danson, Anthony Grafton, Alvin Kernan, and Froma Zeitlin. A year at the marvelous Wissenschaftskolleg zu Berlin was invaluable. The Rektor, Prof. Dr. Wolf Lepenies, the superb staff, and the intense intellectual stimulation of the Kolleg created an ideal space for research and writing—and the fact that Berlin is haunted by ghosts was itself a powerful inducement to reflect on the claims of the dead and the obligations of the living. I have been fortunate in other institutional supports as well, including the extraordinary resources of the British Library, the Getty Library in Los Angeles, and the Houghton and Widener Libraries at Harvard University. The intellectual seriousness and high distinction of my colleagues and students at Harvard have been equally remarkable resources. A residence at the Rockefeller Foundation Study and Conference Center in Bellagio and a Corrour Symposium enabled me to think and write in almost absurdly beautiful surroundings.

Now, as in the past, I have been struck by the remarkable intellectual generosity of scholars. I have had the opportunity to present pieces of this book as lectures, and on each and every one of these occasions I have profited greatly from advice and argument, often pursued in subsequent e-mail exchanges. I particularly want to thank the Medical Anthropology and Cultural Psychiatry Research Seminar at Harvard University; the Seminar on Society, Belief, and Culture in the Early Modern World at the University of London; the Center for Research in Early Modern History, Culture, and Science at the Johann Wolfgang Goethe-Universistät in Frankfurt; the conference on "Rituale Heute" at the University of Zürich; the conference on "Lancastrian Shakespeare" at Lancaster University; the New Europe College in Bucharest, Romania; the Center for Literary Studies at the Hebrew University in Jerusalem; Kyoto University, Tokyo University, and the Suntory Foundation in Japan; and the Indian Institute of Technology and the Indian Academy of Letters in New Delhi.

The list of individuals who have helped me could be extended for many pages, but I will content myself with naming a few whose assistance with this book has been particularly important to me: Homi Bhabha, Natalie Zemon Davis, Philip Fisher, Carlo Ginzberg, Valentin Groebner, Richard Helgerson, David Kastan, Jeffrey Knapp, Joseph Koerner, Lisbet Koerner, Thomas Laqueur, François Laroque, Franco Marenco, J. Hillis Miller, Robert Pinsky, Peter Sacks, Elaine Scarry, Pippa Skotnes, Nicholas Watson, and Bernard Williams. Debora Shuger brought to the whole manuscript her characteristic spiritual intensity, rich learning, and penetrating intelligence. John Maier and Gustavo Secchi have been indefatigable and resourceful research assistants; Beatrice Kitzinger and John Lopez made many valuable suggestions. As always, my sons, Josh and Aaron, have listened patiently, asked crucial questions, and prodded me in new directions. It seems appropriate too, given my subject, to reflect with gratitude on all I owe to my father, who died in 1983, and to my mother, who died—it pains me to write—just as I was finishing this book.

I have left for last my acknowledgment of the deepest bond, the most cherished indebtedness, to the person who has been essential in every way to meeting the challenges and sharing the pleasures of this project: my wife, Ramie Targoff.

HAMLET IN PURGATORY

PROLOGUE

THIS IS a book about the afterlife of Purgatory, the echoes of its dead name. Specifically, it is about the traces of Purgatory in *Hamlet* (1601). Thus described, my project seems very tightly focused, but since Purgatory was a creation of Western Christendom as a whole, I found I could not neatly restrict my account, geographically or culturally: Ireland plays an important role, as do France, Italy, and Germany. But my principal concern is with England; to understand what Shakespeare inherited and transformed, we need to understand the way in which Purgatory, the middle space of the realm of the dead, was conceived in English texts of the later Middle Ages and then attacked by English Protestants of the sixteenth and early seventeenth centuries. That attack, as we will see, focused on the imagination: Purgatory, it was charged, was not simply a fraud; it was a piece of poetry. The terms of this attack in turn, I will argue, facilitated Shakespeare's crucial appropriation of Purgatory in *Hamlet*.

As such sketches often do, this one reverses the order in which this book actually evolved. I began with the notion of writing a book about Shakespeare as a Renaissance conjurer. By the term "conjurer" I simply mean someone who has the power to call forth or make contact through language with those things—voices, faces, bodies, and spirits—that are absent. Shakespeare possessed this power to an extraordinary degree, and I wanted to explore some of its sources. I made starts in several different directions: an essay on *Macbeth* and Shakespeare's great contemporary, Reginald Scot, who blamed witchcraft persecutions on a misplaced faith in poets' metaphors; an essay on the peculiar absence in Shakespeare's drama, even in a play like *King Lear* about extreme old age, of what we would term "natural death"; several essays on

Shakespeare's theatrical appropriation of the Eucharist.[1] Above all, I found myself drawn again and again to the weird, compelling ghost in *Hamlet*, and I set aside the overarching project to concentrate on that single figure.

My goal was not to understand the theology behind the ghost; still less, to determine whether it was "Catholic" or "Protestant." My only goal was to immerse myself in the tragedy's magical intensity. It seems a bit absurd to bear witness to the intensity of *Hamlet*, but my profession has become so oddly diffident and even phobic about literary power, so suspicious and tense, that it risks losing sight of—or at least failing to articulate—the whole reason anyone bothers with the enterprise in the first place. The ghost in *Hamlet* is like none other—not only in Shakespeare but in any literary or historical text that I have ever read. It does not have very many lines—it appears in three scenes and speaks only in two—but it is amazingly disturbing and vivid. I wanted to let the feeling of this vividness wash over me, and I wanted to understand how it was achieved.

I believe that nothing comes of nothing, even in Shakespeare. I wanted to know where he got the matter he was working with and what he did with that matter. And so the broad inquiry that had come to focus more and more sharply on one figure in a single play spread out once again to encompass a dauntingly large field. Many of the key features of this field—the "poetics" of Purgatory in England and the struggle over its existence—do not align themselves conveniently with elements in *Hamlet* or in any of Shakespeare's plays. For example, Prince Hamlet does not worry that he, like his father, may serve a prison term in Purgatory (though he does worry that his soul might go to Hell), and Shakespeare never in his career seems drawn to the argument that ghost stories were cynical devices wielded by wolvish priests to extract wealth from the gullible. But I believe strongly that the historical and contextual work that literary critics do succeeds only if it acquires its own compelling imaginative interest, a powerful gravitational pull that makes it feel almost wrenching to turn back to the thing that was the original focus of interest. And paradoxically it is this independent interest—the fascination that I at least have found in Saint

Patrick's Purgatory and *The Gast of Gy* and the *Supplication of Souls*, along with trentals, indulgences, chantries, and requiem masses— that makes the whole subject seem worthy of *Hamlet.*

For even when in the course of this book I seem to be venturing far away from *Hamlet*, the play shapes virtually everything I have to say. This is in part because *Hamlet* has made so central a contribution to what Joel Fineman calls "the subjectivity effect" in Western consciousness that it has helped to condition the sensibilities of its readers and auditors.[2] In part, too, it is because my interest in what years ago I called a cultural poetics, adapting the term from Clifford Geertz, requires a certain hermeneutical patience, a willingness to suspend direct literary analysis, in order to examine more thoroughly what had been treated as mere background for the canonical work of art. If we are in part the unintended consequences of *Hamlet*, Shakespeare's play, I will suggest, is in part one of the unintended consequences of the theological struggles with which much of this book will be concerned. But for this book to work properly, the reader should understand literary analysis, and specifically the analysis of *Hamlet*, to be suspended in another sense as well, that is, distributed in tiny, almost invisible particles throughout my account.

A FEW years ago, as a fellow at the Wissenschaftskolleg in Berlin, I had a conversation with an urbane Islamicist who was maintaining eloquently that one must put aside one's family and group identifications, no matter how powerful they may be, in order to think and speak as a rational person. I agreed with him, but I found myself thinking, and not for the first time, how slyly amusing and acute Plato was in the *Ion* in pointing to the tension between the work of the rational philosopher and the work of the rhapsode or, let us say, the literary critic. I know, in any case, that I am incapable of simply bracketing my own origins; rather, I find myself trying to transform them, most often silently and implicitly, into the love I bring to my work.

Let me on this occasion be explicit. My father was born in the late nineteenth century. I was the child of what I used to think of as his old age but that I have now, at my point in life, come to think of, rather, as his vigorous middle age. I saw him, in any case, as embodying the life experience not of the generation directly behind me but of two generations back. His own childhood memories seemed to have a quite unusual, almost eerie distance from my life-world. Hence, for example, he told me that when he was very young, he was taken, along with the other boys in his Hebrew school class (his *cheder*) to the apartment of a Jewish railway worker who had been struck and killed by a train. The little children were told by their teacher, whom I can only imagine as a madman, to stand around the mangled corpse—which was placed on great cakes of ice, since it was the summer in Boston and very hot—and to recite the psalms, while the man's wife wailed inconsolably in a corner.

Initiated, perhaps, by this traumatic experience, my father was obsessed throughout his life with death. His own father had died dreadfully, clinging to his son and begging for help, and my father carried the scars of that experience with him ever after. The effect on him was not exactly melancholy, but rather something like a strange blend of wonder and denial. The wonder had a specific origin: my grandfather had died in New York, where my father had taken him in a desperate, last-ditch search for medical treatment. My father then had to bring the body back to Boston by train. The coffin was in the baggage car, and my father was sitting quietly weeping in the club car, when, in New Haven, Connecticut, the entire chorus line of the Ziegfield Follies climbed on board. The chorus girls, leggy, buxom, bejeweled, bedecked in feather boas and wide-brimmed hats, sweetly crowded around my weeping father, kissing and hugging him and trying to cheer him up. It was perhaps my father's purest encounter with the wonderful power of *eros* over *thanatos*.

To this experience of wonder my father conjoined denial. He kept us from celebrating his birthday, refused to retire, working until the week before he died in his eighty-seventh year, and lied about his age even when he entered the hospital. But when we read his will, we found that he had, after all, been thinking about his death. He had left a sum of money to an organization that would say kaddish for him—kaddish being the Aramaic prayer for the dead, recited for eleven months after a person's death and then on certain annual occasions. The prayer is usually said by the deceased's immediate family and particularly by his sons—in Yiddish a son could actually be called a *kaddish,* so that a childless man could be said to die without leaving a *kaddish.* Evidently, my father did not trust either my older brother or me to recite the prayer for him. The effect the bequest had on me, perhaps perversely, was to impel me to do so, as if in a blend of love and spite.

I did not until that moment know that Jews had anything like chantries, and I realized that I did not know why Jews prayed for the dead at all. After all, biblical Judaism has only what seems like a vague and imaginatively impoverished account of the afterlife. The Hebrew Bible speaks of a place called *sheol,* often translated by Christians as "Hell," but it is not a place of torture and has very few of the features of the Christian or classical underworld.[3] It seems to be associated not with torment (or purgation) but rather with privation or depression. "Are not my days few?" complains Job; "cease then, and let me alone, that I may take comfort a little, Before I go whence I shall not return, even to the land of darkness and the shadow of death; A land of darkness, as darkness itself; and of the shadow of death, without any order, and where the light is as darkness" (Job 10:20–22). The phrase "without any order" links this netherworld not with a prison house or penal colony—we are immensely distant conceptually from Dante's circles—but with the state of things before the Creation, when "the earth was without form, and void; and darkness was upon the face of the deep" (Gen. 1:2). The overall focus in the Hebrew Scriptures is not on assuring oneself a more favorable location in this melancholy kingdom, but rather on valuing life: "For him that is joined to all the living there is hope," as Ecclesiastes puts it, "for a living dog is better than a dead lion" (9:4).

There are, however, some biblical expressions, especially in the Psalter, of a hope to be liberated from *sheol:* "Like sheep they are laid in the grave; death shall feed on them; and the upright shall have dominion over them in the morning; and their beauty shall consume in the grave from their dwelling. But God will redeem my soul from the power of the grave: for he shall receive me. Selah"

(Ps. 49:14–15). Or again, "For thou wilt not leave my soul in hell; neither wilt thou suffer thine Holy One to see corruption. Thou wilt shew me the path of life: in thy presence is fullness of joy; at thy right hand there are pleasures for evermore" (Ps. 16:10–11). This faith in the possibility of resurrection—and the Jewish liturgy to this day praises God for raising the dead to life—still does not explain why Jews would offer prayers for the dead.

The answer seems to be that the kaddish, as we know it, is relatively recent. In a sermon preached at St. Paul's on May 21, 1626, John Donne notes that God gave his chosen people, through Moses and Aaron, the most elaborate directions for every aspect of their lives: "what they should eat, what they should wear, how often they should wash, what they should do, in every religious, in every civil action." Yet, Donne continues, "never, never any mention, any intimation, never any approach, any inclination, never any light, no nor any shadow, never any color, any colorableness of any command of prayer for the Dead." There was, to be sure, an ancient custom of remembering the dead, on Yom Kippur, as part of the general ritual of atonement, and there was also a long-standing Hebrew custom of giving alms to the poor or to charitable institutions in memory of the dead. But the Jews adopted prayers for the dead, Donne argues, from the pagans: "After the Jews had been a long time conversant amongst the Gentiles, and that as fresh water approaching the Sea, contracts a saltish, a brackish taste, so the Jews received impressions of the customs of the Gentiles, who were ever naturally inclined to this mis-devotion, and left-handed piety, of praying for the Dead."[4]

In fact, though the left-handed piety of the pagans may be the ultimate origin of praying for the dead, the Jews may well have adopted it from the Christians. The recitation of the mourner's kaddish seems to have originated in the Rhineland in the twelfth century, after the horrors of the First and Second Crusade. In the wake of the mass murders and suicides, the Ashkenazim evidently began to keep memorial books, *Memorbucher*, in which the martyrs, along with benefactors of the community and other worthies, were commemorated. The inscriptions in these books were linked to

the kaddish, and, eventually, the recitation of this prayer was generalized to include all of the dead.

In a recent, often haunting meditation on the kaddish, Leon
Wieseltier acknowledges that the recitation of the mourner's kaddish thus originated precisely at the time that Christianity in the
West formalized the practice of praying for the dead in order to
alleviate their sufferings in Purgatory. "Yet this is, as I say, a coincidence," Wieseltier insists; "I do not believe for a minute that the
one was the cause of the other."[5] It is not my intention to dispute
this flat claim, nor do I have the scholarship to do so, but if it were
a coincidence, it would be an almost miraculous one, since many
of the texts that Wieseltier cites bear a startling resemblance to
the exempla and scholastic arguments of the medieval and early
modern Christians among whom the Jews were dwelling. I suspect,
rather, that the long, twisting path that leads back from my father
and forefathers passes through the Christianity that seemed to
them the embodiment of otherness.[6]

Very few Jews were dwelling among the Christians in early modern England; the entire community had been officially expelled in
1290.[7] But Donne speaks as if he has personally witnessed them
saying the kaddish: "This is true which I have seen," he tells his
London congregation, "that the Jews at this day continue it in practice; For when one dies, for some certain time after, appointed by
them, his son or some other near in blood or alliance, comes to
the Altar, and there saith and doth something in the behalf of his
dead father, or grandfather respectively."[8]

This practice, then, which with a lightly ironic piety I, who
scarcely know how to pray, undertook for my own father, is the
personal starting point for what follows.

❦ 1 ❦

A POET'S FABLE

EARLY IN 1529 a London lawyer, Simon Fish, anonymously published a tract, addressed to Henry VIII, called *A Supplication for the Beggars*. The tract was modest in length but explosive in content: Fish wrote on behalf of the homeless, desperate English men and women, "needy, impotent, blind, lame and sick" who pleaded for spare change on the streets of every city and town in the realm.[1] These wretches, "on whom scarcely for horror any eye dare look," have become so numerous that private charity can no longer sustain them, and they are dying of hunger.[2] Their plight, in Fish's account, is directly linked to the pestiferous spread throughout the realm of beggars of a different kind: bishops, abbots, priors, deacons, archdeacons, suffragans, priests, monks, canons, friars, pardoners, and summoners.

Simon Fish had already given a foretaste of his anticlerical sentiments and his satirical gifts. In his first year as a law student at Gray's Inn, according to John Foxe, one of Fish's mates, a certain Mr. Roo, had written a play holding Cardinal Wolsey up to ridicule. No one dared to take on the part of Wolsey until Simon Fish came forward and offered to do so. The performance must have been impressive: it so enraged the cardinal that Fish was forced "the same night that this Tragedy was played" to flee to the Low Countries to escape arrest.[3] There he evidently met the exile William Tyndale, whose new English translation of the Bible, inspired by Luther, he subsequently helped to circulate. At the time he wrote *A Supplication for the Beggars*, Fish had probably returned to London but was in hiding. He was thus a man associated with Protestant beliefs, determined to risk his life to save the soul of his country, and endowed, as were many religious revolutionaries in the 1520s and 1530s, with a kind of theatrical gift.[4]

In *A Supplication for the Beggars*, this gift leads Fish not only to speak on behalf of the poor but also to speak in their own voice, crying out to the king against those who have greedily taken for themselves the wealth that should otherwise have made England prosperous for all of its people. If his gracious majesty would only look around, he would see "a thing far out of joint" (413). The ravenous monkish idlers "have begged so importunately that they have gotten into their hands more then the third part of all your Realm." No great people, not the Greeks nor the Romans nor the Turks, and no ruler, not King Arthur himself, could flourish with such parasites sucking at their lifeblood. Not only do they destroy the economy, interfere with royal prerogative, and undermine the laws of the commonwealth, but, since they seduce "every man's wife, every man's daughter and every man's maid," they subvert the nation's moral order as well. Boasting among themselves about the number of women they have slept with, the clerical drones carry physical and moral contagion—syphilis, leprosy, and idleness—through the whole commonwealth. "Who is she that will set her hands to work to get three pence a day," the beggars ask, "and may have at least twenty pence a day to sleep an hour with a friar, a monk, or a priest?" (417). With a politician's flair for shocking (and unverifiable) statistics, Fish estimates the number of Englishwomen corrupted by monks at 100,000. No one can be sure, he writes, that it is his own child and not a priest's bastard who is poised to inherit his estate.

Why have these diseased "bloodsuppers" succeeded in amassing so much wealth and power? Why would otherwise sensible, decent people, alert to threats to their property, their health, and their liberties, allow themselves to be ruthlessly exploited by a pack of "sturdy idle holy thieves" (415)? The question would be relatively easy to answer were this a cunningly concealed crime or one perpetrated on the powerless. But in Fish's account virtually the entire society, from the king and the nobility to the poor housewife who has to give the priests every tenth egg her hen lays, has been openly victimized. How is it possible to explain the dismaying spectacle of what Montaigne's friend, Etienne de la Boétie, called "voluntary servitude"?[5]

For la Boétie (1530–1563) the answer is structural: a chain of clientage and dependency extends and expands geometrically, he argues, from a small number of cynical exploiters at the top to the great mass of the exploited below.[6] Anyone who challenges this system risks attack, both from the few who are actually reaping a benefit and from the many who are deceived into thinking that their interests are being served. Individuals may actually grasp that they have been lured into voluntary servitude, but as long as they have no way of knowing who else among them has arrived at the same perception, they recognize that it is dangerous to speak out.

If those who see through the lies could share their knowledge with other, like-minded souls, as they long to do, they could take the steps necessary to free themselves from their chains. Those steps are remarkably simple: what is needed, in fact, is not a violent uprising but a quiet refusal. Since only a minuscule fraction of the society is truly profiting from the system, all it would take, were there widespread enlightenment, is peaceful noncooperation. When the king demands his breakfast, one need only refuse to bring it. He may sputter in rage, but the rage will be as inconsequential as an infant's, provided that the great majority of men and women have collectively determined to be free. But how is that determination to be fostered? How is it possible for those who understand the situation to awaken others, so that all can act in unison? As long as they remain isolated, there is little that enlightened individuals can do, and it is risky for them to open their secret thoughts to others. If only there were little windows in each person, la Boétie daydreams, so that one could see what is hidden inside and know to whom one could safely speak.

For Etienne de la Boétie, the first and fundamental problem is to account for widespread behavior that seems so obviously against interest, and not simply against the marginal or incidental concerns of particular groups but against the central material and sexual preoccupations of all human societies. Why do people allow themselves to be robbed and cheated? Simon Fish is grappling with the same problem, but his answer centers not on social structures or institutions or hierarchical systems of dependency. After all, very few people think of themselves as actually dependent on the lazy, syphilitic monks and friars who shamelessly take advantage of them. These so-called holy men are not conspicuous figures of wealth or might; on the contrary, unarmed and unattended, they dress poorly and go about begging. In Fish's account their place at the center of a vast system of pillaging and sexual corruption relies upon the exploitation of a single core conviction: Purgatory.

ALMS FOR THE DEAD

Fish was not alone in his theory. Elsewhere in the writings of the early Reformers, we find similar claims for the overwhelming importance of the doctrine of Purgatory, a doctrine already long under attack in England by those heretics known as Lollards.[7] "In God's name, tell me," the king asks the impoverished Commonality in the tragedy *King Johan* by John Bale (1495–1563), "how cometh thy substance gone?" To which Commonality replies, "By priests, canons and monks, which do but fill their belly, / With my sweat and labor for their popish Purgatory."[8] Tyndale similarly writes of the churchmen that "[a]ll they have, they have received in the name of Purgatory . . . and on that foundation be all their bishoprics, abbeys, colleges, and cathedral churches built."[9]

The claim obviously serves a Protestant polemical purpose by loading the immense weight of the entire Catholic Church upon one of its most contested doctrines, but in the heated debates of the sixteenth century, at least some English Catholics agreed. Writing in the 1560s in defense of Purgatory, Cardinal William Allen (1532–1594) claims that "this doctrine (as the whole world knoweth) founded all Bishoprics, builded all Churches, raised all Oratories, instituted all Colleges, endowed all Schools, maintained all hospitals, set forward all works of charity and religion, of what sort soever they be."[10] Though it received its full doctrinal elaboration quite late—the historian Jacques Le Goff places the "birth of Purgatory" in the latter half of the twelfth century[11]—the notion of an intermediate place between Heaven and Hell and the system of indulgences and pardons meant to relieve the sufferings of souls imprisoned within it had come to seem, for many heretics and orthodox believers alike, essential to the institutional structure, authority, and power of the Catholic Church.

This degree of importance is certainly an exaggeration, but it is not a complete travesty: by the late Middle Ages in Western Europe, Purgatory had achieved both a doctrinal and a social success. That is, it was by no means exclusively the esoteric doctrine of theologians but part of a much broader, popular understanding of the meaning of existence, the nature of Christian faith, and the structure of family and community. Hence, to cite a single English example, the various fifteenth-century devotional treatises known collectively as *The Lay Folks Mass Book* include for recital after the elevation of the Host a vernacular prayer for the dead. The faithful pray for those souls, "father soul, mother soul, brother dear, sisters souls, sib men and other sere [*relatives and other particular individuals*]," who may be suffering in "Purgatory pain."[12] The prayer—from a text that is not a piece of the official liturgy but a model of private, vernacular faith, intended to be read while the priests conduct the Latin Mass—pleads that bonds shackling these dead be unlocked, so that they can pass from torment to everlasting joy.

The simple English prayer is evidence—to which much more could be added—that the attempt to free souls from the prison house of Purgatory was not exclusively the work of a priestly class of specialists. There *was* such a class, large in numbers, as Fish and other Protestant polemicists stridently insisted, whose maintenance cost a considerable amount of money. But their rituals, though regarded as particularly efficacious, were not the only assistance that the dead could receive, and lay persons could supplement the liturgical ceremonies that their donations sponsored with a variety of less formal (and less expensive) acts on behalf of their loved ones and themselves. In Catholic countries that did not pass through periods of iconoclastic violence, one can still see, particularly in small towns, many traces of this popular piety, often accorded formal, if grudging, recognition by the church. Thus, for

Fig. 1. "40 days of indulgence" Votive plaque beneath image of Virgin, Erice, Sicily. Photo: Stephen Greenblatt.

example, embedded in the stone walls along the narrow lanes of Erice, in western Sicily, there are numerous small, rather crude votive images beneath which elegant inscriptions, dating for the most part from the eighteenth century, promise the remission of periods of purgatorial suffering for those who stand before the images and recite prayers (fig. 1). I asked a local resident once, an elderly woman, whether people still stopped and said the ritual words. No, she replied, not any more. Was that, I inquired, because the practice was now regarded as superstitious? Not at all, she said; the priests now wanted you to pay for prayers in church. To be sure, these prayers were much more powerful, but they were too expensive, and everyone she knew had stopped buying them. But if the price came down, she added, more people would certainly want them.

Along with private fasts and vigils, such prayers—casual, informal, recited in the streets—certainly did not replace the proper intercessory gestures provided for by the "pious bequests" made in large numbers of wills, but they do clearly indicate that the task of assisting the soul's passage to bliss was not entrusted entirely to the certified authorities on the afterlife. Nonspecialists understood that they could do things in their everyday lives to ease the pain of those they loved or to shorten their own anticipated share of postmortem pain.

Charity to the dead, whether performed privately or in public, by lay persons or by priests, began at home. But the effort to alleviate suffering extended beyond the immediate circle of self, family, and friends to "all Christian souls." On All Hallows' Eve, before All Saints' Day (November 1), bells rang throughout the night in English towns and villages, as communities joined in prayers for the whole, vast company of the dead, and on the day following, All Souls' Day (November 2), it was customary to distribute "soul cakes." John Mirk, canon of Lilleshall, Shropshire, in the mid–fifteenth century, lamented that the custom of giving bread for the souls of the dead—"hoping with each loaf to get a soul out of Purgatory"—was in decline, but it evidently survived, at least in rural areas, into the eighteenth century.[13] The *Sarum Prymer* of 1538 includes "A prayer to God for them that be departed, having none to pray for them." These are souls, as the prayer puts it, "which either by negligence of them that be living, or long process of time, are forgotten of their friends and posterity" and therefore "have neither hope nor comfort in their torments."[14] Similarly, the *Sarum Horae* of 1531 tells those who are entering a graveyard that Pope John IV has granted as many days of pardon as there are bodies buried in that place to those who recite a prayer that begins as follows: "All hail, all faithful souls, whose bodies do here and everywhere rest in the dust [*Salvete vos omnes fideles animae, quarum corpora hic et ubique requiescunt in pulvere*]: the Lord Jesus Christ, who hath redeemed both you and us with his most precious blood, vouchsafe to deliver you from pains."[15] Such customs implicitly acknowledge that an ordinary person's principal focus is likely to be personal—the overriding concern is with one's own fate or with the fate of particular, named loved ones—even as they give form to and reward a more capacious sense of connectedness. Though the rituals of everyday life centered on the intimate and familial, they encoded the sense of a larger bond as well, linking the living with the souls of countless previous generations.

One does not need the whole elaborate doctrine of Purgatory, of course, to feel linked to the dead: memory and a sense of the shared human condition will suffice. To be sure, in most traditional cultures this feeling of connectedness acquires a more specific set of topographical references, but this localization had already occurred many centuries before the invention of Purgatory. Christianity had long offered its believers two principal places, Heaven and Hell, in which to situate definitively those who had once lived in the world and had now ceased to exist. Purgatory forged a different kind of link between the living and the dead, or, rather, it enabled the dead to be not completely dead—not as utterly gone, finished, complete as those whose souls resided forever in Hell or Heaven.[16]

It was not possible (or, in any case, not licit in orthodox Christianity) to pray for the souls in Hell, in hope either of mitigating their pain or of augmenting it. The unspeakable tortures of the damned could be contemplated with horror or with fierce satisfaction, but those who suffered for eternity were beyond the effective range of human intervention. Saint Augustine said that even if he learned that his father was burning in Hell, he would not attempt to do anything to succor him, for he knew that he was beyond assistance. The harsh sentiment is echoed in the fourteenth-century *Treatise of the Manner and Mede of the Mass*: "If I knew that my father were wholly held in Hell," the text puts it, I would no more pray for him "than for a dog that was dead."[17]

The blessed similarly had no need of human prayers; their condition, too, was fixed for eternity. The living might hope that their friends and family in Heaven might remember them and offer them some spiritual assistance, but there was nothing that souls in bliss could want in return. A large group of the dead, however, continued to exist in time and to need something that they could get only from the living, something that would enable them to escape from the hideous, dark prison in which they were trapped.

The lay community was obviously never as thoroughly bound up with a general concern for postmortem welfare as were those monastic and conventual communities where, in certain cases, it was customary to pray daily in the actual presence of members of the order who had died. The nineteenth-century ecclesiastical antiquary William Maskell cites such a custom recorded at Durham Abbey: "Also the monks was accustomed every day, to go through the cloister, in at the usher's door, and so through the entry, in under the prior's lodging, and straight into the scentorie garth [*churchyard*], where all the monks was buried, and they did all bareheaded, a certain long space, praying amongst the tombs and throwghes [*sepulchres*] for their brethren souls being buried there, and, when they had done their prayers, then they did return to the cloister."[18] The formal arrangement that facilitated such observances—seats designed to drain off the liquids from the corpses, etc.—may still be glimpsed, for example, in the somber architecture of an underground chapel linked to the cathedral on Ischia, a chapel that must have seemed to the nuns to be a powerful representation of the purgatorial afterlife.

But the practice of burying the dead in the hallowed ground of the churchyard or, in the case of the wealthiest and most powerful parishioners, under the floor or in the walls of the church itself meant that ordinary men and women, including those quite uninterested in theological niceties, worshiped in close proximity to the mortal remains of those whose souls had passed on to their reward or punishment. Even the liberal use of incense, flowers, and sprigs of rosemary could not altogether have masked the smell of decay that medieval and early modern burial practices almost inevitably introduced into the still air of churches.[19] The wall paintings, carved doors and capitals, altarpieces, stained-glass windows, and funeral monuments further reinforced the deep link between Christianity and the fate of the dead.

Not only doctrine, then, but also chants, gestures, images, and the very air that the faithful breathed said the same thing: the border between this world and the afterlife was not firmly and irrevocably closed. For a large group of mortals—perhaps the majority of them—time did not come to an end at the moment of death. The book was not quite shut. One chapter remained to be written, and if the outcome was fixed and settled, the sequence of events, the duration, and the quality of the experience were not. The living could have an ongoing relationship with one important segment of the dead, and not simply a relationship constituted by memory. There were things that the living could do for the dead—and not to do these things, or to delay doing them, or to do some and not others, was also a course of action in this ongoing relationship. The whole social and economic importance of Purgatory in Catholic Europe rested on the belief that prayers, fasts, almsgiving, and masses constituted a valuable commodity—"suffrages," as they were termed—that could in effect be purchased, directly or indirectly, on behalf of specific dead persons.

The blessed souls in Heaven, of course, had no need of suffrages, since they had already attained eternal bliss, while the damned souls in Hell could not make use of them, since they were condemned to an eternity of irremediable torment. But imperfect souls, souls still bearing the stains of the faults they had committed in mortal life, would have to endure excruciating pain. Fortunately, suffrages were available to reduce the intensity and duration of this agony. Masses lovingly paid for and performed in memory of the dead were particularly efficacious, as were the prayers of the poor and sick offered in grateful memory of their benefactor. Similarly, the pious fasts, prayers, and alms of relatives and friends could be directed to relieve the sufferings of a named individual whom they believed to be in Purgatory. Moreover, the pope was the administrator, in effect, of an enormous account of "superabundant satisfactions" left by Christ and further enhanced by the saints and martyrs, an account that could be expended, in the form of indulgences, on behalf of deserving souls.[20] The reckoning in every case was strictly individual and scrupulously proportional to the gravity of the particular sins, but it was possible for individuals after death to receive help from others, just as living debtors languishing in prison could have their debts paid by their friends. "Thus devout prayers said with humility," writes the poet and monk John Lydgate (ca. 1370–ca. 1450), "Delivereth souls out of Purgatory."[21]

Popular religion in the Middle Ages conjured up vivid images of the efficacy of this help. One of the most widely read books in the period, the *Golden Legend* (ca. 1260) by Jacobus de Voragine (Jacopo da Varazze), recounts a vision granted to a warden of Saint Peter's:

Then the angel led the warden to another place and showed him people of both sexes, some reclining on golden beds, others at tables enjoying delicious viands, still others naked and needy, begging for help. This place, the angel said, was Purgatory. Those enjoying abundance were the souls for whom their friends provided plentiful aid, whereas those in need had no one who cared for them.[22]

Though the story ostensibly functions as a justification for the newly instituted Feast of All Souls "on which day those who had no one to pray for them would at least share in the general commemoration," it makes clear the enormous value of acquiring special prayers.

The value is heightened in *The Golden Legend* by the familiar emphasis on the pains of Purgatory. The emphasis, which often seems ghoulish, made perfect institutional sense. Since the ultimate fate of those who reached Purgatory was fixed and immutable—all would eventually reach Heaven—there had to be some reason to induce men and women to busy themselves and give their worldly goods to help the souls who were already imprisoned there or to abridge their own possible future prison terms. The reason was anxiety. Voragine rehearses, for example, the story of Master Silo originally told by the scholastic theologian Peter the Chanter (d. 1197) and found as well in the influential preacher James of Vitry (d. 1240) and the Dominican Stephen of Bourbon (d. 1261).

Master Silo had a colleague, a scholar who was very ill, and Silo asked him urgently to come back after he died and tell him, Silo, how things were with him. Some days after his death the scholar appeared to Silo, wearing a cape made of parchment written all over with sophisms, and woven of flames inside. The master asked who he was and he answered: "I am indeed the one who promised to come back to you." Asked how things were with him he said: "This cape weighs upon me and presses me down more than if I were carrying a tower on my shoulders. It is given to me to wear on account of the pride I had in my sophisms. The flames that flare inside it are the delicate, mottled furs I used to wear, and they torture and burn me." The master, however, thought that this penalty was fairly light, so that the dead man told him to put out his hand and feel how light the punishment really was. He held out his hand and the scholar let a drop of his sweat fall on it. The drop went through the master's hand like an arrow, causing him excruciating pain. "That's how I feel all over," the scholar said.[23]

After all, as Aquinas wrote, the least degree of pain in Purgatory "surpasses the greatest pain that one can endure in this world."[24]

THE PRICE OF PRAYERS

Master Silo's response to the ghost was to abandon the world at once and enter religious life.[25] Others less willing to forsake worldly wealth altogether used at least a portion of that wealth to assure themselves postmortem assistance. There was a range of available packages, as it were, from a simple funeral mass to the popular and moderately priced trental—a set of thirty requiem masses, said on the same day or on successive days—to the extremely expensive chantry, an endowment for the maintenance of a priest to sing daily mass for the founder or for someone specified by the founder, often in an ornate, purpose-built chapel.[26] On the eve of the Battle of Agincourt, queasy at the memory of his usurping father's murder of Richard II, Shakespeare's Henry V reminds God of his lavish acts of contrition:

> Five hundred poor have I in yearly pay
> Who twice a day their withered hands hold up
> Toward Heaven to pardon blood. And I have built
> Two chantries, where the sad and solemn priests
> Sing still for Richard's soul.
>
> (4.1.280–84)[27]

Two chantries were an extravagance, even for a monarch, but there were in this case special circumstances.[28] Aware that his claim to the throne is tainted, Henry in effect is bargaining with God or with the vengeful spirit of the murdered Richard, and the bargaining chips are chantries. "Not today, O Lord," he prays, attempting to distract God from the reckoning he fears will be due,

> O not today, think not upon the fault
> My father made in compassing the crown.
>
> (4.1.274–76)

At this critical moment the king is concerned not with the fate of his soul but with the outcome of the battle: perhaps this served for Shakespeare and his audience as a spectacular, if morally problematical, display of heroic leadership.

Ordinarily, in making provisions for the afterlife, most people, including kings, wanted the sad and solemn priests to pray for their own souls. Faced with the terrifying prospect of purgatorial torment, the wealthy were willing to part with a great deal of money, particularly at the moment that they were forced to part with the world itself. The most spectacular instance of this willingness was that of a king who found himself in a position not altogether unlike that of Henry V—a king, that is, who wore a crown that had been wrested by violence from the legitimate ruler. The king in question was Henry VII, who came to the throne in 1485 by killing the Yorkist king Richard III at the Battle of Bosworth Field.

Henry VII was not an extravagant monarch—he was thought, if anything, to be something of a skinflint—but the magnificent late Gothic chapel he ordered built at Westminster was, according to one architectural historian, "the largest and certainly the most expensive structure ever built for funerary purposes."[29] Three monks of Westminster were to serve as chantry priests, perpetually praying for Henry's soul, and these constant suffrages were to be supplemented by anniversary masses in an impressive number of cathedral, conventual, and university churches. But even these extraordinary efforts to hasten his soul through Purgatory were not enough for a king who evidently thought he might be facing a long prison sentence in the afterlife. During his lifetime Henry founded a hospital and an almshouse whose grateful inhabitants could be counted on to offer up a steady supply of prayers, and in his will he provided for the establishment of two further hospitals, along with other contributions clearly designed to generate suffrages.

Finally, he saw to it that immediately after his death ten thousand masses would be said for the remission of his sins and the good of his soul. Ten thousand masses.

This was the father of the king to whom Simon Fish dedicated his *Supplication of the Beggars*. Somewhere buried in the story of Henry VIII's suppression of the monasteries and seizure of their great wealth is a son's violent repudiation of his father's attempts to ease his soul's torments. Between 1536 and 1539 Henry VIII took back for his own uses what Henry VII had laid out for himself—that, and much more. If his own last will and testament, drawn up and revised before his death in 1547, is any indication, the son by no means repudiated the religious beliefs to which his father adhered. But the terms of this will perhaps betray some ambiguous sign of the influence of *The Supplication of the Beggars* and, in any case, certainly reflect the silencing of the chantries. "We will and charge our Executors," Henry VIII commanded,

> that they dispose and give in alms to the most poor and needy people that may be found (common beggars as much as may be avoided) in as short space as possibly they may after our departure out of this transitory life, *one thousand marks* of lawful money of England, part in the same place and thereabouts, where it shall please Almighty God to call us to his Mercy, part by the way, and part in the same place of our burial after their discretions, and to move the poor people that shall have our alms to pray heartily unto God for remission of our offenses and the wealth of our soul.[30]

"In as short space as possibly they may after our departure": Henry VIII does not want to linger in the fires of Purgatory. Thousands of masses will not be sung to haste him toward Heaven, but a thousand marks could purchase the prayers of many poor people. In the unlikely event that he did not go straight to Hell, he would certainly have needed all of them.

Reformers who were centrally concerned to challenge the doctrine of Purgatory would not have been content with the king's provisions, but at least the money was not going to enrich the priesthood. Protestant polemics of the sixteenth century are virtually obsessed with the amount of wealth wasted in the vain belief that masses can shorten the torment. By this belief, Barnabe Googe, a prolific translator and antipapal polemicist, writes in *The Popish Kingdom* (1570),

> so many altars in the Churches up did rise,
> By this the number grows so great of Priests to sacrifice.
> From hence arose such shameful swarms of Monks with
>   great excess,
> Whom profit of this Mass doth keep in slothful idleness.
> For this same cause such mighty kings, and famous
>   Princes high,
> Ordained Masses for their souls, and Priests continually,
> With great revenues yearly left and everlasting fee,
> An easy way to joy, if it with scriptures might agree.[31]

In this view, the immense outpouring of wealth originated in the desire of kings and princes to secure for their souls an "easy way to joy," and then spread to the whole class of the rich and privileged, eager to attain similar benefits for themselves:

> Straight after these, the wealthy men took up this fancy vain,
> And built them Chapels every one, and Chaplains did retain
> At home, or in their parish Church, where Mass they
>   daily sung,
> For safeguard of their family, and of their children young.
> Both for their friends alive, and such as long before did die,
> And in the Purgatory flames tormented sore doe lie.

The theology focused on the sins and sufferings of individuals, but, as Googe's account suggests, the actual observances had a wider reach. Chantries and other costly ritual practices often served as pious attempts to help whole networks of family and friends, along with the donor himself.

Henry VII's will notwithstanding, enormous bequests of the kind Googe attacks seem in reality to have been on the wane well before the Reformation. According to the historian Christopher Haigh, by the latter part of the fifteenth century "the endowment of chantries on a large scale was clearly a thing of the past in most parts of England."[32] But Googe and his fellow polemicists are certainly correct in claiming that English Catholics invested heavily in suffrages. Medieval wills are full of provisions for the acquisition of prayers, along with almsgiving and other acts of pious benefaction.[33] As we have seen, the monks of Westminster Abbey, who said masses for the kings of England, were especially well-endowed beneficiaries of the belief in Purgatory, but virtually all monasteries and churches in the Middle Ages would have been the recipients of donations in exchange for prayers for the dead.[34]

Theologians assured the faithful that their generous acts of penance and commissioned prayers would not be wasted, even if those for whom the prayers were said went directly to Heaven (or, for that matter, to Hell). Prayers that could not be used by the person for whom they were intended would go to the next of kin.[35] Only if no such person were available would the benefit of those prayers be deposited in the papal treasury, along with the supererogatory virtues of the saints and martyrs, to be dispensed to those who properly paid for them. It was always better to err on the side of excess, since there could be no waste, and since inadequate suffrages would work inadequately.[36]

Catholic texts repeatedly emphasize that the donations on behalf of someone's soul have to be made in the right spirit,[37] but they could also be amazingly explicit about the benefits that money could buy. And though the doctrine fostered familial solidarity and the bonds of charity and remembrance linking the living and the dead, appeals were often made directly to self-interest. Hence, for example, the seventeenth-century English Catholic writer Jane Owen urges her wealthy readers to acts of frankly self-serving generosity: "O how many peculiar *Advocates* and *Intercessors* of the then most blessed Souls (released out of *Purgatory*) might a rich Catholic purchase to himself, by this former means, thereby to plead his cause before the Throne of Almighty God, in his greatest need?"[38] The French Jesuit Etienne Binet, in a text translated into English in the seventeenth century, emphasizes the burning shame that clever, rich people, finding themselves after death in the sulfurous and stinking smoke of Purgatory, will feel when they realize "that the souls of many country clowns, mere idiots, poor women and

simple religious persons go straight up to Heaven, while they lie
there burning." Their shame, in this account, will derive less from
contemplation of their sins than from realization of their stupid
carelessness: "And for a handful of Silver, they might have redeemed many years of torments in that fiery Furnace; and alas,
they chose rather to give it to their dogs and their horses."[39]

Like Owen, Binet warns parents against counting on their children to provide suffrages for them. It is important to make all
the necessary financial arrangements before your death, for your
heirs will only want more money from your estate and will leave
you frying.[40] Moreover, if you are hesitating between relieving a
soul in Purgatory and relieving a beggar or a sick person in this
life, you should consider the absolute certainty of the former
course of action, underwritten by the full faith and credit of the
Catholic Church, and the gross uncertainty of the latter. If you
give to a living person, Binet points out, "you may often fail of your
aim and lose both your money and your labor." Why? "Consider
the men themselves who for the most part are Ungrateful, Deceitful, Wicked, and so far unsatisfied, that you have never done
with them."[41]

There were some, not surprisingly, who thought it unjust that
the wealthy could purchase spiritual benefits denied to the poor.
"It may fall that the pope grant to rich worldly men that they
should go straight to heaven without pain of Purgatory," complains
the fourteenth-century reformer John Wycliffe, "and deny this to
poor men, keep they never so [*however carefully they keep*] God's
law."[42] Wycliffe believed in the existence of Purgatory, though he
rejected prayers for the dead and strenuously objected to the purchase of suffrages. But even among those who concluded that Purgatory was a fable, the charge of unfairness recurs. A poem by the
sixteenth-century Scottish Protestant minister John Wedderburn
(1500?–1556) begins by declaring happily, if somewhat paradoxically, that the fire of Purgatory is at once "false" and extin-
guished—"Of the fals fyre of Purgatorie, / Is nocht left in ane
sponk [*spark*]"—but continues with a complaint that the priests
provided relief from its excruciating pains only to the rich:

> At Corps presence [*Mass*] thay wald sing,
> For ryches, to slokkin [*slake*] the fyre:
> Bot all pure folk that had na thing
> Was skaldit baine and lyre [*scalded bone and flesh*].[43]

The injustice so evident on earth, with the rich living in ease and the poor suffering miserably, is extended by the purchase of suffrages beyond the grave. As the old saying goes, "No penny, no paternoster."[44]

Aquinas evidently discussed the problem, since the *Supplement*, composed by his disciples from notes and added to the *Summa theologica*, addresses it. The rich are not unfairly favored, he concludes, because the expiation of penalties "is as nothing compared with the possession of the kingdom of Heaven, and there the poor are favored."[45] From this perspective, the availability of suffrages to the wealthy is a charitable gesture toward a group whose ordinary chances of reaching Heaven are roughly comparable to those of a camel passing through the eye of a needle. As one might imagine, this argument, however clever, did not quiet all resentment.

In England, as more famously in Germany, the resentment was particularly though not exclusively focused on the sale of indulgences. As early as 1395, the *Twelve Conclusions of the Lollards* articulated some of the key charges against the pope rehearsed by Protestant agitators more than a century later: if the pope actually possesses a vast fund of supererogatory works of virtue, as he says he does, then "he is a treasurer most banished out of charity, since he may deliver the prisoners that been in pain at his own will, and make himself so that he shall never come there."[46] The argument was easily extended from the papacy to other parts of the clerical hierarchy. "Why make ye men believe," asks Jack Upland, the speaker in a poem associated with Langland,

> that your golden trental sung of you,
> to take therefore ten shillings,
> or at least five shillings
> will bring souls out of Hell,
> or out of purgatory?

> If this be sooth, certes,
> ye might bring all souls out of pain;
> and that will ye not,
> and then ye be out of charity.[47]

All of the ill will normally aroused by money changers, usurers, and bankers is thus directed against the pope and the priests with their treasury of unspent suffrages.

To the ordinary feelings awakened by a tantalizing glimpse of hoarded riches were added the fear and anguish deliberately cultivated in the fourteenth and fifteenth centuries by popular preachers. As an esoteric doctrine among intellectuals, Purgatory could be the subject of complex debates about the quantification of quality, the ethics of proportionality, the difference between purgatorial and consummatory fire, the precise jurisdictional claims of the Church Militant, the degree to which souls could be said to undergo their pains "voluntarily," the distinction between pardon "as to the penalty" (*quoad poenam*) and pardon "as to the guilt" (*quoad culpam*), and so forth. But as a popular belief, Purgatory aroused— or at least was meant to arouse—fear. The theologians who teased out the subtle science of the hereafter had, for the most part, a reassuring access to the fund of suffrages; the great majority of Christians did not. The faithful who were most deeply moved by the visions of torment were the most anxious to acquire some remission. To those who lacked the money to pay for such remission, the system of indulgences must have been particularly infuriating. "Why busy ye not to hear / to shrift of poor folk, / as well as of rich," asks Jack Upland; "Why will ye not be at her dirges, / as ye have been at rich men's?"[48]

This anguished sense that priests were covetously holding back a benefit they could be freely distributing made the doctrine of Purgatory—or at least the institutional practices that the Roman Catholic Church had built up around the doctrine—vulnerable. In *A Supplication for the Beggars* Simon Fish takes up the smoldering issue of fairness, but he sidesteps class antagonism by pitting one group of beggars, the blind, ill, or impoverished, against another group, the hypocritical idlers who contrive by "sleights" to exact more and more money. "Nor have they any other color to gather these yearly exactions," Fish writes, "but that they say they pray for us to God to deliver our souls out of the pains of purgatory" (419).

Not everyone is taken in by the fraud. "Many men of great literature and judgment" dare to point out that Purgatory does not exist. Others observe that if there is a Purgatory, and if the pardons that the pope sells for money can in fact deliver souls from its pains, as the Catholic Church claims, then those same pardons given freely, without charge, would surely be equally effective. Moreover, if the pope can deliver one soul from torment, he can presumably deliver a thousand, and if he can deliver a thousand, he can presumably deliver everyone, "and so destroy Purgatory." If he possesses such power and does not use it, if he leaves souls to languish in prison unless he is given money, then the pope is nothing but "a cruel tyrant without all charity." Indeed, if all priests and friars— "the whole sort of the spirituality"—will allow souls to be punished for want of prayers and will "pray for no man but for them that give them money" (419), then they are all tyrants.

Anyone who publicly says such things is taking a serious risk, Fish acknowledges, for the priests are quick to accuse their critics of heresy. In fact, even those who have a clear cause of action against a cleric—for murder, "ravishment of his wife, of his daughter, robbery, trespass, mayhem, debt, or any other offence" (417)— are afraid to seek legal remedy for fear of excommunication. Moreover, there is no recourse to Parliament. If the king himself thought to propose laws in Parliament against the priests, Fish writes provocatively, "I am in doubt whether ye be able: Are they not stronger in your own parliament house than yourself?" (417).

But, if he acts on his own authority, the king has enough power to save his realm and succor his poor starving subjects. He can do so at a stroke by seizing the wealth that the wolvish priests have stolen from the people and using that wealth to relieve the needy. As for the thousands of lazy monks and friars, Fish urges the king to put an end to their racket once and for all: "Tie these holy idle thieves to the carts to be whipped naked about every market town til they will fall to labor that they by their importunate begging take not away the alms that the good Christian people would give unto us sore, impotent, miserable people" (34).

THE DEAD HAND

Fish's anticlericalism may well have struck a chord among impotent, miserable people unable to afford suffrages, but far more important, in a polemic addressed to Henry VIII, was the fact that the English state had for a long time been concerned about the fiscal implications of intercessory institutions like chantries.[49] The concern, which often flared into hostility and covetousness, centered on the fact that over the years a great deal of property had been progressively removed from the tax rolls and given in donation to the church. Ecclesiastical property was, at least in theory, inalienable; hence lands and other goods donated by those wishing to secure prayers for the suffering souls in Purgatory ceased to change hands and became "dead." As early as the thirteenth century, statutes attempted to limit or control what was called *mortmain*—literally, in French, "dead hand": property forever lost to a corporate body that never died and hence never released its iron grip on its rents and income. The statutes helped to produce income for the crown, by imposing costly fines and other charges on those who wished to donate real estate to the church, but they did not stop such donations altogether, nor did they wrest property already in the ecclesiastical dead hand back into taxable social circulation.

Originally devised to restrain gifts to the church for the saying of prayers, by the sixteenth century *mortmain* had become virtually synonymous with such gifts. In Bale's fiercely anti-Catholic play *King Johan*, the character called Sedition announces that he plays many clerical parts:

> Sometime I can be a monk in a long sad cowl;
> Sometime I can be a nun and look like an owl;
> Sometime a canon in a surplice fair and white;
> A chapterhouse monk sometime I appear in sight . . .

Sometime the bishop with a miter and a cope
A gray friar sometime with cut shoes and a rope;
Sometime I can play the white monk, sometime the friar,
The Purgatory priest and every mans wife desire.
This company hath provided for me mortmain,
For that I might ever among their sort remain.[50]

So ineffective have the *mortmain* statutes been, Fish tells the king, so successfully have the priests exploited people's faith and fear, that the realm has been split in two: the temporal kingdom is in competition with what the clergy call the spiritual kingdom, or what would be better termed "the kingdom of the bloodsuppers" (418). And the competitive advantage lies with the priests, for whatever "is once given them cometh never from them again." In the fantastic imagery of *A Supplication for the Beggars* the Catholic Church figures as an enormous maw into which everything—not property alone but the whole moral and political life of the nation—disappears: "O how all the substance of your Realm forthwith, your sword, power, crown, dignity, and obedience of your people, runneth headlong into the insatiable whirlpool of these greedy goulafres [*gluttons*] to be swallowed and devoured" (419).[51]

For Fish, the nightmare is not simply that the kingdom is divided but that it will eventually pass by an inexorable logic into the sole possession of the priests. More stringent *mortmain* legislation will not suffice to avert this end, for unless they come to understand that priests are "cruel, unclean, unmerciful, and hypocrites" (420), pious laymen will only resent attempts to restrict their ability to donate their wealth to the church. "I am as good a man as my father," the lords, knights, squires, gentlemen, and yeomen of England will tell themselves; "Why may I not as well give them as much as my father did?" (420). Until people grasp that the whole system of papal indulgences and pardons is a hypocritical fraud, they will contrive to evade any restrictions in order to purchase remission from purgatorial pain, as their forefathers did before them. Government half-measures will only slow the church's steady accumulation of wealth, not stop it. Or as Tyndale, with a longer view of the same process, puts it, "If men should continue to buy prayer

four or five hundred years more, as they have done, there would
not be a foot of ground in Christendom, neither any worldly thing,
which they, that will be called spiritual only, should not possess.
And thus all should be called spiritual."[52]

The Commodification
of Fables

"If men should continue to buy prayer": for the early-sixteenth-
century reformers, the fuel driving this whole monstrous jugger-
naut is a corrupt dream, the dream that salvation from a temporary
postmortem punishment can be obtained through the purchase
of prayers. "This Purgatory and the Pope's pardons," Fish writes to
the king, "is all the cause of the translation of your kingdom so fast
into their hands" (419–20). And the most remarkable feature of
this immense "translation" is that it is entirely dependent on an
invention. "There is," as Fish flatly and accurately writes, "not one
word spoken of it in all Holy Scripture." "For Purgatory invented
was," as a crude polemic printed in 1570 puts it, "for to persuade
that Popes had power, / to pardon every crime. Not only here
when men doth live, / but also after death."[53] The faithful have
been led to believe, without any scriptural authority, in the existence of a realm between Heaven and Hell and then, still more
fantastically, led to believe that the pope has the power to mitigate
the torments of souls imprisoned in this realm. Driven by fear and
a longing for some protection from the flames, generations of
pious Christians have been lured by a fiction into handing over
their wealth to clerical drones.

In their insatiable craving for riches, these drones also resort to
physical intimidation and coercion. The Henrician reformers
dwell on the notorious case of Richard Hunne, who refused to pay
"mortuary"—the customary gift claimed by a priest on the death
of a parishioner—for his dead infant son. Hunne was accused of
heresy, imprisoned, and then found hanging in his cell on December 4, 1514.[54] (It is worth recalling that Tyndale, Frith, Latimer,
and others who took up the assault on Purgatory were all martyred,
as Fish would certainly have been, had Thomas More gotten his

hands on him.) But Protestant polemicists know that violence is not enough to account for the systematic exploitation of a whole society, from aristocrats and warriors to the simplest of villagers, nor is the limitless venality of a well-organized, complex, bureaucratic institution. The explanation, rather, lies in the way that fables seize hold of the mind, create vast unreal spaces, and people those spaces with imaginary beings and detailed events. The priests' principal power derives from their hold upon the imagination of their flock.

Like Fish, Tyndale does not altogether and explicitly deny that there could be some middle state, between death and judgment. "It seem not impossible haply," he writes with a deliberate flourish of uncertainty, "that there might be a place where the souls might be kept for a space, to be taught and instructed."[55] Such a hypothetical proposition is permissible; the task is to refuse detailed imaginings of the kind that the papists offer: "[Y]et that there should be such a jail as they jangle, and such fashions as they feign, is plainly impossible, and repugnant to the scripture."

Here, as in other aspects of his thought, Tyndale is closely following Luther, who tried at least in his early writings to keep open the possibility of a place of purgation without imagining anything very explicit about it. As a pious young Catholic, Luther—imbued with that aspect of the doctrine that stressed the duty to help those whom one loved—had wanted to free his grandfather from Purgatory and therefore ascended the Santa Scala in Rome on his knees, reciting an Our Father on each step. In this way, it was said, it was possible to save a soul. But when he had arrived at the top, doubt seized him: "Who knows if it is really true?"[56] Despite this doubt, in his "Defense and Explanation of All the Articles," Luther still declares that he personally does not deny the existence of Purgatory: "I still hold that it exists . . . though I have found no way of proving it incontrovertibly from Scripture or reason." But in the absence of such incontrovertible proof, it is wrong, he writes, to force anyone to come to the same conclusion: "My advice is that no one allow the pope to invent new articles of faith, but be willing to remain in ignorance, with St. Augustine, about what the souls in Purgatory are doing and what their condition is."[57]

By 1530 Luther came to denounce the whole notion of Purgatory, but in the "Defense and Explanation," written in 1520, he was still clinging to a minimalist vision of suffering souls: "For us it is enough to know that they suffer great and unbearable pain and crave your help."[58] Any further inquiry is a form of dangerous curiosity, curiosity that leads, as the Puritan divine Thomas Wilcox put it in 1581, to an uncontrolled proliferation of fantasies: "For if one may be suffered in the vain and idle imaginations of his own heart and head to discourse without the warrant of the word, upon this or any other such like point . . . why shall it not be lawful, for others to doe the like? And so by that means, we shall have a whole world of men's fantasies propounded unto us. . . ."[59] The key is to stop rampant speculation, to learn to be lowly wise.

Several prominent English Protestants in the early sixteenth century attempt, like Luther, to hold onto a notion of Purgatory but to strip it of its specificity, its space, its rituals. The great preacher Hugh Latimer writes that there is some middle state, but the souls in it are probably not tortured, even if they sound as though they are in pain: "They need to cry loud to God: they be in Christ and Christ in them." These souls might do something for the living, but the living can do (and need do) nothing for them, for their salvation is assured: "I had rather be in Purgatory," Latimer writes wryly, "than in the bishop of London's prison; for in this I might die bodily for lack of meat; in that I could not; in this I might die ghostly for fear of pain, or lack of good counsel; in that I could not: in this I might be in extreme necessity; in that I could not." It is pointless to endow prayers for the dead, nor indeed would the souls in Purgatory desire such empty gifts: "[W]e see not who needeth in Purgatory; but we see who needeth in this world. . . . I am sure the souls in Purgatory be so charitable, and of charity so loth to have God dishonoured, that they would have nothing withdrawn from the poor here in this world, to be bestowed upon them, which might occasion the dishonour of God."[60] Money wasted on Purgatory is not only withdrawn from the poor; it is withheld from the state: giving money for chantries, trentals, and the like, Latimer writes wittily, is rendering to God that which is

Caesar's. As for the questions that remain about the residual, vague concept of Purgatory, Latimer, like Luther, advises a frank expression of uncertainty: "Now my answer is this: 'I cannot tell' ."[61]

But remaining in ignorance is actually quite difficult. Tyndale notes two particular qualities of the imagination that pull powerfully toward a fraudulent specificity: an extraordinary capacity to shape textual materials in an endless variety of forms and an equally extraordinary capacity to give these forms the illusion of solidity. Mocking the competition among the followers of various scholastic theologians, Tyndale writes that "every man to maintain his doctor withal, corrupteth the scripture, and fashioneth it after his own imagination, as a potter doth his clay." The conventional image of the potter here serves to insist upon radical malleability: "Of what text thou Hell provest, will another prove Purgatory; another *limbo patrum*; and another the assumption of our lady; and another shall prove of the same text that an ape hath a tail."[62] It might seem that the consequence of this absolute interpretive license would be to render Scripture blank or invisible, but for Tyndale its principal corrupting effect is, rather, as he puts it, to materialize or "darken" the Word of God. The false prelates made us "image-servants; referring our deeds unto the person of God, and worshipping him as an image of our own imagination, with bodily work; saying moreover, if we would not do such penance here at their injunctions, we must do it in another world; and so feigned Purgatory, where we must suffer seven years for every sin."[63] Through the imagination, illusions assume the opacity and materiality of bodies, bodies that require "bodily work," and the faithful are thus lured into idolatry.

Purgatory, concludes Tyndale, is "a poet's fable."[64]

THROUGHOUT the sixteenth and seventeenth centuries Protestants of all persuasions return again and again to this set of ideas: not only the fraudulence of Purgatory, its lack of scriptural basis, and its corrupt institutional uses but its special relation to dream, fantasy, and imagination. At one extreme we may take Richard Corbett, a celebrated wit, friend of Ben Jonson, bishop of Oxford and of Norwich, and a sharply satirical anti-Puritan as well as anti-Papist. "Your holy water, purgatory, bulls," Corbett mocks the Catholic priesthood,

> Wherewith you make the common people gulls,
> Are gross abuses of fantastic brains
> Subtly devis'd only for private gains.[65]

At the other extreme, we find the sober, uncompromising Thomas Wilcox, warning that to permit the lawful circulation of "vain and idle imaginations" about Purgatory will inevitably lead to the spread of "a whole world of men's fantasies."[66] So, too, the more moderate divine John Veron, a French-born Protestant, ordained in England and imprisoned for his beliefs under Mary Tudor. Veron's Protestant spokesman Eutrapelus in his dialogue *The Hunting of Purgatory to Death* (1561) argues that the whole doctrine of Purgatory is the lying invention of poetry. His wavering friend Dydimus concedes that he had not realized "that the poets are great liars and that their books be full of lying tales and vain fables: and also that both they and painters, have had always license to feign, whatsoever please them."[67]

An early-seventeenth-century tract spells out the Protestant charge against the Catholic doctrine of Purgatory with painstaking explicitness. The text, published under the pseudonym Nickgroom of the Hoby-Stable, was by Sir Edward Hoby (1560–1617), the eldest son of the great translator of Castiglione and the nephew of Queen Elizabeth's principal adviser, Lord Burghley. Hoby is responding to a defense of Purgatory by the Jesuit John Floyd:

> Such is the notorious folly of your Preacher . . . that he gathereth a Gospel out of a Poem, and that not written historically, or doctrinally, but in pathetical verse, full of Metaphors, Metonymies, Apostrophes, Prosopopeis, and other as well rhetorical figures, as Poetical flowers, which to take in a proper and of rigorous sense, is folly, to urge them as points and articles [of] faith, is such a solemn foolery, that it may seem the next degree to madness. He should know the difference betwixt an

Evangelist, and a Poet, a Gospel and a Poem, rigid truth, and figurative speech, Articles of Faith, and poetical fancies.

Hoby's work is nominally a dialogue, but in response we are given not a defense of Catholicism and not an acknowledgment of the pervasiveness of metaphor, metonymy, apostrophe, and prosopopoeia in Scripture but, rather, a defense of poetry: "Is not this," a character objects, "to shift off their *Idolatrous appeals*, their *mental and imaginary petitions* to the Poet's pen?"[68]

At moments in the Protestant polemic the emphasis falls almost entirely on the emptiness of the fictive imagination, as if "imagined" were inevitably synonymous with "untrue." Cardinal Allen's defenses of Purgatory, writes the acerbic Puritan controversialist William Fulke in 1577, may be compared to "the arguments of those vain fables that were wont to be printed in English of *Bevis of Hampton*, *Guy of Warwick*, and such like, where the arguments show how such a Knight overcame such a Giant, how such a sorcerer wrought such a miracle, which are rolled as confidently as though they were true, and yet there is no man of mean wit so ignorant, but he knoweth them to be feigned fantasies." To Allen's urgent appeal—"Therefore I shall desire all Catholic readers, as they believe this grave sentence of God to come, and fear the rod of our father's correction, that they prevent the same, by lowly submitting themselves unto the chastisement of our kind mother the Church"—Fulke sarcastically replies that it is mere rhetoric. "As for that Prosopopoeia of the mother, opposing her to the father, in word is more rhetorical than Christian in deed, and because it is unfit for the matter, it is more of garrulity than of eloquence." The whole Catholic edifice, Fulke mocks, is an absurd pageant manned by a belligerent impostor: "Now this lusty gallant as though he had fully repaired and fortified the old ruinous and battered towers of *limbus patrum*, with canvas painted walls, he standeth upon his bulwark of brown paper, and crieth defiance to all his enemies."[69]

A "bulwark of brown paper": Protestants sometimes wrote as if the whole doctrine of Purgatory were a stage set, a will-o'-the-wisp, a filthy spiderweb they could simply sweep away. Certainly, by the time of Milton's *Paradise Lost* (1667), it had been swept away in England, so completely that the poet does not feel obliged to condemn or mock it. In Milton's cosmos, there is no purgatorial space at all and no conspicuous refutation of what was once such a central object of Protestant loathing. The nearest thing to an allusion comes in the grotesque fantasy of the fate of those among the horde of "Embryos and idiots, eremites and friars / White, black and gray, with all their trumpery" (3:474–75),[70] who hope through superstitious means to pass disguised into Paradise. Just at the foot of Heaven's ascent, writes Milton, a violent wind sweeps these deluded impostors off their feet and blows them into the "devious air":

> then might ye see
> Cowls, hoods and habits, with their wearers tossed
> And fluttered into rags, then relics, beads,
> Indulgences, dispenses, pardons, bulls,
> The sport of winds: all these upwhirled aloft
> Fly o'er the backside of the world far off
> Into a limbo large and broad, since called
> The Paradise of Fools, to few unknown
> Long after, now unpeopled, and untrod.
>
> (3:489–97)

The indulgences that flutter in the wind, along with all the other rubbish, are all that remains of the elaborate cult of the dead, and what was once a massive, imposing realm has been transmuted into a comic limbo.[71] But this Miltonic perspective, which has shaped our own account of the past, is highly misleading. In early-sixteenth-century England, there was nothing gossamer-like about Purgatory. The great imaginary construction had produced highly tangible results.

Hence at other moments, what is most startling is not the fraudulence of the imaginary place but its power. Tyndale's young follower John Frith writes that when he read the accounts of Purgatory written by those "witty and learned men," Thomas More and the bishop of Rochester, he was struck by the fact that the accounts did not match: "M. More saith, that 'there is no water in Purgatory;' and my Lord of Rochester saith, that 'there is water;' Master More saith, that 'the ministers of punishment are devils,' and my Lord of Rochester saith, 'that the ministers of the punishment are angels;' " and so forth. The conflicting details, Frith concludes, "made mine heart yearn and fully to consent, that this their painful Purgatory was but a vain imagination." The vanity (that is, the emptiness) of the doctrine, the fact that the great prison house is "nothing but man's imagination and phantasy" and its fires a mere piece of "poetry,"[72] does not mean, however, that it is without consequences in the world: purgatorial fire, though a figment of the imagination, brings real gold and silver into the coffers of the Catholic Church.

When in 1545 and 1547, with zealous Protestantism in the ascendant, the English Parliament acted to dissolve the whole system of intercessory foundations created to offer prayers for souls in Purgatory, the lawmakers and bureaucrats found themselves faced with an immense task. They had to strike at colleges, free chapels, chantries, hospitals, fraternities, brotherhoods, guilds, stipendiary priests, and priests for terms of years, as well as at many smaller funds left to pay for trentals (the cycle of thirty requiem masses), obits (the yearly memorial service), flowers, bells, and candles. *Britannia*, the great survey of the realm by the antiquary William Camden, gives as the total number of suppressed foundations 2,374 chantries and free chapels, 110 hospitals, and 90 nonuniversity colleges, a list that modern scholars regard as a substantial underestimation.[73] It would have been a social catastrophe simply to shut down all institutions that had been created in the attempt to provide prayers for the dead.

Government commissioners struggled to separate out the religious functions of such institutions, functions that they wished to ban, from benefits to the community which often seemed manifest and even indispensable. It was one thing to stop the sick from praying for the soul of the founder; quite another to shut down the hospital that the founder had endowed in order to acquire a long-term fund of prayers.[74] In part the task was a legal one: crown lawyers had to figure out how to break a large number of wills, diverting funds from their intended purpose and violating the explicit wishes of the testators. In part it was institutional: to rid itself of Purgatory, English culture had to embark on a huge enterprise of recycling and reorienting. Key aspects of the community's structure had been bound up with its ongoing relationship to souls in the afterlife. If that relationship were to be decisively broken— Protestant reformers hoped to achieve this end—then the ultimate purpose of many significant institutions had to be reconceived and the impulse to assist others channeled in different directions. In part, therefore, the task was also psychological: men and women had to be led to reimagine their own postmortem fate, as well as that of their loved ones.

"I hate dead names"

We can observe the traces of this psychological reimagining in John Donne's remarkable *Devotions on Emergent Occasions* (1623– 1624). Lying ill, brooding on the resemblance between his sickbed and a grave, Donne tells himself that his condition is worse than death:

> In the grave I may speak through the stones, in the voice of my friends, and in the accents of those words which their love may afford my memory; here I am mine own ghost, and rather affright my beholders than instruct them; they conceive the worst of me now, and yet fear worse; they give me for dead now, and yet wonder how I do when they wake at midnight, and ask how I do to-morrow. Miserable, and (though common to all) inhuman posture, where I must practise my lying in the grave by lying still, and not practise my resurrection by rising any more.[75]

"In the grave I may speak through the stones": the phrase invokes tales of ghostly voices surging up uncannily from the grave. It was precisely by means of such voices (or, more accurately, reports of such voices)—along with accounts of voyages to the otherworld and the testimony of those rare individuals who died but then miraculously revived—that the existence of Purgatory was affirmed again and again throughout the later Middle Ages. The purpose of spectral visitations was most often to plead for prayers, almsgiving, pious fasts, and above all masses, in order to obtain some relief from excruciating pain. Less commonly, ghosts returned, as Donne puts it, to "instruct" the living, that is, to issue warnings, disclose hidden wrongs, or urge the restitution of ill-gotten gains.

Throughout the many medieval and Renaissance accounts of these voices or apparitions of the dead, there is a fairly standard pattern.[76] The ghost generally appears shortly after death, while the memory of the deceased, usually a close relative or friend of the living person to whom the vision manifests itself, is still fresh. Ghostly apparitions, then, are quite distinct from the persistence of the dead through fame: hauntings are not about the dream of occupying a place in the memories of future generations, not about the longing to escape from the limitations of one's own narrow life-world, not even about the craving for persistence that leads men to engrave their names on stone tablets. The spectral voice is not for strangers; it is for those who awake at midnight and think about the dead person whom they have loved, and wonder with mingled fear and hope about the fate of that person's soul.[77]

But it is not exactly his own spectral voice that Donne imagines echoing through the stones; it is the voice of his friends. And he does not imagine their words—"the words which their love may afford my memory"—as the prayers that pious Catholics hoped would relieve their sufferings in the otherworld. Rather, by lovingly remembering him after his death, the friends will give Donne's voice at least the semblance of continued existence in this world. Such an existence, however limited, would be preferable, Donne thinks, to his present condition, so leveled by illness that he is his own ghost. In his friends' minds, waking at midnight or thinking about him on the morrow, there is not sweet memory but fear, not gentle closure but ongoing dread.

In the universe conjured up by Donne's *Devotions*, there is ample space for Heaven, and Hell; there is even room for a plurality of worlds; but there is no place for Purgatory. When, in the course of a long work obsessed with death and the afterlife, a ghost makes its appearance, it is only the living Donne himself, gravely ill and hence frightening to his friends, and not the spirit of a dead man who is being purified before rising to bliss. The middle place where such spirits could have been found, by the millions, only a generation or two earlier—and we might recall that Donne was raised as a Catholic and related by marriage to the family of Thomas More— has vanished. To be sure, Donne can invoke it as a metaphor; in Elegy VI, he speaks of kisses he has breathed into "my purgatory, faithless thee." But, declaring that "I hate dead names," he goes on to warn his mistress that she is teaching him to look with "new eyes" and to fall away from his old faith: "[T]hus taught, I shall / As nations do from Rome, from thy love fall." Such a falling away will, he knows, provoke anger and rejection, but he will be armed against their effects:

> [W]hen I
> Am the recusant, in that resolute state,
> What hurts it me to be excommunicate?[78]

Purgatory has become nothing but a "dead name" for Donne, and he is resolute in turning away from it, as he turned away from other aspects of Rome. Yet it leaves a ghostly trace in his writing, and not only in his sardonic reference to his mistress. In his *Devotions* he speaks of three kinds of hearts: the first, suitable to be presented to God, are "perfect hearts; straight hearts, no perverseness without; and clean hearts, no foulness within"; the second, suitable for the devil, are "hearts that burn like ovens," hearts fueled by lust, envy, and ambition, Judas hearts. But there is a third category, one to which Donne himself belongs:

> There is then a middle kind of hearts, not so perfect as to be given but that the very giving mends them; not so desperate as not to be accepted but that the very accepting dignifies them. This is a melting heart, and a troubled heart, and a wounded heart, and a broken heart, and a contrite heart; and by the powerful working of thy piercing Spirit such a heart I have.[79]

This "middle kind" is precisely the category assigned by Catholic tradition to the souls in Purgatory.

Theologians had for centuries pondered the fate of those Christians who were neither completely good nor completely bad, and, in particular, the fate of those at the brink of death burdened with some sins for which they had not done (or had begun but not yet completed) the canonical penance. The sins in question were not the gravest ones, mortal sins for which Hell was the inescapable punishment, but lesser ones ("venial sins," as a distinction fully formulated in the twelfth century put it), for which, if justice were to be satisfied, some punishment was still due.

In Donne's analysis of his spiritual condition, he belongs neither with those whose hearts are perfect nor with those whose hearts are indelibly stained. Contemplating his own death, he recognizes that he stands in urgent need of purgation. But the cleansing for which he hopes has no special place assigned to it in the other-world; it must happen now, in this life, through the healing power of Jesus' sacrifice. "Let thy spirit of true contrition and sorrow," he prays, "pass all my sins, through these eyes, into the wounds of thy Son, and I shall be clean, and my soul so much better purged than my body, as it is ordained for better and a longer life."[80] With this prayer for a spiritual purging that accompanies and surpasses the physical purging prescribed by his doctors, Donne rises from his sickbed like Lazarus from the grave. It is as if the entire Catholic vision of death, reckoning, purgation, and ascent had been compressed, reoriented, and forced into the drama of sickness and recovery in this life.

"Any man's death diminishes me, because I am involved in mankind," Donne writes in the most celebrated passage of the *Devotions*, "and therefore never send to know for whom the bells tolls; it tolls for thee."[81] The famous image here is not historically neutral: the tolling of the bells in Protestant England was a subject of contention.[82] More zealous Protestants wanted to see the custom eliminated as a remnant of popery, and they had a strong case. Traditionally the bells, signaling the passing of a fellow Christian, were a call for prayers that would help speed the newly departed soul through its purgatorial torment. Such assistance would come most naturally from the immediate family of the deceased, but the bells alerted and invoked the assistance of the entire congregation, for all the faithful, living and dead, were bound together. The sound of the bells demarcated a geographical unit of fellow feeling within whose limits prayers were particularly appropriate. The English church instituted restrictions on this practice, but it did not eliminate bell ringing altogether. Donne's image gives unforgettable expression to the shared community of the living and the dead. At the same time it redirects the focus: the dead are no longer a special group imprisoned in a distant penal colony; they are ourselves.

The principal idea, of course, has to do with participation in the human community: "No man is an island, entire of itself; every man is a piece of the continent, a part of the main." But the force of the image of the bells tolling is bound up with its uncanny implication: you may not have realized it, but you are on your deathbed; indeed, you may already be dead. Donne began his work by imagining himself as his own ghost, an image he now immeasurably deepens. But where do these ghosts—all of us, in effect, or at least all of us who have heard the bells toll—reside? In a realm under the earth? In a special place set aside for purgation? No, here in this world, a world that is an enormous charnel house, where we await resurrection.[83] "Where Lazarus had been four days," Donne tells God, "I have been fifty years in this putrefaction; why dost thou not call me, as thou didst him, *with a loud voice*, since my soul is as dead as his body was?"[84]

In a strange, vivid realization of this notion, on February 25, 1631, less than two months before his death, Donne preached his final sermon at St. Paul's wrapped in his shroud. "To the amazement of some beholders," wrote his biographer, Izaak Walton, Donne "presented himself not to preach mortification by a living voice: but, mortality by a decayed body and dying face."[85] The sermon, "Death's Duell," vividly imagines what it calls the body's second death: "the death of corruption and putrefaction, and vermiculation, and incineration, and dispersion in and from the grave, in which every dead man dies over again." As if he is already dead,

Donne politely accepts prayers for his soul, but they are almost without significance: "I thank him that prays for me when the bell tolls, but I thank him much more that catechises me, or preaches to me, or instructs me how to live."[86] There are no ghosts, save the Holy Ghost, no suffrages, save preaching to the living. For the dying Donne there is an almost frantic hope of Heaven; there is an intense fear of Hell and a still more intense fear of putrefaction; but there is no Purgatory.

AS WE HAVE seen in the course of this chapter, the Protestants who attacked the doctrine of Purgatory had worked out an account of the poetics of Purgatory. They charted the ways in which certain elemental human fears, longings, and fantasies were being shaped and exploited by an intellectual elite who carefully packaged fraudulent, profit-making innovations as if they were ancient traditions. In the 1626 sermon at which we glanced in the prologue, John Donne links humans' love for objects of their own making to the legal ruses by which clever men get around real estate restrictions and thence to Purgatory, transubstantiation, the invention of tradition, and the diseased imagination: "For, as men are most delighted with things of their own making, their own planting, their own purchasing, their own building, so are these men therefore enamoured of Purgatory: Men that can make Articles of faith of their own Traditions, (And as men to elude the law against new Buildings, first build sheds, or stables, and after erect houses there, as upon old foundations, so these men first put forth Traditions of their own, and then erect those Traditions into Articles of faith, as ancient foundations of Religion) Men that make God himself of a piece of bread, may easily make Purgatory of a Dream, and of Apparitions, and imaginary visions of sick or melancholic men."[87]

By the nineteenth century the tangle of dream, crafty institutional practice, and material consequences that Donne identifies in this extraordinary passage had hardened into the concept of ideology. But that concept, as modern thinkers have tried to deploy it in a wide range of cultural analyses, has been dismayingly insensitive to the imaginative dimension that most fascinated Donne and his contemporaries. In the Old Testament, Donne remarks, there is no precedent for Purgatory; its foundation stone was laid by Plato, who is the patriarch of the pagan Greek church. "The Latin Church had Patriarchs too for this Doctrine," Donne continues, "though not Philosophers, yet Poets."[88] What we call ideology, then, Renaissance England called poetry.

❧ 2 ❧

IMAGINING PURGATORY

WHAT IF we take the Protestant charge seriously? Not the charge of papal venality or institutional cynicism or conspiracy to defraud—though of course, given the general wretchedness of human beings and the size of the institution in question, there is some evidence that would support all of these accusations. Rather, what if we take seriously the charge that Purgatory was a vast piece of poetry?

From an appropriate distance, the same could be said of all conceptions of the afterlife, and, for that matter, of all religions. By the early eighteenth century, the great Neapolitan philosopher of history, Giambattista Vico, had developed this global perception into what he called a "new science." The first peoples, Vico wrote, "were poets who spoke in poetic characters."[1] What are poetic characters and what are the sentences in which these characters find expression? True poetic sentences are "sentiments clothed in the greatest passions and therefore full of sublimity and arousing wonder" (22). The ancient gods were fashioned out of such sentiments, for in the earliest times the reasoning power of humankind was weak, but the imagination was immensely strong. "In the world's childhood men were by nature sublime poets" (71).

Vico gives some thought to the hypothesis that the gods were invented by mortals whose aim was to cheat and defraud people, but he finds this idea unlikely. His resistance to the notion of an originary imposture is not motivated by sentimentality; he believes, rather, that "it was fear which created gods in the world; not fear awakened in men by other men, but fear awakened in men by themselves" (120). In the first men, "whose minds were not in the least abstract, refined, or spiritualized, because they were entirely immersed in the senses, buffeted by the passions, buried in the body" (118), the pinnacle of fear and wonder was the experience of lightning and thunder. Out of this awe-inspiring, terrifying somatic experience, the first theological poets generated a whole metaphysics: they "created the first divine fable, the greatest they ever created: that of Jove, king and father of men and gods, in the act of hurling the lightning bolt; an image so popular, disturbing, and instructive that its creators themselves believed in it, and feared, revered, and worshiped it in frightful religions" (118). The gods originate not in imposture but in credulity.

Religion in Vico's powerful account is not invented by a group of clever, disillusioned cynics who defraud their gullible neighbors with a fable. It is the invention of the terrorized imagination. Frightened humans create fables with marvelous poetic sublimity, sublimity so great that they believe in their own creations. *Fingunt simul creduntque*—Vico quotes a phrase of Tacitus: "no sooner do they imagine than they believe." Great poetry, the magnificent precipitate of fear, serves a threefold function: it invents "sublime fables suited to the popular understanding"; it perturbs to excess; and it teaches "the vulgar to act virtuously, as the poets have taught themselves" (117). If the theological poets induce the credulous into believing their fictions, it is because they, the poets, have come to believe in these fictions themselves.

For Vico, the fact that the whole enormous structure of belief is based on universal poetic invention is not a source of disillusionment. Instead, it underwrites the very possibility of scientific understanding. For the primacy of human invention lies at the heart of what for him is the great foundational axiom: "[T]he world of civil society has certainly been made by men, and . . . its principles are therefore to be found within the modifications of our own human mind" (96). There is, Vico believes, a mental language common to all nations. Everywhere in the world, he observes, civil society manifests the same three core principles, the universal building blocks of the poetic imagination and therefore of social practice. These principles are, first, divine providence, a fable of the gods; second, marriage, a fable of passions moderated or restrained; and third, burial, a fable of the decaying body and the soul's immortality.

This splendid intellectual edifice is light-years away from what the Catholics and Protestants warring over Purgatory themselves characterized as "snarl" and "counter-snarl."[2] Yet we can apprehend in the Protestant charge that Purgatory was a poetic fable an anticipatory glimmer of the light that Vico was to shine. Of course, the Protestants wanted it to shine, and to shine harshly, in one direction only: at the Catholic doctrine of the middle place of souls and the practices that this place had generated. They would certainly have found Vico's more general claim impious. But the terms of their polemics strikingly anticipate that claim in analyzing the centrality in doctrine and practice of the poetic imagination.

Why were people like Tyndale, Latimer, and Donne confident that their sharp weapon would not turn against their own beliefs? In part the answer lies in the steadfastness of their faith—and, after all, even Vico claims exemption for Christian dogma. In part, too, it lies in the relative belatedness of Purgatory as both a place and a full-fledged doctrine. Hence its poetic inventedness was more glaringly visible than the inventedness, say, of Heaven or of God. Above all, it lies in the absence of a clear scriptural basis not only for Purgatory but also for most of the practices, including indulgences, that were associated with it. With no biblical passages to authorize belief, Protestants could in this one place begin the work that Vico triumphantly universalized.

PICTURING THE AFTERLIFE

Let us accordingly focus less on doctrine than on what Vico would call poetic sublimity. The sublimity in question is not that of great literary masterpieces, of which Dante's *Purgatorio* is the supreme instance. There are surprisingly few references to Dante, hostile or otherwise, in the controversies between Catholics and Protestants, and it is clear that when Frith or Tyndale charges that Purgatory is a fable, he is not thinking of the *Divine Comedy*. Even if these

Protestant writers knew Dante's work—which is unlikely—they would not have been greatly troubled by it, for it does not depend on the reader's belief that the poet is recounting a literal voyage that he personally took. Rather, the massive edifice they wish to dismantle is the effect of hundreds of smaller imaginative interventions, acts of making visible and making articulable that cumulatively made Dante's astonishing achievement possible. The Protestant polemicists of the sixteenth and early seventeenth centuries had, in many ways, a grossly inadequate account of the poetic imagination, for they associated it routinely with lying, but in one respect at least they understood something that we often overlook. They grasped clearly that the imagination was not exclusively the inspired work of a tiny number of renowned poets, though it included that work; it was, they thought, a quality diffused, for good or ill, throughout a very large mass of makers. They saw that it took a sustained collective effort of the imagination to make Purgatory central to the institutional, material, and spiritual practices of everyday life.

There was, for a start, the effort of the imagination to body forth, as Shakespeare puts it, "the forms of things unknown" and to give "to airy nothing / A local habitation and a name" (*A Midsummer Night's Dream* 5.1.14–17). Beginning in the late thirteenth and early fourteenth centuries, alongside traditional images of Heaven and Hell, Purgatory itself begins to be represented in painting, principally as a subterranean cave, a boiling vat, or a dungeon, and artists start to grapple with the depiction of souls who are being tortured and yet have some hope of redemption. In one of the earliest representations, a painted wooden panel from Aachen or Cologne dated 1425, the donor and his family kneel in prayer on either side of a flaming pit that curves back into the distance.[3] Crowded into the pit are the souls of the dead, crying out in pain and begging for help. Their cries are not in vain, for the psalms whose words rise up on banners streaming from the mouths of the donor and his wife are reaching up to the heavens from which four angels descend, carrying attributes of the Works of Mercy: bread for the hungry, clothing for the naked, drink for the thirsty, and a basin for the stranger, the prisoner, or the sick. At the top of the panel, angels are holding a white cloth in which they are carrying up toward the radiant face of Jesus two small naked figures who have been released from their torment.

This panel is not simply a *representation* of the attempt to shorten the term of purgatorial imprisonment; it is an active agent in this attempt. It formed part of an altarpiece before which the donor, the knight Werner von Palant, commissioned masses to be sung daily, except for Tuesdays and Sundays, along with special weekly masses in honor of the Holy Cross and of Mary, and yearly masses in honor of particularly beloved saints. The precise identity of the donor, his wife, mother, and children, secured by the painted coats of arms as well as the portrait likenesses, is crucially important. It is, after all, for their individual benefit and not for a general communal purpose that the knight commits himself to give the chaplain the annual sum of eighteen measures of rye to perform the services. The masses are intended to help them get more quickly and less painfully onto that white cloth being carried up by the angels toward the Savior.

"Good night, sweet prince," Horatio says, bidding farewell to the friend who has just died, "And flights of angels sing thee to thy rest" (*Hamlet* 5.2.302–3).[4] If depictions of the afterlife are any indication, the flying of the angels here is as important as their singing. Angels in flight figure in many images of Purgatory and clearly constitute one of the central ways in which the faithful imagined that assistance would come to them in their distress. In one striking fifteenth-century manuscript illumination to a theological tome, a capital letter *D* is divided in three parts by a wooden cross or *T* (plate 1). In the top segment a lone peasant raises a hoe or rake above his head and is about to bring it down onto the ground for some purpose: whether he is working the field or digging a grave is not clear. "There is no ancient gentlemen but gardeners, ditchers, and gravemakers," says the wry gravedigger in *Hamlet*, "they hold up Adam's profession" (5.1.29–31). The peasant in the illuminated capital is practicing Adam's profession. He swings his implement as if he thought the ground beneath his feet was thick and solid, but in fact he is standing on only a thin ledge, beneath which are two separate chambers. Each of these has a yawning Hell-mouth within which are crowded the suffering figures of the dead, eerily looking out toward the viewer. The images are virtually identical, save for a single differentiating feature: on one side an angel is hovering near the top, reaching out to one of the souls who raises up his hands to be pulled out of the horrible mouth; on the other side a devil blocks the exit, and none of the souls has any hope of escaping.

Illuminations with a particular bearing on Purgatory frequently appear in Books of Hours, the volumes, often lavish and exquisite, that contained the prayers or offices prescribed for the seven stated times of the day allotted by the medieval church to prayer. Not surprisingly, representations of the afterlife are most often conjoined with the office of the dead recited at vespers, particularly with the prayer known as the *Placebo*. At times the images simply depict a funeral, such as the beautiful scene painted by Gerart David of Bruges for Edward, Lord Hastings, of a church interior: nine black-hooded monks are praying by a coffin, lit with many candles, while other religious figures are in the surrounding choir stalls (fig. 2). But very often there are dramatic scenes of suffering and rescue. An illumination later in the same manuscript shows angels helping redeemed souls rise up toward a golden sun in the midst of which God (wearing a crown reminiscent of a papal tiara) stretches out his hands to welcome them. The souls are depicted as naked adults, both male and female. Some are being held in the arms of the angels; others are riding on their backs; one, a woman with very long hair, is standing erect on the angel's outstretched hand (plate 2).

That, of course, is the good news—these images of rescue in effect make sense of the act of praying seven times a day—but the prayer books also feature scenes of unspeakable suffering, such as one in a Book of Hours that belonged to Philip the Fair, archduke of Austria, that depicts the fate of those who are thrust for eternity into the mouth of what appears to be an exceedingly unpleasant cat (fig. 3). Often these scenes of Hell differentiate among the various tortures inflicted forever on different types of sinners— thieves hung over flames; the envious plunged first into vats of ice

Von dem bösen oder vbeln in a[l]er gemainlichait

[Als]

[ode[r]]

[bös]

[zen]

[en]

[der]

[ha]

[w]

[do]

[de]

[ul]

der pin vnd des schaden vnd d[i]

setzet sich wider drier hand g[r]

Plate 1. Initial *D*. Peasant (Adam?) digging above scenes of Purgatory and Hell. Hugo Ripelin von Straßburg, "Compendium theologicae veritatis," Book 3, fol. 64va. Würzburg, Universitätsbibliothek, Cod. M. ch. F. 690.

Plate 2. Souls ascending. Gerart David of Bruges in Book of Hours belonging to Edward, Lord Hastings. Brit. Lib., Add. MS 54,782, fol. 231. By permission of the British Library.

Plate 3. Angel protecting soul from demon. Book of Hours that belonged to
Philip the Fair, archduke of Austria. Brit. Lib. Add. MSS 17,280, fol. 281.
By permission of the British Library.

Plate 4. Hieronymus Bosch, Vision of the Otherworld. Palazzo
Ducale, Venice. By permission of Art Resource.

Plate 5. Tondal suffers a seizure. Simon Marmion (illuminator), *Les Visions du chevalier Tondal* (1475), fol. 7. The J. Paul Getty Museum, Los Angeles.

que bien y entraissent de
front a vne fois dix mille
cheualliers armez tous
a cheual. Celle horrible
beste auoit en sa gueule
deux grans diables tres
hideulz et cruelz a veoir

estoient ces deux diables
en la gueule de celle beste
ensement comme deux cou
lombes et faisoient en
icelle gueule trois portes
Vng merueilleuz feu en
grandeur qui iamaie ne

Plate 6. The beast Acheron, devourer of the avaricious. Simon Marmion
(illuminator), *Les Visions du chevalier Tondal* (1475), fol. 17. The J. Paul Getty
Museum, Los Angeles.

appuru et puis leur fe
uint moult grant lumie
re · Adont deuint lame
toute asseuree / et si tres
pleine de leesse et iope q̃
Incontinent elle fut de

Et en paour par la boie
Et ozendroit suis ie hois
de tout malaise · Ie setoie
oudeurs puantes a mer
ueilles · Et ie ne sens que
toute bonne flaueur ·

Plate 7. The Wicked But Not Very. Simon Marmion (illuminator), *Les Visions du chevalier Tondal* (1475), fol. 33v. The J. Paul Getty Museum, Los Angeles.

Plate 8. The Monk and Guy's widow converse with the soul of Guy de Thurno. Simon Marmion (illuminator), *The Vision of the Soul of Guy de Thurno* (1474), fol. 7. The J. Paul Getty Museum, Los Angeles.

Fig. 2. Funeral. Gerart David of Bruges in Book of Hours belonging
to Edward, Lord Hastings. Brit. Lib., Add. MS 54,782, fol. 184.
By permission of the British Library.

and then into boiling water; the angry stoned by raging demons;
the proud stretched on rotating wheels, and so forth.

Such differentiations in misery are carried over as well into textual accounts of temporary suffering in Purgatory, but they rarely
figure in images. For the visual arts the more pressing and difficult
problem is not to distinguish among various forms of hideous tor-

Fig. 3. Souls in Hell. Book of Hours belonging to Philip the Fair,
archduke of Austria. Brit. Lib. Add. MSS 17,280, fol. 38. By permission
of the British Library.

ment in Purgatory but to distinguish between any of these and the
identical torments of Hell. As we have seen, the principal device is
to reproduce the traditional imagery of Hell but to add an image
of rescue. A French manuscript of the fifteenth century (fig. 4)
shows a rider on a white horse, with two companions, in the presence of three skeletons. The rider holds up his right hand, as if to
ward off the images of death, but at best this will be only a brief
delaying action. At the right, three souls suffer the torments of
Purgatory in a vat filled with red flames. How do we know that the
vat is Purgatory and not Hell? Because above the vat an angel is
lifting up a fortunate soul who has completed the term of suffering, while below a demon thrusts his pronged fork at the burning
figures crowded into a Hell-mouth. A similar scene of a flaming
cauldron, in a Spanish manuscript, shows one of the figures actually struggling to climb out while mass is being said (fig. 5). The
possibility of mitigated punishment or an outright escape is depicted still more clearly in a scene such as one found in the Book
of Hours of Philip the Fair. In two marginal vignettes, intertwined
among beautiful wreaths of leaves, fruits, and flowers, a cadaverous

Fig. 4. Rescue from Purgatory. French Book of Hours (Horae B. Mariae Virginis). Brit. Lib. Add. MS 11,866. By permission of the British Library.

figure of death, holding a spade and a scythe, leads away a wealthy-looking man and a well-dressed woman: such is the inevitable fate of all flesh. But on the same page, inset into the *Placebo,* a white-robed angel holds under one arm a naked figure whose hands are clasped in prayer; the angel's other arm, wielding a long sword, wards off a horned devil (plate 3).

Fig. 5. Gregory conducting Mass. Note soul climbing out of cauldron.
Brit. Lib. Add MS 18193: Hores de Nra Senyora Segons la Esglesia
Romana. By permission of British Library.

On many church walls and portals, sculptured motifs from the
late Middle Ages and early modern period conjoin skulls and cross-
bones—the fate of the body—with the image of the soul, most
often a young woman with long, flowing hair, half-immersed in a
cauldron lapped by flames, her hands clasped in prayer or her eyes
raised to heaven (fig. 6). The clasped hands or raised eyes, signs
in the midst of fear and danger of the hope of salvation, serve to
distinguish such an image from the very similar iconography of a
soul in Hell. Moreover, the figure serves to instruct the worshiper
who happens to look up at it: it simultaneously represents prayer,
motivates it, increases its fervor, and explains one of its principal
benefits.

Images of purgatorial suffering fulfill a complex, multiple function. They are instructions to the viewer's imagination, guiding it
to give an appropriate shape to a concept of purgation that might

Fig. 6. Soul in purgatorial flames. Church in Ragusa, Sicily.
Photo: Stephen Greenblatt.

otherwise seem too abstract and theoretical to generate the proper degree of fear. That fear is at once aroused and mitigated by the prospect of rescue, and the best means of hastening that rescue is depicted in the gesture of prayer. The representational challenge is to fashion a response distinct from the blend of horrified fascination and grim satisfaction with which the viewer is ordinarily invited to regard the agonies of the damned or the complacent pleasure with which the viewer is invited to regard the pious delights of the saved. The ultimate goal is to provoke action, the pious action needed to obtain the supernatural assistance figured in the angels who lift the souls out of their suffering.

On occasion, the assistance comes from still higher powers: on the title page of a mass book of 1521, Hans Holbein the Younger shows Christ and Mary nourishing souls in Purgatory with their blood and milk (fig. 7). The image of Mary's milk flowing into

Fig. 7. Christ and Mary nourishing souls in Purgatory with blood
and milk. Hans Holbein the Younger, *Missale Speciale* (Basel:
Thomas Wolff, März 1521). By permission of the Houghton
Library, Harvard University.

the mouths of suffering souls was widely disseminated, especially
around Naples, while in the North artists tend to favor a different
representation, the Mystic Mass of Saint Gregory the Great. Traditionally, that image made the doctrinal point that the consecrated
Host in the central Christian ritual, the Eucharist, is not merely a

representation or reminder but is miraculously transubstantiated in Christ's body and blood. As Saint Gregory elevates the Host before an altarpiece, the figure of the bleeding Savior appears. In some images, beginning in the fifteenth century, the blood from his wounds flows not only into the chalice used in the celebration of the Mass but also into the mouths of small naked figures standing near the altar.[5] These figures are souls of the dead, suffering in Purgatory, and with the divine assistance of the Mass, the souls begin to ascend out of the flames.

This image of upward movement is perhaps the most brilliant solution to the representational problem posed by Purgatory, since it gets at a crucial way of differentiating the suffering endured for eternity by souls in Hell from that endured by souls whose term of punishment is limited. In an astonishing late-fifteenth-century panel by Hieronymus Bosch, now in the Doge's Palace in Venice, we see naked souls that have been cleansed of their sins lifted by angels toward a long funnel, a kind of birth canal, at whose end figures are emerging into a blinding light (plate 4). It was some such ecstatic movement that the celebrants of Mass or the pious readers of the Books of Hours were encouraged to imagine, for themselves and for those they loved.

"Most of the representations of Purgatory in medieval art," one scholar has concluded, are "illustrations showing the efficacy of intercession."[6] But the visual evidence which we have examined certainly also supports Vico's general hypothesis that a primary motive in the poetic fashioning and dissemination of religious belief was fear. And it is difficult, in the case of Purgatory, to rule out a mercenary motive as well, both for the artists and for the institutions they served. But there were other considerations that helped drive the enterprise. Through its teaching about Purgatory, the church mobilized an impulse of charity toward the dead that could be deployed throughout the lives of the living. The doctrine of suffrages confirmed the power of the Mass and of the ecclesiastical hierarchy, but it also stressed communal solidarity, kindness, love, and solicitous concern for the weak and the wretched. Concern properly began with the fate of one's own soul—after all,

Christians were responsible for their own individual actions—and it could end there too, but the longing for rescue extended to wider circles.

Sermons and images trained people to imagine in vivid detail the miseries of suffering souls, and the church then offered ways to transform empathic identification into generous action. Many of these ways involved religious rituals, but they also included alms to the poor, subsidized education, hospitals for the sick, assistance in giving the indigent a proper burial. A Middle English poem, "The Relief of Souls in Purgatory," in a fifteenth-century devotional compilation is accompanied by a drawing showing souls being pulled out of the purgatorial flames in a bucket. The bucket is drawn by a thick rope that passes through a pulley at the entrance of Heaven and then back down to the earth where it is pulled by a group of priests who are saying Mass at an altar. The drawing, in a manuscript possibly executed for the private use of a Carthusian monk, thus celebrates the power of ritual. But the rope continues past the altar and reaches an individual, evidently a layman, who is giving alms to two poor people, one of whom has an artificial leg.[7]

There was a high cost to all of this, as Protestant reformers indignantly charged: a large clerical hierarchy in the service of the cult of the dead, a steady flow of money into the hands of these soul-specialists, a flowering of religious practices that many figures in the Catholic Church itself regarded as superstitious, and a morbid infusion of death into all aspects of community life. Above all, polemicists tried to discredit the charitable impulse by claiming that the only real beneficiary was the pope. "Purgatory brings Rome more gold a day," goes a satirical jingle from the 1570s, "Than two horse well loaden will carry away."[8] And what does the pope do in exchange for all of this gold? Nothing. "The pope is kin to Robin Goodfellow," Tyndale remarks wryly, "which sweepeth the house, washeth the dishes, and purgeth all, by night; but when day cometh, there is nothing found clean."[9] For, as we have seen, the reformers argue that the whole Catholic mortuary kingdom is a fraud, built around a mere fantasy. "I am wont to call a dream a dream," says one of the characters in Veron's dialogue *The Hunting of Purgatory to Death;* "For, where have they learned those lying tales, and vain fables, that they have preached unto us?"[10]

Protestants struggled therefore to undo the purgatorial imagination. Only by taking the great fable apart, piece by piece, could they hope to liberate people from it. Only by exposing it as a fable could they get the faithful to conquer slavish credulity or at least redirect the most compelling feelings that the cult of Purgatory had deliberately aroused and braided together: hope and fear. The easiest part of the task was to destroy the images: manuscripts were torn up, altarpieces were disassembled and burned, sculpted images of souls praying in the flames were smashed. Or if the images were not destroyed, they were detached gently or violently from their original meaning. All over England, set into the floors of churches, are exquisite monumental brasses still intact, but with the prayer for the donor's soul carefully chiseled away.

Images are vivid but vulnerable. The harder part of the zealots' task was to chisel away a set of powerful stories, for it was in narrative even more than in pictures that the purgatorial poem was created and maintained.

PRISON HOUSE AND THEATER

Souls were imprisoned in Purgatory for a purpose: to be readied for bliss. It was possible, at least in principle, to emphasize the positive outcome and to conjure up a state of being very close to the joys of Paradise. Hence, for example, in the mid-twelfth-century *Vision of Tondal* (or *Tnugdal*) written in Latin in the south German city of Regensburg by an Irish monk, a description of the horrific torments suffered by the damned in Hell is followed by a very different account of two adjacent abodes. Neither of these abodes is explicitly designated as Purgatory—evidently the work's author, Brother Marcus, was unaware of the term—but their function is closely related to that formalized shortly afterward in church doctrine and repeatedly explored in narrative.[11]

Tondal, a dissolute young layman who has collapsed into unconsciousness and whose soul has been granted a vision of the afterlife, is relieved when the stench, screaming, and darkness of Hell give way to a more endurable sight. By an extremely high wall he sees a multitude of men and women, hungry and thirsty, standing exposed to wind and rain. In comparison with what he has just witnessed and in part endured—souls beaten, burned, and mutilated; others raped and devoured by monsters; still others (male and female alike) howling as they give birth to snakes—the suffering of those by the high wall seems light. Tondal asks his angelic guide who they are. "These are the wicked," the angel answers, "but not very." "They have indeed applied themselves to lead a rigorous and virtuous life," he explains, "but they did not give worldly goods generously to the poor as was their duty, and this is why they have merited to suffer the rain for some years, after which they will be brought to a good resting place."[12]

The next abode, reached by a door that opens to them of its own accord, is a still happier vision: a fragrant, flowery meadow filled with joyous souls resting by the fountain of life. Tondal shouts in delight, thinking that he is in Heaven, but the angel corrects him: "The people who dwell here are not totally good: they have been spared the tortures of Hell but do not yet merit to be united to the communion of saints."[13] Purgation, in this account, is a period of waiting, at best in something like Provençal spring, at worst in the equivalent of a blustery season in Dublin.

This vivid account does not depend upon illustrations and for the most part circulated throughout Europe without any, but as it happens, a manuscript of *The Vision of Tondal*, commissioned by Margaret of York, duchess of Burgundy, has miniatures by one of the great Flemish illuminators of the fifteenth century, Simon Marmion of Valenciennes. In Marmion's first miniature, Tondal, a model of elegance in his peach-colored velvet robe and his gold chain, reaches out for some food at the dinner table, when he suddenly suffers a seizure (plate 5). We next see him laid out on the floor, as if dead, surrounded by a crowd of grieving witnesses, while in the air, visible to us but not to these witnesses, winged demons are coming for his soul. In the following miniature, everything has changed: the room has disappeared, along with all of the young man's rich clothes, from his soft cap to his pointed-toe shoes, and Tondal's soul stands completely naked before the ap-

Fig. 8. Tondal and Guardian Angel. Simon Marmion
(illuminator), *Les Visions du chevalier Tondal* (1475), fol. 11v.
The J. Paul Getty Museum, Los Angeles.

proaching fiends. Naked but not alone: he is accompanied and
protected by a beautiful, golden-haired angel arrayed in a long
purple robe (fig. 8). Marmion emphasizes these clothes as
clothes—the robe, from which the angel's altogether human head
and hands emerge, is fastened at the neck by a small gold pin—
and at the same time emphasizes their symbolic status by depicting
the angel's wings as identical to them in color and substance. That
is, clothing in the afterlife is a sign of angelic virtue and power, just
as nakedness is a sign of human vulnerability.

The subsequent miniatures make manifest the consequences of
this vulnerability with a series of unforgettably vivid depictions of
the unspeakable torments to which souls in Hell are subjected.

Fig. 9. The Good But Not Totally Good. Simon Marmion
(illuminator), *Les Visions du chevalier Tondal* (1475), fol. 34v.
The J. Paul Getty Museum, Los Angeles.

Indeed, at one point Marmion, for the most part extremely faithful to his text, transforms a description of two devils stuck into
the cavernous mouth of a horrible beast into an image of the infernal suffering of two miserable humans (plate 6). But the tone
and imagery shift dramatically when Tondal is led by his angelic
guide to the place of purgation. In one of the illuminations, the
angel shows the naked Tondal the wall in which the "wicked but
not very" are standing exposed in niches; in another, he points
through an archway to the meadow where the good but not totally good disport themselves around the fountain of life (plate 7
and fig. 9).

But in both medieval theology and popular literature such relatively mild, even blissful representations of the intermediate zone
between Hell and Heaven are rare. Far more common is the night-

marish landscape of fire, snow, and stinking water, vividly depicted in a characteristic passage from a late-twelfth-century text, recounting a vision that a monk of Evesham, who had fallen into a coma, reported upon returning to consciousness:

> The region of the above-mentioned valley, and the sides of both mountains, which bore this dreadful appearance of heat and cold, were occupied by a crowd of spirits, as numerous as bees at the time of swarming; and their punishment in general was at one time to be dipped in the fetid lake; at another, breaking forth from thence, they were devoured by the volumes of flame which met them, and at length, in fluctuating balls of fire, as if sparks from a furnace, were tossed on high and fell to the bottom of the other bank; they were again restored to the whirlings of the winds, the cold of the snow, and the asperity of the hail; then, thrown forth from thence, as if flying from the violence of the storms, they were again thrust back into the stench of the lake, and the burnings of the raging fire. . . . Of all those then who were there tortured, the condition was this, that for the fulfillment of their purification, they were compelled to pass through the whole surface of that lake from the beginning to the end.

"For the fulfillment of their purification": at moments the process is figured as a kind of ghastly stain-removal, as if the souls were being fed into an enormous washing machine, complete with caustic cleansing solutions and alternating cycles of heat and cold. At other moments it is figured simply as torture in a monstrous penal colony:

> Some were roasted before fire; others were fried in pans; red hot nails were driven into some to their bones; others were tortured with a horrid stench in baths of pitch and sulfur, mixed with molten lead, brass, and other kinds of metal; immense worms with poisonous teeth gnawed some; others, in thick ranks, were transfixed on stakes with fiery thorns; the torturers tore them with their nails, flogged them with dreadful scourges, and lacerated them in dreadful agonies.[14]

This is, let us reiterate, the good news. These are souls destined for Heaven, but they cannot enter its sacred precincts with the burden of even relatively minor sins upon them. Why did God's sacrifice of his own Son not suffice to clean the slate of each soul? Because that sacrifice did not erase individual moral responsibility. If all actions are significant, the argument goes, if virtuous actions are always rewarded and vicious actions punished, if individuals are accountable for their own behavior, then the principle of retributive justice absolutely required that each and every sin, no matter how small, be counted, weighed, and punished. God in this very familiar picture was the supreme judge in a heavenly court.

The invocation of the court of heavenly justice was closely linked to the image of Purgatory as a prison, where, for an appropriate period of time and with a precisely calibrated intensity, punishments would be meted out for sins that had not been fully erased in this life through penitence, fasting, alms, prayer, confession, masses, and other good works. In theory all punishments during the soul's incarceration were various degrees of separation from what was called the Beatific Vision: access to the divine presence for which the imprisoned soul longs and to which it would ultimately rise. But in practice—that is, in the imaginative conception fostered in images and stories—the imprisoned soul was a malefactor, a petty criminal perhaps (serious crimes being punished in Hell) or an improvident debtor, who would be subjected to the most hideous tortures that an unrestrained punitive intelligence could devise. Only when the debt to the divine creditor was fully paid would the soul be released and allowed to go to its destined home.

In keeping with their exemplary nature, the tortures inflicted upon souls in both Purgatory and Hell generally have a theatrical character, as at least one medieval vision of the afterlife renders explicit. In the early-thirteenth-century *Visio Thurkilli*, the peasant Thurkill is led in spirit by Saint Julian into the otherworld, where they are joined by Saint Domninus. There they encounter a fiend who tells them that, as it is Saturday evening, he is hurrying to "our theatrical games" (*ludis nostris theatralibus*).[15] When the saints express their desire to attend these games, the fiend consents but warns them not to bring the peasant, lest he "disclose our secrets to his friends, and thus hinder our work upon earth, and save some from the seats that are even now prepared for them."[16] Julian and Domninus nonetheless manage to bring Thurkill with them, hiding him between them. The theater, a "huge round building (*domus amplissima*) enclosed with dark and antique walls," has in effect a two-tier seating arrangement: innumerable souls of either sex sit on round seats (*sedes*) in cages full of red-hot iron spikes turned inward; above them, on seats fixed into the walls, sit grinning fiends eager for the merry spectacle to begin.

When all of the spectators are assembled, the Prince of the accursed calls out the various sinners who are brought out of their cages one by one and made to perform. Hence, for example, the proud man is dragged out of his seat and brought onto the stage where "in his filthy robes of black he makes a display of all his vanity":

> He stiffens up his neck, tosses his chin, arches his brows, looks askance, shrugs his shoulders, and struts about on tiptoe. The Fiends shriek with laughter. Then his breast swells, his cheeks glow, his eyes sparkle, and striking his nose with his finger he threatens mighty things. Presently, with an air of fashion, he draws out a needle, and loops up his hanging sleeves. But then his clothes burst into flame, and his whole body is set on fire. Fiends whirl around him, tearing him with red hot hooks and prongs: and one of them keeps drenching him with pitch and grease, and at every drench his limbs hiss and crackle, like a frying-pan when cold water is dropped in it.[17]

The demonic guide helpfully explains to the saints that this last is the worst of his torments. Then, piecing the victim's torn body together and nailing it down upon his seat again, the fiends proceed to the succeeding shows—a priest who has neglected his flock, a knight who has spent his life in slaughters and robberies, a corrupt judge, and so forth.

The Cult of Fear

An alternative image-cluster emerged from the conception of Heaven not as a law court but as a place of exceptional purity, a palace, for example, with perfectly polished floors or a sublimely beautiful garden. No one stained with excrement and clad in filthy rags could be allowed into a place so exquisite: such a person would first have to be scrubbed clean and given fresh clothing. Unfortunately, the scrubbing would be unpleasant, or, rather, ordinary scrubbing would not suffice: only cutting, freezing, or burning could remove the residual pollution left by sin. And the principal cleansing agent, fire, would be excruciatingly painful, "more terrible," as Augustine put it, "than anything that a man can suffer in this life."[18] The formulation became standard and was endlessly reiterated, with the precise nature of the principal torture described in vivid detail by theologians and preachers.

The pain of purgatorial fire, according to a Middle English homiletical work, is so great

> that all torments sharp and fell
> that all martyrs han [*have*] suffered here,
> and pains that women when they swell
> of childing thole [*endure*] that to death are near,
> to that pine is not to tell
> but as a bathe of water clear.[19]

"Of all the torments which can be suffered," warns an English Jesuit of the mid–seventeenth century, James Mumford, in the same vein,

> none is more painful than those of fire, and perhaps all the other torments which our world hath, can scarce so bitterly torture a poor creature, as it would be tortured, if it were possibly [*sic*] for it to be kept without consuming in the midst of the merciless flames of a glass furnace, the fire of which would soon as it were penetrate itself with the very inmost parts of that afflicted wretch; his bones would glow like red hot bars of iron, his marrow would scorch him more fiercely than

melted lead, his blood would boil more furiously than high-seething oil, his nails, his teeth, his gristles, his very skull would be like plates of bright flaming brass all on burning fire.[20]

Terrible as it is, Mumford adds, this earthly fire is as nothing—"a kind of painted fire"—compared to the scorching flames of Purgatory.[21]

Representation and reality, here and elsewhere in the literature of Purgatory, exchange positions. The terrible fire was in principle intended to be a convenient image, drawn from ordinary life, of the suffering that a redeemed soul would experience after the death of the body, during the cleansing period in which it was deprived of the vision of God. But the image of bodies in flames is more vivid, more intuitively graspable, and more frightening than the abstract notion of a deprivation or absence. Hence, in sermons and homilies, the imagery becomes increasingly elaborate, demanding ever more attention, until the notion of the Beatific Vision shrinks to near-invisibility. The fire ceases to be a figure for what the preacher understands cannot be represented and instead becomes what he insists is the actual experience of the otherworld: not an image at all, therefore, but a reality—*the* reality—next to which our actual physical experience of being burned (the most intense pain that most of us endure in the ordinary course of life) is mere representation.

The rhetorical strategy here is not without its risk, for it is obviously the church's fire, the fire of Purgatory, that is "painted" (both in words and in the actual paintings that adorned the walls): it would seem rash virtually to call attention to the fact that the handle of a frying pan, imprudently grasped, can inflict more agony than mortals have ever directly known of the whole vast punitive machinery of the afterlife. But writers like Mumford repeatedly take this risk in part to challenge doubt precisely where it is most likely to arise and in part to produce the somatic effect that interests them: not the actual agony of being burned but sickening dread of what might come. Though some churchmen clearly felt that the dread was better aroused through menacing vagueness—talk of what was forbidden or simply too horrible to be disclosed to mortal ears—than through such overly explicit imagery as glass furnaces and scorched marrow, the general goals over a long period of time remained constant: to undermine psychological security, to prevent any serene contemplation of one's own death or that of one's loved ones, to make the stomach churn and the hair stand on end, to provoke fear.

How long could an ordinary person—not so wicked as to deserve Hell but not so preternaturally virtuous as to ascend directly to Heaven—expect to suffer these horrors? One Spanish theologian calculated that an average Christian would have to spend around one to two thousand years in Purgatory.[22] An Italian preacher declares that he cannot guess how much time is allotted to his audience's dead friends and relations, but their prospects are bleak. After all, he points out, Pope Sixtus V granted an indulgence of 11,000 years for the reciting of a certain prayer at Notre-Dame; Gregory XIII conceded 74,000 years to the members of the Confraternity of the Rosary.[23]

What could be done? One answer was to choose Purgatory in this life. As the pain of mere flesh was supposed to be infinitely preferable to the agony suffered by the strange virtual body (*similitudo corporis*) of the soul, and as God was graciously willing to accept the pain of the flesh in place of the pain of the soul, the faithful could elect penance or ardently hope for suffering in this life as a way to lessen the reckoning that would ultimately and inevitably have to be paid.[24] "And he that does a sinful deed," goes the *Cursor Mundi*, a fourteenth-century Northumbrian poem,

> Of heavy penance has he need.
> For it is better here for to mend
> Than in the cleansing fire be brend.[25]

Heavy penance, and for that matter ordinary suffering, in this life could in effect do the beneficial work of purgatorial fire at a much reduced level of pain. As Thomas Tuke puts it, reducing several centuries of complex meditation to a simple formula, "He that dies, while he lives, lives whiles he is dead."[26] In consequence, a pious person should pray, in the words of the fifteenth-century mystic Richard Rolle, "Grant me, lord Jesu, Purgatory for my sins ere I die."[27]

For many Protestant critics, such prayers were contemptible, as was the prudential calculation that lay behind them: "Consider the slavish fear," writes Henry Jones in the mid–seventeenth century, "into which by the Popish Doctrine of Purgatory, the world had been brought; with fear whereof many have all their lives long been held in bondage: being told that all the sorrows in this life, labors, want, banishments, prisons, shame, miseries, calamities, wounds, nay death itself, are nothing to the pains of Purgatory."[28] But in Rolle's traditional and widely shared view, terror of the purgation that lies ahead is an essential agent of moral restraint as well as an inducement to the pious acceptance of tribulation.[29]

From this perspective—a perspective familiar from innumerable paintings, carved capitals, and mosaics still visible on the walls of medieval and Renaissance churches—fear was a gift to be assiduously cultivated.[30] The discourse of Purgatory was meant not only to manage, contain, and ultimately relieve anxiety; it was explicitly meant to arouse it, to sharpen its intensity, to provide it with hideous imagery. "Among all the Passions of the mind," writes a seventeenth-century recusant Catholic, Jane Owen, "there is not any, which hath so great a sovereignty, and command over man, as the Passion of *Fear.*" It is for this reason, she writes, that she has instructed the printer to include at the bottom of every page of her book, *An Antidote Against Purgatory* (1634), the ominous words from Matthew: "Thou shalt not go out from thence, till thou repay the last Farthing."[31]

It is not an accident that the words Owen quotes are monetary as well as monitory. She writes not simply for the faithful but for the faithful who have enough wealth to protect themselves from the worst consequences of their venial sins by acquiring the favorable intercession of souls whom their charitable contributions have helped to reach Heaven. "O how many peculiar *Advocates* and *Intercessours* of the then most blessed Soules (released out of *Purgatory*) might a rich Catholike purchase to himselfe," she writes, urging almsgiving and other means of assisting the dead, "thereby to

pleade his cause before the Throne of Almighty God, in his greatest need."[32] Owen's particular concern is that wealthy parents may
be foolish enough to give everything to their children at the expense of their own souls; it is, she warns, crucial to make those
expenditures that will save one from purgatorial torture even if
those expenditures mean doing less for one's heirs: "Let your own
Souls (which are more near to you, than any Children) HAVE AT
LEAST A *Child's Portion*."[33]

To encourage her readers to lay out, as she puts it, "a great
part of your riches to spiritual usury (as I may term it) for the
good of your Souls," she rehearses four basic principles devised to
arouse the appropriate level of anticipatory dread: first, the pains
of Purgatory are more intense than any pains experienced in
this life; second, the pains of Purgatory for the most part endure
longer than any pains can endure in this life; third, the souls in
Purgatory cannot help or bring ease to themselves; and fourth,
the souls in Purgatory are almost infinite in number. To these principles, which, as Owen acknowledges, may be found in Cardinal
Bellarmine and other Continental sources, she adds a specifically
English argument drawn unexpectedly from Shakespeare's *1
Henry IV*:

> *Sir Iohn Oldcastle* being exprobated of his Cowardliness, and
> thereby reputed inglorious, replied; *If through my pursuit of
> Honour, I shall fortune to loose an Arm, or a Leg in the wars, can
> Honour restore to me my lost Arm, or leg?* In like manner I here
> say to you, *Catholic*: Can your Riches, your worldly pomp and
> pleasures, or antiquity of your House, and Family redeem your
> Souls out of *Purgatory?* Or can this poor weak blast of wind or
> air, which you call your reputation (consisting in other men's
> words, passed upon you) cool the heat of those burning
> flames?"[34]

This strange allusion to Falstaff—remembered by his original stage
name, before Shakespeare was compelled to change it in defer-
ence to the descendants of the Lollard martyr—is an attempt to
awaken fear of the afterlife where it is most mooted, in the skeptical, antiheroic credo of the fat knight.[35] Sensing perhaps that this

is an unpromising line of reasoning, Jane Owen generally sticks to more familiar ground, the testimony of those "eyewitnesses" like Tondal who have died and then, at God's bidding, have revived or who have otherwise been enabled to tour Purgatory for themselves and report on what they have seen to a world that would otherwise have remained skeptical or indifferent.[36]

EYEWITNESSES OF THE AFTERLIFE

The earliest of these eyewitnesses is a pious English layman, Drihthelm, whose vision of the purgatorial beyond in the year 696 is related in Bede's *Ecclesiastical History of England* (before 735). Many of the elements that recur centuries later in accounts of Purgatory—the infernal valley with its merciless flames and its blinding snowstorms, the hideous stench, the screams of the tortured souls—are already present in Bede's account, along with the angelic guide who explains to Drihthelm that he is not, as he thinks, in Hell but rather in a realm where souls are readied to enter the Kingdom of Heaven. The realm, however, is not yet specifically called Purgatory, and it is not a single place. As is still the case in the *Vision of Tondal*, more than four hundred years later, purgation is sharply bifurcated: the souls of the not-entirely-bad (the wicked who repented their sins in time) are tormented by devils, while on the other side of a high wall the souls of the not-entirely-good rest in a bright, sweet-smelling flowery meadow. The formal designation of a third place called Purgatory, situated between Hell and Heaven and devoted to the painful, gradual, and progressive purging of souls destined for bliss, does not occur until the late twelfth century in the reports of other eyewitnesses to the nature of the afterlife.

The most important of these, for the Middle Ages, is the knight Owein, who is the first named visitor to a place specifically called Purgatory. The numerous vernacular accounts of the adventures of "Owein Miles" (*Owein* is a variant of *Ywain*, the name of a knight of the Round Table whose tribulations constitute a kind of Purgatory on earth)[37] all derive from the Latin prose treatise *Saint Patrick's Purgatory* (*Tractatus de Purgatorio Sancti Patricii*), written in the early 1180s by the Anglo-Norman monk H. of Sawtry in Huntingdonshire.[38] Henry (as subsequent chroniclers dub him, for no good reason) explains that he was asked to write the story by a fellow Cistercian, the abbot of Sartis, and that he first heard it from another monk, Gilbert, who had been sent to Ireland in order to locate a site on which to found a monastery. Since Gilbert did not speak Gaelic, he took with him as interpreter and bodyguard the knight Owein, and it was Owein who directly recounted to him the story of his adventures in Purgatory.

Saint Patrick's Purgatory, then, surrounds the vision with a network of names—H. of Sawtry, the abbot of Sartis, the monk Gilbert, Abbot Gervase (who sent Gilbert into Ireland)—names that serve to authenticate the eyewitness account and set it in the context of a larger community among whom the narrative has been circulating. Here, as in other early visionary accounts of the afterlife, direct testimony is evidently less prized than an authorizing medium of transmission. Drihthelm, the English layman who died and then miraculously came back to life, does not directly record what he saw; rather, the Venerable Bede tells his story. Tondal's vision is recounted by Brother Marcus, in response to the request of an abbess, "Lady G." The monk of Evesham's account is in the first person, but the chroniclers who include it make clear that we are being given what, "with incessant tears and groans," he only reluctantly told his fellow monks, who had urgently entreated him to relate for their edification what he had seen.

"The order of ideas must follow the order of institutions" (78), goes one of Vico's canniest aphorisms about the metaphysical imagination. The key institutions in the case of Purgatory were the monasteries, and in particular the houses of the Anglo-Norman Augustinian canons and Cistercians who generated the story of Owein and set it in motion, making copies of *Saint Patrick's Purgatory* and urging preaching friars to cite it in their sermons.[39] The Cistercians had only recently established a substantial presence in Ireland, and it was obviously in their interest to lay claim to the possession and control of an entrance, perhaps the only entrance on earth accessible to mortals, to the otherworld.[40] But the claim was only as good as the belief that was invested in it, a belief that depended not on a doctrinal argument about the necessity of purgation in the afterlife—that argument had been made in a variety of ways at least from the time of Augustine—but rather on the credit accorded a particular narrative about a specific place and a specific repertoire of experiences to be had there. Though credit presumably ran high within the order itself (assuming for the moment that the monks were not joined together in a cynical conspiracy), the claim obviously depended on its ability to extend beyond the confines of the monastic community. But how was belief generated outside the group whose interests it clearly served? How were people not in the immediate orbit of the monasteries induced to credit what they did not and, in the nature of things, could not see?

The answer depends in part on the stunning mobility of texts, a mobility enhanced by vernacular translations. In addition to the 150 surviving manuscripts of the Latin original, there are an equal number of copies in translation, diffused throughout Europe from Madrid to Cracow, Edinburgh to Rome.[41] This remarkable diffusion has led understandably to the claim, often reiterated, that H. of Sawtry's account was "one of the best-sellers of the Middle Ages,"[42] but perhaps the language of the modern book trade is not altogether appropriate here. It is quite possible that broad circulation of the visions at Saint Patrick's Purgatory, like the comparable circulation of *Mandeville's Travels* or Columbus's first letter, represents a response to widespread curiosity. But the Latin *Saint Patrick's Purgatory* and its many translations are closely linked to an institutional program, and they seem to be addressed less to the curious than to those who doubt the very existence of the place described.

THE KNIGHT'S ADVENTURE

The Middle English translations, the most famous of which is *Owayne Miles*—a version in rhymed six-line stanzas in the early-fourteenth-century Auchinleck MS—generally begin with Saint Patrick's discovery of the entrance to Purgatory at Lough Derg, in county Donegal, a discovery that is an implicit response to the problem of innovation and an explicit response to the problem of skepticism. The Cistercians, in this account, were not inventing an entrance to the otherworld; they were guarding a holy site that had been known for centuries. The skepticism that might be expected to greet such a claim—for there is no philological evidence prior to the time that *Saint Patrick's Purgatory* was composed that Purgatory as a specific geographical location was thought to exist, let alone that its entrance could be found in Donegal[43]—is countered by being displaced back to the time of Saint Patrick. Purgatory here does not emerge from a mist of popular credulity and only later, in enlightened times, encounters disbelief. It is explicitly asserted in the face of contemptuous ridicule. The heathen Irish find the missionary saint's account of the afterlife quite simply unbelievable: "They no held it but ribaldry / Of nothing that he said" (stanza 2, lines 5–6). In Raphael Holinshed's late-sixteenth-century rehearsal of the legend, in his *Irish Chronicles*, the skeptical auditors declare flatly, "[W]e dislike not of our liberty." They are not, they tell the saint, inclined to believe "gugawes and estrange dreams."[44] Similarly, in Calderón de la Barca's play *El purgatorio de San Patricio* (ca. 1634), the Irish king Egerio refuses to credit the vision reported by his daughter, who has revived from an apparent death. The vision, the king maintains, is simply an "encanto," an "hechizo," a deceiving "apariencia" designed to lure the credulous into conversion.[45]

Purgatory is haunted, from its origin and then repeatedly in the retellings, with the specter of disbelief, the suspicion that the whole thing is an illusion, a trick, a fiction. In many of the versions, the doubt (which is aroused by Saint Patrick's preaching not of Heaven and Hell—these are assumed to exist—but only of Purgatory) is accompanied by a proposal or challenge:

> And then he preached of Purgatory,
> As he found in his story
> But yet the folk of this country
> Believed not that it might be,
> And said, but if it were so,

> That any man might himself go
> And see all that and come again,
> Then would they believe fayn [*willingly*].[46]

Distressed by this response, Patrick goes to pray in church and falls asleep before the altar. He dreams that Jesus comes to him, gives him a strange book that "speaketh of all manner godspelle [*the Gospels*], / Of heaven and earth and of Hell, / Of God's privity [*secrets*]" (stanza 9, lines 4–6), and leads him into a great desert to a grisly hole, round and black. Patrick is frightened "in his sleeping," but Jesus tells him that this is a place for penance: should a person venture down into the hole, steadfast in belief, he would have to suffer there for only a night and a day and would then be forgiven his sins, thus avoiding the terrible punishments that would otherwise be due to him.

It is part of the peculiar imaginative daring of medieval texts to answer an ontological challenge with a dream, as if the charge of fantasy could be met only on fantasy's own ground. The dream vision serves as a kind of transition between the fictive realm to which the saint's auditors assign his preaching and the reality upon which he insists. This reality begins to assert itself—to harden into the solidity of the material world—when, on awakening, Patrick finds himself in possession of the book of which he has dreamed, a book whose revelation of "God's privity" lies beyond human creation: "there is no clerk that such can write, / Nor never no shall be" (stanza 9, lines 2–3). Furnished with this token of the truth, along with a staff about which he has also dreamed, the saint ventures forth to find the hole. In the earliest English text to mention Saint Patrick's Purgatory, *The South English Legendary* (late-thirteenth-century), he actually appears to create the entrance to Purgatory by tracing it with the staff.[47] In other texts, he simply locates the site. In all versions, however, he proceeds to establish an abbey there, providing an architectural setting for the revelation: at the east end is situated the black hole, "with good stone wall all abouten, / With lock and key the gate to locken" (stanza 23, lines 4–5). The lock and key signal that the setting is institutional as well as architectural, with the entrance to Purgatory controlled by the white-robed monks of the abbey and ultimately by the whole clerical hierarchy.

To this place comes Owein, a knight of Northumberland,[48] eager to repent his sins and determined, against the solemn warnings of the bishop of Ireland, to venture into "Patrickes Purgatorie." The warnings are part of a preparatory ritual that serves to make descent into the hole seem like a solemn, spiritually meaningful decision, not a rash act. Only after a fifteen-day period of ritual "affliction," fasting, and prayer is the knight brought, in a procession with cross and banners, to the hole and told that he will find, below the ground, a hall of stone lit with a wintry light. The emphasis on spiritual discipline, as distinct from ordinary martial courage, continues even when Owein passes through the gate, heads north through the "great field," and reaches the hall. His first encounter is not with the demons of the underworld but rather with thirteen wise men clad in white whose leader counsels him to keep God in his heart, think upon his wounds, and invoke his high name. Only when these wise men leave does the knight, his dread heightened by an earsplitting noise, see the first of the devils, fifty score of them with hideous grinning faces on their backsides as well as their heads.

The peculiar jauntiness of these fiends—who proclaim that the knight has come "To fetch him the joy of Hell / Withouten any ending" (54.5–6)—is not a form of comic relief; rather, like the grimacing faces in Bosch's powerful, singularly anti-Semitic painting of the mocking of Christ, their taunts are set against a sobriety that serves as a sign of spiritual maturity. (We might note that "sadness," even in Renaissance English, had the force of "sincerity" or "seriousness.") In a work that sets out to establish the existence of Purgatory in the face of skepticism and disbelief, mockery is repeatedly marked out as demonic.[49] "Welcome, Owein!" the "master-fiend" cries in mock hospitality, "Nor haddest thou never more mischance / Than thou shall have in our dance, / When we shall play begin" (56.3; 56.4–6). The devils offer to spare him suffering if he follows their advice and turns back, but he refuses and calls upon God, whereupon he is led into "an uncouth land."

The geographical description that follows derives from the tours of Hell familiar from the second-century *Apocalypse of Saint Peter,* the third-century *Apocalypse of Saint Paul,* and other ancient texts in the Christian tradition, texts closely related to both Jewish and classical sources.[50] Through a treeless landscape blows an icy wind, carrying the sounds of screaming. Owein heads north, the traditional direction of Satan's realm, through a serious of discontinuous valleys and fields, past a mountain "red as blood," a filthy, stinking river, a sinister castle filled with torture chambers and fiery pits.[51] In some versions of the story he quite understandably mistakes the place he is in for Hell: "Then wende [thought] the knight he had found / The deepest pit in Hell-ground" (64.1–2). His mistake is corrected, but there is little or no difference between the landscape of Purgatory and the landscape of Hell:

> He saw there lay full a field
> Of men and women that were aqueled [*destroyed*],
> Naked with many a wound,
> Toward the earth they lay deueling [*groveling*],
> "Allas! Allas!" was their brocking [*complaint*],
> With iron bands y-bound;
>
> And began to screech and to wail,
> And cried, "Allas! Mercy, mercy!
> Mercy, God almight!"
> Mercy was there none, forsooth,
> But sorrow of heart and grinding of tooth:
> That was a grisly sight.
>
> (65–66)

These are the tortures of the slothful, and the grisly sights continue, with unrelenting ferocity, through the fields of the gluttons (bitten by toads, snakes, and dragons), the lechers (torn with burning hooks and hanged), the backbiters (grilled on gridirons), the avaricious (broken on a flaming wheel), the usurers (boiled in molten metal), and all the others, many fixed to the ground by red-hot nails driven through their feet, hands, and head, who are penned up within the horrible place.

Initially, though the spectacle of so much pain grieves and frightens him, Owein is simply a wondering observer of a succession of new sights and sounds, and his role of eyewitness (and ear-witness) remains crucial throughout the work: "He heard screech and grede [*cry out*]" (64.6); "There he saw sorrow more" (68.6); "And saw where a wheel trent [*turned*], / That grisly were of sight" (83.2–3); "he nor had never seen before / Haluendel [*half the amount of*] the care" (98.2–3); "He nor saw never ere none such" (96.3). But the demons have already begun to threaten him—"Thou hast been strong lecher apliyt [*truly*], / And strong glutton also" (74.2)—and he pales when he sees stretched out on the instruments of torture some of his acquaintance (79.4). Before long he himself has begun to suffer: drenched in cold, stinking water, scorched by fiery heat, terrified by pits of molten lead, and finally cast into a dark, stinking, burning dungeon where pride—evidently Owein's major sin—is punished.

At the end of a sequence of trials of increasing intensity, Owein is brought by a squadron of demons with sixty eyes and sixty hands to a high, narrow bridge above a pitch-black river that "stank fouler than any hound" (116.4). This is, he is told, the bridge of Paradise, but, if he attempts to cross it, fiends will throw stones at him, a strong wind will blow, and, should he fall, he will be seized by the waiting "fellows" who will teach him "a new play" (119.4). For the river below—"So the dominical [*Sunday reading*] us tell" (123.1)— is the entry of Hell; for anyone who falls off the bridge—"as high as a tower, / And as sharp as a razor" (121.1–2)—there is no redemption. As they have repeatedly done, the demons offer him a chance to turn back. There is no necessity for him to attempt the crossing: "Fly peril, sorrow, and woe," they tell him in the accents of fraudulent solicitude, "And to that stead, there thou come from, / Well fair we shall thee lead" (124.4–6). Though frightened, Owein remembers that God has repeatedly saved him. He ventures out on the bridge, finds that he feels no razor's edge, and manages the perilous passage.

Once he passes through the bejeweled gates of Paradise, he is greeted by a joyous procession of the saved, in which the church hierarchy heavily predominates:

Popes with great dignity,
And cardinals great plenty,
Kings and queens there were,
Knights, abbots, and priors,
Monks, canons and friar Preachers [*Dominicans*],
And bishops that crosses bear.

Friars Minor [*Franciscans*] and Jacobins [*Dominicans*],
Friar Carmes [*Carmelites*] and friar Austins [*Augustinians*],
And nuns white and black. . . .

(38.3)

The knight dwells among them with delight for as long as he is permitted and then is sent, weeping with reluctance and regret, back to the abbey from which he has come, and to life in the world of the flesh. Now a holy man, Owein takes up "scrip [*pilgrim's bag*] and burden [*pilgrim's staff*]" and embarks on a pilgrimage to the Holy Land. On his return—a return, we are told, not to his native Northumberland but to Ireland—he becomes a monk and lives for another seven years before he dies and goes to Paradise.[52] The poem ends with a prayer that marks the full transformation of the once sinful knight:

Now God, for saint Owain's love,
Grant us heaven-bliss above
Before his sweet face! Amen.

(198.4–6)

In the visit to Patrick's Purgatory, the knight experiences for a short time what he would have to endure, were he condemned to a term of purgatorial torture. And for the reader, too, there is a similar vicarious experience of fear. For the knight there is also a certain measure of physical pain. "There are (saith he) who say that the Knight being entered the Hall, was rapt into an ecstasy," *Saint Patrick's Purgatory* notes, "and that in the spirit he saw all these things. The Knight confidently affirmed that it was not so, but that he did see all things with his corporeal eyes, and really felt what he did suffer."[53] But the torments, along with the demonic threats of eternal punishment, vanish in the face of pious steadfastness.

The mistake would be to turn back, to compromise, to refuse to face a suffering that is, in comparison to the actual torments of souls in Purgatory, only dreamlike, virtual suffering—in Mumford's phrase, "a kind of painted fire." There is, to be sure, an alternative course: a chastened, unimaginative life, less heroic but more stable and secure in its daily piety. It is this alternative that the bishop of Ireland initially urges upon Owein, but the knight, acting as the reader's surrogate, insists upon a direct encounter, and the reader accordingly follows him into the black hole.

Marks of Protection, Marks of Pain

To encounter within carefully demarcated boundaries what might otherwise spiral out of control; to know states of extreme suffering and exaltation that are normally inaccessible; to penetrate realms that are hidden from view and to return safely, changed forever by what one has encountered: Owein's journey is in some sense a model of a certain imaginative experience, as it subsequently came to be developed, an experience to which Dante in the early fourteenth century gave the highest expression. To be sure, neither H. of Sawtry's Latin *Tractatus de Purgatorio Sancti Patricii* nor any of the English texts based upon it comes even close to the sublimity of Dante's *Purgatorio*. H. of Sawtry's account gives almost no individuating detail to his adventurous knight or to the souls he encounters, and though subsequent narratives invent a past for him to repent—"He particularly repented of the violation of churches and invasion of ecclesiastical property, besides other enormous sins of which he had been guilty"[54]—Owein's character never attains the vividness (what classical rhetoric called the *enargeia*) that Dante's verse confers on virtually everything it touches.

In an early-fifteenth-century prose text attributed to William of Stranton in the bishopric of Durham, however, one can at least glimpse traces of the impulse to individualize and thereby intensify the voyage through the uncouth land. Unlike the earlier accounts at which we have looked, this one is written in the first person. William enters Saint Patrick's Purgatory on April 14 (Easter Day),

1406.[55] He is greeted by demons who present themselves as his friends and slyly attempt to dissuade him from continuing on his voyage, warning him that he will hurt himself. More disturbingly, he meets his dead sister in the company of the man she had wished to wed, a wedding William had prevented.[56] Blocking a marriage was a sin—Mirk tells confessors to inquire into acts of this kind[57]— for which William needs to repent and be shriven. The need to repent is driven home by a terrible sight that Saint John shows him: pits in which sinners are hideously punished, for a limited duration if they are in Purgatory, forever if they are in Hell. Around these pits, witnessing the tortures, stand those who have been the victims of the sinners' actions.

Among a group of priests being tortured, William sees his uncle (*eme*) who had died sixteen years earlier. The torture consists of his being enclosed in plates of burning iron, "and on the plates were letters and words well written, and through the words were nails of iron all burning smitten into their heads and so into their hearts and into their bodies."[58] The letters, Saint John explains, were "divine service that they should have said and done every day, with great devotion" (101–3), instead of playing, as they did, in fleshly and worldly lusts. Now the words, which would have served as "marks" of protection, as they do for William during his passage through Purgatory, are objects of excruciating pain, pain intensified as the devils rip out the sinners' hearts and tongues, shred them, and fling the flaming pieces back into their faces.[59] William's face, by contrast, is safely marked by his prayers. The marks are signs not simply of pious trust, that is, of an inner condition; they are also the tokens of proper religious practice. For as William of Stranton's vision reveals, faith alone is not enough to ensure an escape from pain. The souls in Purgatory possessed sufficient belief to save them from an eternity of torment, but they failed to realize and implement this belief in acts that would spare them a cleansing suffering after death. William's work ends with a monitory vision of a prioress who has placed an excessive trust in God's mercy. She has been shriven for her sins, but she is condemned to suffer horribly until doomsday, because trust in God's mercy is not the same as a full and proper repentance.

Making Dreams Real

I remarked above that *Saint Patrick's Purgatory* may serve as a model
for a type of literary experience: an expressive pattern of explora-
tion, symbolic suffering, and psychic release that extends from
Dante's *Purgatorio* to Seamus Heaney's *Station Island*. The literary
potential of H. of Sawtry's vision was directly exploited in Marie
de France's *Espurgatoire Seint Patriz* and still more in a series of
remarkable works from the Spanish Golden Age, including Pérez
de Montalbán's *Vida y purgatorio de San Patricio* (1627), Lope de
Vega's *El mayor prodigio y Purgatorio en la vida* (1627), and Calderón
de la Barca's *El purgatorio de San Patricio* (1628).[60] But if by literature we mean only those works that pull away in some sense from
the world, that manifest a certain indifference, if not hostility, to
direct reference, that call attention to their own verbal invention
and the inventedness of the worlds they depict, then the principal
significance of the Latin *Saint Patrick's Purgatory*, along with its
translations and adaptations, lies elsewhere. For, far from occupying a self-enclosed play space, this text attempts to drive its fantasies directly into the earth where it locates the actual cave entrance
that leads into Purgatory. It has nothing to do with the pleasures
of suspended disbelief, a toying with the world and the mind that
enables one to pretend that something is real that one knows is
actually an invention or a clever hypothesis. It uses the devices of
fiction—the central character is a knight from an adventure tale—
but it is not content with "as if" or "suppose." What is really at
stake is not character or style or intensity of vision but the daring
imaginative act of deploying in narrative a place called Purgatory.
The central creative act is to assert that this place actually exists
in the world; its consequence is to make people fear their future
imprisonment, attempt to alleviate their anticipated torture there,
and even visit it as pilgrims.

The idea that the residual stains of sin would have to be purged
after death before the cleansed soul could ascend to Heaven is a
very ancient one. But, as we have already remarked, the identification of a specific place for this purgation—a third place, situated

alongside Heaven and Hell—is quite late.[61] Dating from the early 1180s, H. of Sawtry's *Saint Patrick's Purgatory* is virtually contemporary with the theological formulation that it seems to illustrate; indeed, it considerably anticipates the first pontifical definition of Purgatory, which did not come until a doctrinal discussion between the Latin and Greek churches in 1254. Narrative and doctrine, then, are intimately intertwined.[62]

This doctrinal issue—the dogmatic insistence on the existence of time and progress in a specially demarcated zone of the otherworld—is obviously conceptually crucial, but it does not by itself call forth a narrative such as *Saint Patrick's Purgatory* or exhaust its significance. Why should the story of the knight's passage through the afterlife have seemed important enough to the Cistercians to circulate in so many manuscripts? Why were its tales translated, recycled as exempla and deployed in sermons? Why did monks, theologians, and preachers, with their sophisticated intellectual resources, think they needed Owein the knight? The answer lies in the fact, possibly as apparent then as now, that Purgatory is an innovative work of the imagination. Apparent, but inadmissible. Does it bear repeating that it is all made up, every bit of it? That no one comes back with reports from the dead; that the dreams dreamt by coma victims have no more claim on reality than any other dreams, that the whole elaborate organizing structure of religious belief and practice in the Middle Ages was a sublime fiction? Purgatory is only an extreme and vulnerable instance of something far more widespread: it is palpably invented and obviously new and startlingly phantasmatic, and yet it must somehow pretend to have the compelling vividness and solidity of those things that we actually know to exist. The monks who launched the story were not propounding a doctrine; they were shaping and colonizing the imagination, specifically the imagination of what, if anything, follows the death of the body. Of course, their religion had had long experience in doing this: Heaven and Hell are overwhelmingly impressive predecessors and models, next to which the middle space of souls is a relatively minor, belated innovation. But the very belatedness enables us to view close-up what the antiquity of Heaven and Hell largely obscures: the process by which philosophical abstractions, institutional ambitions, and inchoate fears acquire a local habitation and a name.

This process turns out to rely heavily on literature: the made-up story of Owein—not simply an abstract principle of successive events in time but the adventures of a named hero—helped to make real a place that would have initially seemed to be made up. Why should it have done so? That is, why was the theological claim not by itself sufficient? Or what was there—for that matter, what is there—about literature that made it so serviceable? In part the answer is that narrative is the principal home of eyewitnessing. H. of Sawtry's text is crude, compared to the sophisticated, intellectually supple, and challenging writings of the theologians, but it could claim to record a direct, personal encounter. Of course, such claims do not come with ontological guarantees, at least not guarantees that one could stake one's life on. But as we have already seen, *Saint Patrick's Purgatory* counters skepticism by playing simple yet extremely effective games with reference—setting, for example, Patrick's dream of the mystical staff and book against his waking discovery of these divine tokens in solid reality. To be sure, that claimed discovery is no more tangibly real in any logical sense than the dream, but H. of Sawtry can appeal both in general to the reader's comfortable knowledge of real-life staffs and books and in particular to the purported survival of these same material objects as relics that may still be viewed: "God's Staff, I understand," the Middle English *Owayne Miles* puts it, "Men clepeth [*calleth*] that staff in Ireland / Yet to this ich [*very*] day" (10.40–46). Perhaps the narrator's uncharacteristic phrase "I understand" expresses some reservation about the relic, some lack of absolute confidence that the object men call "God's Staff" is the very staff that Saint Patrick awoke to find in his possession. But the existence of the relic is nonetheless reassuring, for it provides the ordinary material perception upon which the larger claim for the existence of what cannot be seen is built. Two other early English versions of the *Owayne Miles*, in the Cotton and Yale manuscripts, strengthen this link by observing that the staff remains the object of a ritualized display.

Saint Patrick received the "rich staff" and the book, we are told, with good cheer:

> And yet be those rich relics there,
> And at every feast-day in the year
> They been borne in procession
> With full great devotion.
> The archbishop of that land
> Shall bear that staff in his hand.
> Whoso will wyte [*know*] what it hatte [*is called*],
> "Jesu staff" men call it yet.[63]

To some readers, the sight of the staff—or the confident assurance that the staff could in fact be seen—must have reinforced the account elsewhere in the work of a realm that is beyond mortal vision: such, at least, must have been the conviction of those who publicly burned the staff in Dublin in 1538.[64]

But even without the material existence of the relic, the play of dream and waking in the *Owayne Miles* is one of the basic means by which, in Elaine Scarry's phrase, "the verbal arts enlist our imaginations in mental actions that in their vivacity more closely resemble sensing than daydreaming." Analyzing a scene in Proust in which an image from a magic lantern is projected on the walls and door of the narrator's room, Scarry notes that though the fictive wall is just as insubstantial as the fictive magic lantern's image, the image nonetheless has the odd effect of making the wall seem solid: "[B]y the peculiar gravitational rules of the imagination, two or more images that are each independently weightless can nevertheless confer weight on one another."[65] This is the effect that the *Owayne Miles* attempts to achieve (and evidently, for its medieval audience, succeeded spectacularly in achieving) by setting the airy thinness of fictive dreaming over against the thickness of fictive reality.

To this device we may add many others, equally simple and equally effective, beginning with the basic notations of time and space ("near," "soon," "further," and so forth) by which direct witnessing has been narrated at least since Herodotus:

> When he came nigh the stead [*place*]
> He looked up soon anon;
> Strong [*difficult*] it was further to go,
> He heard screech and grede [*shout*].
>
> (64.3–6)

Narrative is the principal textual means of doing what painting does: creating and populating a space.[66] Like the landscapes in medieval painting, the underground realm in the *Owayne Miles* is not organized on the principles of perspective. The hero moves through a sequence of discontinuous spaces, characterized by only the most conventional of topographical features and not rationally linked to one another. Yet what emerges is a distinct and recognizable landscape, the landscape of fear.

Looking at the tiny marks on the page, we cannot see or hear anything other than those marks themselves: the underground realm is obviously inaccessible to our senses. We cannot feel the icy wind or smell the stench from the black river or hear the screams of the tortured, but, we are told, Owein does. He goes where we cannot, passing from one of the hidden spaces to another, and reports to us what he has experienced for himself and what we would experience had we the courage or misfortune to enter the cave. In the course of doing so, he even expresses the wonder that readers must feel at the claim that there are great fields and enormous stone halls below the ground. First the claim is made: "The hall was full selly dight [*marvelously made*], / Such can make no earthly wight / The pillars stood wide." And then Owein responds on our behalf: "The knight wondered," we are told, "that he found / Such a hall in that land, / And open in each side" (44.1–6). The descriptions of what he sees constitute a kind of narrative map or guide, a set of instructions for fashioning an image of the otherworld.

Beginning in the late twelfth century, the church, which had left details of the place of purgation vague, and which had refused or neglected even to specify whether it was a "place" at all, decided to tell people what they could expect to see and experience. But they needed a volunteer: Owein is this volunteer, the one who has gone and returns to bear witness.

The *Owayne Miles* stresses the voluntary, even willful, nature of the hero's decision: "Nay, Owein, friend!" the bishop says, when the knight first proposes to enter Purgatory; "That ich [*same*] way shalt thou not wend" (36.1–2). But his determination to proceed is fixed—"For nought the bishop could say, / The knight would not leten [*abandon*] his way" (37.1–2)—and remains so when the fiends attempt to dissuade him in very similar terms. This sense of overcoming a difficult obstacle helps to rationalize our exclusion from the vision, but once the initial free choice is established, it gives way to its opposite, a sense of directedness and boundedness. Owein does not move freely within Purgatory; he is led. Indeed, his initial experience, after he has rejected the fiends' urging to turn back, is of extreme duress. The fiends build a great fire and then turn on their unwelcome guest: "Feet and hand they bound him hard, / And cast him amidward" (60.1–2). Here, as later, he is saved when he calls on God, but the divine protection does not preclude further unsuccessful demonic attempts to seize him, nor does it ever altogether free him from constraint. When the fiends are not trying to hook him onto the burning wheel or cast him into the filthy river or plunge him into the pit of molten metal or throw him off the narrow bridge, they are leading him "with great pain" from place to place (90.1).

We might imagine that constraint is specifically what it means to be in the hands of demons, but this is not exactly the case. As soon as Owein makes it clear to the bishop that he is adamant in his intention to proceed, he immediately loses all sense of free agency and is led off, just as he is later led off by the demons:

> For naught the bishop could say,
> The knight would not at all abandon his way,
> His soul to amend.
> Then led he him into holy church,
> God's works for to wirche [*perform*],
> And the right law him kende [*taught*].
>
> (37)

For fifteen days he is kept "in affliction / In fasting and in orison," at the end of which time he is brought in a solemn procession to the entrance of the hole.

Why, if it is not a clear marker of the difference between priests and demons, should the *Owayne Miles* emphasize the hero's constraint? The answer seems linked to the other features we have noted that work to establish the solid reality of what might otherwise too patently appear an imaginary realm.[67] The hero is not moving about in a world of his own making but acting according to detailed instructions. Here is the gate, the prior tells the knight,

> And when thou a while ygone hast,
> Light of day thou all forlast [*will lose*],
> Ac [*but*] hold thee even north.
>
> (39.4–6)

Having set his direction, the prior goes on to tell Owein what he should expect: he will come to a field in which he will find a stone hall lit with a faint wintry light. He is to wait there until thirteen men who will give him further instructions join him. It all happens as foretold, and Owein continues to follow their instructions through the rest of his voyage, even as he is being dragged about by the demons.

Obviously, the knight is the nominal object of all of the directives, but equally obviously it is the reader who is their principal recipient. For this is how the great process of invention begins: after centuries in which the faithful were permitted to daydream, as it were, about what their purgation after death might be like, they are now receiving detailed instructions about precisely what they can expect to encounter. Their imagination of the afterlife is no longer indeterminate or free: it is guided, shaped, and constrained in the ways that successful narratives always guide, shape, and constrain the imagination of those who come under their sway.

I have stressed the extent to which the whole project of the medieval narrative was to induce readers to credit the reality of Purgatory, to confer upon it the "givenness" of those things that actually exist. But there is nothing reassuringly familiar about the landscape we are instructed to imagine and very little that is convincing, in the mode of narrative realism, about the knight's experiences. On the contrary, the torture fields littered with gridirons and whirling wheels, the hundreds of thousands of broken bodies, the huge red mountain, the stinking river that runs under the mountain like a bolt from a crossbow, the blast of wind powerful enough to lift the knight into the air, the castle filled with pits of burning metal, the bridge that is "many miles" above the black, burning water: this is the topography of nightmare, not of solid reality. We could simply attribute this to limited narrative gifts: H. of Sawtry is not Tolstoy or Proust. But the *Owayne Miles* has in fact precisely the representational means that it needs to produce its particular desired effect: the perception of a realm in which time and space are warped, the laws of physics are suspended, and the boundaries between the living and the dead are blurred.

The *Owayne Miles* wants to affirm that Purgatory is real, but the reality it depicts is dreamlike: solid things suddenly dissolve, doors open in blank walls, snow and fire together fall from the sky, words have magical effects over objects, creatures are composed out of the parts of different animals, the body is burned or torn to pieces only to be revived in order to submit to further experiments in excruciating pain, and all at once pain gives way to exquisite joy. These elements, so close to our experience of fantasy, distance the *Owayne Miles* from any claim on ordinary reality, but here they work to convey almost effortlessly the nature of the extraordinary reality that is being doctrinally affirmed.

In the seventeenth century there was an attempt to give this dreamlike reality convincing pictorial representation by means of a device that oddly anticipates Proust's shimmering image. In his *Romani Collegi Societatus Jesu Musaeum celeberrimum . . .* (Amsterdam, 1678), the indefatigable Jesuit intellectual Athanasius Kircher claims to have invented the magic lantern. The image of this candlelit slide projector, whose lifelike images left its viewers, he claims, ravished in admiration, shows a band of eight transparencies, including a chicken, a figure of Time with a scythe, a person on his or her knees praying, and so forth. But the transparency that is actually being projected onto the wall is of a soul in Purgatory, burning in fire and imploring help (fig. 10).[68]

Fig. 10. Magic Lantern. Athanasius Kircher, *Romani Collegii Societatus Jesu Musaeum celeberrimum* (1678), p. 125. By permission of the Houghton Library, Harvard University.

The church, even at its most aggressive, did not require that the faithful accept this or that topographical feature of Purgatory as literally true: one was not positively obliged to believe in the existence of the whirling wheel on which "an hundred thousand souls and more" were hanging on hooks, or the hideous, flaming dragons, or the vicious seven-colored fire surging forth from the ground, or even the black toads, newts, adders, and snakes. But each of these frightening elements helped to fill the space upon whose literal existence the church did insist. And their dreamlike qualities doubled back in a satisfying way to confirm the whole movement that the work sketches from skepticism to belief: the pagans regard Purgatory as a dream and declare that they will not believe it until they see it for themselves; Saint Patrick dreams a dream; the dream becomes the reality of the black hole; the hole is said to be the entrance to Purgatory; and Purgatory turns out to have the structure and imagery of a dream. This sounds suspiciously circular, but only because we have left out of our summary a crucial and quite literal structure: the fair abbey, "with power and eke with rich" (21.6), that is constructed around the hole.

THE HOLE IN THE GROUND

The hole or cave enclosed by the abbey's walls at Lough Derg in northern Ulster became one of the important pilgrimage sites of the Middle Ages, attracting penitents many of whom were drawn by the belief—tenacious in spite of official attempts to modify it—that a person who entered this place would have no other Purgatory.[69] There were considerable hardships and risks associated with the pilgrimage, which was represented as an ordeal. The difficulty of the journey itself, the period of fasting and discipline that preceded entry into the cave, and the dangers posed by whatever lay within all combined to make the pilgrimage more like a ritualized martial exploit than a religious journey. Significantly, all of the medieval pilgrims to Lough Derg whose identities are known were male.

The extent to which the dangers were physical was open to question. One authority, Gabriel Pennotus, claims that "they who being truly penitent shall enter into this Purgatory, and do suffer those cruel pains, whether by a real passion, or if only but by an imaginary apprehension [*sive per veram passionem, sive per imaginariam apprehensionem*], shall be purged from all punishments due to them for their sins."[70] Though the Protestant Holinshed speaks of "the old withered worm-eaten legend, loaded with as many loud lies and lewd lines," he nonetheless rehearses Gerald of Wales's old report that "if any be so hardy as to take one night his lodging in any of these inns [the nine caves on the island], which hath been experimented by some rash and hare-brained adventurers, strait these spirits claw him by the back and tug him ruggedly and toss him crabbedly."[71] Still more were the risks psychological: the horrible spectacle of torment, the cries of the sufferers, the hideous grinning of the demons, and the intense fear could undermine a person's sanity. It was said, as Caxton notes, that when a pilgrim returned from the experience of Purgatory, "never shall nothing in this world please him that he shall see nor he shall never be joyous nor glad nor shall not be seen to laugh but shall be continually in wailings and weepings for the sins that he hath committed."[72] Hence, for example, a German pilgrim who visited Lough Derg around 1400 is said to have refused, on his return, to eat anything but bread and salt:

> Nor could he show a cheerful face, but looked all the time as though they would immediately kill him and when they asked him why he was always so sad, he said: If any man among you had seen the tenth part of that I have seen, he could never be happy again all the days of his life. The same monk by the favour of his Abbot became a Hermit in a forest, where he lived a severe hard life, ever thinking of the great misery which he had seen in the aforesaid Purgatory and he lived nearly twelve years longer.[73]

Comparable stories testify not simply to the risks of the pilgrimage to Lough Derg but to the serious, long-term effects, in this life and beyond, that pilgrims were reputed to experience from their descent into the cave.

The Catholic Church, however, was never altogether comfortable with the claims made on behalf of Lough Derg, claims that at times seemed as much to threaten as to substantiate the doctrine.[74] In part the threat lay in an exaggerated faith in the efficacy of the pilgrimage, a faith that seemed to call into question the whole moral logic not only of purgatorial suffering but of penitence and absolution. Popular belief went so far as to imagine that a descent into the hole would settle in advance—and always favorably—the judgment of the soul.[75] In part the threat lay in the opposite direction, in the skepticism provoked by recurring reports that the wonders of Lough Derg were grossly exaggerated, and by complaints that the pilgrimage site was nothing more than a crassly commercial exploitation of vulgar superstitions. "I have spoken with diverse men that have been therein," writes Caxton in 1480, among whom was a "high Canon of Waterford, which told me that he had been therein five or six times. And he saw nor suffered no such things. . . . [save that] in their sleep some men have marvelous dreams. And other thing saw he not. And in likewise told to me a worshipful knight of Bruges named Sir John de Banste that he had been therein in like wise and seen none other thing but as afore is said."[76]

Henry Jones, who in the mid–seventeenth century was the Protestant bishop of Clogher, the diocese in which Lough Derg is situated, assembles considerable evidence of such skepticism and disillusionment. As early as 1240, according to Jones, Vincentius Belluacensis remarks that Saint Patrick's Purgatory was "a mere fable," and in 1265 Saint Bonaventure concurs: "[I]t was fabulously reported that Purgatory was in that place" (*ex hoc fabulose ornant est, quod ibi esset purgatorium*). Their comments suggest that the work of transforming the story (*fabula*) into reality was never complete, that the mystical dream attributed to Saint Patrick remained for at least some observers only a dream, that the attempt to provide eyewitness evidence of the existence of Purgatory was undermined by eyewitness accounts of its supposed entrance. The chorus of complaints gathered by Jones rises in the late fifteenth century: Ponticus Virumnius of Blasius Biragus notes that the site is "nothing agreeable to the Fables commonly related of it"; Joachimus Vadianus reports that the Irish "fable that they that go thither, go into the place of Souls: and that being returned they can no more laugh, which is extremely vain"; and Abertus (*sic*) Krantzius is entirely dismissive: "The Irish remember a Purgatory of a sometime Saint, called Patrick. . . . These dreams and flitting Monsters [*Somnia & monstra*], I thought not good to insert in a discourse of things done, being more like unto old wives Tales."[77]

On Saint Patrick's Day, 1497, the pilgrimage site at Lough Derg was destroyed on orders of the pope, Alexander VI. The space of Purgatory had returned to the precincts of the mind. The demotion was only temporary: the office of Saint Patrick was introduced in the Roman missals in 1522, and pilgrimage resumed, at a slightly different location in Lough Derg, in the sixteenth century. But the uneasiness continued.[78] "Touching the credit of those matters," writes the Jesuit Edmund Campion in 1570, obviously trying to be very careful, "I see no cause but a Christian man, assuring himself that there is both Heaven and Hell, may without vanity upon sufficient information be persuaded that it might please God at some time for considerations to his infinite wisdom known to reveal by miracles the vision of joys and pains eternal." Thus far Campion seems to be heading toward an acceptance of Saint Patrick's Purgatory, basing its "credit" both on the possibility of miracles and on the half-expressed notion that if Heaven and Hell exist, as all Christians believe, then a middle state may also exist. But the wonders reported by pilgrims who visited Lough Derg were not represented as miraculous or exceptional; they were, it was claimed, what all visitors who ventured into the cave could see for themselves. And hence Campion begins to pull back sharply from the legends associated with the pilgrimage site. Miracles might indeed occur, but, he continues,

> that altogether in such sort and so ordinarily and to such persons and by such means as the common fame and some records thereof do utter, I neither believe nor wish to be regarded. . . . a man of indifferent judgment may soon suspect that in the drift and strength of imagination a contemplative person would happily suppose the sight of many strange things which he never saw. Since writing hereof I met with a priest, who told me that he had gone the same pilgrimage and affirmed the order of premises: but that he for his own part saw no sight in the world, save only fearful dreams when he chanced to nod and those he said were exceedingly horrible: further he added that the taste is rated more or less according to the quality of the penitent and that the place seemed to him scarcely able to contain six persons.[79]

Another English Jesuit, Richard Stanihurst, in a Latin account printed in Antwerp in 1587, acknowledges that the stories of visions are not current: "In fact those, who have locked themselves up in this place in our memory, have not felt any terror overcast them save perchance a closer sleep embraced them. But in the first seedtime of religion (the period when miracles are far more frequent) I believe it is true that many horrible and terrible shapes to the sight were wont to appear before the eyes of penitents."[80]

If many Catholics were guarded and uncomfortable about the old legends of Saint Patrick's Purgatory, Protestants were not even remotely concerned to salvage its credit. In Veron's dialogue *The Hunting of Purgatory to Death*, a credulous character named Dydimus expresses some interest in making the pilgrimage. "Did ye never hear of the Purgatory of Saint Patrick," he asks his Protestant friends; "Do ye not remember what books we had of it, when we were little children and went to school?" The dialogue, written in 1561, is looking back at the Catholic instruction that its author and most of his readers would have had. "Ye make me now to remember mine old grandame's tales," replies the skeptical Eutrapelus, who asks whether Dydimus is mocking or dreaming. Dydimus assures his friend that he is in earnest: "It is not a place, to be mocked with all, since that all they, that have been there never laugh after, but lose all their joy." The mention of this legend gives Eutrapelus the opportunity to modulate mockery into source study:

> Then it is like unto the pit and cave of Trophonius, which is in Lebadia, of the which hole or pit, the ancient authors have written in a manner the same, that our dreamers have written of the Purgatory of saint Patrick. Therefore, I doubt not, but that one fable did engender an other.[81]

If the distinctive features of Saint Patrick's Purgatory can be found in classical sources, then the pilgrimage will be disclosed to be a pagan fantasy, the most recent and preposterous of a chain of dreams that have been engendering one another.

Learned Catholics, of course, knew as much about Trophonius's cave—the subterranean chamber in Boeotia whence suppliants who had gone to consult the oracle of Zeus Trophonius always emerged pale and dejected—as did learned Protestants. Faced with the obvious parallels between pagan mythology and Purgatory, Catholic apologists perfectly reasonably observed that classical sources contain a great deal of the teachings in which all Christians must believe, not simply the landscape of Hell and Purgatory. There is a risk in such observations, of course, the risk of confronting the mythic foundations of doctrines that claim to be the literal truth. But believers, whether Catholic or Protestant, could always argue, as the French Jesuit Noel Taillepied does, that anything doctrinally true in the pagan texts derived from the Jews or the Christians. "It were a witless thing," Taillepied wrote in *A Treatise of Ghosts* (1588), "utterly to disregard the view of these Latin and Greek writers. We, who know the truth and have the light of Christianity, ought rather to consider that the truths contained in their teaching concerning the future life are either drawn from us or from that sacred Hebrew tradition, which is fulfilled and incorporated in the Catholic doctrine."[82]

It would, this argument implies, be equally risky for Protestants to push too hard on the skeptical implications of a causal link between paganism and certain Christian doctrines: the skepticism may quickly begin to erode more than the targeted Catholic practices. Hence perhaps the slight queasiness that Veron's spokesman Eutrapelus immediately manifests with his own account of the classical sources of the pilgrimage site's main features. "Our Master doctor" who taught us about Saint Patrick's Purgatory when we were young, he grumbles, must have been "at school with some old rotten witch from whom he did bring this divinity unto us."[83] Another participant in the dialogue objects to railing at such a virtuous and learned man, but Eutrapelus challenges that learning:

> If he had been brought up in humanity, I would think that he had read this, that he did preach unto us, in the poetry of Homer or Virgil, and of other Greek and Latin Poets, or in Plutarch. For, I am sure that any man can find all ye same matter, being in a manner intreated of after the same sort as he hath set it forth unto us, in those ancient authors, and specially in the works of Plutarch, who doth rehearse the marvelous wonders that one Timarchus had seen in the den or cave of Trophonius, which do not differ much from those that we have heard of our master doctor. . . . But to tell, as I think,

I believe, that he hath rather learned this goodly divinity in
the shepherd's calendar, and in Dante, than in any of those
Latin and Greek writers.[84]

Veron does not want to give up the core perception—that Saint
Patrick's Purgatory is a tangle of fictions—but he would rather as-
sociate the Catholic priests with medieval sources (including a rare
allusion to Dante) than with more prestigious classical learning.

For later Elizabethan and Jacobean writers, the pilgrimage site
in Ulster had become part of a repertory of Irish jokes: "Why then,
should all your Chimny-sweepers likewise be Irishmen," asks one
of the characters in Part 2 of Dekker's *The Honest Whore*, to which
the answer is that "S. Patrick you know keeps Purgatory, he makes
the fire, and his Countrymen could do nothing, if they cannot
sweep the Chimneys."[85] In a poem by Ralph Knevet, "Security," the
place serves as a figure of illusion for vain, earthbound Man, who
hopes to ignore all that lies ahead:

> Yet He lives, as if Hell,
> Were but a fable, or a story,
> A place of fancy, that might parallel
> The old St Patrick's Purgatory.
> He mirth recruits with cups, and seldom thinks
> Of Death, until into the grave He sinks.[86]

Saint Patrick's Purgatory may have become a standing joke for
Protestants, but, as Knevet's poem suggests, its patent fictionality
threatened to infect the whole Christian vision of the afterlife with
an air of fable. Moreover, despite the uneasiness of certain Catholics, it continued to attract large numbers of pilgrims, seducing
them into what Protestants regarded as grotesque superstition. In
1632, the state authorities moved to bring not simply the practices
but the place itself to an end. Agents of the earl of Cork and the
lord chancellor rowed to the island and found "four hundred sev-
enty one persons doing such fooleries as is not to be imagined
could be done among Christians."[87] Noting that all attempts at reform had failed, the Privy Council determined that a move simply
to block access to the island would not work, for "the seduced

people will secretly find opportunity to resort thither, and so by stealths continue these superstitious abuses, while the place standeth."[88] Accordingly, on October 25, 1632, James Spottiswoode, bishop of Clogher, came to Lough Derg with a company of twenty well-armed men supplied with demolition tools. It was, he noted in a letter written some days later to the archbishop of Armagh, a good thing that he was so accompanied, since neither the high sheriff of Donegal nor the high sheriff of Farmanagh provided the assistance they had promised. The occasion was inauspicious—"I was forced [to wait], on a rainy day, on a bleak place without any shelter to horse, or man, three hours before we could have the Boat"—but Spottiswoode carried on with his mission.

His account is worth quoting at some length for its sober enactment of a secular ritual of disenchantment, the transformation of a sacred space back into a mute heap of stones and dirt:

> The first thing I searched diligently after, was the Cave, wherein I remembered your Grace enjoined me to dig to the very foundations, and leave no corner unsought, and so I did: I caused to dig about it on all sides, till I came to the Rock but found no appearance of any secret passage, either to the Chapel or to the Lough: neither would the nature of the ground suffer it, in a word this Cave was a poor beggarly hole, made with some stones, laid together with men's hands without any great Art: and after covered with Earth, such as husbandmen make to keep a few Hogs from the rain.
>
> When I could find nothing there, I undermined the Chapel, which was well covered with shingles, and brought all down together. Then we brake down the Circles and Saints Beds, which were like so many Coalpits, and so pulled down some great Irish houses. Thus when I had defaced all saving one Irish house: I came out of the Island myself, and left one half of my men behind to pull that down also so soon as they should see me landed, not sooner; lest if by a storm we were driven back, we might want a place to shelter us.
>
> The country people expected that S. Patrick would have wrought some miracle, but thanks be to God none of my Com-

pany received any other harm but the bad ways, broken caw-
sies, and the dangerous going in a little Boat: Yet our comfort
is, we effected that for which we came thither, which was more
than was expected could be done in so short a time, which
hath wonderfully displeased them that were bewitched with
these fooleries. But that I doe not much stand upon, in regard
I have obeyed the Command of the State.[89]

✣ 3 ✣

THE RIGHTS OF MEMORY

ANYONE who has experienced the death of a close friend or relative knows the feeling: not only the pain of sudden, irrevocable loss but also the strange, irrational expectation of recovery. The telephone rings, and you are suddenly certain that your dead friend is on the other end of the line; the elevator door opens, and you expect your dead father to step out into the hallway, brushing the snow from the shoulders of his coat. These are not merely modern feelings; in fact it is startling that we continue to have them so vividly, since everything in the contemporary world works to suppress them. They were not suppressed in the past.

The brilliance of the doctrine of Purgatory—whatever its topographical implausibility, its scriptural belatedness, and its proneness to cynical abuse—lay both in its institutional control over ineradicable folk beliefs and in its engagement with intimate, private feelings. Reports of hauntings were going to recur from time to time, no matter what churchmen soberly declared. (They continue to recur, for that matter, no matter what intellectuals declare.) Purgatory enabled the church to make sense of these reports, to harness the weird and potentially disruptive psychic energy to its liturgical system, and to distinguish carefully between those experiences that could be absorbed into the moral order (encounters with "good" ghosts) and those that had to be consigned to the sphere of the demonic.[1] The notion of suffrages—masses, almsgiving, fasts, and prayers—gave mourners something constructive to do with their feelings of grief and confirmed those feelings of reciprocity that survived, at least for a limited time, the shock of death. Moreover, the church could find in Purgatory a way to enable mourners to work through, with less psychological distress than they otherwise might experience, their feelings of abandonment and anger at the dead. To imagine the dead in great pain no doubt caused alarm, fear, and pity, but it also served other, murkier needs, needs that could be resolved in organized acts of mercy or even in the delay or withholding of organized acts of mercy.

But there were urgent questions that needed to be resolved before any such acts could be initiated. Virtually everyone recognized the need to distinguish in some way or other between dreams, hallucinations, and fantasies, on the one hand, and real encounters with the dead, on the other. And then once it was established—by whatever means people ordinarily use to reassure themselves that they are in touch with something outside their own mind and heart—that the encounter was real, the question remained how to determine the nature of the being that had returned from the dead. The principal answer lay in the practice of a *discretio spirituum*—a means to distinguish between good and evil spirits—that was particularly important from the late fourteenth through the seventeenth century.[2] A ghost is forced to submit to a rigorous cross-examination centered on six key questions: *Quis? Quid? Quare? Cui? Qualiter? Unde?* In another, simplified version of this judicial ritual, there are three questions—*Nomen? Causas? Remedium?*—followed by a formula:

> We immediately beg you through Jesus Christ, you spirit, to say who you are, and if there is one among us to whom you wish to respond, to name him or point him out with a sign: "Is it this one, N.?" "Or perhaps that one, N.?" And so forth, while naming everyone else present, for it is understood that he will not respond to each one of them. If a voice or a noise is heard when someone is named, it is that person who is to question him, by asking him of which man he is the soul, why he has come, what he wants, if he wishes suffrages, either in masses or in alms. And how many masses? Six, ten, twenty, thirty, one hundred? Said by which priests? Regulars or secu-

lars? Or in fasting; what kind? How much? By whom? As for almsgiving, to the profit of whom should they be given? In hospices or in leprosaria? Or to beggars and poor? And what sign will he give of his liberation?[3]

The use of experts versed in the *discretio spirituum*, along with the stylized narrative recounting of apparitions in *exempla* (illustrative stories intended for sermons), *mirabilia* (collections of marvels), *miracula* (collections of miracles), and the like, brought some order and meaning to the violent, spectral eruptions. Each person, Jean-Claude Schmitt writes,

> could situate himself in the continuous chain of relatives, witnesses, informants, preachers, and authors who assured the transmission of tales, and to these tales each person could add that of his own dreams. Thus the living made the voice of the dead their own, a voice which, strong with the authority conferred upon it by its supernatural origin, reminded them of all the norms of Christian society.[4]

Fortified with their questions, *Nomen? Causas? Remedium?*, the living come to know with whom they are dealing and what remains to be done. In this way, as Schmitt remarks, apparitions of the dead were "banalized." This banalization was not an isolated phenomenon:

> It responded to a general strategy, whose goal was to create a Christian mode of edifying familiarity with death and the dead, orchestrated moreover by the increased ritualization of funeral services, by the valuing of the space of the cemetery as a holy space in the heart of the community of the living, through participation in the burial services of the dead and, within the privileged classes, through the daily reading of the book of hours.[5]

The doctrine of Purgatory, as we have seen, occupied a place at the center of Christendom's ritualized strategies of familiarity, containment, and control. These strategies extended to the precise calculation of the number of masses or quantity of alms that might be required in relation to the probable number of years of purgatorial suffering, an "accounting of the hereafter" that Jacques Chiffoleau has related to the rise in the later Middle Ages of double-entry bookkeeping.[6] By these means, the living no longer need to feel paralyzed with anxiety and uncertainty in the face of spectral visitations.

The problem is that, *discretio spirituum* and double-entry bookkeeping notwithstanding, those visitations always had about them something disorderly, threatening, and wild. The emphasis in the surviving records upon clerical formulas and bureaucratic procedures inevitably falsifies the profound emotional disturbance that the doctrine of Purgatory and its attendant rituals attempted to relieve. It is difficult at this distance to take the human measure of this disturbance—medieval narrative conventions, as well as doctrinal considerations, allowed very little scope for the articulation of particularized, individualized existential dread—but there are at least a few documents from the period that enable us to register its intensity.

The Voice in the Bedroom

One of the most remarkable and compelling of such documents describes a haunting that took place in 1323 (or 1324) in the town of Alès, near Avignon, in southern France. The core of this account is a succinct report written in the first person by a celebrated Dominican prior, Jean Gobi, and presented to Pope John XXII. Copies of this report, which is in effect the transcript of a scholastic *disputatio* between the cleric and the specter, began to circulate almost immediately, as did brief sketches in letters sent by various figures in (or in close contact with) the papal court in Avignon. It was by this means that the story probably first reached England: the pope's chaplain, Jean de Rosse, canon of Hereford (and later bishop of Carlisle), sent a version to Walter Reynolds, bishop of Worcester (and, after 1327, archbishop of Canterbury).[7] By the latter half of the fourteenth century, a longer description of the encounter, now no longer a deposition but rather a third-person narrative of a full-fledged conversation between the prior and the ghost, had been written, probably by someone in Bologna, and was also soon in wide circulation.[8]

Judging from its many copies, paraphrases, and vernacular translations (including French, High and Low German, Catalan, Gallic, and Swedish), this narrative aroused considerable interest, appearing in Middle English in the fourteenth century in both prose and rhyme versions. *The Gast of Gy* (as these English versions of the narrative are titled) recounts that in the period immediately after the death on December 16 of a prosperous, well-regarded bourgeois named Gui de Corvo, his widow is terrified, day and night, by the sound of something moving in her bedroom.[9] Though she cannot see any figure, she understands that the source of the noises is supernatural, but she does not know whether they derive from the ghost of her husband or from some fiend's deceitfulness ("faynding [*feigning*]" in the verse version; "gylerie [*guile*]" in the prose). At her wits' end, the haggard woman goes to the prior of the Dominicans in Alès and asks for help. She can no longer conceal what she has seen and heard, she explains, adding a significant detail: the spirit is haunting her bed, the same bed in which her husband died.[10]

In the prose translation of *The Gast of Gy*, the widow characterizes the visitation as a "wonder." The term, echoed by the prior who speaks to his fellow Dominicans of the "wonderful case" and eventually goes in person to witness "that wonderful thing," seems carefully chosen to convey uncertainty about the nature or origin of the spirit.[11] The uncertainty plays off the work's initial claim that it is going to relate a "miracle," a term it defines with some precision, following Augustine, as a high or "uncustomable" thing that exceeds man's ordinary faculties for the purpose of strengthening faith. Jesus Christ, the opening passage continues, ordained such an indescribable miracle in Alès, so that "we might have greater certainty of the life that is to come."[12] But those to whom the ghost first appeared are anything but certain about the nature and purpose of their encounter, and they do not dare to characterize it as a miracle. The term they use instead is a way at once of acknowledging and suspending judgment upon the preternatural quality of the event, its apparent violation of the laws of nature, its uncanniness.

A wonder is not necessarily a miracle—it does not explicitly or definitively have God's hand in it—and its strangeness may derive from a variety of sources, sacred and profane. The emotion of wonder is an experience that precedes a secure determination of good or evil; the person who wonders does not know whether to approach or to flee, to follow or to fight. The play of conflicting impulses is carried over even into what the prior intends as entirely reassuring words to the anxious widow: "Be not awondered of this case," he says, because "Our Lord is wonderful in his works."[13] It is not clear why recognizing that God's works are wonderful should make the widow cease to wonder. In fact, as the narrative makes clear, the prior himself is deeply "awondered" and deeply anxious. (The narrative will repeatedly make clear the limitation of the prior's understanding.) He hurries off to ring the chapter bell in order to consult his brethren—for, in this as in other cases, he explains, the counsel of many wise men is better than the counsel of one man alone. Following the advice of the other friars, he chooses the wisest among them—a master of theology and a master of philosophy. In the event, these scholars play no further part as advisers, either in theological or philosophical matters; it suffices that he is accompanied by scholars of any kind (indeed, in the verse text, instead of a philosopher there is a master of geometry). Together they go off to consult the mayor, who assigns two hundred men, armed "from top to toe," to accompany the prior to the scene of the haunting and to follow his orders.[14]

The cast of characters then widens out from the widow to the prior to intellectuals within the church to the civic authority that provides whatever protection weapons can afford in such cases. A circular path, which is also an institutional itinerary, leads from the bedroom to the monastery to the chapter house within the monastery to the city and then back to the bedroom. The ghost's appearance originates as a private, intimate event, but it comes to involve the whole society in the experience of wonder before it returns to the privacy of the domestic space. Albertus Magnus characterized wonder as like a systole of the heart, and something of this effect of heart-stopping astonishment seems to be produced in Alès by the ghost of Gy. The ghost in the bedroom is first of all a figure of fear, fear to his widow and to the entire community, but he (or it) is also a figure of intense curiosity. Though the return of a dead person arouses terror, the collective impulse is not to flee from and not even simply to ward off the weird apparition, but rather to approach and find out what it is and what it wants. Everyone recognizes, however, that this approach has to be extremely cautious. The community, responding as it might to an invader from another planet, mobilizes a detachment of armed men.

Comparable instances of extreme precaution in other recorded hauntings confirm the dread associated with ghosts, a dread that evidently led the inhabitants of a village in Brittany, whose deceased baker was returning to help his wife and children knead their dough, to smash open his tomb and break the legs of the corpse.[15] As this action suggests, the wandering of ghosts, like the wandering of vagabonds, was central to the fear they aroused. This spectral vagrancy, which could in exceptional cases manifest itself as virtual ubiquity, violated the most fundamental principles of physical as well as moral order, and it had to be stopped.[16]

In his first-person report to the pope, Jean Gobi makes clear that, as he undertook his investigation, he harbored two principal suspicions as to the nature of the haunting: fraud (*fictitium*) and diabolical illusion (*illusio daemonis*). It is with regard to this first suspicion that he deploys the men, assigning them to search every inch of the house (including the roof tiles) and the neighboring dwellings, evacuating the nearby inhabitants, and stationing guards in those places where deception was most likely to be staged: on the solarium above the bedroom where the spectral voice was heard and on the house's principal roof beam. The figure he most suspects of fraud, of course, is the widow, and he therefore orders an old woman of good reputation to sit with her on the bed and keep her under surveillance. In the *Gast of Gy*, by contrast, all of these precautions have vanished. The prior fears not human fiction—the fabrication of a false marvel for some motive or other, probably pecuniary—but demonic deceit. He does not assume that the uncanny noise is, in all likelihood, a ghost come to plead for suffrages; he strongly suspects, rather, that it is the devil up to his old, malevolent tricks.

The preparation and deployment of the armed men therefore are not directed against human deception but against spiritual menace. The prior accordingly counsels the soldiers to go to confession, hear Mass, and receive communion. (Communion, the text takes care to note, cannot be commanded or dispensed automatically, as it were, but is given only to those who elect to take it: "And all that then would housel take / He houseled soon for God's sake."[17] The men thus purified in spirit are placed in groups of three—to honor the Trinity—around the doors and the windows of the house and in the garden. Meanwhile, the prior has taken further measures to shore up his spiritual defenses. He himself confesses his sins and then sings a requiem mass. The mass is for all the dead—"For Christian souls both more and less"[18]—but the prior focuses his spiritual attention on one soul in particular: "And in his mind then took he Gy / And prayed for him full specially."[19] By so channeling the benefit of the mass, the prior is in effect addressing in advance the possibility that the ghost of Gy has not been sung to rest properly with a requiem.

Before he ventures to conjure the spirit, the prior takes one further precaution: unbeknownst to anyone else, he hides "God's body"—that is, a consecrated wafer—under his clothing. (The prose version, following the Latin closely, is more specific: "And the prior took privily with him that no man wist [knew]: the box with God's flesh and his blood, and hanged it privily before his breast under his scapular as worshipfully as he might.")[20] Thus secretly as well as publicly armed and defended, he enters the house, accompanied by the two scholars and the household servants. Reciting prayers and sprinking holy water, he comes to the innermost chamber, where at his request the trembling widow is brought in to point out the bed where her husband died. Though crazed with fear, the widow also expresses love for her husband, a love that is all the more striking in the context of a literature that usually veers off into misogynist complaints about women's forgetfulness:

> The woman was full mazed and mad,
> She trembled then, so was she rad [*frightened*];
> Unto the bed soon she him told [*took*],
> The care was at her heart full cold;
> But in her way yet as she was,
> She said, "Sir prior, ere ye pass,
> I pray you for the love of me
> And as in deed of charity,
> That ye would bid some holy bead
> And make prayers in this stead
> For his soul, that noble man."[21]

In this moment, the institutional makes contact with the individual: the tangled emotions of a frightened, grieving widow call for the ritual performance of the religious specialist.

In response to the woman's urgent request, the prior begins to pray: he reads the Gospel of John and then sits down to recite the special prayers for the dead, the *Placebo* and the *Dirige*, along with the seven Penitential Psalms, the litany, and the *Agnus Dei*. At the third repetition of the *Agnus Dei*, they hear "a feeble voice . . . as of a child, saying 'Amen' ."[22] Though everything about this first encounter seems designed to offer reassurance—the feeble sound, the child's voice, and the "Amen" in answer to a prayer that begs the Lamb of God, who takes away the sins of the world, to have pity on us—the men are all afraid.

A manuscript illumination from 1474, attributed to Simon Marmion (the same artist who painted the beautiful scenes from the *Vision of Tondal*), captures the tension of this moment (plate 8). The prior, directly facing the widow, makes an emphatic gesture with his hands; behind them are four witnesses, three citizens and another priest. All are staring intently, but their gazes are not directed to the same place, for the exact location of the spectral voice is evidently unclear to them. Two candles burn in brass candlesticks on a high cabinet covered by a spotless white cloth at the back of the room. The candles are not strictly necessary for light, since the sky, glimpsed through the window next to the cabinet, reveals that it is still day. They suggest, rather, something like an altar, but there is no religious image behind them, and this is very much a domestic interior. To the left there is a carved wooden bench, adorned with matching cover and pillows, on which has been laid two heavy black books, no doubt the prayer books that have been used to conjure the ghost of Gy. And further to the left, behind the bench, we glimpse the marriage bed, its curtains drawn back. But the center of the scene, remarkably enough, is sheer vacancy, the empty space between the prior and the widow.

The illuminator brilliantly grasps the essential truth of his text: it is what has failed to make itself visible, what is only heard, that lies at the heart of the drama. When in response to the prior's conjuration, the ghost consents to answer any questions put to him, as far as he is able, his spectral voice causes all of the armed men to come running, each with a weapon in his hand, in the expectation of seeing "some ghastly thing."[23] But there is nothing to see. Bidding the men to be still, the prior then puts to the disembodied voice the crucial question: "Art thou an evil ghost or a good?"[24]

DEBATING WITH THE DEAD

There follows a long, intricate debate that stages some of the most difficult issues raised by the Catholic doctrine of the suffering ghosts in Purgatory. This is a theological text quite different from the narrative of Owein's adventures in the Purgatory of Saint Patrick. To be sure, the ghost of Gy declares that he is suffering in hot "cleansing fire," and he describes the foul fiends, grinning and gnashing their teeth, that try to seize upon him and other souls after death. But there is no tour of the otherworld, no grisly description of torture chambers with their chains and racks, no dark, stinking river, no heroic tests of faith and endurance imposed on one who would reach the narrow bridge to Heaven. There are also no skeptics who deny the very existence of Purgatory: the existence of a middle space between Heaven and Hell is assumed, though its precise location is among the issues that are disputed. The most insistent question is how to determine whether this ghost is, as he claims, a denizen of Purgatory, and behind the question is an attempt to sort out the precise moral meaning of that middle space and the best method to relieve the sufferings of those who are condemned to spend time there. These are problems that greatly exercised theologians, but *The Gast of Gy* gives them an unusual dramatic force by emphasizing the wary skepticism of the prior and, still more, as we shall see, by turning the debate into an unusual love story.

To the question of whether he is a good or evil ghost, the spirit of Gy gives a double answer. "I am the gast of Gy," he declares "with eger mode [*passionate intensity*]," and proceeds to propound what is in effect a syllogism. I, the ghost of Gy, am a creature of God; God looked upon all he had created and saw it was good; *ergo*, "I am a good ghost."[25] At the same time, he adds, "I am evil for mine evil deed"[26] and hence must suffer pain. Therefore, as the prose translation puts it bluntly, "I am a wicked ghost," adding as an explanatory afterthought, "as unto my wicked pain that I suffer."[27] The prior quickly concludes that this ambiguous answer proves that the ghost is unambiguously wicked, for if he were good, he could never characterize his pain as wicked.

> All pain is good (that prove I thee)
> That ordained is in good degree.[28]

This is the first of a succession of exchanges in which the prior shows that he is clever, skeptical, and sharp, that he has a learned interest in doctrinal distinctions, that he has a fine prosecutor's eye for contradictions in testimony, but also that he is limited, rigid, insensitive to human and spiritual suffering, and repeatedly, even embarrassingly wrong. The ghost readily concedes that from the point of view of God the pain that he is suffering is good, for it is justly given by divine judgment in punishment for his sins. But the pain is nevertheless ill to him to whom it is given—only a theologian comfortably abstracted from the reality of suffering could blithely call it "good." What the ghost actually experiences is unmistakably "evil pain," justly inflicted upon him for his evil deeds, and therefore, until such time as he is cleansed, men may call him an "evil spirit."

The primacy of experience is reaffirmed when the prior asks the ghost to disclose the identity of some of the souls in Heaven and some of those in Hell—to give him, in effect, what Dante (like Tondal and others) so unforgettably provides. But Gy cannot oblige: someone who has actually been in those places would be able truthfully to give such a report, but no soul in Purgatory could possibly do so. For though he is destined for Heaven, he has not yet attained it, and though he is suffering, his torments do not take place in Hell: "I was never there nor never shall be."[29] The prior is once again certain that he has caught the ghost in a lie, one that will expose his fiendish nature. For, he observes, though the Hebrew prophets were men of flesh and blood, they nonetheless were able to speak openly—"in field and town"—of Christ's incarnation, death, and resurrection, events that they never saw with their own eyes. Surely, a "clean spirit," as the ghost claims to be, should be able to see still more than these mere mortals could. But the ghost replies that the prior is wasting his words, for there is no likeness between prophets and souls in Purgatory. The former were given the gift of the Holy Spirit, so that they could preach of what had not yet come to pass; the latter have no such gift. They are simply set to suffer "for certain space" until their sins are cleansed.[30] No miraculous visions are granted them; the only angels that the ghost himself has seen are those who are his keepers, and they will tell him nothing until he is brought out of his pain.

The prior is more convinced than ever that he has caught the ghost in a trap, for "books bear witness" (line 503) that spirits, and even fiends, sometimes tell mortal men who is saved and who is damned. But the ghost replies that neither spirits nor fiends have the power to disclose anything that touches on the "privities of heaven," unless God authorizes it or an angel chances to mention it. As the angels he has encountered have told him nothing, he has no way of knowing who is in Heaven; and as there is "no likeness to tell / Between me and the fiends in hell," he has no way of knowing who is eternally damned.[31] "I pray thee now, / Tell me," the prior then abruptly asks, in the manner of a wily prosecutor springing a trap, "In what stead art thou?" (lines 525–26). When the disembodied voice replies, "I am here in Purgatory," the prior declares, with heavy irony, that the ghost is telling him that this place, the bedroom in Alès, is the place where the souls of all the dead are being purged in terrible fires. But the ghost has an answer to this obvious absurdity: there are two purgatories, one common and the other individual (or "departable").[32]

Double Purgatories

This is a surprise revelation, and one of doubtful orthodoxy. In the sixth century Gregory the Great taught that the souls of the dead would endure Purgatory on this earth. He tells the story of a priest who went frequently to the baths—this was still a world in close contact with the culture of ancient Rome—and one day offered to the bathhouse attendant the gift of two loaves of bread. The attendant sadly declined the gift, explaining that he could not eat it because he was in fact dead: "In the form in which you see me now I used to be in charge of these baths and because of my sins I have been sent back here after my death."[33] To be of any help, he added before disappearing, the food should be offered to God and not to him. The priest obliged and was gratified, when he returned to the baths after a week of masses, to find that the attendant had vanished, presumably because he had completed his term of suffering. In this very early conception, then, souls are compelled to return for their purgatorial suffering to the places where they had most sinned. But the church had gradually abandoned Gregory's vision of the afterlife, and by the early fourteenth century, when the spirit of Gy returned to his house in Alès, souls condemned to Purgatory should all by rights have been doctrinally penned up in the single enormous prison house.[34]

Hence when the ghost tells Jean Gobi that he is suffering in two distinct purgatories, the prior declares flatly that he is a liar, for he obviously cannot be here in familiar human surroundings and at the same time burning with the other suffering souls in "common" Purgatory. True, the ghost agrees, but he is not telling a "fable" or claiming to be in two places at once: by day he is condemned to suffer in the bedroom; by night he is confined in fire with all the other souls. (Both the verse and the prose English texts, for some reason, reverse the temporal scheme of the Latin source, which specifies that the ghost haunts the bedroom at night and is penned up in common Purgatory during the day.) The afterlife by this account does not necessarily mark the immediate severing of all relations to the familiar spaces of this world. The dead have departed; their souls have gone off to other realms, and their bodies are beginning to decompose. But, in the immediate wake of his death, the ghost of Gy and his anguished widow are in daily contact in the very place where they were most intimate. For this contact to achieve a coherent meaning, it evidently must be mediated by the church—by herself the widow was not able to make out any words that the ghost might have been speaking, not even his name, but heard only frightening sounds—yet it is not contained by the ecclesiastical setting or doctrinal orthodoxy.[35]

There is one further dispute about the location of Purgatory. When the ghost declares that common Purgatory is located in the center of the earth, the prior challenges him on the grounds that it is impossible for two distinct places (here, "the midst of the earth," and common Purgatory) to exist in the same geographical location. The problem once again is with a violation of the elementary laws of physics, and the challenge thus voices at least a touch of rational skepticism about the existence of Purgatory. But, as befits a question asked by a churchman who does not actually doubt its existence, skepticism is staged in such a way as to be easily answerable. The ghost replies that physical and spiritual realms can coexist in the same place, just as the body and soul coexist in a single person, and then—as if uneasy with the highly unorthodox spiritualization of Purgatory that this answer potentially implies— he shifts to a different kind of orderly coexistence, entirely physical in character: rain, hail, sleet, and snow may all exist together in the same air.

Accounts of Purgatory, as we have already seen, repeatedly grapple with the belatedness of the doctrine and the evident difficulty that many people had in believing it. How is it possible to make the complex mental construct seem compellingly real and to confer on the gossamer, insubstantial image of souls an illusion of materiality? Unlike the *Owayne Miles*, *The Gast of Gy* does not depict the confounding of the mockery of infidels, nor does it attempt to represent in gruesome detail the agonies of the condemned. On the contrary, the ghost never assumes material form. The strategy instead is to represent doubts: Is the voice that of a purgatorial spirit or a demon? Can there be two distinct purgatorial spaces? How much does a soul in Purgatory actually know, and when does he come to know it? The doubts are never permitted to undermine the existence of Purgatory; indeed, they implicitly affirm the reality of the main territory by skirmishing fiercely around its periphery.

Thus the debate never turns directly on whether Purgatory exists, and it veers away from a discussion of its precise location—the prior evidently coming to accept the existence of a double sphere—to the best means of alleviating the pain of souls condemned to suffer there. The ghost expounds upon the relative merits of prayer, fasting, alms, and the gracious intercession of Mary, "the empress of hell."[36] Above all, he extols the efficacy of Christ's Passion—that is, of the Mass—in mitigating suffering. Do souls know what is done for them by the living, the prior asks, to which the ghost replies that they do. Then, the prior demands, resuming his best prosecutorial manner, Can you say what Mass I sang today? "Thou sang of Saint Spirit," the ghost answers. Once again the prior pounces, certain that he has caught the voice in a lie: he sang not the Mass of the Holy Spirit but a requiem mass. And once again the ghost, insisting that he is not a liar, appeals to an existential reality that is beyond the grasp of his inquisitor. It is true enough, he concedes, that it was a requiem, but the prior should know that when you ask a person a question, the answer that comes most quickly from the mouth is what lies nearest the heart.[37] In his life on earth, scrambling after worldly wealth, he had most offended the Holy Spirit, the ghost explains, and therefore he stands most in need of prayers that directly compensate for this offense. When the prior sang today's mass, he added a prayer to the Holy Spirit, and it was this prayer, more than all of the others that he recited, that actually gave the ghost some direct, personal comfort. Hence, the voice concludes, his answer was not at all a lie.[38]

What is at stake in this sparring? The putative issue is the attempt to determine whether the spirit in the bedroom at Alès is good or evil, but after the prior's suspicions have been repeatedly dashed, the case inevitably begins to seem closed. (There can be no absolute certainty, of course, only a tissue of probabilities.) Yet the debate goes on and on long after most readers will have come to the conclusion that they can, in Hamlet's phrase, take this ghost's word for a thousand pounds. Something else seems to be motivating the argument. In part it addresses, with subtle indirection, the lingering skeptical doubts that laymen—the "lewd men" for whom the work was written—must have had about the whole elaborate business. Hence the prior asks the voice how it is possible for a ghost, having no body, to suffer in flames, a form of suffering that could afflict only flesh-and-blood creatures. This is the kind of question—as distinct from inquiries about which prayers are most efficacious—that reason and common sense would advance not only against the doctrine of Purgatory in particular but also against any claim that the souls of the dead can experience physical pain or pleasure. The fact that the predictable, perfectly orthodox answers to such questions come directly from the ghost, rather than from the official representative of the church, gives them a rhetorical edge in allaying skepticism.

Late in the dialogue it seems finally to strike the prior that he has been bending his eye on vacancy, to paraphrase Gertrude in *Hamlet,* and holding discourse with the incorporeal air. "I marvel me," he says to the disembodied voice,

> How thou to speak has such pouste [*power*]
> And has no tongue nor other thing,
> That instrument is of speaking.

(Lines 1511–14)

The ghost concedes that just as a carpenter cannot cut wood without an ax, so a human being cannot speak without a tongue. But such tools—axes and tongues—are used only as a result of an intention to use them, that is, an immaterial impulse given to the body by the invisible soul. Therefore, if the body is but an instrument of the soul, in which "virtue, might, and mind" actually reside, then after death the soul may find the power to speak properly without the help of the body. Then, as if slightly uneasy with the vagueness of this explanation and casting about for another, more decisive way to show the prior that his "saws are false," the ghost adds that, after all, the Holy Writ plainly witnesses that God and his angels bright speak wisely, and *they* do not have mouths or tongues. The dogmatic incontestability of Scripture closes this particular question.

This overarching strategy—the ceding of authority from the prior to the ghost, in order to recast institutional dogma as firsthand experience—is apparent at many points in the debate; indeed, as the prior loses argument after argument, it comes to seem one of its most striking characteristics. Yet the ghost appears to be something more than a conventional spokesman for doctrinal correctness. As we have already seen, his presence in the bedroom entails the elaboration of a double Purgatory that sits awkwardly with church orthodoxy. If there is a rhetorical advantage to the insistence on the superiority of the ghost's existential stringency over the prior's institutional knowledge, the persuasive power is purchased at a fairly high price: the prior's specialized knowledge, his mastery of the *discretio spirituum,* is revealed to be a rather feeble, unreliable instrument for determining the nature and origin of ghosts.

More than seventeen hundred lines into a poem of some two thousand lines, the interrogator is still expressing variations on doubts that he had already many times articulated and that had each time been forcefully answered. Of course, these doubts could be seen as an admirable manifestation of the prior's proper wariness—the institution cannot let down its guard—but the specter voices impatience that it is difficult for the reader not to share. Since you claim, the prior tells the ghost, that you are always in flames,

> Then think me, that this house and we
> Should burn all for the fire of thee,
> Since that it is so hot and keen.

(Lines 1753–55)

The whole course of the work insists that we share in the ghost's exasperation: "Now is well seen," he replies, "That in thee is full little skill" (lines 1756–57).

He had just finished answering the same question, the spectral voice complains—"right now told I thee"—and he does not conceal his frustration when he reiterates the explanation. "But, certainly, this shalt thou understand," he concludes, as if talking to a particularly slow learner,

> If all houses in every land
> In a place were burning sheer,
> It might not be so hot a fire
> As I now suffer night and day.
>
> (Lines 1782–85)

Once again the ghost's actual experience is set against a merely theoretical, abstract doubt. There turns out to be nothing in the prior's imposing institutional position that gives him a privileged insight into the afterlife.

This surprising limitation is made explicit when the prior asks the ghost what "manner of folk" is revealed in Purgatory to have lived the best lives. One might anticipate an answer in praise of clerics or cloistered monks and nuns, or at least those who practice celibacy, but the ghost does not respond by celebrating any particular mode of life. It is impossible to determine in this world, he says, whether a man's works will be judged evil or good, worthy of joy or pain. The prior is evidently dissatisfied with this answer and asks again "which is the most perfect degree / Of all" earthly professions (lines 1664–65).

> "In every state I see," he says,
> "Some things to lack [*to fault*] and some to praise;
> Therefore I will praise no degree,
> Nor none shall be dispraised for me."
>
> (Lines 1667–70)

All men in all places, he concludes, should "serve God with all their might, / In what degree so they be dight" (lines 1673–74).

This refusal to grant special praise to the religious is intensified when, in response to the prior's question, the ghost names three sins that God most sternly and immediately punishes. The first of these is cohabitation without the sacrament of the holy church; the third is manslaughter conjoined with perjury. The second is left discretely unspecified, "But clerks full kindly know it may" (line 1850), that is, churchmen by their nature may know it. The apparent discretion is, of course, only an invitation to the reader to fill in the blank with one or another clerical sin: simony, sodomy, fornication. The charge casts a shadow over the clergy, a shadow that darkens as the work nears its conclusion.

"Tell Us Some Marvel"

After responding to the lengthy series of questions, the ghost finally disappears, leaving his widow with the parting injunction that she live in chastity, and that she celebrate for her own soul and for him three hundred masses: one hundred dedicated to the Trinity or the Holy Spirit, one hundred to the Virgin, fifty to Saint Peter and fifty requiem masses. Hastening to carry out his instructions, the widow immediately employs all of the priests, monks, and friars of the town to sing the multiple masses all on a single day, and she also arranges for a priest to sing daily masses for her husband's soul until Easter. These measures seem to be effective: she is no longer tormented by the ghost. But she remains terrified and does not dare to enter her bedchamber. Therefore, twelve days after Christmas, on the Feast of the Epiphany, she consults once again with the prior, who decides to return to the house, this time in the company of twenty Augustinian and Minorite friars. Singing the *Placebo* and the *Dirige* and intoning the words "Requiescant in pace" (as if they feared that there was more than one specter), they become aware of the ghost, whose presence in the bedroom is signaled by the sound of a broom sweeping across the pavement. The friars are frightened, but once again the voice is meek, like that of a man who "had been sick." With the exhaustion and querulousness of such a person, the ghost asks why the prior and his companions are once again disturbing him:

It is not long, since I told thee
All that thou would ask of me.
What should I now say to you here?

(Lines 1969–71)

The prior asks him for a sign or a wonder. He has gathered, he says, friars and other folk to bear witness so that they can "declare" the case before the pope. "And therefore," he adds, "tell us some marvel, / That we may trow withouten fail" (lines 2001–2). The ghost responds with barely suppressed anger: "I am not God," he says, and only God and his angels can perform marvels. But, he continues, if they wish to preach better than they have before, they should speak out most especially "[a]gainst the sin of simony" (line 2012). It is as if churchmen preaching against their own abuses would be the greatest marvel that the ghost could tell those who have come to interrogate him.

There follows a longer list of sins, but the rhetorical effect of beginning here, with the clerical traffic in sacred things, is unsettling. This is the culmination of the steady erosion of the prior's position, the gradual evacuation of the *discretio spirituum*, and the transfer of moral authority from the powerful cleric to the miserable ghost. The transfer, as I have suggested, may serve a strategic purpose, affirming the reality of Purgatory through the testimony of the ghost rather than the pronouncements of the church, but it is difficult to believe that this is its only purpose.

Something seems to have happened in the passage from Jean Gobi's deposition to *The Gast of Gy*. Most obviously, the work has greatly expanded in length, which enables it to explore a range of theological issues related to the afterlife and to the invisible powers about which the ghost can claim to testify with eyewitness authority. Hence, for example, the dialogue addresses the question, much debated in the church, of whether a demon can interfere with the consecration of the Host by exploiting the weaknesses of sinful priests, and the still more vexed question of whether souls after death would be immediately granted the Beatific Vision or would have to wait until their ascension to Heaven.[39] But the sheer number of vernacular translations suggests that the interest of the longer work extended well beyond a clerical audience, and this broader reach is perhaps linked to the weakening of the prior's authority and the assault on clerical abuses that we have remarked.[40]

Did early readers consciously perceive these subversive features? It is possible that the strategy of attributing the crucial doctrinal claims to the ghost rather than to the prior necessarily weakened the power of the interrogator and unleashed critical elements without entailing an explicitly satirical stance toward the clerical hierarchy. The attacks on the prior for his lack of skill and even the jibes at the priesthood for sodomy and simony could be relished without being altogether acknowleged.

Yet an odd feature of the Queen's College, Oxford, manuscript in which the prose version of *The Gast of Gy* is found suggests that there may have been some more conscious recognition of the heterodox elements: at the end of the text the fourteenth-century scribe ("Jenkyn by name," as he signs himself) wrote the words *Explicit Johannes Mandeville.* John Mandeville was the presumed author of one of the most brilliantly disquieting works of the period, *Mandeville's Travels*, a version of which is adjacent in the Queen's College manuscript to *The Gast of Gy.* The adjacency may simply have confused the scribe: the author of a veiled antipapal satire, as the editor of *The Gast of Gy* remarks, "would hardly be the writer or translator of a serious religious tract."[41] But, alternatively, the scribe may have noticed in the religious tract he had just copied a satirical strain that linked it in his mind to a travel book whose eyewitness account of distant lands allowed its author a comparable license to criticize and unsettle.

It would be a mistake to exaggerate the anticlerical implications: *The Gast of Gy* is a pious work that confirms both the overarching claim that Purgatory exists and the particular claim that certain rituals of the Catholic Church possess the power directly to relieve the sufferings of imprisoned souls. The dialogue with the ghost manifests nothing of the skeptical relativism and surprising tolerance articulated in *Mandeville's Travels.* On the contrary, when the prior asks why God allows Saracens, Jews, and pagans to exist, the ghost replies that their existence permits Christians to fight against them and thereby make manifest a commitment to the true faith. That faith is securely lodged within the "holy church" (lines 1129, 1844, etc.): what most vexes the fiends of Hell, the ghost declares, is the sacrament of God's Body, and what most comforts souls in pain are masses and prayers recited by priests. The immediate efficacy of these prayers is vividly demonstrated when, after providing a long series of answers, the ghost urges that any further questions be asked quickly, for the time is fast approaching when he must go "to suffer pains in other place" (line 1208). The prior charitably asks if there is anything that he and the rest of the company can do to provide relief, and the ghost replies that "the five joys of Our Lady" might be a great help. After the prior and his fellows kneel and devoutly recite the prayers—" 'Gaude virgo, mater Christi' / With the five verses following fully" (lines 1221–22)—the ghost responds as if he has been given a fast-acting medicine:

> . . . "Well have ye comforteth me:
> My pain is somedeal passed now,
> That I may better speak with you."
>
> (Lines 1226–28)

The particularity of the ghost's request is important here, for it is not only the general efficacy of prayer that is established by *The Gast of Gy* but the specific needs of suffering souls. Beneath the umbrella of the *discretio spirituum*, what much of the dialogue is struggling to tease out is the vexed relation between the overarching category of the souls of the dead, pent up en masse in Purgatory, and individual souls, those recently deceased family members and friends whose voices still echo in the ears of their loved ones. In principle there is no apparent reason why a good Christian should not care equally for all of the virtuous dead, or why the church should not strive evenhandedly to relieve the sufferings of all Christian souls. But, while it concedes that the dead have a collective claim to attention, *The Gast of Gy* gives powerful expression to a very different sense, one based on the spiritual specificity of sin and guilt and the psychological specificity of grief.

From time to time the reader is reminded that there is a "common Purgatory" where the ghost suffers in the company of millions of others, but the work stresses Gy's special, highly individuated place of torment. As we have already seen, out of all the prayers in the Mass that the prior has sung that day, the ghost seizes upon those to the Holy Spirit, since those are the prayers he particularly needs, but the issue is addressed more directly. In singing Mass, the ghost explains, a priest should pray first "specially for his friends' sake" (line 968) and then, after he has helped those to whom he is "most holden," he should pray for everyone. Thus, he adds by way of illustration, he himself has been freed of four years of penance as a result of prayers made on his behalf by a cousin, a poor friar, whom he had helped, when he was still in life. Thanks to his friend's kindness, he will be finished with his term of suffering at Easter.

The prior seems to have some difficulty grasping the principle of individuation. What helps most to hasten a soul out of Purgatory? he asks again, to which the ghost replies that masses said by holy men, especially masses dedicated to the Virgin, are particularly effective. The answer disquiets the prior: the Office of the Dead, he says, was therefore "made in vain," since other masses are evidently of more avail than the requiem mass. No, the voice explains, the requiem is useful "when any men for all will pray" (line 1036); it was instituted for "lewd men here in land" (line 1037) who fail to understand that souls need other, special prayers. When the prior, pursuing the issue in an attempt to get more details, asks whether mortals help when they recite the *Placebo* and the *Dirige*, two sequences of psalms and anthems, the ghost erupts with passionate eagerness, as if his interlocutor has finally hit on something important:

> The voice answered him on high
> (With great force out gan he burst)
> And said: "Ah, prior, and thou wist,
> How greatly that it may them gain,
> Then hope I, that thou would be fain
> Oft for to bid that blessed bead
> For thy friends, that are dead.
>
> (Lines 1096–1102)

What excites the ghost is less that these prayers have general validity than that their many individual parts include virtually all of the possible categories in which particular souls in Purgatory may find themselves: young or old, poor or powerful, virgin or married or widowed, in holy orders or "lewd." There is something in them for everyone: "In which degree so he is in, / Their lessons shall to wealth him win" (lines 1141–42).

Prayers here do not function principally as expressions of the piety of the cleric or congregant; they function as spiritual medicines charitably donated to souls in pain. And each medicine works best when it is sharply focused on a particular ailment afflicting a particular person. Hence the priest is encouraged to have specific souls in mind when he prays, and hence too those prayers are most effective that directly address the specific sins that these souls are condemned to expiate. The spiritual disposition of the priest is no more relevant to the cure than the spiritual disposition of a physician would be to the efficacy of his prescriptions. To be sure, the ghost notes in answer to one of the prior's questions, the inward state of a priest is relevant to his ability to perform the Mass, for unclean thoughts and deadly sins enable fiends to interfere and mar the proper "making" of God's Body. But this is only to say that the most precious medicine must be well and cleanly made.

The discussion of the Mass gives the prior—who, unbeknownst to everyone, has a consecrated Host hidden under his scapular— the occasion to ask one of his most sly prosecutorial questions: since the time that the ghost went "out of this world," has he ever seen "that solemn sight" (line 1294) of the sacrament? "Yea," the voice replies,

> "I see it yet,
> For on thy breast thou bears it;
> In a box thou hast it brought."

> (Lines 1297–99)

The entire company is astonished, but the prior is not willing to concede the accuracy of the ghost's spiritual vision: if the ghost knew that "God's Body" was hidden in the box, why didn't he, as

one of God's creatures, do honor to it? "I have it honored in my
kind," the voice responds with quiet dignity,

> "With all my might and all my mind,
> Since first that thou it hither brought,
> All if thou perceived it not."
>
> (Lines 1311–14)

What follows is the most dramatic moment in the dialogue, the
moment in which the complicated theological debate turns decisively into an exorcism. The prior takes the sacrament "out of his
clothes, where it was laid," and says that if the ghost actually believes that this is God's Body, then he must submit to its power. "I
command thee," the prior continues, to "go with me plain pace"
(line 1325) to the outermost gate of this place and hence to leave
the house. The ghost, who has until this point remained singularly
independent of the prior's power, concedes that he is "bound,"
but not, he adds, "to follow thy person." Rather, "with my lord fain
will I wend / that thou holdest betwixt thy hands" (lines 1329–30).
Carrying the consecrated wafer, the prior then proceeds toward
the gate. He is able to see nothing, but once again he hears coming
after him a noise like that of a broom sweeping a pavement. At his
command that the ghost show himself, there is only silence.

THE SECRET

The route toward the gate passes through the bedroom. As the
prior and the ghost approach the bed on which the widow is lying,
the woman begins to gnash her teeth, grimace, and cry aloud as
if she were mad, before falling into a swoon. In the comparable
scene in the deposition, Jean Gobi reports that her terror in effect
broke the sacred spell through which he was leading the ghost
to the door. In the silence after she faints, the prior and his companions hear a voice lamenting as it passes through the house,
and then for the remainder of the night, they hear nothing. In *The
Gast of Gy*, by contrast, the scene of panic leads to a renewal of
the very personal questioning with which the prior had begun his
interrogation.

Just after the ghost identified himself by name, the prior had accused him of slandering himself and his wife: during his life, he and his wife were deemed to be "true in faith, of noble fame" (line 293), but now lewd folk—the people who in every land say that evil spirits walk abroad—will conclude that "Gy was evil in all his life, / And therefore torments he his wife" (lines 297–98). Gy responds that he has slandered neither his wife nor his body. He suggests that the prior should imagine someone who borrows a coat and then suffers horrible pain on its account: just so, the spirit has used Gy's body as its clothing and is now enduring torments as a consequence of that body's wickedness. The body itself—dead and buried—is not suffering at all, but it will share in the bliss that lies at the end of the purgatorial imprisonment, so the soul is anything but unkind.

Why, the prior goes on to ask, is the ghost condemned to suffer some of his pains in the house where he lived? "For in this place I sinned most" (line 592), the voice replies, adding that since, though he was shriven, he performed no penance during his lifetime, he must now do penance for his sin. Ordinarily so wary and suspicious, the prior had seemed contented with these answers, and the dialogue shifted to theological matters. But now, with the widow writhing in fear on the bed, he resumes the intimate interrogation. Invoking Christ's Passion, the prior demands to be told "why it is and for what thing" (line 1369) the ghost is tormenting his wife. The voice replies that she knows the answer as well as he. The prior then turns to the widow:

> "In the name of God, dame, I thee pray,
> Tell unto me all thy thought."
> And she lay still and answered not.
>
> (Lines 1376–78)

The woman's distress is so intense that many of those standing around her bed weep for her, as she begins to crawl on her knees and to cry out to Jesus to help her.

The spectacle only intensifies the prior's determination to discover the reason for the haunting. "Why is thy wife thus travailed here?" he demands of the ghost. The voice once again redirects the question away from himself: I told you just now, he says, that she knows the answer, and if you want to know more, then "Ask herself; she can thee say" (line 1396). The prior gazes at the woman and urges her to speak frankly to him, promising to help her:

> "To save thyself of sare [*sorrow*]
> Tell me the cause of all thy care,
> And out of bale I shall thee bring."
>
> (Lines 1399–1401)

But the cause remains a secret—"She lay and answered him nothing" (line 1402)—and the frustrated interrogator stands as one amazed.

At this point of impasse, with his personal prestige and the spiritual power of his institution at stake, the prior musters a tremendous conjuration. By God's might and power, he intones, and by the virtue of his body and of his mother, mild Mary, and by the sweet milk he sucked from her, and by the tears she shed when she saw that her son was slain, and by all hallows, tell me the precise truth—"the certain sooth"—of this marvel. Tell me "why thy wife has all this pain" (line 1415). At last he gets at least a partial answer: their mutual suffering is for "an unkindly sin," that is, a sin against kind, that they committed together "here in this stead." But what was the sin, the prior urgently asks, so that married couples can be warned not to commit it in deed or thought? The ghost refuses to answer, not because he resists the power of the church but because he is obedient to a higher power than his interrogator possesses. God does not wish the sin to be revealed, the voice says, because the wife and her husband, while he was still alive, had both confessed and received absolution for it, though they have not yet completed their penance. God has forgiven their sin—it has in effect been erased—and it would be a violation of the sanctity of confession to disclose it now. But the ghost can say one thing to married couples: let them always keep "the rule of wedding" and "duly do both day and night" (lines 1445–46).

What is it that they have done? Taken too much pleasure in the marriage bed? Or the wrong kind of pleasure? Or—in light of the fact that this is a work that makes no mention of any children—

have they contrived to prevent conception or to terminate preg-
nancy? Somewhere perhaps behind *The Gast of Gy* is one of the
foundational stories of Purgatory, a story rehearsed in the Middle
English versions of the popular *Trental of St. Gregory*. The mother
of a certain pope, we are told, had committed lechery as a young
woman and had murdered her child. She felt remorse, but as she
was the pope's mother, she was ashamed to reveal her sin to her
confessor. When she died, the pope, celebrating Mass, saw a creature emerging from a strange, uncanny darkness:

> So ragged, so twisted, so dreary, so evil,
> As hideous to behold as hell-devil;
> Mouth and nose, ears and eyes,
> Flamed all full of fury lies.[42]

The pope asks who this hideous creature is, and she replies that
she is his mother. She confesses her crime and says she can be
delivered by "a true Trental / Of ten chief feasts of all the year."[43]
Gregory performs the cycle of thirty masses for the dead and at
the end of twelve months he sees a comely lady dressed and
crowned like a queen. He thinks she is the Virgin, but in fact she
is his mother, newly delivered from Purgatory.[44]

In *The Gast of Gy*, as in the story of Gregory the Great's mother,
an "unkindly sin" leads to a haunting. But Gy and his wife are in
far less dire circumstances, for they have been shriven, and they
are spared the shame of public disclosure. The prior's failure to
discover the precise nature of the sin is a tribute to the efficacy
and the privacy of confession. It is not, of course, that the church
is excluded from the secrets of the marriage bed; on the contrary,
the work stages in dramatic terms the legitimacy of its interest in
the married couple's most intimate secrets and shameful acts.
Moreover, the very refusal to disclose the details produces a certain
invasive power of implication, as if it were inviting all readers to
bring to confession any act that might possibly fall outside the dis-
creetly unspecified "rule of wedding." Yet the preservation of the
secret also turns the work's attention away from the public, visible
institution and directs it instead at the intimate bond between the
deceased husband and his grieving widow.

The focus on this bond is the culmination of the strategy that we have repeatedly noted in *The Gast of Gy*, its insistence on the personal, the particular, and the experiential against the more abstract and theoretical concerns of the clerical interrogator. At the moment when the ghost and his widow refuse to reveal their sin, they turn to one another and speak directly, without the mediation of the prior. "Good Gy, for love of me," the woman says, weeping as she lies on the marriage bed, "say if I shall saved be" (lines 1459–60). Will she suffer forever for the sin they committed, she asks, a sin for which God was "not paid"? The ghost comforts her: the penance is nearing its end, he says; "thou shall be saved for certain" (line 1467). The prior now intervenes to reclaim control of the discourse by channeling this reassurance of salvation toward the practice of piety: he tells the woman that she should give alms every day, for alms "may sins waste." The ghost characteristically personalizes this counsel by telling his wife that when she gives these alms, she should "think on me" (line 1478).

Something about this request—the ghost's attempt to find some relief of his pain directly through the pious thoughts of his wife— seems to nettle the prior. Why did the ghost not come with the story of his life to "men of religion," he demands, rather than to his wife, since he must know perfectly well that such men were wiser and better at praying to God than women were? The ghost's response is the clearest, most powerful statement in the poem of the primacy of the personal and the intimate:

> The voice answered then unto this
> And said: "I loved more my wife
> Than any other man alive,
> And therefore first to her I went."
>
> (Lines 1488–91)

The loss of all of his worldly possessions, the crossing of the boundary between life and death, the encounter with vengeful fiends, the dismaying recognition of the sins of his flesh, the commencement of unspeakable torments—none of these ghastly experiences has severed his deepest mortal passion: "I loved more my wife / Than any other man alive." Hence in his pain he turns not to the spiritual experts—priests and monks and friars—to whom he might appeal for succor; he turns to the woman he loved.[45]

"Think on me," he entreats her, when she performs deeds of charity, and that will "allay some of my pain" (line 1479). Being "thought on" by his wife or by any other living person is not simply a matter of sentimental remembrance; rather, it is an active memory, the directing of a beam of spiritual healing through the power of mental concentration. But it is not in order to be thus remembered and to obtain suffrages that the ghost is haunting his widow's bedroom. Rather, he says, when he was condemned to suffer penance in this place, he asked God's permission to warn his wife, so that she could escape what he is now forced to endure. God graciously gave him leave "for to grieve / And for to torment her" (lines 1498–99). For what looks like cruelty—the terrible fear that he has aroused in her, the writhing, screams, and grimaces that his presence has provoked—is in fact the purest expression of his love. Only by suffering pain for her sins here and now in this life, as a result of his intervention, can his wife be spared the horrible suffering he is experiencing in the afterlife.

This, then, is the psychological and emotional logic of Purgatory, as depicted by *The Gast of Gy*. The church, with its clerical hierarchies, its specialized knowledge of prayer, its elaborate rituals, and above all its miraculous ability to make God's Body, is massively present. Without the powerful conjuring of the prior there would be only vague terror at the sound of a broom scraping along the ground. Yet the center around which this enormous institutional structure is deployed is not the high altar in the church or the papal court of Avignon or the royal throne; it is the bedroom in a bourgeois house in a provincial town. That is, the symbolic core is the relationship between a husband and a wife. That relationship involves guilty secrets as well as love: the couple share the knowledge of something they have done against the "rule" of marriage, and this knowledge continues, along with their love, after they have been severed by the hand of death. The agony Gy suffers in his bedroom is the direct consequence of the nameless sin that he has committed there with his wife, and his wife is terrified that after death she will suffer the fate of her husband. But the haunting that increases her terror is also the key to a release from it. Her intense psychological distress now will obviate later torment, and the alms that she gives in her husband's memory will not only allay some of his pain but also will work to cancel her own sins. The doctrine of Purgatory, in this account, is a way of organizing, articulating, and making sense of a tangle of intense, intimate feelings in the wake of a loved one's death: longing, regret, guilt, fear, anger, and grief.[46]

Surviving manuscripts suggest that *The Gast of Gy* had its greatest impact in the fourteenth century, though the gorgeous illuminated copy was produced for Margaret of York as late as 1474. Around 1500, a Scots writer, possibly William Dunbar, wrote a short comic interlude called *The Droichis [Dwarf's] Part of the Play*, which is said to be the earliest extant specimen of dramatic verse in Scots.[47] "Hiry, hary, hubbilschow!" the dwarf declares as he struts onto the scene, claiming that he is a giant who can wrestle with bears. Eventually, he will identify himself as "Wealth," accompanied by his three boon companions, Welfare, Wantonness, and Play, but before he reveals his name, he plays with several other shapes he claims that he has assumed during his immensely long existence. I am "the naked Blind Harry," he says, who has long been among "ferlys" in faery land, or a sergeant out of Sultan-land, or—yet another alternative shape—"the spirit of Gy."

In the early sixteenth century, then, the ghost who had appeared almost three hundred years earlier in the south of France was still sufficiently well-known that he could be lightly alluded to—linked to the fabulous and the exotic—in a popular entertainment. His renown evidently long continued, at least in Scottish circles: a century later, David Lyndsay relates that in his youth he amused King James V, sometimes singing and dancing, sometimes "playing farces on the floor,"

> And sometimes like a fiend, transfigured
> And sometimes like the grisly Gast of Gy;
> In diverse forms oftimes disfigured,
> And sometimes disguised full pleasantly.[48]

"Sometimes like the grisy Gast of Gy": the poor, disembodied voice of the purgatorial spirit who loved his wife has become entertainment.

The Souls' Book

By the middle of the sixteenth century Christendom had decisively ruptured, and in England the state church had moved to abolish the whole elaborate system of suffrages, offerings, chantries, requiem masses and other means to assist the dead in their pain. A century later Hobbes could write coolly that "all the histories of apparitions and ghosts alleged by the doctors of the Roman Church" are "old wives' fables."[49] How did it all come to an end? How were the dead killed off? And did they go quietly?

Let us return to Simon Fish's *Supplication for the Beggars.* John Foxe, the Protestant martyrologist, offers two different accounts of how Fish's incendiary tract reached the hands of Henry VIII. In one account, the king was conversing with his footman, Edmund Moddys, when their talk turned to religion and "the new books that were come from beyond the seas." Moddys offered to put the king in contact with men who would show him a book "as was a marvel to hear of." The men were two merchants, George Elyot and George Robinson, who presumably had access to a copy of Fish's book smuggled into England from abroad, or who may even have smuggled it in themselves. The king had the book read out to him, made a long pause, and remarked, "If a man should pull down an old stone wall, and begin at the lower part, the upper part thereof might chance to fall upon his head."[50] The meaning of this gnomic comment evidently is that Henry grasped that belief in Purgatory was so foundational that, if the risks of institutional chaos were to be avoided, many other aspects of Catholic dogma would have to be dismantled first, or perhaps that he foresaw that he would have to establish the principle of royal supremacy before he could safely meddle with the wealth of the monks and friars. The king in this account put the book away in his desk and told the merchants to keep their interview with him a secret.

In the other account, it was sent—Foxe does not say by whom—to the king's intimate friend Anne Boleyn, whose personal position and family fortunes depended on the fate of the Reformation; she then brought it to the king. After Henry "kept the book in his bosom" three or four days, the story goes, he contacted Fish's wife and, promising a safe conduct, told her he wished to see her husband. Trusting one of Henry's promises was probably the rashest thing Fish ever did, but his book's suggestion that the crown seize monastic wealth had obviously delighted the king, who "embraced him with loving countenance," talked with him for three or four hours, and even took him hunting. For once the king was as good as his word, giving Fish his signet ring as a token of his protection and instructing his lord chancellor, Sir Thomas More, not to touch the fugitive. The king, however, had neglected to say anything about Fish's wife, whom More promptly moved to interrogate.[51]

Brilliant, learned, politically adroit, and passionately committed to the Catholic Church, More was deeply anxious about the spread of poisonous heresies and determined to stop it. He had known about Fish and his dangerous book for some time. Only a few months after *A Supplication for the Beggars* appeared, though busy with high affairs of state and on the brink of his elevation to the lord chancellorship, More wrote a substantial reply, divided into two long books, *The Supplication of Souls.* The length is characteristic of More's polemical writings, most of them disastrously misconceived as rhetorical performances, but it may also reflect a peculiarly personal stake.

In *Utopia* (1516) More had slyly satirized the idleness of friars, and he had imagined radical measures to solve the problems of poverty, homelessness, and hunger in England. In Utopia, More's imaginary traveler pointedly observes, everyone works, none more so than the members of the religious orders, who "allow themselves no leisure" but devote their full time to good works (*boniis officiis*). Lest the reader think that these are sacramental good works, such as saying masses for the dead, More spells out in detail the tasks undertaken by the Utopian equivalent of monks and friars: "Some tend the sick. Others repair roads, clean out ditches, rebuild bridges, dig turf and sand and stone, fell and cut up trees, and transport wood, grain, and other things into the cities in carts."[52] The consequence of this universal work ethic stands in startling contrast to the miseries so widespread at home: "In Utopia there is no poor man and no beggar."[53]

Years after writing these words, when he encountered Fish's vision of an England in which "idle people be set to work" and even the poorest wretches "have enough and more than shall suffice us"(422), More must have glimpsed a crudely distorted reflection of his own earlier self. This glimpse of a dangerous, heretical double would help to explain not only the sharp reduction of concern in *The Supplication of Souls* for the plight of the poor but also the melancholy absence of the deft irony, playful wit, and mirth that More cultivated throughout the darkest moments of his life, even onto the scaffold where he lost his head. Confronted by Fish's boisterous, coarse voice, railing against the corrupt clergy and pleading on behalf of the dispossessed, the visionary author of the century's greatest work of social criticism is transformed, apart from a few flashes of mordant comedy, into an anxiously defensive spokesman for the Catholic clerical establishment.

If in *The Supplication of Souls* More does not altogether repudiate his earlier social criticism, his attempt to give the lie to each of the reformer's claims forces him to turn in a strikingly different direction. Where Fish declares that the number of beggars has of late greatly increased, More argues that if people remembered the past rightly, they would "think and say that they have in days past seen as many sick beggars as they see now."[54] Poor householders, to be sure, have in recent times "made right hard shift for corn"(121), but "very few" are dying of hunger, and the source of their plight is certainly not the begging of the friars and other clerics. The "beggars' proctor" (that is, official agent or fundraiser), as More dubs Fish, has got all his facts wrong in a reckless attempt to slander the church: the church does not in fact possess a third part of the lands of the realm; there are not 52,000 parish churches in England; every household does not make a quarterly contribution of one penny to each of the five mendicant orders; the friars do not receive annual donations totaling 43,333 pounds, 6 shillings, and 8 pence, and so on. Fish's solemn enumeration of economic statistics is "mad," More writes, or, rather, it is a pack of lies enabling the slanderer to bring in "his ragman's roll of his rude rhetoric against the poor friars" (125).

The heretic's lies, in More's account, extend beyond his tendentious assessment of England's economic woes. *A Supplication for the Beggers* tries to persuade the king that the Catholic Church is a school of sedition and rebellion, but *The Supplication of Souls* counters that the exact opposite is the case. In Germany, More observes, Luther's heretical books sparked a peasant rising that quickly spread from attacks upon the spirituality to murderous attacks upon princes and magistrates. In England heretics like Sir John Oldcastle, espousing seditious views similar to those advanced by the beggars' proctor, provoked comparable disorders during the reign of Henry V. The author of *A Supplication for the Beggers* impudently lectures the king, implying that he is weak and incompetent; Catholic clerics, by contrast, understand that "there is nothing earthly that so much keepeth themselves in quiet rest and surety as doth the due obedience of the people to the virtuous mind of the prince" (128).

Churchmen, moreover, have no such power over laymen as the heretic claims they do, in Parliament or in the nation's courts, nor, More writes, do they routinely accuse their critics of heresy. Richard Hunne, More writes, was already suspected of heresy before he brought a suit against the church, and he was not murdered by the bishop's henchman: "the man hanged himself for despair, despight, and for lack of grace" (135). The beggars' proctor may claim that "all the world knows" Hunne was murdered, but "we dare be bold to warrant you that in heaven, hell, and here among us in Purgatory of all that this man so boldly affirmeth the contrary is well and clearly known" (134). As for the charge that the clergy corrupt the morals of the kingdom, and the proposal that they should be compelled to marry in order to generate legitimate offspring, such notions, "so merry and so mad," are enough "to make one laugh that lieth in the fire" (153). But unfortunately the beggars' proctor is not making a tasteless joke; he is in deadly earnest.

"To make one laugh that lieth in the fire": More's cruel figure of speech—cruel because the burning of heretics was an ongoing reality that More himself was actively furthering at the time—is not merely a playful hyperbole; it is a glimpse of the theatrical strategy that he adopts to counter the theatrical strategy of his heretical enemy. If *A Supplication for the Beggers* speaks in the voice of the poor, *The Supplication of Souls* speaks in the voice of the dead burning in purgatorial fire.[55] And, like Fish's beggars, the dead, as More conceives them, have very few reasons to laugh. The reader encounters a desperate appeal for help, comfort, and pity from "your late acquaintance, kindred, spouses, companions, playfellows, and friends." These former intimates are crying out not because they are dead, not even because they are abiding the "grievous pains and hot cleansing fire" of Purgatory, but because they have become "humble and unacquainted and half-forgotten suppliants." They had once been able to count on relief and comfort from the private prayers of virtuous people and, still more, from "the daily Masses and other ghostly suffrages of priests, religious, and folk of Holy Church" (111).

More's own father, it is worth noting, had in his last will and testament arranged, at considerable expense, for these suffrages, not only for himself but also for his three wives, the former husbands of his second and third wives, his parents, and other named dead people, including King Edward IV, as well as "all Christian souls."[56] Now those who had made comparably careful arrangements for the alleviation of their agonies fear that this consolation and help will vanish, for "certain seditious persons" (111) have spread pestilent doubts about the very existence of Purgatory and the efficacy of the Holy Church's good works on behalf of the dead.

THE CLAIMS OF KINSHIP

The Supplication of Souls, then, begins with the dead crying out, like the ghost of Gy, begging for suffrages. The suffering souls know that their loud lamentings will be disturbing to the living, who desire understandably to take their ease, and who have buried the dead precisely so that the dead will remain buried. But the dead now have no choice, for they fear that they are being forgotten. Though they have been good souls who have "long lain and cried so far from you that we seldom broke your sleep" (111–12), they must now make their existence and their agonies known.[57] They do so in order to counteract the pernicious influence of *A Supplication for the Beggars*, an influence that threatens not only the souls of the dead but also the souls of the living.

Indeed, after initially speaking for their own plight, the dead in More's book affirm that they, after all, are not the real victims of the anonymous author's venom, for when their purgatorial punishment has ceased, they will be "translated" to heavenly bliss. It is the living who run the real risk, for they will find, "for lack of belief of Purgatory, the very straight way to hell" (113). To lure unsuspecting readers down this path is indeed the whole purpose of the wicked anonymous author, whose identity, More's dead souls declare, is not unknown to them, both because certain of his associates before their deaths repented their heresies, returned to the true faith, and are now companions in Purgatory, and because "our and your ghostly enemy the devil" has visited Purgatory in person to brag about his agent on earth.[58] With his "enmious [*hostile*] and envious laughter gnashing the teeth and grinning" (114), the devil delights in the virulent power of the book that will deceive many simple readers.

In order to combat this satanic adversary, Book 2 of *The Supplication of Souls* launches into an extended defense of the doctrine of Purgatory, an odd enterprise, perhaps, for souls who profess to be suffering from its tormenting fires, but one presumably justified both by their concern for misguided mortals and by their fear of being forgotten. Though reason alone, they claim, would lead inevitably to the idea of a process of purgation after death, much of this defense consists of rather strained interpretation of key biblical citations, especially verses from the Second Book of the Maccabees and from Paul's First Epistle to the Corinthians.[59] In 2 Maccabees, Judas Maccabeus orders prayers on behalf of certain sinful Jewish soldiers who had been killed:

> All men therefore praising the Lord, the righteous judge, who had opened the things that were hid, betook themselves unto prayer, and besought him that the sin committed might wholly

be put out of remembrance. Besides, that noble Judas exhorted the people to keep themselves from sin, forsomuch as they saw before their eyes the things that came to pass for sins of those that were slain.

Not only does this passage clearly show prayers for the dead—a practice that the ancient Hebrews were often claimed not to follow—but it goes on to depict a monetary "sin offering" that the church claimed strikingly anticipated indulgences:

And when he had made a gathering throughout the company to the sum of two thousand drachmas of silver, he sent it to Jerusalem to offer a sin offering, doing therein very well and honestly, in that he was mindful of the resurrection; For if he had not hoped that they that were slain should have risen again, it had been superfluous and vain to pray for the dead. And also in that he perceived that there was great favour laid up for those that died godly, it was an holy and good thought. Whereupon he made a reconciliation for the dead, that they might be delivered from sin. (2 Macc. 12:41–46)

In the passage from 1 Corinthians, Paul writes that "other foundation can no man lay than that is laid which is Jesus Christ." He then expands upon this image:

Now if any man build upon this foundation gold, silver, precious stones, wood, hay, stubble; Every man's work shall be made manifest: for the day shall declare it, because it shall be revealed by fire; and the fire shall try every man's work of what sort it is. If any man's work shall be burned, he shall suffer loss: but he himself shall be saved; yet so as by fire. (1 Cor. 3:11–15)

The problem, as More understood quite well, is that none of the scriptural passages—and the difficult, enigmatic ones I have quoted are by far the most relevant—comes very close to the Catholic Church's doctrine of Purgatory.[60] To be sure, 2 Maccabees speaks reasonably plainly about prayers for the dead (though not about a place called Purgatory), but none of the Maccabean books were a part of the Hebrew canon, and many Christians, including the Reformers, relegated them to the Apocrypha. Paul's First Epistle to the Corinthians was certainly canonical, but it said nothing about prayers for the dead, and its words of warning—about a fire that would test the worth of each man's work, whether built of gold, silver, and fine stone, or of wood, hay, and stubble—do not in any obvious way refer to Purgatory or assert the existence of real as distinct from metaphorical fire.

From time to time, when the strain of attempting to prove the existence of Purgatory by natural reason or scriptural interpretation becomes too great, More's souls appeal to the witness of "the old holy doctors" (194) and to the dogmatic authority of the Holy Church. Heretics claim that the Book of Maccabees is apocryphal, but "since the Church of Christ accounteth it for Holy Scripture, there can no man doubt thereof," for everyone who affirms himself to be a Christian, from "the noble doctor and glorious confessor" Saint Augustine to the archheretic Luther, must necessarily believe that "the church cannot fail surely and certainly to discern between the words of God and the words of men" (182). Without such an absolute assurance, "then stood all Christendom in doubt and unsurety whether St. John's Gospel were Holy Scripture or not, and so forth of all the New Testament" (183). Of course, as More concedes, including the Second Book of Maccabees in the canon will not settle the issue once and for all, since even that book does not mention Purgatory, but there are other ancient tenets of the Christian faith, such as the Virgin Birth, that are not "plain proved" by Holy Scripture and yet cannot and must not be doubted. One fact alone should be enough "to stop the mouths of all the proud, high-hearted, malicious heretics": "The Catholic Church of Christ hath always believed Purgatory"(195).

It was precisely this flat claim, as More himself knew, that the heretics challenged, just as they challenged his scriptural readings. On a few occasions in the long treatise, More's souls reach beyond textual arguments and dogmatic pronouncements to appeal to the experience of the living. Nothing can enable you to "conceive a very right imagination of these things which ye never felt," they concede, but you may be able to grasp the nature of purgatorial suffering if you consider a ship wallowing about in high seas. A small number of passengers are so well "attempered of themselves" that they feel "as lusty and as jocund" as if they were on land. Others are anything but jocund: "But then shall ye sometimes see there some other whose body is so incurably corrupted that they shall walter and totter and wring their hands and gnash the teeth, and their eyes water, their head ache, their body fret, their stomach wamble, and all their body shiver for pain, and yet shall never vomit at all: or if they vomit, yet shall they vomit still and never find ease thereof" (189). If the former figure the saved in Heaven and the latter the damned in Hell, how shall we imagine the souls in Purgatory? They are the passengers who feel horrible at first and yet who are, after a vomit or two, "so clean rid of their grief that they never feel displeasure of it after." Such is the middle state, the betwixt-and-between condition of More's speakers.

But the problem remains of convincing readers, poisoned by *A Supplication for the Beggers*, that Purgatory actually exists, for dogmatic appeals to the authority of the church, strained textual interpretation, and metaphors masquerading as realities are precisely what Fish's book attacked as mainstays of Roman Catholic hypocrisy. As a last resort, the souls in More's text can point to the testimony of ghosts. "For there hath in every country and every age apparitions been had," they say, "and well-known and testified by which men have had sufficient revelation and proof of Purgatory, except such as list not to believe them; and they be such as would be never better if they saw them" (196). To be sure, it would be impious to demand to see such apparitions for oneself; they are rare precisely so that people can believe by faith. Those stubborn enough to reject the well-authenticated stories of such apparitions and to demand further proof deserve the punishment they will undoubtedly receive after death when they will "to their pain see such a grisly sight as shall so grieve their hearts to look thereon" (197).

More knew that it was possible to be skeptical about ghost stories. In the colloquy "Exorcism, or the Specter" (1524), his friend Erasmus tells the tale of a gullible priest who is tricked into believing that he has encountered a ghost, a gullibility More himself mocks in similar terms in the dedication to his translation (1506) of Lucian's *Philopseudes*. But in his translation of a life of Pico della Mirandola, More renders apparently straightforwardly Savonarola's report that "Picus had after his death appeared unto him, all compassed in fire: and showed unto him, that he was such wise in Purgatory punished for his negligence, and his unkindness."[61] The sermons and homiletical literature with which More and most of his contemporaries were well acquainted are filled with stories of this kind, many deriving from voluminous collections of exempla such as the *Dialogus miraculorum* (*Dialogue on Miracles*) compiled between 1219 and 1223 by Caesarius of Heisterbach or the *Scala Coeli* compiled by none other than Jean Gobi.[62] Hence, for example, Gobi recounts that before his death a powerful abbot demands that the monks elect his young nephew to succeed him. One day the newly elected abbot is walking in a garden past a beautiful fountain from the midst of whose waters he is startled to hear terrible cries and groans. When he demands, in the name of Christ's Passion, who is making these noises, a voice replies, "I am the soul of your uncle boiling in these waters in excruciating pain for having demanded that you succeed to my diginities." Astonished by these words, the nephew declares that it is scarcely believable that anyone could be burning in such cold water, to which the spectral voice responds by ordering him to cast into the fountain a copper candlestick. When the candlestick immediately melts, the young man at once resigns his position, whereupon the groans from the fountain cease.[63]

The rhetorical problem, from More's point of view, must have been that most of these stories are too obviously homiletical. They provide a lively way of castigating particular sins, often with the satirical edge that we encountered in *The Gast of Gy*, but they carry about them the slightly stale air of the pulpit. Thus, in one typical Middle English sermon, a group of boys are singing psalms over the body of a priest. When the children reach the verse "Thou shalt keep thy tongue from all falsehood," the dead body suddenly arises and says, "Forsooth, ye say sooth. And forasmuch as I have not done so, but slandered my even-Christian [*fellow Christians*] and harmed them with my tongue, therefore I am in woe enough.

See now how that I am tormented in that member." Predictably enough, he then opens his mouth and shows the boys that his tongue is on fire. Once the point is made, the lesson is over: "And when the body had said thus, he laid him down again and did no more harm."[64]

Such neatly illustrative ghosts make, as More understood, no more powerful a claim upon the living than do the names of strangers inscribed on tombstones and effigies. Such names are instances of what Jean-Claude Schmitt calls "cold memory."[65] More was interested in warm memory or, rather, to shift the metaphor to the one Shakespeare uses in *Hamlet*, "green" memory. After a month or two, when memory ceased to be green, ghosts were less and less likely to appear, or, if they did appear, less and less likely to seem anything but an instructive fantasy. More's souls do not speak about sin; they speak about connectedness: "Remember what kin ye and we be together," they cry to the living, "what familiar friendship hath ere this been between us: what sweet words ye have spoken and what promise ye have made us. Let now your words appear and your fair promise be kept" (228).

This appeal, of course, would work best on those who had recently lost loved ones, and More knows that he cannot assume such fresh losses for most of his readers. Therefore the spirits in *The Supplication of Souls* acknowledge the anomalousness of what must be for many a belated and unwelcome return. Its untimeliness, they say, was due to the unprecedented and disastrous interruption of suffrages caused by Fish's malign pamphlet. More's souls then proceed to do what ghosts ordinarily did when they appeared to living relatives, friends, and members of religious communities: first they give an account of their particular situation in the afterlife and provide a description more generally of the nature of Purgatory, and then they appeal for particular actions to be performed on their behalf. More's text does not end, however, with the promise that often accompanied the appeal for suffrages, the souls' promise to return and report on the effect that these suffrages have had. Perhaps More recognized that readers were unlikely to profit from a second long ghostly discourse, or perhaps he did not know whether his work would, as he fervently hoped, actually shore up the old faith in Purgatory and thereby liberate his imagined souls from their agonies. His ghosts close instead with a promise of reciprocity: if the living help the souls of the dead, in Purgatory, to reach bliss in Heaven, then the dead, in Heaven, "shall set hand to help you thither to us" (228).

The communal commitment to caring and assistance that conjoins the living and the dead runs in both directions: after all, as we have seen, the ghost of Gy returns not only to beg suffrages but also to offer counsel to his wife. "The body of charity that links the members of the Church," writes Thomas Aquinas, "is valuable not only to the living but also to the dead who have died in a state of love [*caritas*]. . . . The dead live on in the memory of the living, . . . and so the suffrages of the living can be useful to the dead."[66] The dead in turn, as Le Goff summarizes the position of the Dominican Stephen of Bourbon and others, can be useful to the living: "[I]t is advantageous to pray for souls in Purgatory, because, once they reach Paradise, they will pray for those who have helped them out."[67] Such a mutual exchange is what More's souls propose: they will benefit from the suffrages provided by the living, in return for which they will reward the living with their prayers. These prayers will of necessity be efficacious, for the dead in Purgatory are already assured of God's special favor: "[W]e stand sure of his grace" (227). Not only are the living helping their loved ones; they are also helping themselves.

The centuries-old model here, which More would have understood from firsthand experience at the court of Henry VIII, is gift giving by those who sought to acquire influential friends, friends who have the ear of the all-powerful ruler. But these are better than friends; they are kinsfolk whose integrity is guaranteed—after all, these are the souls of the saved—and whose gratitude toward those who have helped them is reinforced by the terrible intensity of their suffering. Together the living and the dead form a perfect community of mutual charity and interest.

In More's view Fish and other heretics were bent on destroying this precious sense of community; all that would be left would be ignorant selfishness and greed, a world in which each generation would be cut off from the last. To prevent this disaster, More desperately reminded his readers of the powerful claims upon them not only of the Catholic Church but also of their own personal ghosts. Simon Fish does not himself specifically challenge the existence of ghosts, but English Protestants were beginning to do so. "Let no man . . . be moved by those deceitful spirits," writes Miles Coverdale, "which, as they say, do appear unto men, and desire their help, praying that masses, pilgrimages, and other like superstitious ceremonies, may be done for them; for even the same night-bogs, like as they in old time were among the heath, so are they now also among the Turks. Neither is it a wonder, if the devil can disguise himself in the form of a dead man, seeing he can transfigure himself into an angel of light."[68] In a work that dates from the late 1540s, *A Confutation of Unwritten Verities*, Archbishop Cranmer (or someone in his entourage) assembled a set of scriptural and patristic passages to show that "apparitions of the dead be unsufficient to prove truth." Many men dream that they see the dead, writes the Greek Church Father Chrysostom in one of these passages, but such apparitions are not to be credited. If a man sees a ghost, as Cranmer's text notes in a marginal gloss, he may be certain that "it is not the soul of the dead that saith, I am such a man's soul, but the devil counterfeiteth the dead to deceive the living: for souls departed the body cannot walk here on earth." There is no point in trying to distinguish between real ghosts and demons disguised as ghosts; there is no exit, no route back from the place where the dead are locked away. In order to make it more difficult for the devil to introduce deceits and frauds, "God hath shut up that way, neither doth he suffer any of the dead to come again hither."[69]

In *The Supplication of Souls*, More is aware of the problem, which, as we saw, was discussed in *The Gast of Gy*: how could apparitions leave the prison house of Purgatory at all in order to appear on earth, if they are meant to be burning in fires? The souls explain that "we carry our pain with us" (221);[70] indeed, their pain is intensified by their witnessing the ongoing life of the living. The guardian devils ("our evil angels") whom God commands to accompany the souls back to the earth compel some of their miserable prisoners to watch their own funerals, forcing them to stand invisible in the midst of the crowd of mourners and "to look on our carrion corpse carried out with great pomp" (220). Other souls are forced to look at the gold they have left behind and to contemplate "our late wives so soon waxen wanton and, forgetting us their old husbands that have loved them so tenderly and left them so rich, sit and laugh and make merry and more too sometimes with their new wooers, while our keepers in despight keep us there in pain to stand still and look on"(222).

More characteristically does not imagine dead wives looking on at their husbands' carousals, but only dead husbands returning, like the ghost of Gy, to see their wives. Indeed, More's miserable ghosts are forced to witness the pleasures, including sexual pleasures, of their widows. This scene, more than any other he invokes in his long work, seems to conjure up a passionate spectral outburst:

> Many times would we then speak, if we could be suffered, and sore we long to say to her, "Ah wife, wife, ywisse this was not covenant, wife, when ye wept and told me that if I left you to live by, ye would never wed again. We see there our children too, whom we loved so well, pipe, sing, and dance, and no more think on their fathers' souls then on their old shoes, saving that sometimes commeth out "God have mercy on all Christian souls." But it commeth out so coldly and with so dull affection that it lieth but in the lips and never came near the heart. (222)[71]

Vows are broken, mourning is forgotten, life resumes its round of heedless pleasures, and even piety takes the form of cold lip service. The dead in their individuality, their intense suffering, their urgent claims on personal remembrance, are consigned to oblivion or become at best an anonymous, generalized category, the "all Christian souls" casually invoked in a ritual phrase by thoughtless children.

Against this terrible indifference the suffering souls in More's text cry out, passionately claiming the right to be remembered and the rites of memory. They claim something more tangible as well: the alms that will relieve them of some of their pains. Seeing themselves forgotten by their wives, their children, and their friends, the dead are consumed with regret that they left so much behind them and "had not sent hither more of our substance before us by our own hands" (222). Looking around them, they see that those who had arranged during their own lifetimes to give away their wealth to the church in anticipation of their postmortem sufferings are in far better condition than those who are now counting on the goodwill of their heirs and executors. That goodwill has always been threatened by the ordinary power of greed: "[C]atch every man what he can and hold fast that he catcheth and care nothing for us" (222). But it has of late been disastrously eroded by the malicious mockery of heretics who "make a game and a jest now of our heavy pains" (226).

The ghosts return again and again to their terrible problem: they are screaming in pain and pleading for help, but their enemies say not only that they are not suffering but that they do not exist at all. How can they make their existence manifest? How can they enable the living to imagine and to credit fully what they are enduring? "If ever ye lay sick and thought the night long and longed sore for day while every hour seemed longer than five," they cry out in a passage that anticipates Donne's sickbed *Devotions*, "bethink you then what a long night we silly [*helpless*] souls endure that lie sleepless, restless, burning, and broiling in the dark fire one long night of many days, of many weeks, and some of many years together" (225).

But even as they elaborate on this similitude—"You walter peradventure and tolter in sickness from side to side and find little rest in any part of the bed: we lie bounded to the brands and cannot lift up our heads," etc.—they seem to hear the derision of their enemies, who "laugh at our lamentation because we speak of our heads, our hands, our feet, and such our other gross bodily members as lie buried in our graves and of our garments that we did wear which come not hither with us." What can they do? How else can they make any person on earth conceive "in his imagination and fantasy" what "we bodiless souls do suffer"? Without using the language of the body, it would be impossible, "much more impossible than to make a born blind man to perceive in his mind the nature and difference of colors" (226). Only if the living conceive of their dead in the familiar terms of the body will they be able to remember their loved ones and do what they can to help them. "Our wives there," More's dead cry out from the otherworld, "remember here your husbands. Our children there remember here your parents. Our parents there remember here your children. Our husbands there remember here your wives" (223–24).

Here More imagines dead wives speaking out, not to lament their surviving husbands' pleasures but to regret their own past delight in gorgeous clothing, jewels, and cosmetics. This "gay gear" is now burning hot upon their tormented bodies, so that, looking back on their lives, they wish that their husbands "never had followed our fantasies, nor never had so cockered us nor made us so wanton, nor had given us other ouches [*brooches*] than onions or great garlic heads" (224). For them, of course, such thoughts come too late, but they have a generous desire to save others as well as to help themselves. "We beseech you," they cry out from beyond the grave to their living husbands, "since ye gave them us, let us have them still. Let them hurt none other woman but help to do us good: sell them for our sakes to set in saints' copes, and send the money hither by mass pennies and by poor men that may pray for our souls" (224).

How can you show that you remember the dead, that you care for your departed wives and husbands and children, that you are not cruelly indifferent to their sufferings? Give money to the church for the recitation of prayers. Since masses for the dead were closely linked to almsgiving, it would in principle have been possible for More to reject Fish's premise entirely and to claim that the doctrine of Purgatory was in fact a strong incentive to charity, but instead he chooses to set the dead against the living.[72] More's poor souls understand themselves to be in direct competition with Fish's beggars:

> If ye pity the poor, there is none so poor as we that have not a brat [*rag*] to put on our backs. If ye pity the blind, there is none so blind as we which are here in the dark, saving for sights unpleasant and loathsome, till some comfort come. If

ye pity the lame, there is none so lame as we that neither can creep one foot out of the fire, nor have one hand at liberty to defend our face from the flame. Finally, if ye pity any man in pain, never knew ye pain comparable to ours, whose fire as far passeth in heat all the fires that ever burned upon earth as the hottest of all those passeth a fained fire painted on a wall. (225)[73]

More was a savvy politician who must have grasped perfectly well that it would be rhetorically wiser to point out that the church *did* care for the hungry and the sick, often in the same moment in which it was caring for the dead, but he accepts Fish's challenge. Why? It is possible that he simply blundered, drawn into a trap by his overwhelming sympathy for the suffering souls. But perhaps, too, his rhetorical position was hardened by the fact that he could not use the one overwhelmingly obvious argument against Fish: namely, that Henry VIII was probably the least likely person in England to redistribute the wealth of the church to the poor. Instead, More argues that the miseries of the poor are vastly exceeded by the unspeakable miseries of souls in Purgatory, and the good that alms can do for the living is vastly exceeded by what the same alms can do for the dead. Moreover, the money that is donated for the relief of souls is proof that the giver is not a heretic who dismisses the flames of Purgatory as mere "fained fire" and "taketh in his heart that story told by God for a very fantastic fable" (227). Consequently, the souls declare, as if their supplication were an investment prospectus, whatever you give "shall also rebound upon yourself an inestimable profit" (227).

Fish's ally, the young reformer John Frith, took special note of this particular passage. As we saw in chapter 2, Frith was one of those who charged that Purgatory was a tangle of dreams and fantasies. But, quoting the impassioned appeal for pity in *The Supplication of Souls*, he wryly conceded at least part of More's argument: "Verily, among all his other poetry it is reason that we grant him this; yea, and that our fire is but water in comparison to it, for, I ensure you, it hath alone melted more gold and silver, for our spirituality's profit, out of poor men's purses, than all the goldsmiths' fires within England, neither yet therewith can the raging heat be assuaged, but it melteth castles, hard stones, lands and tenements innumerable."[74] Therefore, Frith concedes with rueful irony, we must grant that "this fire is very hot."

But, though *The Supplication of Souls* reiterates the appeal for money, it would be a mistake to conclude with Frith that its principal aim was to augment the church's revenues. More's concern is to counteract a serious and potentially damaging attack upon the church, an attack launched against what the scholarly humanist More knew perfectly well was one of its most vulnerable doctrines. Simon Fish spoke in the name of the poor and dispossessed, but he does not seem a tenderhearted philanthropist, and it is unlikely that his concern lay with their plight.[75] His book takes the form of a petition to the king, to whom it offers in effect a convenient, morally upright political cover for a cynical course of action Henry had probably already been contemplating, just as Henry was loudly professing that it was his moral scruples that impelled him to seek a divorce from Catharine of Aragon. Fish's own motives were almost certainly not mercenary; rather he was offering the king and the nation a kind of bait to embark on a path that would lead to a reformed religion.

More understood the bait and struggled to avert the danger by recalling his readers to their deep and ancient religious loyalty. Money is important, to be sure, as both Fish and More agree, but for More it is a sign of remembrance. "Let never any slothful oblivion raze us out of your remembrance," the souls cry; "Remember what kin ye and we be together"; "remember how nature and Christendom bindeth you to remember us"; "remember our thirst while ye sit and drink; our hunger while ye be feasting; our restless watch while ye be sleeping; our sore and grievous pain while ye be playing; our hot, burning fire while ye be in pleasure and sporting. So might God make your offspring after remember you" (227–28).

❧ 4 ❧

STAGING GHOSTS

THE GHOSTS who cry out desperately in the pages of More's *Suppli-cation*, for fear that they are being forgotten, the ghosts who are consigned to oblivion by skeptics and reassigned to Hell in the writings of the triumphant Protestants, the ghosts who are increasingly labeled as fictions of the mind—these do not altogether vanish in the later sixteenth century. Instead they turn up onstage.

Not only onstage, of course: reports of hauntings occur from time to time throughout the sixteenth and seventeenth centuries, as they continue to do in the present. In the late 1570s, for example, Henry Caesar, the vicar of Lostwithiel in Cornwall, affirms that a conjuror had brought back the deceased Cardinal Pole at the request of Sir Walter Mildmay.[1] So, too, ghosts perennially appear in ballads: "My mouth it is full cold, Margaret," laments the ghost of Clerk Sanders in one of these ballads; "It has the smell now of the ground."[2] But there is always something suspect about such apparitions: they are specimens of "folk beliefs," to be savored or despised, or evidence of fraud, or signs of residual Catholic "super-stition." Henry Caesar was long suspected of being a papist sympa-thizer: in church he wore a cope and turned his face away from the congregation when he read the divine service.[3] Popular bal-lads, too, were hiding-holes for old believers. A broadside of 1616 tells of three ghosts that arise from their graves to announce the imminence of doomsday. One ghost, "most seemly clear and white," praises the Lord; another, "gnashing of his teeth together," hideously cries, "Woe, woe unto you, wicked men!" But the middle ghost, "all in fire," calls for repentance. Either an unexamined tradition has brought with it this third, manifestly purgatorial ghost, like wreckage carried downstream from an ancient ruin, or the ballad-monger has deliberately preserved a figure from the banished system of faith.[4] What is gone, in any case, is legitimate, sanctioned belief in ghosts, the ghosts featured in stories told from the pulpit by friars and priests who had culled them from the great collections of exempla.

The major exception in Elizabethan and Jacobean public space is the theater, where ghosts make frequent appearances.[5] As early as 1559, in a translation of Seneca's *Troas* Jasper Heywood adds a long, grim speech by the "spright" of Achilles:

> Now mischief, murder, wrath of hell draweth near,
> And dire Phlegethon flood doth blood require:
> Achilles' death shall be revenged here.[6]

Such menacing tirades, adapted from a Senecan drama abundant in vengeful ghosts, become a regular feature of late-sixteenth-century English drama. The ghost of Gorlois, surging up from "Pluto's pits and glooming shades," chilled the spectators of *The Misfortunes of Arthur* by Thomas Hughes and other law students of Gray's Inn:

> Come therefore blooms of settled mischief's root,
> Come each thing else, what fury can invent,
> Wreak all at once, infect the air with plagues,
> Till bad to worse, till worse to worst be turned.
> Let mischiefs know no mean, nor plagues an end.[7]

At about the same time, the late 1580s, in *Locrine* (probably by Thomas Peele), the ghost of Albanact appeared to the man who had killed him in battle—"For now revenge shall ease my lingering grief, / And now revenge shall glut my longing soul"[8]—while in Thomas Kyd's *Spanish Tragedy* the ghost of the slain Andrea sat down in the company of Revenge to watch the whole ghastly bloodletting.

There are occasional comic ghosts—Will Summer in Thomas Nashe's *Summer's Last Will and Testament*, for example, or the spirit of Jack in Peele's *Old Wives' Tale*, who returns to aid the stranger who generously paid for his Christian burial—but the predominant theatrical figures of the dead are spirits from the underworld who, like the ghost of Thyestes in Seneca's *Agamemnon*, long to see the stage run with blood. "Antonio, revenge," cries the ghost of the murdered Andrugio to his son, in John Marston's *Antonio's Revenge* (1601),

> I was empoisoned by Piero's hand;
> Revenge my blood. Take spirit gentle boy.
> Revenge my blood.[9]

Only a spectacular act of vengeance—on the night that the murderer was going to marry Andrugio's widow, in the midst of the festivities, the villainous Piero is taken by surprise, tortured, and stabbed to death—can appease the rage in the murdered man's spirit. An eager spectator of the killing, the ghost declares himself satisfied and proud of his dutiful son:

> 'Tis done, and now my soul shall sleep in rest.
> Sons that revenge their father's blood are blest.
>
> (5.3.114–15)

Such figures may have helped to fuel contemporary complaints that the theater was unchristian, but they did not seem to arouse a specifically theological anxiety.[10] No one, even among the most rabid Puritan antitheatricalists, could imagine them to be secret agents for the pope's Purgatory. Their ancestry is manifestly classical rather than Catholic: they derive not only from Seneca but also from Aeschylus (who presents the ghost of Darius in the *Persae* and of Clytemnestra in the *Eumenides*) and Euripides (who presents the murdered Polydorus in the *Hecuba*). Hence the attacks upon them, when they come, are more literary than doctrinal. The anonymous *A Warning for Fair Women* (ca. 1599) begins with a debate among Tragedy, Comedy, and History. Tragedy scolds History for being noisy, all drums and shouting, and Comedy for being slight and childish. Comedy responds by mocking Tragedy's penchant for the story of some "damned tyrant" who stabs, hangs, poisons, smothers, or cuts throats to obtain the crown. "Then, too, a filthy whining ghost," the mockery continues,

> Lapped in some foul sheet or a leather pilch,
> Comes screaming like a pig half-sticked,
> And cries, "Vindicta! Revenge, Revenge!"
> With that a little rosin flasheth forth,
> Like smoke out of a tobacco pipe or a boy's squib.[11]

Comedy is interested in showing how Tragedy's spookiest effect is produced, and still more interested in showing that the effect is cheap.

Marlowe's Succubus

In keeping with this disdain, two of the greatest playwrights of the age, Marlowe and Jonson, show surprisingly little interest in the popular stage figure of the ghost. Jonson's fundamentally comic and satiric sensibility is almost completely averse to it, as is manifestly demonstrated by his abortive attempt to introduce one at the beginning of his wooden tragedy *Catiline,* and by the contempt he voices in *Poetaster.*[12] Marlowe's sensibility was less obviously antipathetic. But though there would have been ample scope for spectacular hauntings in the two parts of *Tamburlaine, The Jew of Malta, Edward II,* and, above all, *Dido, Queen of Carthage,* he eschews all representation of ghosts in these plays. To be sure, the villainous Jew Barabas, impatiently waiting at midnight under the walls of his expropriated house, thinks of himself as one of the specters who, according to a popular belief that Horatio also recalls in *Hamlet,* keep watch over buried treasure:

> Now I remember those old women's words,
> Who in my wealth would tell me winter's tales,
> And speak of spirits and ghosts that glide by night
> About the place where Treasure hath been hid.
> And now methinks that I am one of those,
> For whilst I live here lives my soul's sole hope,
> And when I die here shall my spirit walk.[13]

But a moment later, after his daughter Abigail has thrown him the bags of gold and jewels that he has hidden under the floorboards—"Father, here receive thy happiness"—all talk of ghosts vanishes in an effusion of satisfied greed: "O girl, O gold, O beauty, O my bliss!" (2.1.54).

The exception in Marlowe is *Doctor Faustus*, where, along with grapes out of season, devils with fireworks, and horses that turn into straw, the magician conjures up what seem to be the spirits of the dead. "Then, Faustus, as thou late didst promise us," declares the German emperor, Charles the Fifth,

> We would behold that famous conqueror
> Great Alexander and his paramour
> In their true shapes and state majestical,
> That we may wonder at their excellence.[14]

Sending Mephostophilis to do his bidding, Faustus sets conditions for watching the spectacle. This will not be an interview, he makes clear, like Saul's anxious interrogation of the spirit of Samuel or Jean Gobi's demanding theological clarification from the ghost of Gy. Rather, it will be a spectacle, like a masque or play:

> My lord, I must forewarn your majesty
> That when my spirits present the royal shapes
> Of Alexander and his paramour,
> Your grace demand no questions of the king,
> But in dumb silence let them come and go.
>
> (4.1.92–96)

"When my spirits present the royal shapes": the spirits under Faustus's command will take on the forms of Alexander and his paramour, miming them with uncanny verisimilitude. Marlowe's principal source, *The History of the Damnable Life, and Deserved Death of Doctor John Faustus* (1592), makes the point explicit, adding a detail that explains why the likeness is so accurate: "I am ready to accomplish your request in all things, so far forth as I and my spirit are able to perform," Faustus tells the emperor; "Yet your majesty shall know that their dead bodies are not able substantially to be brought before you, but such spirits as have seen Alexander and his paramour alive shall appear unto you in manner and form as they both lived in their most flourishing time."[15] These will not be the shades of the ancient conqueror and his mistress—their bodies somehow reanimated or their souls reclothed in flesh—but rather cunning and persuasive representations, fashioned by actors who have directly observed those whom they are presenting. The representations will not have actual bodies: when the emperor, ravished by the sight, goes to embrace them, Faustus has to remind him that "these are but shadows, not substantial" (4.1.103). They are masterfully detailed illusions, down to the "little wart or mole" on the neck of the fair lady, but they are not human beings, either living or dead.

What are they, then? They are not specifically identified as anything other than "spirits," but there is at least a strong suggestion that they are demons, at once infinitely alluring and destructive. "To glut the longing" of his heart's desire, the doomed magician, eager to distract himself from tormenting thoughts of repentance, asks that the Helen whom he has recently conjured up be his paramour. In the play's most famous scene, he gets his wish, and his words mark his own decisive violation of the injunction to be silent:

> Was this the face that launched a thousand ships
> And burnt the topless towers of Ilium?
> Sweet Helen, make me immortal with a kiss.
> Her lips suck forth my soul. See where it flies!

(5.1.93–96)

Somewhere behind this celebrated moment of suicidal ecstasy there may be traces of the tangled tradition of spectral returns that we have been examining, but these traces have become so faint as to be all but invisible. This is no ghost come from Purgatory or even a spirit from classical Hades; this is something else: a succubus.

SHAKESPEARE'S SPIRITS

Of the leading Renaissance English playwrights, it is only Shakespeare who fully participates in the popular vogue for presenting ghosts onstage.[16] Indeed, "participates" is an inadequate term: Shakespeare's celebrated ghost scenes—easily the greatest in all of

English drama—are signs of a deep interest that continues through virtually his entire career. He saw that he could draw upon a range of traditions, including not only the classical Hades and the popular Hell but also the banished realm of Catholic Purgatory. He saw, too, that uncertainty—including perhaps his own uncertainty—about the very possibility of ghosts was itself valuable theatrical capital. More than anyone of his age, Shakespeare grasped that there were powerful links between his art and the haunting of spirits.

The richest and most complex exploitation of the theatrical capital Shakespeare found in ghosts is in *Hamlet*, which is the subject of the next chapter and the subtext of this entire book, but it is important to grasp how frequently and insistently the figure of the ghost recurs throughout his plays. The questions the figure raises, at once theological, psychological, and theatrical, are ones to which Shakespeare never provides definitive answers; rather, he prefers to keep the issues alive by staging ghosts in a variety of guises and from shifting perspectives.[17] Each of these stagings has its own distinct and subtle meanings, but there are three fundamental perspectives to which Shakespeare repeatedly returns: the ghost as a figure of false surmise, the ghost as a figure of history's nightmare, and the ghost as a figure of deep psychic disturbance. Half-hidden in all of these is a fourth perspective: the ghost as a figure of theater.

Shakespeare was clearly fascinated by what we might call evacuated ghost beliefs, beliefs attributable to panic, superstitious dread, or psychological projection. This fascination may have seemed sufficiently characteristic of him to induce the printer, hoping to increase sales of a decidedly creaky comedy, *The Puritan: or, the Widow of Watling Street*, to publish it in 1607 with the ascription "Written by W. S." (The ascription seems to have led the editors of the Third Folio of Shakespeare's *Works* [1664] to include it in their text.) The plot of the comedy, whose style does not remotely resemble Shakespeare's, hinges on an attempt by the clever scholar, young George Pyeboard, to persuade a wealthy London widow that her deceased husband, a grasping Puritan, lies in Purgatory and will suffer there unless she and her daughters change their marriage plans. "Widow, I have been a mere stranger for these parts that you live in," George declares, launching his strategy, "nor did I ever know the Husband of you, and Father of them, but I truly know by certain spiritual Intelligence, that he is in Purgatory." The widow responds with the appropriate Protestant religious zeal: "Purgatory? tuh; that word deserves to be spit upon; I wonder that a man of sober tongue, as you seem to be, should have the folly to believe there's such a place." But George persists:

> Well Lady, in cold blood I speak it, I assure you that there is a Purgatory, in which place I know your husband to reside, and wherein he is like to remain, till the dissolution of the world, till the last general Bonfire: when all the earth shall melt into nothing, and the Seas scald their finny labourers: so long is his abidance, unless you alter the property of your purpose, together with each of your Daughters theirs, that is, the purpose of single life in yourself and your eldest Daughter, and the speedy determination of marriage in your youngest.[18]

The resolution of this sly device does not concern us, but it is of interest that the play could have been passed off as Shakespeare's, since it suggests that his name may have been associated with stories of Protestants confronted by purgatorial spirits, stories obviously relevant to *Hamlet.*

Alternatively, his name may have been associated with the staging of false or fraudulent ghosts. Yet Shakespeare never depicts unreal ghosts as deliberate deceptions, only as mistakes or delusions. If this type of depiction associates his plays at least in part with a skeptical challenge to ghost sightings—one that was perfectly compatible with Catholicism as well as Protestantism[19]—it does not constitute evidence of full-scale skepticism, nor does it link Shakespeare at all with the Protestant argument that ghosts, when they are not simply frauds, are demons. (That argument is given dramatic currency in Marlowe's Helen.) What it does suggest is that Shakespeare was fascinated by the way in which disoriented or anxious people construct desperate explanatory hypotheses—his contemporary Gascoigne called them "supposes"—about their world.[20]

Hence, to take a relatively minor instance, in one of his earliest plays, *The Comedy of Errors*, Shakespeare folds belief in ghosts into a range of other fearful fantasies—witches, sorcerers, fairies, goblins, and the like—that arise from the screwball confusion that besets the characters. In the giddy scene at the end of the comedy, the two sets of twins who have been constantly mistaken for one another are finally brought onstage together. "I see two husbands," declares Adriana, staring at Antipholus of Ephesus and his identical twin, "or mine eyes deceive me." She is offering in effect two hypotheses for the weird double image she is seeing: either two husbands or an optical illusion. To these hypotheses, both of which, as we know, are incorrect, the duke adds a third:

> One of these men is *genius* to the other:
> And so of these, which is the natural man,
> And which the spirit? Who deciphers them?
>
> (5.1.332–35)

The duke begins with a seemingly definitive explanation—one that has the advantage of that impressive-sounding term *genius*, highly appropriate for the classical setting—but immediately runs into difficulty.[21] The two figures before his eyes do not have the convenient marks that distinguish between representation and reality, the former more faded, schematic, or intangible than the latter. Instead they each make the identical strong claim to reality, just as the two servants, the twin Dromios, proceed to do:

DROMIO OF SYRACUSE. I, sir, am Dromio. Command him away.
DROMIO OF EPHESUS. I, sir, am Dromio. Pray let me stay.

> (5.1.336–37)

It is at this point of heightened confusion that Antipholus of Syracuse suddenly notices his father, whom he believes to be far away, and raises the possibility that he is seeing a ghost: "Egeon, art thou not? Or else his ghost" (5.1.338). No sooner is this possibility voiced than it is laid to rest: though they return several times to the possibility that they are dreaming, the characters begin to sort out that they are seeing something no more (or less) amazing than identical twins. What looked like spirit—*genius* or ghost, hallucination or dream—is flesh.

Shakespeare liked this scene sufficiently well that he wrote another version of it in *Twelfth Night,* playing once again with the uncanniness of twins. "Do I stand there?" asks Sebastian, gawking at Cesario, who appears to him, as to everyone else, to be his perfect double.

> I never had a brother,
> Nor can there be that deity in my nature,
> Of here and everywhere. I had a sister,
> Whom the blind waves and surges have devoured.
> Of charity, what kin are you to me?
> What countryman? What name? What parentage?
>
> (5.1.219–24)

The solution to the mystery is so obvious—a simple change of clothes will turn Cesario back into his twin sister, Viola—that Sebastian seems remarkably dim-witted. Yet the quick and resourceful Viola is also utterly perplexed, as she answers the flurry of questions and tentatively speculates that she may be seeing a ghost:

> Of Messaline. Sebastian was my father;
> Such a Sebastian was my brother, too.
> So went he suited to his watery tomb.
> If spirits can assume both form and suit
> You come to fright us.
>
> (5.1.225–29)

If the phrase "both form and suit" is not merely a hendiadys for "suitable form," the issue here is not only whether the spirits of the dead can return to the fleshly form they once possessed but also whether they can dress as if they were again alive.[22] Sebastian's reply confirms that he is a spirit, but only in the sense in which everyone alive is a spirit. He picks up the issue of suit as dress or costume—intensely important in this play of cross-dressing and disguise—to turn it into a reference to the flesh in which his spirit has been clothed from the moment of conception:

A spirit I am indeed,
But am in that dimension grossly clad
Which from the womb I did participate.
Were you a woman, as the rest goes even,
I should my tears let fall upon your cheek,
And say "Thrice-welcome, drowned Viola."

(5.1.229–34)

There are no ghosts in *Comedy of Errors* or *Twelfth Night*, only perplexing, unnerving resemblances that turn out to have an entirely naturalistic explanation. Though both comedies are deeply sensitive to the tragic potential built into their plots, in neither is the audience for even one moment induced to share the fear: the character's alarm—"You come to fright us"—is an occasion for laughter, qualified perhaps by a measure of compassion. Thinking that you are seeing a ghost is revealed to be a false surmise. It is a desperate hypothesis advanced, in bafflement and rising panic, to account for the extraordinary apparition of someone one does not expect to see. Ghosts are the effects of anxious misreading.

In *A Midsummer Night's Dream* Theseus gives an account of such misreadings, which he attributes to the overheated imagination or "shaping fantasies" that link lunatics, lovers, and poets. The madman, he says, "sees more devils than vast hell can hold"; the frantic lover sees "Helen's beauty in a brow of Egypt." And the poet in effect combines the phantasmatic powers of both:

The poet's eye, in a fine frenzy rolling,
Doth glance from heaven to earth, from earth to heaven,
And as imagination bodies forth
The forms of things unknown, the poet's pen
Turns them to shapes, and gives to airy nothing
A local habitation and a name.

(5.1.5–17)

This account in effect sketches the whole basis of the Protestant use of the term "poetry" to characterize Purgatory. It gets at the cosmic reach of the poetic imagination, its bold assigning of form to what in fact is utterly unknown, its capacity to create virtual bodies, its fashioning of nothing into a specific, named place where these shapes may dwell. All of this constitutes a brief for withholding belief: "I never may believe / These antique fables, nor these fairy toys" (5.1.2–3).

Yet, of course, *A Midsummer Night's Dream*, itself an antique fable, playfully undermines Theseus's skepticism by bringing "fairy toys" onto the stage. The fairies are not exactly ghosts, but they are not exactly *not* ghosts either. Robin Goodfellow urges haste because the dawn is not far off,

> At whose approach ghosts, wand'ring here and there,
> Troop home to churchyards; damnèd spirits all
> That in cross-ways and floods have burial
> Already to their wormy beds are gone,
> For fear lest day should look their shames upon.
> They wilfully themselves exiled from light,
> And must for aye consort with black-browed night.
>
> (3.2.382–88)

Two different types of spirits are quickly sketched here: the first are the ghosts of those who have been buried in churchyards; the second are the ghosts of those who have not received proper funerals. (In the latter category are those who have drowned and hence have died without proper ceremonies, and those who have committed suicide and hence have been buried at crossroads, where men will walk disrespectfully upon their graves.) Catholic and Protestant theologians would have assigned these spirits a place in the otherworld: the aim, as we have seen, was to lock away the dead securely in a sphere from which they could seldom, if ever, return. But the universe of *A Midsummer Night's Dream* is hyperanimated, especially at night, by restless wanderers.

Oberon, the fairy king, goes out of his way (slightly awkwardly, since Robin must surely grasp the point already) to differentiate himself and his fellow fairies from spirits that have to spend their days in wormy beds. "But we are spirits of another sort," he rejoins,

> I with the morning's love have oftmade sport,
> And like a forester the groves may tread

> Even till the eastern gate, all fiery red,
> Opening on Neptune with fair blessèd beams
> Turns into yellow gold his salt green streams.
>
> (3.2.389–94)

It is not clear whether Oberon is saying that the fairies are a special
type of ghosts permitted to remain at large during the whole day;
or that they are granted a few daylight hours (until dawn gives way
to the actual appearance of the sun); or that they are not ghosts at
all. Having made a self-congratulatory distinction of some kind or
other, he nonetheless agrees that the tasks he has assigned should
be done quickly:

> But notwithstanding, haste; make no delay;
> We may effect this business yet ere day.
>
> (3.2.395–96)

This prudent haste leaves a lingering doubt about how sharp the
difference actually is between ghosts and fairies.

Perhaps in the contentious atmosphere of the sixteenth century
there would have been room for heated controversy about even
such an absurd issue or at least for a sense of grave annoyance on
the part of one concerned group or another. Pious Catholics and
Protestants alike could well have felt that their beliefs about the
afterlife were being mocked. Shakespeare gives the spirit of mockery a local habitation and a name in the person of Puck, but the
playwright is not eager to pick a quarrel. Indeed, Shakespeare is
extraordinarily good throughout his career at knowing just how
far he can go without, as it were, getting the police called; compared with Marlowe and Jonson, he is a marvel of prudence. Here
in *A Midsummer Night's Dream* all controversies are made moot by
the pervasive suggestion, fully articulated in the epilogue, that the
whole spectacle is unreal:

> If we shadows have offended,
> Think but this, and all is mended:
> That you have but slumbered here,
> While these visions did appear;

And this weak and idle theme,
No more yielding but a dream.

(Epilogue 1–6)

Spectral Dreams

But dreams, as Shakespeare understood, are hardly as innocent as Puck's sly apology suggests. In its zany, indirect way, the play is a devastating critique of those—like the polemicists against Purgatory—who view the imagination as the diametrical opposite of the truth. After all, in *A Midsummer Night's Dream*, there are strong hints that dreams and idle fantasies reveal truths that waking consciousness, naively confident in its own grasp of reality, cannot recognize or acknowledge. Bottom actually *was* in the arms of the fairy queen, and he *is* precisely the ass that his dream depicts him to be. Even the fantastic imagery of poor Hermia's nightmare—"Methought a serpent ate my heart away, / And you sat smiling at his cruel prey" (2.2.155–56)—turns out to anticipate Lysander's sadistic cruelty a few moments later. And these are, after all, only the dreams of a play in which we are assured that every Jack will have his Jill. It is the game of *A Midsummer Night's Dream*—indeed, the deep game of virtually all of Shakespeare's comedies—to contain, just barely, the wild and destructive energies that they release, yoking them like boisterous, unruly horses to the traces of the conventional marriage plots. No comparable constraints govern the histories and tragedies, plays in which dreams of terror at once prophesy the future and are haunted by ghosts.

The uncanny power of these spectral dreams depends in part on their reality claim. Shakespearean comedies tend to emphasize their fantastic nature, figured in moonlit Athenian woods or the seacoast of Illyria. By contrast, the histories and tragedies alike insist that the terrible events they depict are historically real, an insistence that intensifies the weirdness of their ghostly dreams. In an early history, *Richard III*, and an early tragedy, *Julius Caesar*, ghosts figure not as false surmises or colorful folk beliefs but as something else, something altogether more ominous. What this something else is, however, is difficult to specify. It would not be accurate to characterize them as figures from the late medieval theological imagination, and it is also misleading and evasive to call them mere classical conventions. Their classical lineage is indeed important, but precisely because Greek and Roman histories, as well as plays, include, as part of the fabric of historical actuality, curses, omens, prophetic dreams, and ghosts.

To get at their peculiar force, or to make that force seem something other than quaint, I want to make a detour to two dreams of terror, dreams dreamt during the 1930s and brought together by Charlotte Beradt in *The Third Reich of Dreams*. The first is the dream of a doctor in 1934:

> It was about nine o'clock in the evening. My consultations were over, and I was just stretching out on the couch to relax with a book on Matthias Grünewald, when suddenly the walls of my room and then my apartment disappeared. I looked around and discovered to my horror that as far as the eye could see no apartment had walls anymore. Then I heard a loudspeaker boom, "According to the decree of the 17th of this month on the Abolition of Walls. . . ."

The second is the dream of a lawyer in the same period:

> Two benches were standing side by side in Tiergarten Park, one painted the usual green and the other yellow [in those days, Jews were permitted to sit only on specially painted yellow benches]. There was a trash can between them. I sat down on the trash can and hung a sign around my neck like the ones blind beggars sometimes wear—also like those the government makes "race violators" wear. It read, "*I Make Room for Trash If Need Be.*"[23]

In hindsight these dreams had a horrible premonitory power, but their significance extends beyond this power. They bear witness to the deep, inward experience of malevolent absolutism, its ability to penetrate the mind, in sleep, in fantasy, in the fictions we daily and nightly create, even as it could also penetrate the body.[24] Terror experienced in sleep, as in waking reality, had an important function in the ability of the Third Reich to carry out an inherently difficult program of mass murder, difficult because so many people needed to be confused, disoriented, deceived, and made to feel absolutely powerless, even in the face of incontrovertible evidence of unappeasably violent malice against them. Of course, for the most part the victims *were* absolutely powerless, but it was important for the murderers to carry out their crimes in orderly fashion, to keep the greater part of their victims from attempting to resist or escape or simply from running about in a mad, blind panic.[25] Terror served to block many of the ordinary, self-protective responses of conscious, sentient people marked out for elimination and at least partially aware that they were so marked. Deeply terrified people seemed to act as if they were in a dream, as if they were caught in an immobilizing light, as if they were already dead.[26]

"Terror is not simply dreamed," Reinhart Koselleck remarks about these traces of the wounded inner lives of the German Jews in the 1930s; "the dreams are themselves components of the terror." What is perhaps most striking about the dreams I have quoted, however, is not their terror but rather their weird, grim wit, a terrible, mirthless laughter deeply in touch with the process by which the psychological and structural malevolence of the Nazis would eventually realize itself fully in the world.[27] The sudden removal by decree of the protective walls around the individual and the whole community of which the individual is part, the radical loss of both the dreamer's professional identity as a surgeon and his cultural identity as a reader of books on German high art, the transformation of a person into litter or something less than litter: these are visionary apprehensions of murder in the making, apprehensions conveyed, as dreams so often do, with poetic deftness. The intimations of grotesque humor in several of the details—the bellowing loudspeaker with its bureaucratic language, for example, or the sign that those designated as human refuse must place around their own necks—do not detract from the terror Koselleck sees in the dreams; if anything, the details intensify the terror by undermining the dignity of tragic pathos. But I think that the dreams tell us something important about the nature of the imagination under extreme terror and direct us to the special function of dreams and ghosts in *Richard III*.

Productions of *Richard III* in the late twentieth century (including, notably, Ian McKellen's successful film, along with the stage
production on which it was based) have almost routinely interpreted Shakespeare's play, first performed in 1592 or 1593, as the
imagining of a monstrous state uncannily like the Third Reich.
The link is not merely a matter of costumes and set design cleverly
imposed on an old text in order to confer upon it an air of moder-
nity; the interpretation works because *Richard III* is in fact a brilliant depiction of a radically illegitimate regime of terror, a regime
headed by a twisted, perverse, and utterly ruthless monster who
nonetheless exercises a weird charisma. Shakespeare's Richard
capitalizes on every bit of weakness, vulgarity, greed, and fear in
those around him. He is personally bold and resourceful, but he
cannot do what he wants to do alone; he depends upon the frightened, foolish, opportunistic, or soulless complicity of henchmen.
And, though his evil is apparent to everyone, though he is the killer
of children, he has, as he himself grasps and exploits, a perverted
charm, an almost pornographic and vividly theatrical allure conjoining eros and disgust. He is a kind of waking nightmare, and he
excites dreams of terror in others.

Richard's words and actions bear comparison to the nightmares
of the Third Reich at which we have briefly looked. They share
an extraordinary current of grotesque comedy. In *Richard III*, the
comedy lies in part in the startling frankness with which malice is
expressed. "Your eyes drop millstones when fools' eyes fall tears,"
Gloucester observes of his hired assassins; "I like you, lads"
(1.3.351–52). Or again, after hinting broadly that he wants Buck-
ingham to get rid of the two royal children in the Tower, Gloucester becomes exasperated: "Cousin, thou wast not wont to be so
dull. / Shall I be plain? I wish the bastards dead" (4.2.18–19). This
lurid murderousness is at the same time repeatedly conjoined by
Gloucester and his henchmen with the pretense of legality, a pretense that it is clear no one actually credits for an instant. "Who
is so gross / That cannot see this palpable device?" exclaims the
scrivener hired to copy the document that, like the Nazi decrees,
gives to arbitrary violence the form of legality, "Yet who so bold but
says he sees it not?" (3.6.10–12). The point is underscored in the

next scene, in which Gloucester, pretending to be engaged in pious meditation, is drawn with exquisitely hypocritical reluctance to accede to an entirely fraudulent public outcry for his coronation. We are never allowed to lose sight of what is actually happening—a twisted, utterly unscrupulous, homicidal politician is seizing royal power—but the spectacle of this seizure, like the earlier spectacle of Gloucester's seduction of Lady Anne, is compelling and perversely comic.

Still more important than the comedy is the uncanny transformation of fantasy into reality. In *Richard III*, as elsewhere in Shakespeare, dreams are not decorative touches or mere glimpses of individual psychology. They are essential to an understanding of power. One of the characteristic signs of power, and in particular of illegitimate power, is its ability to provoke nightmares, to generate weird images, to alter the shape of the imagination. Hence Gloucester is depicted from the very beginning of the play as trafficking in "drunken prophecies, libels and dreams" (1.1.33), and he figures centrally in the nightmares of his brother George, duke of Clarence, who has been imprisoned in the Tower. Clarence, who does not know that it is by means of Gloucester's secret contrivance that he has been arrested, awakens from a miserable night's sleep, a night, he tells the lieutenant of the Tower, Brackenbury,

> So full of fearful dreams, of ugly sights,
> That as I am a Christian faithful man,
> I would not spend another such a night
> Though 'twere to buy a world of happy days,
> So full of dismal terror was the time.
>
> (1.4.3–7)

Clarence's dream, as he recalls it, begins with the fantasy of escape:

> Methoughts that I had broken from the Tower,
> And was embarked to cross to Burgundy,
> And in my company my brother Gloucester,
> Who from my cabin tempted me to walk
> Upon the hatches.
>
> (1.4.9–13)

At this point the dream plunges abruptly, with the suddenness with which the walls fall down in the doctor's dream, into nightmare:

> As we paced along
> Upon the giddy footing of the hatches,
> Methought that Gloucester stumbled, and in falling
> Struck me—that sought to stay him—overboard
> Into the tumbling billows of the main.
> O Lord! Methought what pain it was to drown.
>
> (1.4.16–21)

The details that follow make clear one crucially significant difference between the dreams of terror in the Third Reich and the dreams that Shakespeare imagines: the former are Kafka-like nightmares of those for whom the historical process that is removing the protective walls around them or turning them into litter is fundamentally incomprehensible; the latter, by contrast, are the nightmares of the collaborators. It is not only those who were complicit with the tyrant who suffer, of course; Gloucester's rise to power, with its "ruthless butchery" (4.3.5), has many victims. But the innocent victims in this play do not seem to have hideous dreams. Such at least is the significance in part of the very odd glimpse that the murderers Dighton and Forrest provide of the two young princes in the Tower just before they are smothered:

> "O thus," quoth Dighton, "lay the gentle babes";
> "Thus, thus," quoth Forrest, "girdling one another
> Within their alabaster innocent arms.
> Their lips were four red roses on a stalk,
> And in their summer beauty kissed each other.
> A book of prayers on their pillow lay."
>
> (4.3.9–14)

Clarence, by contrast, is dismally aware of his own guilt, and his nightmare manifests a queasy soulsickness expressed symbolically as an inability to die quickly and represented in startlingly physical terms as an inability to vomit.[28] "Often did I strive / To yield the ghost," he says, shudderingly recalling the pain of drowning,

> but still the envious flood
> Stopped-in my soul and would not let it forth
> To find the empty, vast, and wand'ring air,
> But smothered it within my panting bulk,
> Who almost burst to belch it in the sea.
>
> (1.4.36–41)

The soul—imagined as a ghost penned up inside his body—longs "[t]o find the empty, vast, and wandering air" precisely because it feels the opposite: not emptiness, but horrible pressure; not vastness, but claustrophobic confinement; not wandering, but immobility and smothering. But when, in Clarence's dream, his soul does finally escape his body, the torment only intensifies, as he encounters the shades of those he has betrayed and murdered.

Those shades—first "my great father-in-law, renownèd Warwick" (1.4.49) and then Edward, Prince of Wales, a "shadow like an angel, with bright hair, / Dabbled in blood" (1.4.53–54)—are the denizens of a classical Hades, "the kingdom of perpetual night" (1.4.47), which Clarence has reached in his dream by passing "the melancholy flood, / With that sour ferryman which poets write of" (1.4.45–46). Upon seeing Clarence, "false, fleeting, perjured Clarence," the murdered Prince of Wales shrieks, "Seize on him, furies! Take him unto torment!"

> With that, methoughts a legion of foul fiends
> Environed me, and howlèd in mine ears
> Such hideous cries that with the very noise
> I trembling waked, and for a season after
> Could not believe but that I was in hell,
> Such terrible impression made my dream.
>
> (1.4.55–63)

How "real" is any of this supposed to be within the world of the play or the minds of the spectators? What is the status of the "shadows" of the dead Warwick and Edward? Clarence's vision is carefully and repeatedly marked as a dream, horribly vivid but distinctly unreal. And within the general unreality of the dream-state, the vision is further distanced by its use of classical figures like the sour ferryman Charon and the Furies, figures whom "poets write of." Yet the distance of these poetic fictions from reality is uncertain, the boundary marking off dream space from the play's actual lived world distinctly porous. Recognizing, as Clarence does, that it is only a dream does not completely free him from the "terrible impression" that it made upon him, an impression confirmed and seconded by his interlocutor Brackenbury:

> No marvel, lord, though it affrighted you;
> I am afraid, methinks, to hear you tell it.
>
> (1.4.64–65)

If there is a small measure of reassurance in Brackenbury's solidarity—the dream would frighten anyone and therefore it presumably need not be interpreted as a specific prognostication of the fate of the dreamer—the reassurance vanishes immediately with the entrance of the two murderers sent by Gloucester to dispatch his older brother.

There is an odd sense in which these figures are a continuation, a congealing into flesh, of Clarence's nightmare. When he tries to dissuade them from carrying out their orders and killing him, they resume, at a highly implausible level of detail, the enumeration of the charges against him begun by the ghosts:

SECOND MURDERER. Thou didst receive the sacrament to fight
    In quarrel of the house of Lancaster.
FIRST MURDERER. And, like a traitor to the name of God,
    Didst break that vow, and with thy treacherous blade
    Unripped'st the bowels of thy sov'reign's son.

> (1.4.191–95)

These words articulate the queasy guilt feelings that resonate within Clarence's complaint against the king at whose command he has been imprisoned:

> Ah, Brackenbury, I have done these things,
> That now give evidence against my soul,
> For Edward's sake; and see how he requites me.
>
> (1.4.66–68)

The murderers are not phantasmatic embodiments of Clarence's bad conscience, however, but rather figures from a nightmare into which he awakens—that is, figures from the play's representation of literal reality. "How cam'st thou hither?" Brackenbury asks one of them, who replies, with the dogged literalism that Shakespeare often associates with his clowns, "I came hither on my legs" (1.4.81–83). These are not now oneiric shadows but stubbornly material beings who have come to actualize Richard's violent design and the victim's premonitory vision: after stabbing Clarence, the assassin, to finish him off, drowns him in a malmsey butt, thereby fulfilling in the flesh the dream's horrible image. Clarence has now in reality been forced, as he had put it, to "yield the ghost" (1.4.37), and at the end of the play, as we will see, he actually appears as a ghost.

But what are we to make of this "fulfillment"? Later in *Richard III* Hastings mocks Stanley's dream—"He dreamt the boar had razed off his helm" (3.2.8)—only to find that it prefigures his end: "Off with his head" (3.4.76). "I, too fond, might have prevented this," laments Hastings when his death sentence is pronounced, "Stanley did dream the boar did raze our helms, / But I did scorn it and disdain to fly" (3.4.81–83). Neither the murderers in the Tower, acting on Gloucester's orders, nor Gloucester himself, condemning Hastings, knows the content of the ominous dreams, so there is no question of any deliberate matching of the imagined death. There is a secret, ironic appropriateness, a kind of grim wit, in the deaths of both Clarence and Hastings, but the wit does not seem to belong to any of the characters, not even to that master of grim wit Richard, duke of Gloucester. Some other principle is at work, but what?

The answer lies within the dreams, but it is difficult to pluck out the heart of their mystery. They have, as we have seen, something to do with the terror that Richard produces—but what exactly is their significance? It is easy enough to assimilate them to the experience of fear in people who were struggling to comprehend terrible events. But they interest us, in both theater and archive, as something more than the expressions of fear. In hindsight, they seem to possess a prophetic power, and as such they speak to an anxious apprehension of something beyond *raison d'état*, a longing to grasp what we might call the poetic or tragic structure of history. It is this secret structure that fascinated Shakespeare, and it is this structure that he associated not only with dreams but also and especially with ghosts.

"Why, then, I do but dream on sovereignty," Gloucester had reproached himself in his great soliloquy in *3 Henry VI* (*Richard Duke of York*),

> Like one that stands upon a promontory
> And spies a far-off shore where he would tread,
> Wishing his foot were equal with his eye,
> And chides the sea that sunders him from thence,
> Saying he'll lade it dry to have his way—
> So do I wish the crown being so far off.
>
> (3.2.135–40)

Dreaming here means idly indulging in wish-fulfillment fantasies, but its meaning is transformed in the course of the soliloquy, as Richard proceeds to contemplate his own misshapen body, itself the incarnation, as he and everyone in the play imagine it, of a particularly malevolent dream. "I'll make my heaven to dream upon the crown" (3.2.168), Richard proclaims, explaining to himself that he can realize his ambition through his theatrical gifts:

> Why, I can smile, and murder whiles I smile,
> And cry "Content!" to that which grieves my heart,
> And wet my cheeks with artificial tears,
> And frame my face to all occasions.
>
> (3.2.182–85)

Theatrical performance here—the art of the hypocrite—is the making of dreams into realities.

If dreams in Shakespeare are not inevitably fulfilled, they are like curses always eerily powerful and disturbing, disturbing precisely in the manner of Clarence's nightmare. Clarence does not fully understand, even in his dream, the historical reality in which he is trapped. He dreams not that his brother pushed him overboard but rather that his brother "stumbled, and in falling / Struck me—that sought to stay him—overboard / Into the tumbling billows of the main" (1.4.18–20). He knows that there is some relation between the things he has done and the fate that seems to be overtaking him, but all he conjures up are the cursing figures of vengeful ghosts. It is only in the terrible moments before he is murdered that he learns, from the murderers themselves, that his brother is in fact his mortal enemy: " 'Tis he that sends us to destroy you here" (1.4.231). And, even then, the awful reality is more than he can accept: "It cannot be, for he bewept my fortune" (1.4.232). But the truth of Clarence's dream does not depend upon historical accuracy; its truth is the experience of terror registered in the imagination. In the course of the play, this dream-experience is hardened, as it were, into public, waking reality, not only in Clarence's own fate but also in the fate of the entire kingdom. This hardening of dream into reality is, in effect, what Shakespeare calls history. And the dream is itself always a significant part of this history.[29]

There is no strict dividing line for Shakespeare between the private and the public, between the bedchamber and the throne room, between the imaginary and the actual. In Tudor law, it was treason "to compass or imagine" the death of the king. This peculiar commingling of fantasy and reality pervades *Richard III* and manifests itself in the force of dreams. Even when Gloucester is wooing, nightmares are close by, for terror is not restricted to the public sphere. "Your beauty," he lies to Lady Anne, "did haunt me in my sleep / To undertake the death of all the world / So I might live one hour in your sweet bosom" (1.2.122–24). When he proposes a place for himself in Anne's bedchamber, the lady replies, "Ill rest betide the chamber where thou liest."

GLOUCESTER. So will it, madam, till I lie with you.
LADY ANNE. I hope so.
GLOUCESTER. I know so.

(1.2.112–14)

After she is married, Anne recalls this exchange and acknowledges that she has

> proved the subject of mine own soul's curse,
> Which hitherto hath held mine eyes from rest—
> For never yet one hour in his bed
> Did I enjoy the golden dew of sleep,
> But with his timorous dreams was still awaked.

$$(4.1.80-84)$$

It is, as these lines suggest, not only those around Gloucester who experience bad dreams but also Gloucester himself. "We do not know the dreams of the enthusiasts, the victors," remarks Koselleck; "they dreamed as well, but hardly anyone knows how the content of their dreams related to the visions of those that were crushed by these temporary victors."[30] Shakespeare obviously pondered this question and thought about the kind of dreams that Gloucester would have. "No sleep close up that deadly eye of thine," Margaret curses him,

> Unless it be while some tormenting dream
> Affrights thee with a hell of ugly devils.

$$(1.3.223-24)$$

From Anne's account, we can conclude that here, too, Margaret's curse was fulfilled, and that the victor had dreams of terror remarkably similar to those of his victims. But the dreams turn out to center not on ugly devils but on ghosts.

The dreams in *Richard III* culminate in the last act. On the eve of the Battle of Bosworth Field, Gloucester, now crowned Richard III, and his adversary, Henry, earl of Richmond, are both depicted in their tents, making last-minute plans for the morning's bloody encounter. King Richard repeatedly calls for a bowl of wine: "I have not that alacrity of spirit," he tells his henchman Ratcliffe, "Nor cheer of mind, that I was wont to have" (5.5.26–27). Richmond, too, remarks that he has "troubled thoughts" (5.5.57), but when they drop off to sleep, the two opponents have radically contrasting visions. To Richard come the ghosts of those he has killed. "Let me sit heavy on thy soul tomorrow," each of them cries, bidding the tyrant to "despair and die." To Richmond they turn with blessings, prayers, and encouragement.

The ghosts here appear to Richard and Richmond in dreams, just as they earlier appeared to the sleeping Clarence. But now they have materialized into actors visible to both characters, and that materialization seems to confirm them as something more than psychic projections. To be sure, they have a psychological significance: Richmond, the future Henry VII, is buoyant, hopeful, and unafraid; Richard is suspicious, self-hating, and terrified. But Richmond has virtually no psychological depth, and Richard's psychology is continually absorbed into political theology. The confidence of the one and the terror of the other are significant here not principally as signs of character—for Richard is in fact repeatedly depicted as bold and courageous, so that his terror is not a sign of ordinary timorousness, while Richmond confesses anxiety just before he drops off to sleep—but rather of the objective historical process. Richmond awakens from his dream confident and refreshed; Richard awakens shaking with fear:

> By the Apostle Paul, shadows tonight
> Have struck more terror to the soul of Richard
> Than can the substance of ten thousand soldiers.
>
> (5.5.170–72)

Political terror, the terror Richard inspired in others, has passed, through the agency of those he has murdered, into his own soul, and this passage marks the imminent fall of the regime.

Richard's nightmare derives from Shakespeare's chronicle sources. In Edward Hall's *The Union of the Two Noble . . . Families of Lancaster and York* (1548), we are told that "the fame went" that on the eve of the Battle of Bosworth Field the king had "a dreadful and a terrible dream,"

> for it seemed to him being asleep that he saw diverse images like terrible devils which pulled and haled him, not suffering him to take any quiet or rest. The which strange vision not so suddenly strake his heart with a sudden fear, but it stuffed his head and troubled his mind with many dreadful and busy Imaginations. For incontinent after, his heart being almost damped, he prognosticated before the doubtful chance of the

battle to come, not using the alacrity and mirth of mind and of countenance as he was accustomed to before he came toward the battle. And lest that it might be suspected that he was abashed for fear of his enemies, and for that cause looked so piteously, he recited and declared to his familiar friends in the morning his wonderful vision and terrible dream.[31]

In Hall, as we see, Richard's nightmare was of devils, an idea Shakespeare echoed early in the play in Margaret's hope that some tormenting dream affright him "with a hell of ugly devils." In the play's climactic scene, however, Shakespeare turned the figures in the tyrant's dream into ghosts. So, too, did the anonymous author of a contemporary play on the same subject, *The True Tragedy of Richard III*. There, at the comparable moment before the battle, the tyrant reveals that he has been having horrible nightmares:

> The hell of life that hangs upon the Crown,
> The daily cares, the nightly dreams,
> The wretched crews, the treason of the foe,
> And horror of my bloody practise past,
> Strikes such a terror to my wounded conscience,
> That sleep I, wake I, or whatsoever I do,
> Methinks their ghosts comes gaping for revenge,
> Whom I have slain in reaching for a Crown.
> Clarence complains, and crieth for revenge.
> My Nephews bloods, Revenge, revenge, doth cry.
> The headless Peers comes pressing for revenge.
> And every one cries, let the tyrant die.[32]

These figures—accompanied by a "screeching Raven" that "sits croaking for revenge" and other conventional furnishings—serve to link *The True Tragedy* with the conventions of Senecan revenge tragedy. But the ghosts of the tyrant's victims in this play do not actually appear onstage; they do not need to, because they serve only as emblems of the villain's "wounded conscience." They function in exactly the way that the devils function in Hall's account of Richard's vision:

But I thinke this was no dream, but a punction and prick of his sinful conscience, for the conscience is so much more charged and aggravate as the offence is greater and more heinous in degree, which prick of conscience although it strike not always, yet at the last day of extreme life it is wont to shew and represent to us our faults and offences and the pains and punishments which hang over our heads for the committing of the same, to th'entent that at that instant we for our deserts being penitent and repentant may be compelled lamenting and bewailing our sins like forsakers of this world, jocund to depart out of this miserable life.[33]

Conscience in Hall's account is not simply a psychological element; it is an objective moral function, designed to produce (or at least to offer the opportunity for) repentance and hence to enable one to make a good end or alternatively to confirm one's own damnation.

Shakespeare uses many of the same materials but shapes them to a different end. To be sure, his Richard, like the Richard of Hall or of the *True Tragedy*, understands his dream as the voice of conscience:

> My conscience hath a thousand several tongues,
> And every tongue brings in a several tale,
> And every tale condemns me for a villain.
> Perjury, perjury, in the high'st degree!
> Murder, stern murder, in the dir'st degree!
> All several sins, all used in each degree,
> Throng to the bar, crying all, "Guilty, guilty!"
>
> (5.5.147–53)

But Shakespeare's Richard rallies and manages to harden his heart: "Let not our babbling dreams affright our souls," he tells his followers. "Conscience is but a word that cowards use," he informs them, "Devised at first to keep the strong in awe" (5.6.38–40).

The terms that Shakespeare's Richard employs here have a very specific resonance for the sixteenth century: they conjure up a popular image of Machiavelli. A few years before *Richard III*, Marlowe's *Jew of Malta* (ca. 1590) began with a prologue spoken by Machevil, who gleefully declares, "I count Religion but a childish Toy, / And hold there is no sin but Ignorance" (lines 14–15). In *Richard* Shakespeare obviously echoes and even exaggerates the demonic qualities Marlowe associated with Machiavelli, but he also echoes and intensifies the subversive power of the figure: the dismissal of conscience as a mere word, the challenge to the whole structure of conventional morality, the skepticism about theologically based claims to secular power, the Nietzschean questioning of the constraints implanted in individuals to make them obedient social and political subjects.

This subversive power is at once released in *Richard III*—allowed to strut about on the stage and in the imagined kingdom—and then defeated, in effect, by ghosts. We could say correctly, of course, that it is Richmond's army that defeats Richard, and we all remember the tyrant's famous last line: "A horse! A horse! My kingdom for a horse!" (5.7.13). Yet Shakespeare is careful not to leave the play simply as the triumph of the stronger army or the tragedy of a king without a horse; it is the ghostly visitation on the night before the battle that condemns Richard to destruction and confers legitimacy as well as victory on Richmond.

The power of the ghosts to bless as well as to curse, to reassure as well as to terrify, marks the central difference between the nightmares of the Third Reich and the nightmares in Shakespeare's tragedy: terror as Shakespeare imagines it at once falls short of the dimension realized by the Nazis and reaches beyond the psychological and political dimension it possesses for the modern world. *Richard III* seems almost innocent in its imagination of monstrous evil when compared with the actual accomplishments of our contemporary historical monsters. The ghosts that haunt the characters in *Richard III* are the play's principal emblems of the intertwining of psychological terror, Machiavellian politics, and metaphysics. They are precipitates of fear, emblems of alliances and enmities, and an element in the moral structure of the universe, a universe that is not, the play repeatedly insists, merely neutral, indifferent, or empty. By bringing the ghosts onstage and having them address the two sleeping adversaries, Shakespeare suggests that the dead do not simply rot and disappear, nor do they survive only in the dreams and fears of living individuals: they are an ineradicable, embodied, objective power. They function as the memory of the murdered, a memory registered not only in Richard's troubled psyche—"Is there a murderer here?" he asks in a panic upon awakening; "No. Yes, I am" (5.5.138)—but also in the collective consciousness of the kingdom and in the mind of God. And, in their mode of blessing—something inconceivable in the Senecan ghosts croaking for revenge—they function as well as the agents of a restored health and wholeness to the damaged community.

THE SPIRIT OF HISTORY

Six or seven years after Shakespeare wrote *Richard III*, he returned in *Julius Caesar* to the idea of an apparition who appears to the man who murdered him and bears the burden of history. This apparition too is not represented as a fantasy, and though it is associated with dream, it is not emptied of reality. On the contrary, the play is careful to set its appearance in the context of other spectacular signs of what Cassius calls "the strange impatience of the heavens" (1.3.61), signs that include ghosts that "shriek and squeal about the streets" (2.2.24). Interpreting these prodigies as instruments of "fear and warning / Unto some monstrous state," Cassius, drawing the superstitious Casca into his conspiracy, names the threat in terms that have the odd effect of identifying the living Caesar with a menacing apparition:

> Now could I, Casca,
> Name to thee a man most like this dreadful night,
> That thunders, lightens, opens graves, and roars
> As doth the lion in the Capitol;
> A man no mightier than thyself or me
> In personal action, yet prodigious grown,
> And fearful, as these strange eruptions are.
>
> (1.3.71–77)

Casca does not need to be particularly brilliant to grasp the meaning of Cassius's allegory: " 'Tis Caesar that you mean, is it not, Cassius?" (1.3.78).

Julius Caesar treats intimations of metaphysical horror with a ruthless irony already implicit in Cassius's words: Caesar, when we see him in person, is all too human. Yet at the same time the omens and portents turn out to be true, and after his death Caesar proves with a vengeance to be "prodigious grown." From this perspective, the tragedy would seem to stage the defeat of skepticism, the humbling of political rationality by the conjoined power of dreamers, soothsayers, augurers searching the entrails of animals, and shrieking ghosts. "You know that I held Epicurus strong, / And his opinion," Cassius tells his aide-de-camp on the eve of the battle of Philippi; "Now I change my mind" (5.1.76–77). Everything Epicurus stood for—radical materialism, the mortality of the soul, the absence of metaphysical rewards and punishments, the triumph of clear-eyed reason over the night-birds of superstitious fear—crumbles as Cassius recounts the ominous presages he has witnessed. And the defeat in Brutus is still more crushing. He had been strikingly indifferent to the signs that had terrified everyone else— "The exhalations whizzing in the air," he remarked coolly, "Give so much light that I may read by them" (2.1.44–45)—and now a comparable moment of reading turns into terror at the sight of Caesar's ghost:

> How ill this taper burns! Ha! Who comes here?
> I think it is the weakness of mine eyes
> That shapes this monstrous apparition.
> It comes upon me. Art thou any thing?
> Art thou some god, some angel, or some devil,
> That mak'st my blood cold and my hair to stare?
>
> (4.2.326–31)

The lines trace a seesaw of conflicting responses: a dimming of the candlelight by which he is reading (a dimming sometimes taken as the sign of a ghost's presence) leads Brutus to look up. Startled, he sees someone—it is a "who," not a "what," that he perceives—

and then immediately calls into question the legitimacy of his perception. But his attempt to attribute the shaping of the monstrous apparition to the weakness of his eyes is shaken by its approach: "It comes upon me." Once again he questions whether what he is seeing is real—"Art thou any thing?"—but the mode of direct address (as opposed, that is, to asking, "Is it any thing?") belies the very attempt to challenge its reality. He is in the presence of something, something that is producing the effects of terror in his body, but he does not know what it is. "Speak to me what thou art," he demands again, and he receives a strange answer, an answer that is quite distinct from the three options—god, angel, or devil—that he has advanced: "Thy evil spirit, Brutus" (4.2.332–33).

Presumably, in performance the actor will by his appearance make it clear that his identity is what the stage direction says it is: "the Ghost of Caesar." Yet the stage directions, in this as in other Shakespeare texts, cannot reliably be ascribed to Shakespeare's own authorship; it is striking, in any case, that the figure identifies himself not as Caesar's ghost but rather in terms that seem to claim that he is part of Brutus. The answer Brutus gets calls into question the relationship between the republican assassin and the man—perhaps his own father—whom he has killed; between the projections of the mind or the eyes and the weird supernatural forces that seem to exist objectively in the cosmos of the play; between inside and outside.

The exchange that follows does not explore these questions any further. Instead, adhering closely to the account Shakespeare read in Plutarch, it displays Brutus's stoical calm, once he has recovered from the initial shock of the encounter:

> BRUTUS. Why com'st thou?
> GHOST. To tell thee thou shalt see me at Philippi.
> BRUTUS. Well; then I shall see thee again?
> GHOST.   Ay, at Philippi.
> BRUTUS. Why, I will see thee at Philippi then.
>
>   (4.2.334–37)

With that, the ghost vanishes. In the wake of a disappearance that Brutus finds frustrating—"Ill spirit, I would hold more talk with thee" (4.2.339)—he rouses his three attendants and verifies that, though (as he affirms) they cried out in their sleep, they saw nothing. The cries, of which the attendants were not conscious, seem to confirm that the apparition was not merely a figment of Brutus's imagination but was actually in the tent. But the fact that they saw nothing—quite unlike the monstrous apparitions that were widely seen before the assassination—reinforces the odd sense not only that this haunting is for Brutus alone but also that it was somehow a part of him, his evil spirit.

When, near the end of the play, Brutus encounters the bodies of Cassius and Titinius, he names the ghost of Caesar as the cause of the suicides. It is as if the huge military enterprise of which he is the leader—"Ride, ride, Messala, ride, and give these bills / Unto the legions on the other side" (5.2.1–2)—is only a shadow play, behind which lurks the monster he had tried to destroy:

> O Julius Caesar, thou art mighty yet.
> Thy spirit walks abroad, and turns our swords
> In our own proper entrails.
>
> (5.3.93–95)

And when a few minutes later the battle has turned decisively against him, he confides to his officer Volumnius that the murdering spirit has come now for his own life:

> The ghost of Caesar hath appeared to me
> Two several times by night—at Sardis once,
> And this last night, here in Philippi fields.
> I know my hour is come.
>
> (5.5.17–20)

Running on his sword, Brutus conceives of his suicide as the laying of the ghost—"Caesar, now be still"—and his dying words return to the strange identification of assassin and victim that the specter had disclosed: "I killed not thee with half so good a will" (5.5.50–51).

What does this suicidal identification reveal? In part it is the confirmation of a half-hidden psychological element in Brutus, a quality of epic self-regard and a capacity to envision himself as the

savior of Rome that link him to the megalomaniac he has murdered. In part it is the climactic enactment of a death-drive in Brutus, a desire to reach a point of absolute, rocklike stillness, that
repeatedly surfaces throughout the play in his words and actions.
And in part it is the final expression of Brutus's fantasy of a clean
killing, a decisive, final, and pious act of civic liberation: "Let's be
sacrificers, but not butchers, Caius" (2.1.166). In the end Brutus
hopes that by turning the sacrificer into the sacrificial victim, he
will be able at last to make Caesar "be still."

But nothing in the play—let alone in the subsequent history of
Rome—suggests that the spirit that appeared to Brutus at Sardis
and at Philippi could be laid to rest by this suicide. The ghost of
Caesar bears a superficial resemblance to the vengeful ghosts who
turn up in Elizabethan revenge plays, but it is no accident that
he does not mouth the bloodthirsty curses that always mark these
Senecan hauntings. He is frightening and powerful not as the
agent of the conspirators' end but as the name for a political and
social upheaval that no one, least of all Brutus, can fully control or
even comprehend. In the interval between the time that he is
drawn into the conspiracy to kill Caesar and the actual killing,
Brutus feels a kind of soulsickness that he describes in a remarkable soliloquy:

> Since Cassius first did whet me against Caesar
> I have not slept.
> Between the acting of a dreadful thing
> And the first motion, all the interim is
> Like a phantasma or a hideous dream.
> The genius and the mortal instruments
> Are then in counsel, and the state of man,
> Like to a little kingdom, suffers then
> The nature of an insurrection.
>
>   (2.1.61–69)

The self-analysis is brilliant, but like virtually all of Brutus's subtle
reflections on himself and his world, it is fatally flawed. For it implies that the soulsickness will be healed once the dreadful thing
has been done, but what in fact happens is that the condition only

intensifies and spreads. Now the inner insurrection becomes a civil war, and the phantasm comes to haunt the entire realm. The apparition in *Julius Caesar*, surging up as if it were a figure in Brutus's hideous dream, tells us virtually nothing about the afterlife; it does not even seem to come from anything we might call an otherworld. Rather, it is the restless spirit of this world, and the only message that it bears is a history lesson: "[T]hou shalt see me at Philippi."

A DEEP PSYCHIC DISTURBANCE

The mistaking of a living person for a ghost, which we have seen in *The Comedy of Errors* and *Twelfth Night*, has a disenchanted, faintly comic air, even when Shakespeare deploys it in tragedy, as he does in *King Lear*. "Come not in here, nuncle," the Fool cries, running out from the hovel in which he has sought shelter from the terrible storm:

> Here's a spirit. Help me, help me! $(3.4.38-39)$[34]

Kent does what the decent characters instinctively do again and again in this cruelest of plays: he reaches out to the sufferer. "Give me thy hand," he says to the Fool, and then asks the question that also echoes on the battlements at Elsinore, "Who's there?" "A spirit, a spirit," repeats the Fool, "he says his name's poor Tom." But Kent does not at all fear he is encountering a ghost:

> What art thou that dost grumble there i' the straw?
> Come forth.
>
> $(3.4.40-43)$

The naked man who crawls out of the straw—Edgar, disguised as the Bedlam beggar—is all too human, a poor, bare, forked animal.

There is a second scene in *King Lear* in which a character—not a fool, in this instance, but a madman—mistakes a living person for a ghost. Even here there are distant echoes of the comedy of false surmise developed in *The Comedy of Errors* and in *Twelfth Night*, but Shakespeare takes the undercurrents of desperation, confusion, and loss that run through those farcical scenes and gives them an almost unbearable intensity and pathos. Having returned to

England to fight against her sisters' conjoined powers, Cordelia is reunited with her ruined, mad father and speaks to him for the first time when he awakens from a deep sleep after the terrible night of storm and madness. "You do me wrong to take me out o' th' grave," Lear says,

> Thou art a soul in bliss, but I am bound
> Upon a wheel of fire, that mine own tears
> Do scald like molten lead.

> (4.6.38–41)

The imagery of his suffering places Lear in Hell or Purgatory—as we have seen, their pains were indistinguishable—but these realms of misery are not for him located in the otherworld; they are here and now, his waking reality. Hence he can accuse Cordelia of wronging him by taking him out of the grave.

"Sir, do you know me?" Cordelia asks, to which Lear responds, as if he is encountering a ghost: "You are a spirit, I know. Where did you die?" The eerie power of these words lies in their conjoining of madness—"Still, still, far wide!" (4.6.43), Cordelia exclaims—and truth. The truth is not only that Cordelia *is* a spirit, if by this one means an autonomous living being (something that her overbearing, narcissistic father had found difficult to grasp), but also that she has already in some sense been destroyed and made into a ghost by Lear himself. Behind Lear's mad question—"Where did you die?"—lies the hideously rash moment in which he has undone his daughter: "Better thou / Hadst not been born than not t'have pleased me better" (1.1.231–32).

Yet if Cordelia is from that moment undone—symbolically turned into a ghost—it is only in the special sense in which human existence in *King Lear* has been turned into a purgatory in which demonic figures with names like Goneril, Regan, Edmond, and Cornwall are given leave to torment flawed souls. The play insists with fierce yet humane stringency that purgatorial suffering is the condition of life, not afterlife. Lear's belief that he and his daughter are dead is a sign of his madness, evidence that he is "still, still, far wide." The play is not set in the realm of the dead but in historical Britain; the torturers are not demons but sons and daughters, and the ultimate prospect is not salvation but nothingness: "I know when one is dead and when one lives," howls Lear, holding his dead daughter in his arms, "She's dead as earth" (5.3.234–35). Lear's mad fantasy that Cordelia is a revenant is belied at the play's close by his terrible recognition that there are no returns from the dead:

> Thou'lt come no more.
> Never, never, never, never, never.
>
> (5.3.282–83)

A moment later, when the old man loses consciousness, Edgar tries desperately to call him back to life: "My lord, my lord. . . . Look up, my lord." But the deeply loyal Kent finds this attempt to revive Lear grotesquely cruel:

> Vex not his ghost. O, let him pass. He hates him
> That would upon the rack of this tough world
> Stretch him out longer.
>
> (5.3.287–89)

"Vex not his ghost": the words at once pick up the strange sense that Lear's existence is purgatorial and underscore the bleak humanism that locates his terrible suffering in "this tough world."

IF LEAR's mistaking his daughter for a ghost—"You are a spirit, I know. Where did you die?"—is a false surmise, like the anxious misapprehension that makes Antipholus mistake his father for a ghost in *The Comedy of Errors* and Viola mistake her brother for a ghost in *Twelfth Night*, its symbolic truth-telling links it still more closely to a different Shakespearean perspective. While equally skeptical about the "actual" existence of ghosts, this alternative perspective is less interested in error than in imagination, fantasy, or what we might call the revelatory power of psychic disturbance. Take, as the greatest instance of this power, the ghost of Banquo in *Macbeth*. Whatever else it is, Macbeth's belief that the murdered thane is sitting in his chair is not a mistake, an incorrect hypothesis advanced to account for an unexpected encounter. In the Shakespearean ghost sightings we have thus far been examining, everyone sees the figure whom one panicky character or another incorrectly identifies as a ghost; in the banquet scene no one else sees the apparition. The vision of the bloody corpse is Macbeth's alone; all the others at the ghastly dinner party see only a vacant chair.

"The table's full," Macbeth observes, when Ross requests that he sit down. "Here is a place reserved, sir" (3.4.45), says Lennox, pointing to a chair that to Macbeth's eyes is occupied, though he evidently does not yet see by whom. To this point Macbeth perceives only a mildly comic bit of social awkwardness: the host goes to sit down at his own table and finds that there is no place for him. The moment marks what for the newly crowned Macbeth should be the resumption of the social role in which he has cast himself: "You know your own degrees; sit down" (3.4.1), he has declared, casually alluding, as his guests arrive, to the established, hierarchical order he himself has in secret murderously violated. "Ourself will mingle with society," he adds, somewhat uncomfortably using the royal *we*, "And play the humble host" (3.4.3–4). But his performance as humble host has been momentarily interrupted by the sudden, unexpected appearance of an uninvited guest. I am referring to the arrival not of the ghost, who shatters the whole occasion, but of one of the murderers, to whom Macbeth, uttering his fraudulently hearty banalities, turns in midline:

> Here I'll sit, i'th'midst.
> Be large in mirth. Anon we'll drink a measure
> The table round. [*To* FIRST MURDERER] There's blood
>   upon thy face.

$$(3.4.9–11)$$

The astonishing muttered aside is a vivid instance of a rhetorical effect produced again and again in *Macbeth*, an expression of psychic and social dissociation. Macbeth in particular is repeatedly depicted as "rapt," suddenly absent from the ongoing social discourse and caught up in secret thoughts or dark plans, while Lady Macbeth abets this dissociation by counseling fraud and concealment: "[L]ook like the innocent flower, / But be the serpent under't" (1.5.63–64). But the effect is also an expression of unbearable tension and pain: in these weirdly disjunctive lines of blank verse, it is as if a loose rope is suddenly yanked tight or a needle plunged into unsuspecting flesh. For an instant, Macbeth experiences not tension but pleasure: the blood on the man's face, he is happy to learn, is the murdered Banquo's. But when he hears that Banquo's son Fleance has escaped, pleasure gives way to feverish anxiety:

> Then comes my fit again; I had else been perfect,
> Whole as the marble, founded as the rock,
> As broad and general as the casing air,
> But now I am cabined, cribbed, confined, bound in
> To saucy doubts and fears.
>
> (3.4.20–24)

This sense of incompleteness and vulnerability is covered over by a resumption of the rituals of hospitality, to which Macbeth adds a hypocritical expression of concern for Banquo's absence. But the cover is a very thin one; we have been permitted a sickening glimpse of the seething, claustrophobic fear that lies beneath.

It is our awareness of this fear, our knowledge of what Macbeth is hiding within, that conditions the eruption that follows when Lennox points out the chair that has been "reserved" for the king. "Where?" Macbeth asks. "Here, my good lord" (3.4.46–47), Lennox replies, and now at last Macbeth sees clearly who or what it is that occupies his place. "Which of you have done this?" (3.4.48), he demands. For a moment Macbeth seems to be asking who has played some horrible practical joke upon him, as if one of the guests had managed to place in his chair a full-size, uncannily life-like effigy such as was made for the queasy time between the death of a king and the coronation of his successor.[35] But his next words, spoken to the horrible figure he alone sees, makes it clear that the word "this" in the question "Which of you have done this?" refers not to the weird apparition but to Banquo's murder.

Assuming wrongly that everyone can see what he sees—the corpse of a man who has been repeatedly stabbed and has had his throat cut—Macbeth at first instinctively tries to lay the blame on someone else, as he had earlier blamed Malcolm and Donalbain for the murder of Duncan. But the thing in the chair seems to be leveling a direct accusation at him:

> Thou canst not say I did it. Never shake
> Thy gory locks at me.
>
> (3.4.49–50)

Lady Macbeth, who was not informed of the plot to kill Banquo and Fleance (in order to keep her "innocent"), cannot know who it is whom Macbeth thinks he sees. Insofar as she grasps at all what is going on, she could only conclude that Macbeth believes that he is haunted by the ghost of Duncan. Therefore, urging the company to stay seated and not to take note of the "fit," she tries to sleek over (to use one of her terms) what her husband's words threaten to disclose by returning to the psychological strategy she had earlier used, when urging him to screw his courage to the sticking-place: "Are you a man?"[36] She then offers in effect a theory:

> This is the very painting of your fear;
> This is the air-drawn dagger which you said
> Led you to Duncan.
>
> (3.4.60–62)

By invoking the air-drawn dagger—about which Macbeth has told her—she is attempting to recall him to his own skeptical conclusion that there was "no such thing," that it was but

> A dagger of the mind, a false creation
> Proceeding from the heat-oppressèd brain.
>
> (2.1.38–39)

Distanced from the effects of his own imagination, Macbeth could go on to imagine himself, stealthily approaching Duncan's chamber, as a kind of allegorical figure, "withered murder" moving "towards his design . . . like a ghost" (2.1.52–56). To use the figure of the ghost as an image is precisely not to fear ghosts.

We have, then, two starkly conflicting possibilities: either the apparition is something real in the universe of the play—the spirit of the murdered Banquo come to haunt the man who has ordered his assassination—or it is the hallucinatory production of Macbeth's inward terror. Macbeth never calls what he sees a "ghost"; it is, in his words, a "thing" or a "sight."[37] When he attempts to drive it off, he uses something close to Lady Macbeth's language: "Hence, horrible shadow, / Unreal mock'ry, hence!" (3.4.105–6). But the act of addressing a shadow reveals the extent to which it seems to him anything but unreal. He expresses astonishment not that the others cannot see it—he never securely grasps that they do not—but rather that they are not terrified as he is, though he prides himself on his manly courage. As if in a desperate display of that courage, he repeatedly addresses the specter, challenging it to speak: "Behold, look, lo—how say you? / Why, what care I? If thou canst nod, speak, too!" (3.4.68–69). Lady Macbeth, by contrast, drives home the shameful spectacle of her husband's unmanning:

> O, these flaws and starts,
> Impostors to true fear, would well become
> A woman's story at a winter's fire
> Authorized by her grandam.
>
> (3.4.62–65)

Ghost stories are a peculiar kind of narrative entertainment passed down from one generation of women to another, designed to produce an effeminate miming of fear at an unreal threat: "When all's done," she says with barely concealed disgust and impatience, "You look but on a stool" (3.4.66–67).

Which is it? There are ample grounds for thinking that the specter might be real. Stories circulated throughout the Middle Ages and the Renaissance of ghosts visible to only a single person, and there were stories, too, of murdered spirits returning to haunt and destroy their murderers. "It will have blood, they say. Blood will have blood" (3.5.121). *Macbeth* in effect sanctions such stories by literally representing the penetration of the ordinary world by demonic spirits: the familiars and visions invoked by the witches, Hecate, the dark forces that turned Duncan's horses "wild in nature" (2.4.16) so that they ate each other. It is at least possible, then, within the terms of the tragedy, that a specter only Macbeth can see has come to haunt him. Yet the play cunningly goes out of its way to unsettle any attempt to determine what substantial claim to reality the intimations of the otherworld—the world of ghosts, air-drawn daggers, mysterious sounds, disruptions of the natural order, spirits, and goddesses—actually possess.[38]

Macbeth sees the spirit of "blood-baltered Banquo" (4.1.139) a second time, smiling at him triumphantly in the pageant of the eight kings that the witches conjure up out of the cauldron. But what are the witches and what connection do they have to Banquo's ghost? The witches, visible to both Macbeth and Banquo, are given many of the conventional attributes of both Continental and English witch lore: they are associated with tempests, and particularly with thunder and lightning; they are shown calling to their familiars and conjuring spirits; they recount killing livestock, raising winds, sailing in a sieve; their hideous broth links them to birth-strangled babes and blaspheming Jews; above all, they traffic in prognostication and prophecy. And yet though their malevolent energy apparently informs action—"I'll do, I'll do, and I'll do" (1.3.9)—it is in fact extremely difficult to specify what, if anything, they do or even what, if anything, they are.

"What are these," Banquo asks when he and Macbeth first encounter them,

> So withered, and so wild in their attire,
> That look not like th'inhabitants o'th'earth
> And yet are on't?
>
> (1.3.37–40)

Macbeth echoes the question, "Speak, if you can. What are you?" (1.3.45), to which he receives in reply his own name: "All hail, Macbeth!" (1.3.46). Startled by the titles with which they proceed to greet him, Macbeth falls silent, and Banquo resumes the interrogation:

> I'th' name of truth,
> Are ye fantastical or that indeed
> Which outwardly ye show?
>
> (1.3.50–52)

The question is slightly odd, since Banquo has already marveled at an outward show that would itself seem entirely fantastical: "You should be women, / And yet your beards forbid me to interpret / That you are so" (1.3.43–45). But "fantastical" here refers not to the witches' equivocal appearance but to a deeper doubt, a doubt not about their gender but about their existence. They had at first seemed to be the ultimate figures of the otherworld—Banquo initially remarked that they did not look like earthlings—but now their very "outwardness," their existence outside the mind and its fantasies, is called into question. Like the ghost, then, the witches in *Macbeth* are constructed on the boundaries between hallucination and spiritual reality and between fantasy and fact, the border or membrane where the imagination and the corporeal world, figure and actuality, psychic disturbance and objective truth meet. The means normally used to secure that border are speech and sight, but it is exactly these that are uncertain: the ghost, visible only to Macbeth, repeatedly enters and exits without speaking; the witches, as Macbeth exclaims, are "imperfect speakers" (1.3.68), and at the moment he insists that they account for themselves, they vanish.

The play that begins with the witches ends with Birnam Wood come to Dunsinane and with Macduff, a man not of woman born, hunting for Macbeth, in fear that the tyrant might be killed by someone else:

> If thou beest slain and with no stroke of mine,
> My wife and children's ghosts will haunt me still.
>
> (5.8.2–3)

Is this merely a figure of speech? And, if so, what kind of reality-claim do such figures make? Virtually everything in *Macbeth* transpires on the border between fantasy and reality, a sickening betwixt-and-between where a mental "image" has the uncanny power to produce bodily effects "against the use of nature," where Macbeth's "thought, whose murder yet is but fantastical" can so shake his being that "function / Is smothered in surmise, and nothing is / But what is not" (1.3.139–41), where one mind is present to the innermost fantasies of another, where manhood threatens to vanish and blood cannot be washed off and murdered men walk. If these effects could be securely attributed to a metaphysical agent, we would at least have the security of a defined and focused fear. Alternatively, if ghosts and witches could be definitively dismissed as fantasy, fraud, or metaphor, we would at least have the clear-eyed certainty of grappling with human causes in an altogether secular world. But instead Shakespeare achieves the remarkable effect of a nebulous infection, a bleeding of the spectral into the secular and the secular into the spectral.

Lady Macbeth is confident that if her husband grasps that the thing he sees in his chair is a painting of his fear, a projection of something inside him, then he will be the master of the situation. But—as she herself later finds in her sleepwalking—the things inside you are more wicked than demons and more terrifying than the old stories authorized by grandam. Macbeth has said from the beginning that he is willing to risk the punishments of the otherworld; it is the "poisoned chalice" (1.7.11) of this life that worries him. The ingredients of that chalice include the "terrible dreams" (3.2.20) that shake him nightly, dreams not of the afterlife but of the here and now, including the maddening thought that the worldly benefit of his crime will be reaped by the heirs of Banquo. "Better be with the dead," he tells his wife,

> Whom we to gain our peace have sent to peace,
> Than on the torture of the mind to lie
> In restless ecstasy.

> (3.2.21–24)

Like Lear's wheel of fire, Macbeth's imagery of torture transfers the horrors of souls in the otherworld to the experience he has condemned himself to live in this one. It is, the play repeatedly shows, no consolation to locate ghosts in the human imagination. If you are tormented by the threat of judgment, do not fear the life to come; fear this life. "We still have judgement here" (1.7.8). If you are anxious about losing your manhood, it is not enough to look to the bearded hags on the heath; look to your wife. "When you durst do it, then you were a man" (1.7.49). If you are worried about demonic temptation, fear your own dreams: "Merciful powers, / Restrain in me the cursèd thoughts that nature / Gives way to in repose" (2.1.7–9). If you are concerned about your future, scrutinize your best friends: "He was a gentleman on whom I built / An absolute trust" (1.4.13–14). And if you dread spiritual desolation, turn your eyes on the contents not of the hideous cauldron but of your skull: "O, full of scorpions is my mind, dear wife" (3.2.37).

SKEPTICISM AND WONDER

The ghost as the projection of fear, the ghost as the spirit of history, the ghost as the shadowy embodiment of deep psychic disturbance: these three modes of representation are the principal ways that Shakespeare brought the dead onto the stage. But what kind of theatrical response do they constitute to the great sixteenth-century change in the relations between the living and the dead? What would an audience, even remotely alert to the conflicting Protestant and Catholic positions, make of these figures? None of Shakespeare's ghosts (or even the illusions of ghosts) is a demon, disguised as the wandering soul of the departed; none is a purgatorial spirit, begging for suffrages from the living. They do not greatly resemble the ghosts depicted in ballads or in public inquiries into popular superstitions, nor do they conspicuously come from a classical Hades.

What are they, then? Perhaps part of the answer lies in a brief comment by Reginald Scot in his great *Discoverie of Witchcraft* (1584), a book that Shakespeare seems to have encountered.[39] "I for my part have read a number of their conjurations," Scot observes wryly of the witches whose power he denies, "but never could see any devils of theirs, except it were in a play."[40] Scot's programmatic, skeptical agenda seems very far from Shakespeare's contradictory, slippery, and complex deployment of spirits. Still, without aligning himself with principled disbelief, Shakespeare seems to have staged ghosts, as Scot's wry remark suggests, in a spirit of self-conscious theatricality. That is, his ghosts are figures who exist in and as theater, figures in whom it is possible to believe precisely because they appear and speak only onstage. The audience is invited to credit their existence in a peculiar spirit of theatrical dis-avowal: "I know very well that such things probably do not exist, and yet. . . ."

But Scot looks forward to the day in which the whole tangle of fraud, credulity, and vicious persecution will shrivel into quaint folklore: "[I]n time to come, a witch will be as much derided and contemned, and as plainly perceived, as the illusion and knavery of Robin Goodfellow."[41] Shakespeare does not want his audience to deride and contemn the illusion and knavery of Robin Good-fellow or witches or ghosts. He wants, rather, to persuade his audi-ence to credit them, but only in the special sense in which an audi-ence playfully credits what it sees in the theatrical space of fictions. In the late romances, Shakespeare often highlights the fictive ele-ment, as when *Cymbeline* brings together ghosts, fairies, and witches in a dirge sung over the body of a living young woman who has been mistaken for a dead young man. The rustic Guiderius and Arviragus find what they think is the lifeless body of the youth—Innogen in disguise—whom they have come to love. "If he be gone he'll make his grave a bed," Guiderius says sadly; "With female fairies will his tomb be haunted" (4.2.217–18). Then, turning to the corpse, he adds, as if Shakespeare were thinking back to the lines about the "wormy beds" from *A Midsummer Night's Dream*, "And worms will not come to thee." The words have the slight air of an apotropaic charm, a warding-off made explicit in the antiph-onal lines at the end of the celebrated dirge, "Fear no more the heat o'th'sun":

> No exorcisor harm thee,
> Nor no witchcraft charm thee.
> Ghost unlaid forbear thee.
> Nothing ill come near thee.
> Quiet consummation have,
> And renownèd be thy grave.

(4.2.277–82)

"Quiet consummation": the mourners acknowledge that the youth's corpse will be consumed, but their beautiful prayer is for an end like the slow fading of flowers, and they pray, too, that his soul be granted a comparably quiet vanishing. Their fear is not that the youth's ghost will return to haunt them; rather, their obsequies imagine a sweet sleep after death that could be threatened by unwanted company or malevolent interference.

The dirge in *Cymbeline* provides a quirky anthology of possible beliefs about the afterlife, beliefs involving female fairies, exorcists, witches, and unlaid ghosts. To these, as befits a play that self-consciously braids together ancient British folklore and classical antiquity, is added yet another possibility: the ancestor spirits that were honored in ancient Roman households. At the nadir of his fortunes, the hero, Posthumus Leonatus, goes to sleep and has a vision of his deceased family. To the sound of solemn music, the figures of his father, mother, and brothers enter, in the somewhat ambiguous words of the elaborate stage direction, "*as in an apparition.*" Circling round the sleeping Posthumus, they address themselves to Jupiter and complain bitterly that the thunder-master has not behaved justly toward the worthy young man. The king of the gods should have been kind to an orphan; instead, he has allowed a succession of misfortunes to befall him. "Peep through thy marble mansion. Help," implores the spirit of Posthumus's father,

> Or we poor ghosts will cry
> To th' shining synod of the rest
> Against thy deity.
>
> (5.5.181–84)

Ghosts, then, in this vision, are deceased family members who have no direct power to help the living, but who remain deeply involved in the honor and fortunes of the household. They cannot undo injuries, but they can lodge complaints against the all-powerful god who has permitted these injuries to occur. They make a loud noise to try to catch the attention of a divinity who seems to have locked himself away complacently in his marble mansion. And if Jupiter does not open his "crystal windows" (5.5.175) and look at what has been going on, the ghosts threaten to stir up trouble in the "shining synod" (5.5.183) of the other, lesser gods.

Evidently, this spectral threat is effective, for while he has been silent through the litany of complaints and anguished questions, the king of the gods now angrily rouses himself. The stage direction calls for an impressive show of divine force: "*Jupiter descends in thunder and lightning, sitting upon an eagle. He throws a thunderbolt. The ghosts fall on their knees.*" He may have had his windows shut, but he has clearly been nettled by the noise from the celestial streets:

> No more, you petty spirits of region low,
> Offend our hearing. Hush! How dare you ghosts
> Accuse the thunderer, whose bolt, you know,
> Sky-planted, batters all rebelling coasts?
>
> (5.5.187–90)

"Petty spirits of region low": in his complaint, Posthumus's father Sicilius had boasted of his ancestry, but Jupiter puts the family in its place.

This is, in effect, a political model of spectrality: the ancestor spirits have no control over events, but, if they are sufficiently well-born (as these are), they can cause enough disturbance in the outer regions of the court to catch the attention of the ruler. After making clear that he will not allow himself to be threatened (though the display of power suggests precisely that he has been), Jupiter then tries pacification:

> Poor shadows of Elysium, hence, and rest
> Upon your never-withering banks of flowers.
> Be not with mortal accidents oppresed;
> No care of yours it is; you know 'tis ours.
> Whom best I love, I cross, to make my gift,
> The more delayed, delighted. Be content.
>
> (5.5.191–96)

Jupiter wants the ghosts to stop their racket: "Rise, and fade" (5.5.200), he commands, giving them a written token of his favorable intentions in order to make them go away. Though they have registered his anger—"his celestial breath," they say, "Was sulphurous to smell" (5.5.208–9)—the ghosts are pleased with the assurance they have obtained: "Thanks, Jupiter" (5.5.213).

Cymbeline borders so often on self-parody that it is difficult to say how seriously Shakespeare intended any of this to be taken. His scene of spectral intervention is dressed in classical garb—set, as we have seen, against the rustic talk of fairies and witchcraft—but it also seems a displaced version of certain Catholic ghost beliefs: the special ongoing link between the living and the dead in their own families; the concern that the souls of the dead have for the fate of their descendants; the hope that these souls will intervene with God on behalf of those they love. Even the tablet or book given by Jupiter to the ghosts and then laid by them on the sleeping Posthumus's breast seems to recall the mysterious book that, in the *Tractatus Sancti Patricii,* persuaded the saint that he had not merely been dreaming about Purgatory.

But when he awakens to find the divine token—"What fairies haunt this ground? A book? O rare one!" (5.5.227)—Posthumus does not have a certainty comparable to Patrick's, for the text seems to him utterly opaque:

> 'Tis still a dream, or else such stuff as madmen
> Tongue, and brain not; either both, or nothing,
> Or senseless speaking, or a speaking such
> As sense cannot untie.

$$(5.5.238-41)$$

Perhaps this skepticism and bafflement, not unmixed with an odd current of half-belief, wryly represents Shakespeare's own attitude toward the whole, weird, tangled cultural inheritance, the mingling of folk beliefs, classical mythology, and Catholic doctrine. For all his doubts, his character decides to hold onto the odd, incomprehensible text, "[i]f but for sympathy" (5.5.243). And, of course, within the zany plot of the play, it turns out to be speaking the truth.

The deep link between ghosts and the power, pleasure, and justification of the theater is the thread that runs through the contradictory materials we have been examining: false surmises, panicky mistakes, psychological projections, fairies, familial spirits, vengeful ghosts, emblems of conscience, agents of redemption.[42] There is no straightforward chronological narrative here, no linear move from skepticism to classical "quotation," or from credulity to disenchantment, or from mystification to irony (or the reverse of any of these trajectories). Predictably, there is more scope for ghosts in tragedy than in comedy, but even this generic distinction is not straightforward. The mistake that makes us laugh in *The Comedy of Errors* carries a stab of pain in *King Lear,* while the ruthlessly disenchanted city of *Julius Caesar* and the Machiavellian court of *Richard III* have scope for "real" ghosts called into question in *Macbeth.* What there is again and again in Shakespeare, far more than in any of his contemporaries, is a sense that ghosts, real or imagined, are good theater—indeed, that they are good for thinking about theater's capacity to fashion realities, to call realities into question, to tell compelling stories, to puncture the illusions that these stories generate, and to salvage something on the other side of disillusionment.

In a play written near the end of Shakespeare's career, *The Winter's Tale,* Antigonus is commanded by Leontes to bear the infant daughter, whom he falsely believes to be a bastard, to a "remote and desert place" (2.3.176) and abandon her there. Bound by the strictest of oaths to carry out the cruel order and feeling himself accursed in doing so, Antigonus, having landed on the seacoast of Bohemia, relates a strange dream. The passage is long, but it needs to be quoted in full because its significance is bound up with the sense that we are hearing a story, specifically a ghost story:

> Come, poor babe.
> I have heard, but not believed, the spirits o'th'dead
> May walk again. If such thing be, thy mother
> Appeared to me last night, for ne'er was dream
> So like a waking. To me comes a creature,
> Sometimes her head on one side, some another.
> I never saw a vessel of like sorrow,
> So filled and so becoming. In pure white robes
> Like very sanctity she did approach
> My cabin where I lay, thrice bowed before me,
> And, gasping to begin some speech, her eyes
> Became two spouts. The fury spent, anon
> Did this break from her: "Good Antigonus,
> Since fate, against thy better disposition,

Hath made thy person for the thrower-out
Of my poor babe according to thine oath,
Places remote enough are in Bohemia.
There weep, and leave it crying; and, for the babe
Is counted lost for ever, Perdita
I prithee call't. For this ungentle business
Put on thee by my lord, thou ne'er shalt see
Thy wife Paulina more." And so with shrieks
She melted into air. Affrighted much,
I did in time collect myself and thought
This was so, and no slumber. Dreams are toys,
Yet for this once, yea superstitiously,
I will be squared by this. I do believe
Hermione hath suffered death, and that
Apollo would—this being indeed the issue
Of King Polixenes—it should here be laid,
Either for life or death, upon the earth
Of its right father. Blossom, speed thee well!

(3.3.14–45)

The speech is carefully constructed to frame the apparition as a fiction, very much like the winter's tale "of sprites and goblins" (2.1.28) that the precocious Mamillius tells his mother Hermione earlier in the play. Such scare stories—"There was a man dwelt by a churchyard," the little boy's begins—are suitable for the children of indulgent parents who will pretend to be afraid of ghosts, but the mature, sober Antigonus is properly skeptical of them: "I have heard, but not believed." Yet no sooner does he register his skepticism then he launches into a full-scale recounting of his dream, an experience of haunting so intense, vivid, and convincing that he thinks to himself, "This was so, and no slumber." This conviction—Antigonus's certainty that he actually has seen a specter in white robes, the ghost of Hermione—lasts for only an instant, before his mind recovers its adult skepticism: "Dreams are toys." Yet its influence is enough to lead him to follow the ghost's instructions, even as he nervously registers his awareness that he is acting superstitiously.

There is a game being played here—a toying with the boundary between dream and reality, credulity and skepticism—but what exactly is the game? Though Antigonus is a minor character, Shakespeare sketches enough of his psychological state to suggest a heightened susceptibility to illusion, something that the play explores more fully in Leontes' psychotic suspicion. The benevolent Antigonus has tried to save the innocent babe but instead finds himself bound by the most solemn oaths to abandon her to almost certain death. His deep unhappiness is intensified by the miserable setting: the deserted coast, the threat of wild animals, ominous skies that lead the mariner to grumble that "the heavens with that we have in hand are angry" (3.3.5). Everything in his situation, then, makes him susceptible to horrible dreams and more likely to regard them with superstitious awe. To the extent that *The Winter's Tale* is centrally about horrible consequences of taking fantasies as realities—the whole cause of Leontes' viciously false accusation against his wife[43]—then we are meant to distance ourselves from Antigonus's dream and to think of his ghost story as a psychological projection. There is no weeping, shrieking woman in pure white robes; there is only Antigonus's guilt. The need for such skepticism is confirmed when Antigonus reveals, after relating his dream, that he believes Leontes' charge of adultery—"this being indeed the issue / Of King Polixenes"—and thinks that the spectral vision was conveying Apollo's will that the bastard infant be returned to the earth of "its right father."

Yet though the audience is amply warned not to credit the ghost of Hermione, it is at the same time strongly induced to do so. In the scene directly preceding Antigonus's vision, Hermione collapses and is carried offstage, and a moment later Paulina returns with the news that "[t]he Queen, the Queen, / The sweet'st, dear'st creature's dead" (3.2.198–99). Antigonus, already at sea, has had no way of hearing of this death, so the ghostly apparition seems to have revelatory rather than merely psychological power. This power is immediately, apparently definitively reinforced when the specter's prophetic words, "thou ne'er shalt see / Thy wife Paulina more," are horrifyingly realized in Antigonus's gruesome end: "*Exit, pursued by a bear.*"

Which is it, then? Is the ghost real or unreal? In some sense the end of the play tilts back toward unreality: the statue breathes and moves; Hermione is alive. If the audience listens very closely, it will hear a minor character mention that "privately twice or thrice a day, ever since the death of Hermione" (5.2.95–96), Paulina has visited the secluded house where the statue was supposedly being created. The tiny detail is just enough to enable someone who wishes to believe that there was no ghost, and that Hermione has been sulking for sixteen years, to explain how she has been receiving food. But the explanation is little more than a joke at the expense of anyone who is worrying about the whole issue of the ghost story. This is, after all, a winter's tale: self-consciously fictive, flamboyantly theatrical. Where do we get ghost stories and lost children who are miraculously recovered and statues that magically come to life? In the theater. The theater is the place, as Shakespeare understood, where those things are permitted that the authorities have ruled illicit and have tried to banish from everyday reality. "If this be magic," as Leontes says, "let it be an art / Lawful as eating" (5.3.110–11).

What is being made lawful here, within the theater's specially demarcated space of make-believe? The magic of the statue that comes to life and, behind this, only half-hidden, the magic of the corpse that comes to life. And behind these stories lie certain other stories that had been labeled as magic. Hence there is an odd echo of the Catholic Mass in the awestruck description of the oracle of Apollo:

> I shall report,
> For most it caught me, the celestial habits—
> Methinks I so should term them—and the reverence
> Of the grave wearers. O, the sacrifice—
> How ceremonious, solemn and unearthly
> It was i'th'offering!
>
> (3.1.3–8)

And there is an odd, faint echo too, perhaps, of the old cult of the dead, less in the ghost that dooms Antigonus than in a peculiar exchange between Leontes and Paulina. In the wake of Hermione's death, Leontes has determined never to remarry, for the sight of a new wife, inevitably less perfect than the one he had unjustly injured, would, in his fantasy,

> make her sainted spirit
> Again possess her corpse, and on this stage,
> Where we offenders mourn, appear soul-vexed,
> And begin, "Why to me?"

(5.1.57–60)

Paulina agrees and enters into the fantasy:

> Were I the ghost that walked I'd bid you mark
> Her eye, and tell me for what dull part in't
> You chose her. Then I'd shriek that even your ears
> Should rift to hear me, and the words that followed
> Should be, "Remember mine."[44]

(5.1.63–67)

There is nothing notably Catholic or purgatorial about this vision, and yet it strangely recalls Thomas More's vision of the dead husbands looking in horror at the remarriage of their wives and shrieking to make themselves heard. And, as we have seen, what they want is to be remembered: "Let never any slothful oblivion raze us out of your remembrance"; "Remember what kin ye and we be together"; "Remember how nature and Christendom bindeth you to remember us" (227–28). "Adieu, adieu, Hamlet. Remember me" (1.5.91).

ꙮ 5 ꙮ

REMEMBER ME

"ADIEU, adieu, Hamlet. Remember me" (1.5.91). If Thomas Lodge's recollection in *Wit's Misery and the World's Madness* (1596) is to be credited, an earlier Elizabethan play about Hamlet—the so-called Ur-*Hamlet*—featured a pale ghost that cried "like an oyster-wife, 'Hamlet, revenge.' "[1] Presumably, this was the play alluded to in 1589 by Thomas Nashe, complaining about "trivial translators"—rank amateurs who "could scarcely latinize their neck-verse if they should have need"—who read "English Seneca" by candlelight and then come forth with "whole *Hamlets*, I should say Handfuls of tragical speeches."[2] Assuming that this earlier play was not by the young Shakespeare, then we must credit someone else with the single most important alteration to the old story: neither the history of Hamlet by Saxo Grammaticus in the late twelfth century nor its retelling by François de Belleforest in the sixteenth makes any mention of a ghost.

There would scarcely have been a reason to do so. Saxo's narrative is closely related to the great Norse sagas of violence, cunning, and revenge: Feng is envious of his older brother's good fortune and resolves to slay him. The fratricide is not a secret act; Feng justifies it by claiming that Horwendil was a brute who had been abusing his gentle wife Gerutha. Young Amleth is too young and weak to attempt the revenge that the social code manifestly demands. His task, then, is to survive until he is capable of killing his uncle, but his uncle knows the social code perfectly well and can be expected to snuff out Amleth's life at the first sign of menace. Amleth's solution is to feign madness: "Every day," Saxo writes, "he remained in his mother's house utterly listless and unclean, flinging himself on the ground and bespattering his person with foul and filthy dirt."[3] Though Feng is suspicious, the wily Amleth manages to elude the many traps set for him and eventually to accomplish his great task: he burns Feng's followers to death and runs Feng himself through with his sword. "O valiant Amleth," exclaims Saxo, "and worthy of immortal fame."[4]

The introduction of a ghost, changing the whole nature of the tale, strongly implies that in the Ur-*Hamlet*, the play performed in the 1580s, the murder was hidden, and that the son's obligation to act was not assumed by everyone but, rather, was proclaimed to him by the spirit of his dead father. Possible confirmation that these plot elements were already in place before Shakespeare wrote his play is provided by the strange German version of the tragedy, *Der Bestrafte Brudermord, oder: Prinz Hamlet aus Daennemark,* whose earliest surviving text, in a manuscript of 1710, seems to have been derived from one of the plays performed by the English players who toured in Germany in the latter decades of the sixteenth century. "I cannot rest until my unnatural murder be revenged," declares the highly Senecan Geist, as he departs, to which Prinz Hamlet replies, "I swear not to rest until I have revenged myself on this fratricide."[5] *Der Bestrafte Brudermord* has many elements that come from Shakespeare, but it also seems to contain traces of the earlier Hamlet play—and one of those elements may well be the ghost crying for revenge.

Shakespeare's Ghost, too, cries out for vengeance: "If thou didst ever thy dear father love," he tells his groaning son, "Revenge his foul and most unnatural murder" (1.5.23–25). But his parting injunction, the solemn command upon which young Hamlet dwells obsessively, is that he *remember.*

> Remember thee?
> Ay, thou poor ghost, while memory holds a seat
> In this distracted globe. Remember thee?
> Yea, from the table of my memory
> I'll wipe away all trivial fond records,
> All saws of books, all forms, all pressures past,

> That youth and observation copied there,
> And thy commandment all alone shall live
> Within the book and volume of my brain
> Unmixed with baser matter.
>
> (1.5.95–104)

Does the emphasis in the spectral command fall on "remember" or on "me"? Hamlet's response to the "poor ghost" teases out both terms, with his first repetition emphasizing the memory that holds a seat in his brain and the second insisting that all the contents of that memory, save one, will be wiped away. Contemplating Hamlet's wild and whirling words in the wake of the Ghost's departure, Coleridge remarked that "the terrible, by a law of the human mind, always touches on the verge of the ludicrous."[6] Perhaps the law extends to this anxious insistence on remembrance, since it seems faintly ludicrous to imagine that Hamlet would or could ever forget the Ghost. Or, rather, Hamlet's reiterated question precisely picks up on what seems to him the absurdity of the Ghost's injunction: "Remember thee?"

What is at stake in the shift of spectral obligation from vengeance to remembrance? In terms of plot, very little. When Hamlet first adjures the Ghost to speak—"Speak, I am bound to hear"— the Ghost's response, implicitly strengthening the force of the word "bound," is a call for action: "So art thou to revenge when thou shalt hear" (1.5.6–7).[7] Hamlet hears this call and urgently demands the information that will enable him immediately to heed it:

> Haste, haste me to know it, that with wings as swift
> As meditation or the thoughts of love
> May sweep to my revenge.
>
> (1.5.29–31)

Meditation and love figure the spectacular rapidity of thought, not only the virtually instantaneous leap of the mind from here to the moon but that leap *intensified* by the soul's passionate longing for God or for the beloved. It is as if the desire for haste is so intense that it erases the very person who does the desiring: the subject of the wish has literally vanished from the sentence. Yet the metaphors Hamlet uses have the strange effect of inadvertently introducing some subjective resistance into the desired immediacy, since meditation and love are experiences that are inward, extended, and prolonged, experiences at a far remove from the sudden, decisive, murderous action that he wishes to invoke. Later in the play Hamlet will famously complain that conscience—here consciousness itself—"does make cowards of us all," that the "native hue of resolution / Is sicklied o'er with the pale cast of thought," and that "enterprises of great pith and moment . . . lose the name of action" (3.1.85–90). This corrosive inwardness—the hallmark of the entire play and the principal cause of its astonishing, worldwide renown—is glimpsed even in his first frantic response to the Ghost, and it is reinforced by the Ghost's command, "Remember me." From this perspective, what is at stake in the shift of emphasis from vengeance to remembrance is nothing less than the whole play.

THE QUESTIONABLE SHAPE

The anxious sentries on guard duty as the play begins do not use the word "ghost" to describe what they have seen for two successive nights. Barnardo asks only, "Have you had quiet guard?" to which Francisco replies, "Not a mouse stirring" (1.1.7–8). Horatio is less reticent: "What," he asks, "has this thing appear'd again tonight?" (1.1.19).[8] "This thing": the words assume nothing, admit nothing. If the sentries have speculated about the nature of what they have seen, or think they have seen, Horatio is keeping a skeptical distance:

> Horatio says 'tis but our fantasy,
> And will not let belief take hold of him
> Touching this dreaded sight.
> Therefore I have entreated him along
> With us to watch the minutes of this night,
> That if again this apparition come
> He may approve our eyes and speak to it.
>
> (1.1.21–27)

Thing, fantasy, dreaded sight, apparition, and finally, simply "it" (32): none of the terms, not even "apparition," directly engages with the possibility of a supernatural visitation, though Marcellus's hope that Horatio may "approve our eyes and speak to it" comes close.

Horatio is evidently regarded as a valuable presence on the battlements because he is a "scholar," and, as such, he might be able to resolve the crucial question that hung, as we saw with *The Gast of Gy*, over all apparitions. How was it possible to distinguish the weird, exceptional, and deeply unsettling visitations of tormented souls pleading for help from the weird, exceptional, and deeply unsettling visitations of demons bent on spreading corruption, lies, blasphemy, and heresy? Demons were clever, and it had long been understood that they were capable of insinuating themselves into human communities by pretending that they were souls in pain. What is the reason, asks one of the early church fathers, Saint John Chrysostom, that demons love to dwell in tombs? "They would fain suggest to the multitude a pernicious opinion," his answer goes,

> as though the souls of the dead become Daemons, which God forbid we should ever admit into our conception. . . . "The possessed themselves," it is replied, "cry out, I am the soul of such a one." But this too is a kind of stage-play, and devilish deceit. For it is not the spirit of the dead that cries out, but the evil spirit that feigns these things in order to deceive the hearers.[9]

How is it possible, then, to protect oneself from deception, to unmask the stage play?

If an apparition appeared more than once, as the dreaded sight does in *Hamlet*, any alterations in its appearance might provide some guidance.[10] The second apparition was often marked by a costume change: the spirit, which at first appeared in the clothing of everyday life and with the age and features that the mortal body possessed at the time of death, might now be clad in white. It would declare in this way that it had been cleansed of its mortal stains, with the aid of the suffrages offered by the faithful, and was now bound for Heaven.[11] But there is no such reassuring change when the soldiers see the spirit return to the battlements, and Horatio attempts to determine its nature through a version of the questions asked in the *discretio spirituum*:

> If thou hast any sound or use of voice,
> Speak to me.
> If there be any good thing to be done
> That may to thee do ease and grace to me,
> Speak to me.
> If thou art privy to thy country's fate
> Which happily foreknowing may avoid,
> O speak!
> Or if thou hast uphoarded in thy life
> Extorted treasure in the womb of earth—
> For which, they say, you spirits oft walk in death—
> Speak of it, stay and speak.
>
> (1.1.109–120)

These are the traditional questions—*Quis? Quid? Quare? Cui? Qualiter? Unde?*—and each of Horatio's hypotheses, starting with the offer of suffrages, can be traced to the ghost lore with which we have been concerned.

But when the thing first appears before his eyes, "in the same figure like the King that's dead" (1.1.39), Horatio does not initially address it as a ghost, though he is forced to concede the astonishing likeness. "Looks it not like the King?" the sentinel Barnardo repeats, "Mark it, Horatio"; to which Horatio, marking it, replies, "Most like; it harrows me with fear and wonder" (1.1.41–42). The triple repetition of the word "like" hammers away at the unnerving resemblance of the thing they are all witnessing to the king whose body they have seen interred. In attempting to interrogate the apparition, Horatio immediately questions its right to this resemblance or, for that matter, its right to appear at all:

> What art thou that usurp'st this time of night,
> Together with that fair and warlike form

> In which the majesty of buried Denmark
> Did sometimes march?
>
> (1.1.44–47)[12]

Horatio urgently conjures an answer—"By heaven, I charge thee speak"—but the thing that bears the "figure" or "form" of the buried king is silent and stalks away.

As soon as it is gone, Barnardo returns to the skepticism that Horatio, now pale and trembling, had initially expressed: "Is not this something more than fantasy?" (1.1.52). The apparition then surges up against the background not of credulity but of disbelief. Having begun with a theory of psychological projection, Horatio now believes in its objective reality, a reality to which he bears witness, as if he were being deposed in court:

> Before my God, I might not this believe
> Without the sensible and true avouch
> Of mine own eyes.
>
> (1.1.54–56)

For the fourth time in some fifteen lines, the likeness to the dead Hamlet is reiterated, now by Marcellus: "Is it not like the King?" Horatio's words in response—"As thou art to thyself" (1.1.57–58)—are an emphatic confirmation, but a strange one. The strangeness—if one stops to reflect upon it—has to do with an erasure of the sense of difference that enables one to distinguish between likeness and identity: Marcellus is not "like" himself; he *is* himself. Since Horatio does not seem to be saying that the apparition *is* the old king—for by the sensible and true avouch of his own eyes he knows that the old king is dead and buried—his words "As thou art to thyself" have a different implication: they raise the possibility of a difference between oneself and oneself. The possibility will not be fully explored until much later in the play, where Ophelia is "[d]ivided from herself" (4.5.81) and Hamlet "from himself be ta'en away" (5.2.171). But the issue is already latent in the opening moments, when the sentinel calls out in the darkness, "[I]s Horatio there?" and Horatio replies, "A piece of him"

(1.1.16–17). *Hamlet* is a play of contagious, almost universal self-estrangement.

But the question of the apparition's uncanny likeness to the king is a special one, as the nervous repetitions of the same observation suggest. Marcellus *should* look like himself, but nothing should any longer look like "buried Denmark." For the trembling witnesses all know what they do not need to say: that the corpse of "the King that's dead" can no longer resemble the king that they all saw when he was alive. The king's actual body, were they to exhume it, would bear the signs and the smell of decay.[13] They are seeing something else, then, something perhaps that the Catholic Pierre Le Loyer, in a 1586 book on apparitions, calls a "phantasmal body":

> It is certain that Souls cannot return in their body, which lies in the grave, reanimating it and giving it the movement and life it has lost. And hence, if they return perchance to this world by the will of God and appear to us, they take not a real but a phantasmal body. And those who believe that they return in their true body deceive themselves greatly, for it is only a phantom of air that they clothe themselves in, to appear visibly to men.[14]

Horatio seems to be getting at this sense of the phantasmal (as distinct from merely fantastic) status of the apparition when he pleads with it to remain—"Stay, illusion" (1.1.108)—and he seems to confirm this status when, trying to strike at it with his partisan, he finds that it is "as the air invulnerable" (1.1.126). But what is the nature of this "illusion"?

"Illusion" marks a difference between what they are all witnessing and what they know to be reality—in this case, the decaying corpse. There is nothing imaginary about that corpse, even if they do not see it before their eyes: they know that it is the inevitable consequence of death. What they are seeing is not physical reality, however lifelike the resemblance: instead, as their responses suggest, the apparition on the battlements is a kind of embodied memory.[15] It has, Horatio immediately observes, usurped a particular form, the form in which the king "[d]id sometimes march"

(1.1.47). Indeed, Horatio can specify the recollection implied by "sometimes" more precisely:

> Such was the very armour he had on
> When he th'ambitious Norway combated.
> So frowned he once, when in an angry parley
> He smote the sledded Polacks on the ice.
>
> (1.1.59–62)

But what kind of memory could this possibly be? Memory depends upon a certain fading or dulling of the sense impression, but the apparition is too vivid. " 'Tis strange" (1.1.63).

This sense of strangeness is immediately reinforced, in a different, more psychological register, when, in his first soliloquy, Hamlet discloses himself as tortured by obsessive recollections. Horatio and the nightwatch are terrified by the repeated appearance of an uncanny figure that startlingly recalls the old king; Hamlet is driven to thoughts of suicide by comparably unbidden, repeated inward recollections. He cannot get his dead father out of his mind:

> So excellent a king, that was to this
> Hyperion to a satyr, so loving to my mother
> That he might not beteem the winds of heaven
> Visit her face too roughly! Heaven and earth,
> Must I remember?
>
> (1.2.139–43)

Evidently, the answer to this question is yes, since his mind immediately and involuntarily continues to grapple with the same tormenting images of parental intimacies:

> Why, she would hang on him
> As if increase of appetite had grown
> By what it fed on, and yet within a month—
> Let me not think on't.
>
> (1.2.143–46)

Just as the Ghost on the battlements returns not in the semblance of the poisoned man whose flesh has hideously crusted over but in the complete armor of the powerful warrior-king, so, too, the memories that force themselves into the prince's consciousness—scenes of his father's love for his mother and his mother's desire for his father—are at least on the surface agreeable. But they are all the more tormenting in that they remind Hamlet of the magnitude of his loss and the shock of his mother's hasty remarriage. And he cannot keep the images from pressing themselves vividly upon him, experiencing them as a strange form of compulsion: "Must I remember?"

COMPULSIVE REMEMBRANCE

Such compulsion was difficult for Renaissance theorists of memory to explain naturalistically, that is, without recourse to a notion of supernatural agency. Plato and Aristotle had set the principal terms for understanding memory, but those terms focused on storage and search functions, not on involuntary hauntings. Plato's most influential metaphor for memory was that of wax in which an impression is left. The metaphor expresses beautifully the way in which the mind can keep the image of something that is no longer present. It conveys, too, subtle variations, gradations, and effacements of impressions, some cut deeply, virtually permanently, into the medium of memory, some others only lightly, most slowly losing their original distinctness of outline and eventually fading altogether. There are variations as well, as the metaphor suggests, in the medium itself: in some people memory is like warm wax, barely holding any impression at all; in others it is hard and dry, difficult to imprint but, once imprinted, remarkably stable; in still others, it is a well-tempered medium between these extremes.

But the unwilled, ghostly return and renewal of an old impression cannot be easily accommodated to this scheme—how could the impression be renewed without a material body to reinscribe it in the wax?—nor does it fit comfortably with Plato's other great metaphor for memory, the aviary. To be sure, we can imagine ghosts flitting and swooping, like birds in a huge cage, but the metaphor, as it is developed in the *Theaetetus*, is not about uncanny returns from oblivion but about frustrating evasions. Plato evidently felt obliged to supplement his primary image of the wax in order to convey what that image conspicuously misses: the sense that memories often seem alive, fluttering, and elusive. The aviary metaphor keeps a notion of storage—there is a particular place, a container, for those things that are recalled—but it eschews any notion of systematicity, the sense (later developed by Saint Augustine and others) that memory is like a treasure-house or strongbox with distinct compartments where one can look for particular objects. In the aviary, one must grope after memories that seem anxiously determined to fly out of one's grasp.

For Aristotle it is the possibility of making a deliberate search—whether we think of it as lunging about in an aviary or reading wax tablets or sorting through the compartments in a strongbox—that distinguishes the memory of humans from those of all other animals capable of remembering. Any animal, Aristotle observes, that perceives time can have memories, but among those animals with memories, only humans have the power of recollection. This is because recollection is a "mode of inference," and inference involves deliberation, and deliberation implies reason, and reason is uniquely human. These incisive reflections enable Aristotle to explain, for example, why "things arranged in a fixed order, like the successive demonstrations in geometry, are easy to remember, while badly arranged subjects are remembered with difficulty" (718). But they seem to make his account of memory even less compatible than Plato's with any notion of haunting.

Yet Aristotle—who observes that the moving force of recollection is particularly powerful in "persons of melancholic temperament" (720)—comes closest to the central issue immediately raised by the ghost in *Hamlet*, an issue inseparable from the ghost as memory and memory as ghost: the perception of likeness. For Aristotle this perception is the way one knows, when one is contemplating a mental image or *phantasm* that it is in fact a memory—the remembrance of something that belongs irrevocably to the past—and not something that fully exists in the present. The mind is aware of a ratio between what is imagined and what actually once existed: a memory is grasped as a likeness, as he puts it, "relative to something else" (716). To be sure, this likeness also could in some sense be said to exist, but it is, Aristotle writes, like a painting—that is, both an object in itself and a likeness of something else.

When Horatio goes, in the company of Marcellus and Barnardo, to relate to Hamlet what they have seen on the battlements, he is startled by the prince's sudden declaration, "My father—methinks I see my father." What follows is a brilliant exchange, almost comic, about the boundary between memory and haunting.

> HORATIO. O where, my lord?
> HAMLET. In my mind's eye, Horatio.
> HORATIO. I saw him once. A was a goodly king.
> HAMLET. A was a man. Take him for all in all,
>   I shall not look upon his like again.
> HORATIO. My lord, I think I saw him yesternight.
> HAMLET. Saw? Who?
> HORATIO. My lord, the King your father.
> HAMLET. The King my father?
>
> (1.2.183–91)

What buckles under the pressure of the apparition is the notion of likeness (and hence of difference) that underwrites Hamlet's recollection of his father, or, rather, the ratio of likeness and difference threatens to collapse: "I knew your father," Horatio tells Hamlet, "These hands are not more like" (1.2.211–12).

At the end of *Richard III*, as we have seen, the bloody tyrant is terrified by the ghosts of those he had murdered—

> By the Apostle Paul, shadows tonight
> Have struck more terror to the soul of Richard
> Than can the substance of ten thousand soldiers—
>
> (5.5.170–72)

but the contrast between shadow and substance marks his stubborn hold on what he takes to be the reality principle. Richard clings tenaciously to a distinction between the images in his mind and the hard realities of the actual world, a distinction that enables him to rally his spirits in order to urge his men into battle: "Let not our babbling dreams affright our souls" (5.6.38). So, too, in *Julius Caesar* Brutus is horrified by the "monstrous apparition" in his tent, but a moment later he too recovers his poise: "Why, I will see thee at Philippi then." The contrast to *Hamlet*, where there is no rallying of spirits and no recovery of poise, is extreme; indeed, in the case of *Julius Caesar*, the contrast seems deliberate. Polonius memorably recalls that he once played Caesar and was killed in the Capitol, and Horatio invokes Caesar's assassination just after the first apparition of the ghost:

> A little ere the mightiest Julius fell,
> The graves stood tenantless, and the sheeted dead
> Did squeak and gibber in the Roman streets.
>
> (1.1.106.7–9 [Q2 only])

In 1769 Lady Mary Wortley Montague speculated that by these allusions Shakespeare intended "to captivate our attention by demonstrating that the poet was not going to exhibit such idle and frivolous gambols as ghosts are by the vulgar often represented to perform."[16] This may well be true, but Shakespeare seems also to be emphasizing the particular horror and intensity of the apparition in *Hamlet*, in contrast to his own depiction of Brutus's stoical response to Caesar's ghost. The soldiers Marcellus and Barnardo are "distilled / Almost to jelly with the act of fear" (1.2.204–5), and Hamlet vows to wipe away "[a]ll saws of books, all forms, all pressures past" from his mind.

Hamlet has made the Ghost's command his watchword:

> Now to my word:
> It is "Adieu, adieu, remember me".
> I have sworn't.
>
> (1.5.111–13)

The commandment, he proclaims, will live "all alone" in his brain; everything else will be erased. He has made it into an oath upon which he can swear and a watchword that he will daily reiterate. With no stabilizing hold on a distinction between shadow and substance, such as we saw in Richard III, and no stoical apathy, such as we saw in Brutus, Hamlet submits to an uncanny and yet actual link between himself and his dead father, a link manifested in terror, commandment, and the inescapable obligation to remember.

THE FADING OF REMEMBRANCE

But as the tragedy unfolds, Shakespeare weirdly and unexpectedly conjoins memory as haunting with its opposite, the fading of remembrance. If *Der Bestrafte Brudermord*, along with Saxo Grammaticus and Belleforest, are any indication, there was no precedent in the Hamlet story for the softening of the hard edge of memory into what Shakespeare's play (like More's *Supplication*) repeatedly characterizes as dullness. When Hamlet speaks of sweeping to his revenge, the Ghost commends him in terms that bespeak his own fear of oblivion:

> I find thee apt,
> And duller shouldst thou be than the fat weed
> That rots itself in ease on Lethe wharf
> Wouldst thou not stir in this.
>
> (1.5.31–34)

And it is with this forgetfulness that Hamlet comes to charge himself: "A dull and muddy-mettled rascal" (2.2.544). "How all occasions do inform against me," Hamlet berates himself in a soliloquy dropped from the Folio text, "And spur my dull revenge!" (Q2:4.4.9.22–23).

It is difficult to know exactly what to make of these self-accusations, since they do not correspond to what the play actually depicts. That is, we do not see Hamlet dicing, wenching, or otherwise behaving as if he has forgotten his father's death and resumed the agreeable amnesia of ordinary existence. He has, to be sure, assumed an "antic disposition"—a disposition far removed from the customary solemnity of mourning—but this consists of behavior such as mad speech and an indifference to dress entirely consistent with an *excess* of remembrance, precisely such an excess as we later see unsettle the mind of the grief-crazed Ophelia. If, in the case of Hamlet, this madness is at least in part a deliberate performance (though not perhaps as completely willed and controlled as Hamlet himself would like to believe), it is not because, in the absence of real feelings, he is merely miming the symptoms of extreme grief. On the contrary, the court of Denmark has from the beginning been preoccupied with Hamlet's ostentatious mourning—that is, with the complete absence in him of any sign of a natural dulling of remembrance.[17]

At the same time, Hamlet's strange behavior in the wake of his encounter with the Ghost—what Claudius calls his "transformation"—is not easily read by those around him as the unequivocal sign of deep, unappeasable loss. If, as the princely avenger does in Saxo and Belleforest, Hamlet pretends to be mad in order to deflect his uncle's suspicion, his ruse is a complete failure, as indeed it logically had to be, given the shift in the plot from an open to a secret murder. In the sources, where the murder is a public event, feigned madness is a plausible ruse, since it would lull the murderer into a false sense of security. But a protagonist who has discovered a hidden crime and wishes to take revenge would obviously be wise to conceal any sign of unusual disturbance, any indication that he is troubled by feelings other than the ordinary, conventional symptoms of grief. As soon as he learns of the murder, a truly cunning avenger, of the kind Saxo celebrates, would begin to feign psychic healing, not madness. Hamlet's antic disposition instead sufficiently arouses Claudius's wary interest to lead him to send hastily for Rosencrantz and Guildenstern. He wants to use Hamlet's friends, he explains, to discover

> What it should be,
> More than his father's death, that thus hath put him
> So much from th'understanding of himself.
>
> (2.2.7–9)

"More than his father's death": Claudius thus suspects that mourning is not the only or even the principal reason why Hamlet's behavior is so much altered, and in this suspicion he is joined by Gertrude, Polonius, and Ophelia.[18]

It is not Hamlet alone, then, who believes that there has been some dulling of his intense grief, some interruption or diminution of mourning and remembrance by other thoughts and emotions. Virtually everyone around him speculates on the possible source of this interference: disappointed love, frustrated ambition, his mother's overhasty remarriage. The revenge plot would seem to posit that the actual cause of this dulling is a shift from mourning to rage: that is, grief turns into the imperative to avenge his father.[19] Claudius seems to suspect as much, though he obviously cannot and does not fully articulate to Polonius what he thinks Hamlet's motive might be:

> There's something in his soul
> O'er which his melancholy sits on brood,
> And I do doubt the hatch and the disclose
> Will be some danger.
>
> (3.1.163–66)

But Claudius's suspicion is only partially accurate. If Hamlet were entirely bent on vengeance, he could hardly berate himself for dullness, since he would be fulfilling his father's command and his own pledge to sweep to his revenge.

What has intervened to deflect a direct course of action and to blunt the sharp edge of remembrance? Most obviously, despite attempts at something like the *discretio spirituum*, he is in the grip of continued doubts about the precise nature of the Ghost and hence about the trustworthiness of the Ghost's account of the murder in the garden. "The spirit that I have seen / May be the devil" (2.2.575–76). This suspicion—the fear that the devil is manipulating the weakness and melancholy that he recognizes in himself in order to damn his soul—leads Hamlet to seek some further verification, some independent evidence of his uncle's guilt. Only after "The Mousetrap" provokes Claudius's anger and alarm are Hamlet's doubts about the Ghost's reliability resolved: "I'll take the Ghost's word for a thousand pound" (3.2.263–64). When, a few minutes later, he does not avail himself of the opportunity to kill Claudius at prayer, it is not because he still questions the truth of the Ghost's revelation but because he does not wish to take his uncle "in the purging of his soul" (3.4.85). He wishes instead to kill him

When he is drunk asleep, or in his rage,
Or in th'incestuous pleasure of his bed,
At gaming, swearing, or about some act
That has no relish of salvation in it,

(3.3.89–92)

and so send him straight to Hell. Indeed, immediately afterward, in his mother's closet, Hamlet thinks he may have caught his uncle precisely in such an act—spying behind the arras—and does not hesitate to run him through: "Is it the King?" (3.4.25).

Though he turns out to have taken Polonius's life rather than Claudius's—the play would else be over—the killing allies Hamlet for a brief moment with the figure of Fortinbras, whose "unimprovèd mettle hot and full" (1.1.95) leads him to violent action, heedless of the consequences, in order to recover his father's lost lands.[20] If to remember a father who has been killed is to sweep thoughtlessly to revenge—as we later see Laertes also try to do— then Hamlet's eruption of murderous rage is a fine instance of filial memory. The rash and bloody sword thrust through the arras—"How now, a rat? Dead for a ducat, dead" (3.4.23)—would seem to signal his complete absorption in the urgent task of fulfilling his father's ghostly command. But the exchange that directly follows calls that absorption and the nature of remembrance into question.

Hamlet begins, to be sure, by dwelling lovingly on his father's picture. "See what a grace was seated on this brow," he tells his mother,

Hyperion's curls, the front of Jove himself,
An eye like Mars, to threaten or command,
A station like the herald Mercury
New lighted on a heaven-kissing hill;
A combination and a form indeed
Where every god did seem to set his seal
To give the world assurance of a man.
This *was* your husband.

(3.4.54–62)

Pious remembrance might very well take the form of such intense idealization. But there is something oddly unconvincing about this perfervid eulogy: the metamorphosis of a particular man into a painted combination of classical deities might alternatively be viewed as a characteristic way of forgetting. More telling, perhaps, Hamlet's meditation on his father's picture is only the rhetorical prelude to an elaborate, nauseated vision of his mother's sexual intimacies with her new husband:

> Nay, but to live
> In the rank sweat of an enseamèd bed,
> Stewed in corruption, honeying and making love
> Over the nasty sty.
>
> (3.4.81–84)

Even more than his doubts about the origin of the Ghost, this obsessive, fascinated loathing seems to stand between Hamlet and full remembrance, or so at least the Ghost's sudden appearance in the closet suggests.

That appearance interrupts Hamlet in the midst of an ungovernable rant against his uncle:

> HAMLET.   A murderer and a villain,
>   A slave that is not twenti'th part the tithe
>   Of your precedent lord, a vice of kings,
>   A cutpurse of the empire and the rule,
>   That from the shelf the precious diadem stole
>   And put it in his pocket—
> QUEEN GERTRUDE. No more.
> HAMLET. A king of shreds and patches—
> *Enter* GHOST
>
> (3.4.86–93)

According to a stage direction found only in the First Quarto, the Ghost appears now clad not in his complete armor—and not with the precious diadem and other symbols of his kingship—but in his nightgown. He is, in this staging, a figure not of the battlements nor of the throne room, but of the closet or the bedroom. The detail of the nightgown, adopted by most editors of the play, would correspond not only to the intimacy of the setting of this particular scene but also to the fantasies on which Hamlet's mind queasily dwells. Perhaps, too, for an audience that still recalled the old tales, the transformation from armor to nightgown would lightly echo those multiple hauntings in which spirits from Purgatory displayed their progressive purification by a gradual whitening of their robes. But, however much Hamlet is now persuaded that he has encountered an "honest ghost," he does not imagine that this visitation is benign, or that the Ghost has come to demonstrate spiritual progress or to request prayers.

Hamlet's response is a confused succession of terror, guilt, and pity, each passion cutting across what he has barely been able to articulate. At first, deeply alarmed, he prays for supernatural protection:

> Save me and hover o'er me with your wings,
> You heavenly guards!
>
> (3.4.94–95)

The prayer—in a reiterated first person that does not include Gertrude—seems to indicate that Hamlet instinctively senses that the apparition is for him alone and that he is personally menaced by it, as by a demonic spirit.[21] But then almost in the same breath, he goes on to address the Ghost as a "gracious figure" and to express a sense of guilt. "Do you not come your tardy son to chide?" What can this question, asked by one who has only a moment before killed the man he thought was his uncle, possibly mean? Why does he intuit that his father's spirit has come to chide him for tardiness, as one who "lapsed in time and passion, lets go by / Th'important acting of your dread command?" (3.4.98–99). "Lapsed in time and passion" is an ambiguous phrase, poised between the reproach of coolness and the reproach of excess. Perhaps Hamlet himself, wild with fear and guilt, trembling in the presence of his mother, his father's spirit, and the corpse of the man he has just murdered, does not know whether it is for too little passion or too much that he deserves reproach. He knows that he has failed to fulfill the

"dread command" that he has undertaken to place at the very center of his being—"Remember me"—and it is this command that
the Ghost's response recalls:

> Do not forget. This visitation
> Is but to whet thy almost blunted purpose.
>
> (3.4.100–101)

"Do not forget": the Ghost's return is a reminder, an injunction
to sharpen what has become dull. Polonius's bleeding body would
seem ample evidence that Hamlet's purpose was hardly blunted,
but perhaps remembrance and revenge are not as perfectly coinci-
dent as either the prince or the Ghost had thought. The Ghost's
apparition in the closet is strangely suffused with tenderness, pity,
and love as well as fear and guilt. "Look you how pale he glares,"
Hamlet says to his astonished, uncomprehending mother; "His
form and cause conjoined, preaching to stones, / Would make
them capable" (3.4.116–18). Capable of what? Not of hurting, for
stones are already capable of that, but of feeling, melting, weeping.
Such, at least, is the implication of Hamlet's plea that the Ghost
not look upon him,

> Lest with this piteous action you convert
> My stern effects.
>
> (3.4.119–20)

We are closer to tears at this moment than to blood, closer to *The
Gast of Gy* than to Seneca. To be sure, this ghost has appeared not
to his wife but to the son from whom he demands vengeance. Yet
what we see—what Hamlet sees not only here but also, in his imagination, again and again—is a gesture of spousal tenderness and
solicitude:

> But look, amazement on thy mother sits.
> O, step between her and her fighting soul.
> Conceit in weakest bodies strongest works.
> Speak to her, Hamlet.
>
> (3.4.102–5)

What is it that Hamlet is supposed to remember? What does it mean to keep his memory from becoming dull? How is he to fulfill the command, "Remember me"?

In *The Gast of Gy* the tangle of terror, guilt, grief, love, and, above all, remembrance—"Think on me"—is eventually resolved into a series of ritual actions: three hundred masses, one hundred dedicated to the Trinity or the Holy Spirit, one hundred to the Virgin, fifty to Saint Peter, and fifty requiem masses. In *Hamlet* the Senecan revenge plot seems to rise up from the twisted ruins of the purgatorial system, but in what sense can it actually occupy the same place? Sticking a sword into someone's body turns out to be a very tricky way of remembering the dead. The closet scene is the last time that Hamlet—or the audience—sees the spirit of his father. It has already in some sense started to vanish. In the first act, though it spoke only to Hamlet, the Ghost was seen by Horatio, Marcellus, and Barnardo; now Hamlet seems to his mother to be bending his "eye on vacancy" and talking to "th'incorporal air" (3.4.108–9). Despite Hamlet's urgent entreaties, Gertrude sees and hears nothing or, rather, more devastatingly, she sees and hears what exists:

HAMLET. Do you see nothing there?
QUEEN GERTRUDE. Nothing at all, yet all that is I see.
HAMLET. Nor did you nothing hear?
QUEEN GERTRUDE. No, nothing but ourselves.

(3.4.122–24)

There is something almost frantic about Hamlet's desire to have his mother see what he sees, as if he senses that his own memory traces are at stake:

Why, look you there. Look how it steals away.
My father, in his habit as he lived.
Look where he goes even now out at the portal.

(3.4.125–27)

The nineteenth-century editors who were uneasy about "steals away," proposing without any evidence that Shakespeare must have written "stalks," were in their way sensitively registering the inglorious fading of remembrance.[22]

The Ghost not only vanishes from view here, never to return, but he also almost vanishes from speech. Hamlet, to be sure, reproaches himself one further time—in a soliloquy dropped from the Folio version of the play—for "[b]estial oblivion, or some craven scruple / Of thinking too precisely on th'event" (4.4.9.30–31) that has kept him from acting. Fortinbras and his army march off to do battle "even for an eggshell," Hamlet bitterly observes;

> How stand I, then,
> That have a father killed, a mother stained,
> Excitements of my reason and my blood,
> And let all sleep.
>
> (4.4.9.46–49).

Somewhat later, there is a similar enumeration of his wrongs, with a small but telling difference: Claudius, Hamlet tells Horatio, "hath killed my king and whored my mother" (5.2.65). Not "my father" but "my king": here, as through the whole length of the play following the Ghost's final apparition, the remembrance of the dead has become depersonalized. In Hamlet's speeches, there are no more melancholy broodings on his father's nobility or manly virtue, no more loving descriptions of his appearance, no more tortured recollections of the love he bore for his mother. When for the last time the prince invokes his father as father, it is in a context that oddly conjoins memory—an impression stamped in wax— and bureaucracy: "I had," Hamlet tells Horatio, in explaining how he sent his old school friends to their deaths, "my father's signet in my purse" (5.2.50). And for the others the former king has simply become a point of reference, a marker of time. "How long hast thou been a grave-maker?" the prince asks one of the gravediggers; "Of all the days i'th'year," the man replies, "I came to't that day that our last King Hamlet o'ercame Fortinbras" (5.1.130–33). This is what it means to be well and truly buried.

Even at the play's close, where we might most expect it, there is no restrospect, no final glance back at the warrior king whose treacherous murder has set the destructive train of events in motion. In the confused, violent melee at the play's close, Hamlet does not even declare to the horrified bystanders the meaning of his actions. "The King, the King's to blame" (5.2.263), gasps the dying Laertes, but the blame of which he speaks is the poisoning of the drink that has killed Gertrude, and of the sword that will in a matter of moments kill both Hamlet and himself. Laertes will die without any knowledge of Claudius's crime against old Hamlet. When the dying prince stabs his "murd'rous" uncle with the poisoned sword and forces him to swallow the remaining potion, no one but Horatio could possibly think that the murder in question is that of the former king. The courtiers' shouts of "Treason, treason!" must refer to the killing of the elected king, Claudius, or perhaps to the poisoning of the queen and the prince; not, in any case, to what they must believe to have been the accidental death of his predecessor. When the prince finishes off Claudius, he himself thinks not of his father's spirit in the afterlife but of his mother's:

> Drink off this potion. Is thy union here?
> Follow my mother.
>
> (5.2.268–69)

At the moment that his command is finally fulfilled, old Hamlet has in effect been forgotten.

Remembering the dead, then, is vastly more complex, contradictory, and difficult than it had first seemed.[23] The tragedy ends without a last reckoning, a moment, however brief, in which the revenger—agent of what Francis Bacon calls "wild justice"[24]—discloses the nature of the crime that he has now punished. Hamlet begins to make such a disclosure—the audience is deliberately led to expect that he is about to do so and hence about to speak one last time about his father—but he is carried off, as if to a prison, without being able to deliver his speech:

> You that look pale and tremble at this chance,
> That are but mutes or audience to this act,
> Had I but time—as this fell sergeant Death

Is strict in his arrest—O, I could tell you—
But let it be.

                              (5.2.276–80)

"Let it be" and "the rest is silence" form between them the father's requiem, as well as the son's.

There are, however, two important qualifications to this climactic oblivion. First, Hamlet adjures Horatio, poised amidst the general carnage to commit suicide, to stay alive:

If thou didst ever hold me in thy heart,
Absent thee from felicity a while,
And in this harsh world draw thy breath in pain
To tell my story.

                              (5.2.288–91)

Through Horatio Hamlet's story will live on, and insofar as that story involves the remembrance of his father, so, too, the memory of the Ghost will survive in narrative. But Horatio, of course, never himself hears the Ghost speak, and even if we imagine that Hamlet has related what he was told, the friend's narrative cannot and will not be an intimate, personal act of remembering the beloved father. There is, however, a second way in which the Ghost may be said to be present at the end of the play, and that is inside of his son. When Hamlet first receives his father's dread command, he repeats it to himself, in his own voice, as if he wants to ventriloquize the Ghost's words by making them his "word":

Now to my word:
It is "Adieu, adieu, remember me".
I have sworn't.

                              (1.5.111–13)[25]

At the close Hamlet does not speak of his father, but he twice bids farewell to Horatio in a strange phrase: "I am dead" (5.2.275, 280). The phrase simply picks up on what Laertes has told him—"Hamlet, thou art slain" (5.2.256)—and elsewhere in his final speech Hamlet speaks of himself not as a person who is already dead but as one who is dying: "O, I die. . . . I cannot live. . . . He has my dying voice. . . . O, O, O, O!" (5.2.294–301). But, in the context of the play as a whole, the reiterated expression "I am dead" has an odd resonance: these are words that are most appropriately spoken by a ghost. It is as if the spirit of Hamlet's father has not disappeared; it has been incorporated by his son.

Dark Hints

"When the ghost has vanished," says Goethe's Wilhelm Meister, in what is probably the most influential of all readings of *Hamlet,* "what do we see standing before us? A young hero thirsting for revenge? A prince by birth, happy to be charged with unseating the usurper of his throne? Not at all!" The tragedy is more inward: "A fine, pure, noble and highly moral person, but devoid of that emotional strength that characterizes a hero, goes to pieces beneath a burden that it can neither support nor cast off."[26] Generations of critics have agreed, responding in effect to the startling Shakespearean shift from vengeance to remembrance. But what motivated this unprecedented shift? Where did it come from? How did it connect successfully with a popular London audience in 1601? And why, more specifically, is the injunction to remember spoken by a ghost? The overwhelming emphasis on the psychological dimension, crowned by psychoanalytical readings of the play in the twentieth century, has the odd effect of eliminating the Ghost as ghost, turning it into the prince's traumatic memory or, alternatively, into a conventional piece of dispensable stage machinery. ("When the ghost has vanished," Goethe's account tellingly begins.) But if we do not let the Ghost vanish altogether, we can perhaps begin to answer these questions, by recognizing that the psychological in Shakespeare's tragedy is constructed almost entirely out of the theological, and specifically out of the issue of remembrance that, as we have seen, lay at the heart of the crucial early-sixteenth-century debate about Purgatory.

More's souls are in a panic that they will be forgotten, erased by "slothful oblivion." They are heartsick that they will fade from the minds of the living, that their wives will remarry, that their children will mention them only, if at all, "so coldly and with so dull affection that it lies but in the lips, and comes not near the heart" (149). They are harrowed above all by the fear that their sufferings will cease even to be credited, that their prison house will be dismissed as a "fantastic fable," and that their very existence, in its horrible, prolonged pain, will be doubted. It is this fear that seems to shape Shakespeare's depiction of the Ghost and of Hamlet's response.

The Ghost makes clear to Hamlet that he is in what Thomas White's early-seventeenth-century text called "the middle state of souls,"[27] not damned for eternity but forced to suffer torments in a "prison-house" designed to purge him of the crimes he had committed in his life:

> I am thy father's spirit,
> Doomed for a certain term to walk the night,
> And for the day confined to fast in fires
> Till the foul crimes done in my days of nature
> Are burnt and purged away.
>
> (1.5.9–13)

"For a certain term"—the bland phrase, which looks at first as though it serves only to fill out the syllables of a line of blank verse, is in fact significant, since it helps to set up the theological claim of the word "purged."[28] In a mid-eleventh-century report on moans that had been heard to rise out of the crater of Stromboli, Jotsuald explained that the souls of sinners were being tortured there *ad tempus statutum,* for a certain term.[29] "In purgatory my soul hath been / a thousand years in woe and teen," the "Imperator Salvatus" says in the Chester mystery play *The Last Judgment* (ca. 1475);

> As hard pains, I dare well say,
> in purgatory are night and day
> as are in hell, save by one way—
> that one shall have an end.[30]

In church teachings, the excruciating pains of Purgatory and of Hell were, as we have seen, identical; the only difference was that the former were only for a certain term.

That one difference, of course, was crucial, but the Catholic Church laid a heavy emphasis upon the horrors of purgatorial torments, so that the faithful would be as anxious as possible to reduce the term they would have to endure. The intensity of the anguish is brilliantly represented in the greatest of English morality plays, *Everyman* (ca. 1495), where God sends his agent Death to demand of the hero "a sure reckoning / Without delay or any tarrying."[31] Everyman frantically begs for time, for his "book of reckoning" is not ready, but Death will grant him only the briefest of respites. Still, the interval is enough for the penitent to begin to scourge himself: "Take this, body, for the sin of the flesh!" (613). The grotesque spectacle of a dying man scourging himself makes sense only in the context of a desperate, last-minute attempt to alter the "reckoning" by substituting penitential pain in this life for the far more terrible pain that lies ahead. "Now of penance I will wade the water clear," declares Everyman, intensifying his blows, "To save me from purgatory, that sharp fire" (618–19).

Everyman has thus narrowly escaped one of the worst medieval nightmares, a sudden death.[32] This nightmare, of course, is the fate that befalls Hamlet's father: the horror is not only the fact of his murder, at the hands of his treacherous brother, but also the precise circumstances of that murder, in his sleep, comfortable and secure. Contemplating killing Claudius at prayer, Hamlet remembers that Claudius took his father "grossly, full of bread, / With all his crimes broad blown, as flush as May" (3.3.80–81). Hamlet continues with lines that are perfectly orthodox, from a theological point of view, but extremely strange in the wake of what he has witnessed and heard:

> And how his audit stands, who knows save heaven?
> But in our circumstance and course of thought
> 'Tis heavy with him.

> (3.4.82–84)

The phrase "circumstance and course of thought" is a hendiadys, or nearly so: it means something like circumstantial or indirect course of thought. But Hamlet has precisely had a more direct testimony, which he has professed, only a minute before, to credit absolutely: "I'll take the Ghost's word for a thousand pound" (3.2.263–64). That is, his father's ghost has told him quite explicitly how his audit stands, but once again Hamlet has "forgotten," as he earlier forgot that a traveler has in fact returned from the bourns of the death's undiscovered country.

Having just glanced indirectly at the question of where his father resides in the afterlife, and having avoided directly naming Purgatory, Hamlet goes on to ask himself, with regard to murdering his uncle, "[A]m I then revenged / To take him in the purging of his soul, / When he is fit and seasoned for his passage?" (3.4.84–86). The word "purging" is striking here, since it links prayer in this world (and the preparation or seasoning of a soul for the "passage" to the other world) to the purgation that may or may not follow. Similarly, a few minutes earlier, in response to Guildenstern's saying that the king is "distempered" (a word that recurs in Hamlet) with "choler," Hamlet jokes, "Your wisdom should show itself more richer to signify this to his doctor, for for me to put him to his purgation would perhaps plunge him into far more choler" (3.2.279–81). Here purgation has a meaning in humoral medicine, but the joke is a deep one, since for Hamlet to put the king to his purgation would mean to kill him, and that would, in Hamlet's account, plunge him into choler, that is, into the rage of infernal punishment and torture.

These strange, angry jests seem like a series of anxious, displaced reflections on the middle state in which the Ghost is condemned to suffer as a result of being taken "full of bread." Old Hamlet's condition is a grievous one—the term of his sufferings or their intensity vastly increased—because of the way he was dispatched, unprepared for death:

> Cut off even in the blossoms of my sin,
> Unhouseled, dis-appointed, unaneled,
> No reck'ning made, but sent to my account
> With all my imperfections on my head.
> O horrible, O horrible, most horrible!
>
> (1.5.76–80)

That he can speak of "imperfections" presumably means that his sins were not mortal; after all, he will eventually burn and purge away his crimes. But his inability to make a proper reckoning and his failure to receive the Catholic last rites weigh heavily against him.[33]

When he first encounters the apparition, Hamlet envisages only two possibilities for the Ghost's origin:

> Be thou a spirit of health or goblin damned,
> Bring with thee airs from heaven or blasts from hell,
> Be thy intents wicked or charitable,
> Thou com'st in such a questionable shape
> That I will speak to thee.
>
> $\qquad$ (1.4.21–25)

Nothing Hamlet says in the wake of his fateful exchange with his father's spirit explicitly acknowledges a third possibility, a middle state between Heaven and Hell, a place within the earth where souls are purged. But "there are more things in heaven and earth, Horatio," he tells his Wittenberg friend, as the Ghost moves restlessly beneath the stage, "Than are dreamt of in our philosophy" (1.5.169–69). And a moment later, hearing the Ghost's voice once again, he addresses it directly in words that would have been utterly familiar to a Catholic and deeply suspect to a Protestant: "Rest, rest, perturbèd spirit" (1.5.183).[34]

There is, moreover, something suspect (or at least strange), as scholars have long noted, about the precise terms of Hamlet's response to Horatio's remark, "There's no offense, my lord":

> Yes, by Saint Patrick, but there is, Horatio,
> And much offence, too. Touching this vision here,
> It is an honest ghost, that let me tell you.
>
> $\qquad$ (1.5.139–42)

The assertion that the Ghost is "honest" seems to mark Hamlet's acceptance of its claim that it has come from a place of purgation, and that acceptance may in turn be marked by the invocation— unique in Shakespeare's works—of Saint Patrick, the patron saint of Purgatory. By the eighteenth century Warburton thought the invocation of Patrick must have been made "at random,"[35] but a specific association with Purgatory would have probably seemed obvious to a late-sixteenth-century audience. "I come not from Trophonius care [*sic*], for then I should be loathed," declares a character in John Grange's *The Golden Aphroditis* (1577), "[n]or from S. Patrick's purgatory."[36] In the first chapter, we examined a number of these allusions, all of which make clear the strong association between Saint Patrick and Purgatory, along with the association, to which we will return, between Purgatory and fiction.

To the Saint Patrick allusion in *Hamlet*, whose association with Purgatory was remarked as early as the 1860s by the learned German philologist Benno Tschischwitz, we can add another, a few lines further on, that has not, to my knowledge, been noted. When Hamlet adjures his friends to take an oath that they will not reveal what they have seen, the Ghost, from under the stage, cries "Swear." When they shift ground to a new position, the Ghost once again cries out beneath them, and Hamlet asks, "*Hic et ubique?*" (1.5.158). The Latin tag here has never been adequately explained.[37] The words obviously refer to restless movement, a certain placelessness, comparable in *Othello* to Roderigo's description of Othello as "an extravagant and wheeling stranger / Of here and everywhere" (1.1.137–38). The use of Latin—besides suggesting that Hamlet is, like his friend Horatio, something of a scholar—may also convey a theological resonance, one evidently in Shakespeare's mind at the time that he wrote *Hamlet*. In *Twelfth Night*, a play of the same year, Sebastian, baffled by the appearance of his double, declares that there cannot be "that deity in my nature / Of here and everywhere" (5.1.220–21). The words refer in jest to the divine power to violate the laws of physics, a power that became an issue in the Reformation in a dispute over the Lutheran doctrine of Christ's Ubiquity. If this resonance is present in *Hamlet*, as it well may be, the prince's jest is deepened by a disquieting association of his father's ghost with the omnipresence of God.

But I believe that there is a further theological resonance to these words, specifically relevant to Purgatory. Traditional Catholic ritual in England included a prayer, at which we briefly glanced in the first chapter, to be recited for the dead who had been laid to rest in the churchyard. God's mercy and forgiveness of sin are begged on behalf of all of those souls here and everywhere (*hic et ubique*) who rest in Christ.[38] The point is not only that such pleas for the dead make use of the key phrase *hic et ubique* but also that they are specifically connected to a belief in Purgatory. In *The Catholic Doctrine of the Church of England* (1607), the Protestant Thomas Rogers, ridiculing this connection, quotes the papal indulgence from the Sarum *Horae Beatissimae Virginis Mariae:* "Pope John the Twelfth hath granted to all persons, which, going through the churchyard, do say the prayer following, so many years of pardons as there have been bodies buried since it was a churchyard."[39] The prayer begins "Avete, omnes animae fideles, quarum corpora hic et ubique requiescunt in pulvere" ("Hail all faithful souls, whose bodies here and everywhere do rest in the dust"). In the context of the Ghost's claim that he is being purged, and in the context, too, of Hamlet's invocation of Saint Patrick, the words *hic et ubique*, addressed to the spirit who seems to be moving beneath the earth, seem to be an acknowledgment of the place where his father's spirit is imprisoned.

There is a famous problem with all of these heavy hints that the Ghost is in or has come from Purgatory: by 1563, almost forty years before Shakespeare's *Hamlet* was written, the Church of England had explicitly rejected the Roman Catholic conception of Purgatory and the practices that had been developed around it. The twenty-second of the Thirty-Nine Articles declares that "[t]he Romish doctrine concerning Purgatory, Pardons, Worshipping, and Adoration, as well of Images as of Reliques, and also invocation of Saints, is a fond thing, vainly invented, and grounded upon no warranty of Scripture, but rather repugnant to the word of God."[40] This fact alone would not necessarily have invalidated allusions to Purgatory: there were many people who clung to the old beliefs, despite the official position, and Elizabethan audiences were in any case perfectly capable of imaginatively entering into alien belief systems.[41] Hence the spectators could watch the Lupercalia in *Julius Caesar* or Lear's solemn invocation of Hecate, and Shake-

speare's plays frequently (and not unsympathetically) represent
the monks and friars from the outlawed Catholic orders. But the
theater, like the press, was censored, and, though the censors were
often slipshod in some respects, they were acutely sensitive to con-
troversial political and doctrinal questions. It was, as we saw in the
last chapter, possible in the Elizabethan theater to represent the
afterlife in many different ways, and it was possible (indeed, perfectly orthodox) for Shakespeare to absorb some of the imagery
of Purgatory into the representation of ordinary life. But it would
have been highly risky to represent in a favorable light any specifically Roman Catholic doctrines or practices, just as it would have
been virtually impossible to praise the pope.

A playwright could ridicule Purgatory, as Marlowe does in *Doctor
Faustus*: when the invisible Faustus snatches food and drink away
from the pope, the baffled archbishop of Rheims speculates that
it may "be some ghost crept out of purgatory and now is come
unto your holiness for his pardon."[42] So, too, in a pamphlet written
about 1590, *Tarlton's News Out of Purgatory*, the anonymous author
pretends that he left the theater, in order to avoid the huge crowd,
walked in the nearby fields, and, falling asleep under a tree, was
astonished to be approached by the ghost of the popular Elizabethan clown, Richard Tarlton. "Ghost thou art none," he told Tarlton, "but a very devil, for the souls of them which are departed, if
the sacred principles of theology be true, never return into the
world again till the general resurrection." But Tarlton saucily replied that he resided not in Heaven or Hell but in "a third place
that all our great grandmothers have talked of." "What, sir," the
clown continued, "are we wiser then all our forefathers? and they
not only feared that place in life, but found it after their death: or
else was there much land and annual pensions given in vain to
morrow-mass priests for dirges, trentals, and such like decretals of
devotion."[43] As this and many similar moments in Tudor and Stuart
texts bear witness, belief in Purgatory could be represented as a sly
jest, a confidence trick, a mistake, or what Knevet, in a poem
quoted in chapter 2, calls "a fable or a story, / A place of fancy."
But it could not be represented as a frightening reality. *Hamlet*
comes closer to doing so than any other play of this period. But

Shakespeare, with his remarkable gift for knowing exactly how far he could go without getting into serious trouble, still only uses a network of allusions: "for a certain term," "burned and purged away," "Yes, by Saint Patrick," "*hic et ubique.*"

Moreover, even were these allusions less cautiously equivocal, there remains a second famous problem: souls in Purgatory were saved. The fact that old Hamlet died suddenly and hence without time for last rites—"unhouseled, dis-appointed, unaneled"—left him with a heavy burden of earthly sins that had painfully to be burned away after death, but he could not possibly commit new sins. The trouble is that Purgatory, along with theological language of communion (houseling), deathbed confession (appointment), and anointing (aneling), while compatible with a Christian (and, specifically, a Catholic) call for remembrance, is utterly incompatible with a Senecan call for vengeance.[44] Such a call for vengeance—and Hamlet understands that it is premeditated murder, not due process, that is demanded of him—could come only from the place in the afterlife where Seneca's ghosts reside: Hell.

Uncertainty and Interrogation

It would be quite possible for an audience not to notice this problem at all—after all, this is a play, not a theological tract, and there are many comparable contradictions that are simply ignored throughout Shakespeare and Elizabethan drama—were it not for the fact that Hamlet notices it and broods about it. Even before the Ghost has uttered a syllable, Hamlet anticipates the problem and articulates the key question that the *discretio spirituum* was meant to address.

> Angels and ministers of grace defend us!
> Be thou a spirit of health or goblin damned,
> Bring with thee airs from heaven or blasts from hell,
> Be thy intents wicked or charitable,
> Thou com'st in such a questionable shape
> That I will speak to thee.
>
> (1.4.20–25)

The initial injunction functions like the prophylactic prayers that precede Jean Gobi's encounter with the ghost, and the paired options that follow make clear that Hamlet goes into the encounter fully understanding the dangerous ambiguity that characterized all spectral returns. But there is an odd sense in which Hamlet leaps over the questions that were traditionally asked of "questionable" apparitions. This is precisely not the beginning of a clerical interrogation: in the almost unbearable intensity of the moment, he acknowledges the ambiguity only to brush it aside as irrelevant. "I'll call thee Hamlet," he declares impetuously, before the Ghost has named himself, "King, father, royal Dane" (1.4.25–26).

The desperate impatience that Hamlet expresses is to know why the Ghost has returned, not whence it has returned. Indeed, he addresses the apparition not as a spirit at all but as a "dead corpse" that has burst out from its tomb:

> Let me not burst in ignorance, but tell
> Why thy canonized bones, hearsèd in death,
> Have burst their cerements, why the sepulchre
> Wherein we saw thee quietly enurned
> Hath oped his ponderous and marble jaws
> To cast thee up again.
>
> (1.4.27–32)

This is not an image of Jonah miraculously cast up from the belly of the fish; rather, it is as if Hamlet pictures his father vomited forth, like something undigested, from one of those horrible mouths that artists painted to represent Hell or Purgatory. Hamlet had been deeply mourning his father, seeking him, as his mother said, in the dust. But this vision of his father out of the grave, weirdly intact and clad in armor, is hideous. Instead of "cerements" (that is, grave clothes), the First Quarto reading is "ceremonies." The alternative calls attention to something in any case insistently present in the lines: a sense of shattered ritual, a violation of what it means for a corpse to be "canonized," "hearsèd," quietly laid to rest in its sepulchre. The violation, Hamlet thinks, must have a meaning, and, horribly shaken "with thoughts beyond the reaches of our souls" (1.4.37), he is willing to risk his life to find out what the meaning is.

It is only when he has discovered this meaning, when he has received the Ghost's charge to revenge and to remember, that Hamlet returns to the question of the Ghost's status.

> The spirit that I have seen
> May be the devil, and the devil hath power
> T'assume a pleasing shape; yea, and perhaps,
> Out of my weakness and my melancholy—
> As he is very potent with such spirits—
> Abuses me to damn me.
>
> (2.2.575–80).[45]

The test he devises to establish the veracity of the Ghost's accusation—"The play's the thing / Wherein I'll catch the conscience of the King" (2.2.581–82)—seems to satisfy Hamlet, but it notoriously leaves the question of the Ghost's origin unanswered.

My intention here is not to rehearse a long series of debates by Eleanor Prosser, Christopher Devlin, Miriam Joseph, Peter Milward, Roy Battenhouse, and others whose intricate arguments, for me at least, are not completely evacuated by the fact that they are almost certainly doomed to inconclusiveness.[46] In the ingenious attempt to determine whether the apparition is "Catholic" or "Protestant," whether it is a spirit of health or a goblin damned, whether it comes from Purgatory or from Hell—as if these were questions that could be decisively answered if only we were somehow clever enough—the many players in the long-standing critical game have usefully called attention to the bewildering array of hints that the play generates.[47] Perhaps most striking is simply how much evidence on all sides there is in the play, and not only from those scenes in which the status of the Ghost is being directly discussed. Hence, for example, Ophelia tells her father that the distracted Hamlet appeared to her in her chamber

> with a look so piteous in purport
> As if he had been loosèd out of hell
> To speak of horrors. . . .
>
> (2.1.83–85)

Spirits loosed out of Hell do not normally have "piteous" looks; it is as if Ophelia had begun by thinking of purgatorial suffering and then shifted in midstream to a figure from a pagan or Christian Hell.

The issue is not, I think, simply random inconsistency. There is, rather, a pervasive pattern, a deliberate forcing together of radically incompatible accounts of almost everything that matters in *Hamlet*. Is Hamlet mad or only feigning madness? Does he delay in the pursuit of revenge or only berate himself for delaying? Is Gertrude innocent or was she complicit in the murder of her husband? Is the strange account of the old king's murder accurate or distorted? Does the Ghost come from Purgatory or from Hell?— for many generations now audiences and readers have risen to the challenge and found that each of the questions may be powerfully and convincingly answered on both sides. What is at stake is more than a multiplicity of answers. The opposing positions challenge each other, clashing and sending shock waves through the play. In terms of the particular issues with which this book has been concerned, a young man from Wittenberg, with a distinctly Protestant temperament, is haunted by a distinctly Catholic ghost.

We have already encountered comic versions of such a haunting in *Tarlton's News Out of Purgatory* and *The Puritan: or, the Widow of Watling Street*. But Shakespeare was virtually unique in understanding and giving dramatic expression to its tragic potential. What I have called Hamlet's Protestant temperament is something more than his suspicion that the Ghost may be a devil—a suspicion, after all, that a Catholic could have shared. His sensibility appears more suggestively in a strange exchange that occurs after Hamlet has murdered the eavesdropping Polonius. "Now, Hamlet, where's Polonius?" Claudius asks. "At supper." "At supper? Where?" "Not where he eats," Hamlet replies, "but where a is eaten" (4.3.17–20). The significance of these words extends beyond the cruel and callous joke about Polonius; the supper where the host does not eat but is eaten is the Supper of the Lord. Protestant polemicists had returned throughout the sixteenth century to the moment of eating God's Body; it was for them a way of mocking what they took to be the crude materialism of the Catholic doctrine of transubstantiation. Hence they dwelt with a violent gleefulness on the persistence and what we might call the embarrassments of matter.

If God was actually bread, they tirelessly jested, it meant that God could be eaten by worms, flies, or mice, that the divine body could decay and rot, or that, passing through the intestines, it could be transformed into excrement.

If a comparable theological resonance in Hamlet's weird jest seems implausible—for Polonius is a far cry from the body of God—the next lines make it sound again: "A certain convocation of politic worms are e'en at him. Your worm is your only emperor for diet" (4.3.20–22). Scholars duly note the allusion to the Diet of Worms, where Luther's doctrines were officially condemned by the Holy Roman Emperor, but the question is what work the allusion is doing. Two answers have been proposed—showing that Hamlet was a student at Wittenberg and marking the earliest date for the play's events—but its principal function, I think, is to echo and reinforce the theological and, specifically, the Eucharistic subtext, not only in the bitter jest that was just spoken but in the reverse riddle that follows: "A man may fish with the worm that hath eat of a king, and eat of the fish that hath fed of that worm." "What dost thou mean by this?" Claudius asks, and Hamlet replies, "Nothing but to show you how a king may go a progress through the guts of a beggar" (4.3.27–31).

Somewhere half-buried here is a death threat against the usurper-king—and Claudius understands perfectly well that the rapier thrust at the rat behind the arras had been aimed at him rather than Polonius—but the rage in Hamlet's words reaches beyond his immediate enemy to touch his father's body, rotting in the grave. And if these words are, as I am suggesting, a grotesquely materialist reimagining of the Eucharist, they would seem to touch his father's spirit as well and hence to protest against the ghostly transmission of patriarchal memory and against the whole sacrificial plot in which the son is fatally appointed to do his father's bidding. But how is it possible to reconcile this apparently skeptical, secular protest with Hamlet's obsessive quest to fulfill precisely the task that the Ghost has set him?

The answer is that a skeptical, secular insistence on irreducible corporeality paradoxically originates in an attempt to save the Eucharist from the taint of the body. It is only by ritually defiling the

Host, by imagining the sacrament passing through the belly of the beast, by dwelling on the corruptibility of matter and its humiliating susceptibility to the exigencies of the food chain that one can liberate the spirit. If Christ's Glorified Body, or, rather, Christian faith in that Body, is to be saved from material contamination, it must be pried loose from the visible church, separated off from the grossly physical bread and wine, reserved entirely for the realm of the spirit. Mockery of the material leftover, the matter subject to consumption and rot, is a way of insisting that Christ—single, whole, and beyond corruption—dwells in Heaven at the right hand of his Father. This is the logic of Protestant polemics against the Mass, and this, too, is the logic that seems to drive Hamlet.[48]

Even before he learned of his mother's adultery and his father's murder, Hamlet had been sickened by the "too too solid" (or "sallied" or "sullied") flesh, flesh whose terrible weakness is strikingly figured by the recycling of leftovers: "Thrift, thrift, Horatio. The funeral baked meats / Did coldly furnish forth the marriage tables" (1.2.179–80). In Hamlet's bitter jest, food prepared for his father's funeral has been used for his mother's marriage, a confounding of categories that has stained both social rituals in the service of thrift. At issue is not only, as G. R. Hibbard suggests, an aristocratic disdain for a bourgeois prudential virtue,[49] but a conception of the sacred as incompatible with a restricted economy, an economy of calculation and equivalence. Such calculation has led Gertrude to marry Claudius, as if he were his brother's equal: "My father's brother," Hamlet protests, "but no more like my father / Than I to Hercules" (1.2.152–53). Her remarriage, like the re-use of the funeral baked meats, is a double defilement: it has sullied Gertrude's flesh and, since "[f]ather and mother is man and wife; man and wife is one flesh" (4.3.53–54), it has retroactively stained old Hamlet by identifying his noble spirit with the grossness of the "bloat King" (3.4.166). The source of the pollution, according to the Ghost, is unbridled sexual appetite:

> lust, though to a radiant angel linked,
> Will sate itself in a celestial bed,
> And prey on garbage.
>
> (1.5.55–57)

The disgust provoked by the leftovers is here intensified by the image of the person who, though sated, continues to eat and to eat garbage—not simply filth or refuse, but, literally, "entrails."

The time is out of joint, and the spirit of the father has charged his son with setting it right. But the task becomes mired in the flesh that will not melt away, that cannot free itself from longings for mother and lover, that stubbornly persists and resists and blocks the realization of the father's wishes. And the task is further complicated by the father's own entanglements in the flesh. When alive, old Hamlet was not exempt from the thousand natural shocks that flesh is heir to, and even after death he carries about him a strange quasi-carnality, for he was taken "grossly, full of bread, / With all his crimes broad blown, as flush as May" (3.3.80–81). "Full of bread"—the words distinguish between someone living in the midst of his ordinary life and someone who, anticipating death, puts his spiritual house in order through fasting.

Hamlet is disgusted by the grossness whose emblem here is the bread in his father's stomach, a grossness figured as well by drinking, sleeping, sexual intercourse, and above all perhaps by woman's flesh. The play enacts and reenacts queasy rituals of defilement and revulsion, an obsession with a corporeality that reduces everything to appetite and excretion. "We fat all creatures else to fat us, and we fat ourselves for maggots. Your fat king and your lean beggar is but variable service—two dishes, but to one table. That's the end" (4.3.22–25). Here, as in the lines about the king's progress through the guts of a beggar, the revulsion is mingled with a sense of drastic leveling, the collapse of order and distinction into polymorphous, endlessly recycled materiality. Claudius, with his reechy kisses and paddling fingers, is a paddock, a bat, a gib, and this unclean beast, like the priapic priest of Protestant polemics, has poisoned the entire social and symbolic system. Hamlet's response is not to attempt to shore it up but to drag it altogether into the writhing of maggots. Matter corrupts: "if you find him not this month," Hamlet says, finally telling Claudius where to look for Polonius's corpse, "you shall nose him as you go up the stairs into the lobby" (4.3.35–36).

The spirit can be healed only by refusing all compromise and by plunging the imagination unflinchingly into the rank corruption of the ulcerous place. Such a conviction led the Reformers to dwell on the progress of the Host through the guts of a mouse, and a comparable conviction, born of intertwining theological and psychological obsessions, leads Hamlet to the clay pit and the decayed leftovers that the gravediggers bring to light. "How abhorred my imagination is," Hamlet says, staring at the skull of Yorick; "My gorge rises at it" (5.1.173–74). This is the primary and elemental nausea provoked by the vulnerability of matter, a nausea that reduces language to a gagging sound that the Folio registers as "Pah." This revulsion is not an end in itself; it is the spiritual precondition of a liberated spirit that finds a special providence in the fall of a sparrow, sacrificially fulfills the father's design, and declares that the readiness is all.

BOUNDARY DISPUTES

But the problem is that the father's design is vengeance; vengeance, moreover, demanded by a spirit that seems to come from the place that was for Protestants a supreme emblem of the corruption of the Catholic Church. What can be made of this? The point surely is not to settle issues that Shakespeare has clearly gone out of his way to unsettle or render ambiguous. I am concerned, rather, with the particular uses that the playwright made of the struggle between Simon Fish and Thomas More and its aftermath. Those uses are not necessarily direct. Two chantry acts—1545 (Henry VIII's last Parliament) and 1547 (Edward VI's first Parliament)— resolved that struggle by abolishing the whole elaborate Catholic intercessory system, with its chantries, lights, obits, anniversaries, confraternities, stipendiary priests, and the like, with which English men and women had done suffrages for the sake of the dead in Purgatory and in anticipation of their own future condition as dead people.[50] The brief reign of the Catholic Mary Tudor evidently did little to revive this system, and it is extremely difficult to gauge the extent of residual belief in Purgatory among the great mass of English men and women at the century's end.[51]

In the funeral service in the first Edwardian prayer book (1549), the dead person was still directly addressed: the priest is instructed to cast earth upon the corpse and to say, "I commend thy soul to God the father almighty, and thy body to the ground, earth to earth, ashes to ashes, dust to dust." In the 1552 revision, which was later confirmed by Queen Elizabeth and used throughout Shakespeare's lifetime, the words have changed decisively. The dead person can no longer be addressed. Instead, the priest says to the bystanders around the grave, "We therefore commit his body to the ground, earth to earth, ashes to ashes, dust to dust."[52] These are the words that anyone in late-sixteenth- and seventeenth-century England would have heard. Yet the continued outpouring of polemical literature, reviving the old arguments of Fish and More and rehearsing them again and again throughout the reigns of Elizabeth and James, suggests that the boundary between the living and the dead was not so decisively closed.

The security of the boundary was inevitably called into question by the appearance of ghosts. The apparition in *Hamlet* immediately triggers at least some elements of the traditional rituals in response to hauntings that we have discussed. Hence, for example, the soldiers Marcellus and Barnardo have recourse to an expert: "Thou art a scholar—speak to it, Horatio. . . . Question it, Horatio" (1.1.40, 43). Horatio, like the prior confronting the ghost of Gy, duly initiates a series of questions that follow the logic of the *discretio spirituum*:

> What art thou that usurp'st this time of night,
> Together with that fair and warlike form
> In which the majesty of buried Denmark
> Did sometimes march? By heaven, I charge thee speak.
>
> (1.1.44–47)[53]

And Hamlet similarly echoes the formal cross-examination's litany of *Cur? Causas? Remedium?*: "Say, why is this? Wherefore? What should we do?" (1.4.38).

These rituals were, as Schmitt and others have argued, part of a sustained attempt to tame death, to contain it in the ceremonies of the church and the churchyard. We might note the prominent place in *Hamlet* given to the ritualization of the funeral service, both in the reference to the sepulchre in which the corpse of old

Hamlet was "enurned" and still more in Ophelia's burial service, marked by Laertes' reiterated question, "What ceremony else?" But the priest's response makes clear that, in his view, the holy space of the cemetery would be violated by the full rites that Laertes demands, and is in danger of pollution even from the maimed rites that he and his fellow priests are being forced to perform:

> Her obsequies have been as far enlarged
> As we have warrantise. Her death was doubtful,
> And but that great command o'ersways the order
> She should in ground unsanctified have lodged
> Till the last trumpet. For charitable prayers,
> Shards, flints, and pebbles should be thrown on her,
> Yet here she is allowed her virgin rites,
> Her maiden strewments, and the bringing home
> Of bell and burial.
>
> (5.1.208–16)

The proper funeral that is being invoked here (and partially denied to Ophelia) seems far closer to the full Catholic ritual of interment, with the ringing of bells and attendant ceremonies, than to the simple burial for which zealous Protestants were calling.[54] And it is clear from this and the subsequent exchange that what is at stake is not only the communal social judgment upon Ophelia, suspected of suicide, but also the communal ritual assistance given to the dead by the living—that is, the requiem masses and other "charitable prayers" designed to shorten the soul's purgatorial suffering and hasten its ascent to Heaven. "God 'a' mercy on his soul," the mad Ophelia had prayed for her own murdered father, "And of all Christian souls, I pray God" (4.5.194–95)

"Must there no more be done?" Laertes insistently asks, to which the priest responds with a harsh refusal:

> No more be done.
> We should profane the service of the dead
> To sing sage requiem and such rest to her
> As to peace-parted souls.
>
> (5.1.217–21)

"Lay her i' th' earth," Laertes orders, glancing both at the charge of pollution and at the trajectory of his sister's soul:

> And from her fair and unpolluted flesh
> May violets spring. I tell thee, churlish priest,
> A minist'ring angel shall my sister be
> When thou liest howling.
>
> (5.1.221–25)[55]

This dispute over Ophelia's funeral ceremony is an instance of an overarching phenomenon in *Hamlet*: the disruption or poisoning of virtually all rituals for managing grief, allaying personal and collective anxiety, and restoring order.

The source of this poisoning in the play is Claudius, who usurps not only the kingship but also the language of Protestant mourning. "Why should you shed tears immoderately for them who have all tears wiped from their eyes?" asked a seventeenth-century preacher in a typical funeral sermon; "Why should you be swallowed up of grief for them who are swallowed up of joy?" "God allows us tears; Jacob wept over his dead father; tears give vent to grief," the preacher concedes, "but there is no reason we should grieve excessively for our pious friends, they receive a Crown, and shall we mourn when they have preferment?"[56] "To persever / In obstinate condolement," Claudius tells his nephew in similar accents,

> is a course
> Of impious stubbornness, 'tis unmanly grief,
> It shows a will most incorrect to heaven,
> A heart unfortified, a mind impatient,
> An understanding simple and unschooled.
>
> (1.2.92–97)

In 1601, when Shakespeare wrote *Hamlet*, Protestant preachers had been saying words to this effect for fifty years, trying to wean their flock away from Purgatory and prayers for the dead and obstinate condolement.[57] The argument seemed won: the chantries were all silent. But why should Shakespeare—who sympathetically rehearses the same sentiments in *Twelfth Night*, albeit in the mouth of the fool[58]—have given the Protestant position to his arch-villain in *Hamlet?* And why should his Ghost—who might, after all, have simply croaked for revenge, like the Senecan ghosts in Kyd—insist that he has come from a place where his crimes are being burned and purged away?

THE FIFTY-YEAR EFFECT

Perhaps there is what we might call a fifty-year effect, a time in the wake of the great, charismatic ideological struggle in which the revolutionary generation that made the decisive break with the past is all dying out and the survivors hear only hypocrisy in the sermons and look back with longing at the world they have lost. Perhaps, too, Shakespeare's sensitivity to the status of the dead was intensified by the death in 1596 of his son Hamnet (a name virtually interchangeable with Hamlet in the period's public records) and still more perhaps by the death of his father, John, in 1601, the most likely year for the writing of *Hamlet*. When in April 1757, the owner of Shakespeare's birthplace in Stratford-upon-Avon decided to retile the roof, one of the workmen, described as of "very honest, sober, and industrious character," found an old document between the rafters and the tiling. The document, six leaves stitched together, was a "spiritual testament" in fourteen articles. The testament was a formulary, conspicuously Catholic in content; written by the celebrated Italian priest Carlo Borromeo, it was translated, smuggled into England by Jesuits, and distributed to the faithful. If genuine (for the original has disappeared), the copy discovered in Stratford belonged to John Shakespeare. In it the devout Catholic acknowledges that he is mortal and born to die "without knowing the hour, where, when, or how." Fearing that he may be "surprised upon a sudden," the signer of the testament declares his pious intention to receive at his death the sacraments of confession, Mass, and extreme unction. If by some terrible "accident" he does not receive these sacraments (that is, if he dies "unhouseled, dis-appointed, unaneled"), then he wishes God to pardon him. His appeal for spiritual assistance is not only to God, the blessed Virgin, and his guardian angel; it is also to his family: "I

John Shakspeare," reads article XII, "do in like manner pray, and beseech all my dear friends, Parents, and kinsfolks, by the bowels of our Savior Jesus Christ, that since it is uncertain what lot will befall me, for fear notwithstanding lest by reason of my sins, I be to pass, and stay a long while in Purgatory, they will vouchsafe to assist and succor me with their holy prayers, and satisfactory works, especially with the holy Sacrifice of the Mass, as being the most effectual means to deliver souls from their torments and pains; from the which, if I shall by God's gracious goodness, and by their virtuous works be delivered, I do promise that I will not be ungrateful unto them, for so great a benefit."[59] There is a clear implication to be drawn from this document: the playwright was probably brought up in a Roman Catholic household in a time of official suspicion and persecution of recusancy.[60] And there is, for our purposes, a further implication, particularly if we take seriously the evidence that Shakespeare conformed to the Church of England: in 1601 the Protestant playwright was haunted by the spirit of his Catholic father pleading for suffrages to relieve his soul from the pains of Purgatory.

Shakespeare, in any case, is likely to have encountered *A Supplication for the Beggers*, since it was reprinted in Foxe's *Acts and Monuments* (1563), copies of which were widely distributed in official sites, including, by government order, every cathedral and all the houses of archbishops and bishops in the realm. Shakespeare also may well have read More's *Supplication of Souls*. Like the Ghost of old Hamlet, More's poor souls cry out to be remembered, fear the dull forgetfulness of the living, disrupt the corrupt ease of the world with horrifying tales of their sufferings, lament the remarriage of their wives.[61] But all of this and more Shakespeare could have got from texts other than More's or from his own not inconsiderable imagination. Rather, these works are sources for Shakespeare's play in a different sense: they stage an ontological argument about spectrality and remembrance, a momentous public debate, that unsettled the institutional moorings of a crucial body of imaginative materials and therefore made them available for theatrical appropriation.

Personification and Its Discontents

To grasp the significance of this unsettling, let us return to Fish's pamphlet. In reprinting *A Supplication for the Beggers*, Foxe provides a brief account of Fish's life, conveniently omitting More's claim that before his death Fish "repented himself, and came into the church again, and forswore and forsook all the whole hill of those heresies out of which the fountain of that same good zeal sprang."[62] After he reprints Fish's *Supplication*, Foxe glances briefly at More's answer "under the name and title of the poor silly souls pewling out of Purgatory."[63] Foxe does not undertake in this place to refute More's theology; instead he ridicules his art.

More makes the dead men's souls, Foxe writes, "by a Rhetorical *Prosopopoeia*, to speak out of Purgatory pinfold, sometimes lamentably complaining, sometimes pleasantly dallying and scoffing, at the author of the Beggers' book, sometimes scolding and railing at him, calling him fool, witless, frantic, an ass, a goose, a mad dog, an heretic, and all that naught is" (viii). Foxe wryly speculates that so much testiness must be the result of the heat in Purgatory, and he professes to be concerned that the souls' lack of charity may bring them to Hell rather than to Heaven. He confesses, however, that he is not, after all, terribly concerned, for he does not think there is any such place as "Purgatory at all (unless it be in M. More's Utopia) as Master More's Poetical vain doth imagine" (ix). "[U]nless it be in M. More's Utopia": Purgatory, as Hugh Latimer had sardonically remarked in a sermon preached in 1536, is a "pleasant fiction."[64] It is, in Foxe's account, a no-place, a piece of poetry with no more claim to reality than More's famous imaginary commonwealth. Elsewhere Foxe will speak of the pope's conspiracies and cunning frauds, but not here. All of the passionate claims to remembrance, the institutional structures, the dogmatic elaborations by sophisticated theologians, the popular superstitions, the charges of heresy, the indulgences, the confraternities and masses and chantries, the tales of ghostly apparitions: all are for a moment at least deposited not in the realm of lies but in the realm of poetry.

The rhetorical advantage of this polemical game is that Foxe can proceed to play not the committed ideologue but the judicious critic. *Prosopopoeia*—personification, the making of what is absent to speak—is the rhetorical device that lies behind all haunting. Quintilian had written of the figure *prosopopoeia* that it "gives both variety and animation to eloquence in a wonderful degree," so that it is "allowable even to bring down the gods from heaven and evoke the dead." But, he warned, "our inventions of that sort will meet with credit only so far as we represent people saying what it is not unreasonable to suppose that they may have meditated."[65] Hence, in Foxe's account of *The Supplication of Souls*, More, "the author and contriver of this Poetical book," should be censured "for not keeping *Decorum Personae*, as a perfect Poet should have done." "They that give precepts of Art," Foxe explains, "do note this in all Poetical fictions, as a special observation, to foresee and express what is convenient for every person, according to his degree and condition, to speak and utter." Therefore, he continues, if by More's own account the souls in Purgatory are made clean and wholesome by their sufferings, then he should not have depicted them railing "so fumishly" against their enemies. They should, after all, be on their way to becoming more charitable, not less.

The point here is not to make a serious argument against Purgatory—that has been done by many, he notes, including John Frith—but to make fun of it, to expose it to ridicule. More had tried to exploit horror, fear, and guilt; Foxe tries to blow these away with laughter. Indeed, he proposes to treat *The Supplication of Souls* as a comedy. "It maketh me to laugh," he writes, "to see ye merry Antiques of M. More," whose devil arrives in Purgatory "laughing, grinning, and gnashing his teeth." But then he begins to worry about those teeth: how could the evil angel, "being a spiritual and no corporal substance," have "teeth to gnash & a mouth to grin?" And where exactly, he wonders, was More standing to see the devil open his mouth so wide that the souls of Purgatory all saw his teeth? It must, he decides, have been in Utopia, "where M. More's Purgatory is founded."[66]

This polemical performance seems very far indeed from Shakespeare's *Hamlet*, which probes precisely the fears, longings, and confusions that Foxe attempts to ridicule. The Ghost comes from Purgatory bewailing his failure to receive full Christian last rites but then demands that his son avenge his death, thereby initiating a nightmare that will eventually destroy not only his usurping brother but also Polonius, Ophelia, Laertes, Rosencrantz, Guildenstern, Gertrude, and his own son. He tells Hamlet not to let "the royal bed of Denmark be / A couch for luxury and damnèd incest" (1.5.82–83) but then warns his son not to taint his mind or let his soul contrive anything against his mother. Hamlet receives the most vivid confirmation of the nature of the afterlife, with its "sulph'rous and tormenting flames" (1.5.3), but then, in a spectacular and mysterious act of forgetting, speaks of death as the "undiscovered country from whose bourn / No traveller returns" (3.1.81–82). These are the kinds of representational contradictions that Foxe mercilessly mocks. To notice, publish, and circulate them throughout the realm is to declare that key theological principles and emotional experiences cannot hold together, and that the institution that generated them is bankrupt, worthy only of contempt and laughter.

But in *Hamlet* the same contradictions that should lead to derision actually intensify the play's uncanny power. And it is precisely Foxe's comedy that helped make Shakespeare's tragedy possible. It did so by participating in a violent ideological struggle that turned negotiations with the dead from an institutional process governed by the church to a poetic process governed by guilt, projection, and imagination. Purgatory exists in the imaginary universe of *Hamlet*, but only as what the suffering prince, in a different context, calls "a dream of passion" (2.2.554). Indeed, there is a striking link between Hamlet's description of the player who

> in a fiction, in a dream of passion,
> Could force his soul so to his whole conceit
> That from her working all his visage wanned,
> Tears in his eyes, distraction in's aspect,
> A broken voice, and his whole function suiting
> With forms to his conceit,

(2.2.529–34)

and the Ghost's description of the effect that his tale of torment would have on Hamlet:

> I could a tale unfold whose lightest word
> Would harrow up thy soul, freeze thy young blood,
> Make thy two eyes like stars start from their spheres,
> Thy knotty and combinèd locks to part,
> And each particular hair to stand on end
> Like quills upon the fretful porcupine.
>
> (1.5.15–20)

The link is the astonishingly palpable physiological effect of spectral fiction, dream, tale: "And all for nothing" (2.2.534).

Of course, within the play's fiction, Hamlet does not know that Purgatory is a fiction, as the state-sanctioned church of Shakespeare's time had declared it to be. On the contrary, he is desperate to establish the veracity of the Ghost's tale—"I'll take the Ghost's word for a thousand pound" (3.2.263–64), he exults after the play-within-the-play—and hence to establish that the Ghost is in reality his father's spirit and not the devil. But this reality is theatrical rather than theological; it can accommodate elements, such as a Senecan call for revenge, that would radically undermine church doctrine. At the same time, it can offer the viewer, in an unforgettably vivid dream of passion, many of the deep imaginative experiences, the tangled longing, guilt, pity, and rage, evoked by More. Does this mean that Shakespeare was participating in a secularization process, one in which the theater offers a disenchanted version of what the cult of Purgatory once offered? Perhaps. But the palpable effect is something like the reverse: *Hamlet* immeasurably intensifies a sense of the weirdness of the theater, its proximity to certain experiences that had been organized and exploited by religious institutions and rituals.

Not all forms of energy in Shakespeare's theater, of course, have been transferred, openly or covertly, from the zone of the real to the zone of the imaginary. Plays can borrow, imitate, and reflect much of what passes for everyday reality without necessarily evacuating this reality or exposing it as made-up. But the power of Shakespeare's theater is frequently linked to its appropriation of weakened or damaged institutional structures. It is conceivable that Shakespeare, with his recusant family background, his education in Stratford by teachers linked to Campion and the Jesuits, his own possible links to Lancashire recusants, felt a covert loyalty to these structures and a dismay that they were being gutted. *Hamlet* may provide a suitably disguised articulation of this dismay in the speech of the messenger who rushes in to tell Claudius to save himself from the rioters, a speech peculiar enough to provoke eighteenth-century editors to elevate the character to "Gentleman." "The rabble call him lord," the messenger reports,

> And, as the world were now but to begin,
> Antiquity forgot, custom not known,
> The ratifiers and props of every word,
> They cry, "Choose we! Laertes shall be king."
>
> (4.5.98–102)

It is a bit strange to invoke antiquity and custom in defense of the regime of the upstart Claudius; they seem more suitable as the ratifiers and props of the Catholic Church, whose apologists, like Thomas More, frequently likened the way its doctrines evolved over time to the way in which words gradually acquire their stable meanings.

We do not, however, need to believe that Shakespeare was himself a secret Catholic sympathizer; we need only to recognize how alert he was to the materials that were being made available to him. At a deep level there is something magnificently opportunistic, appropriative, absorptive, even cannibalistic about Shakespeare's art, as if poor, envious Robert Greene had sensed something more important than he knew when he attacked the "upstart crow, beautified with our feathers." In the case of Purgatory, important forces had been busily struggling for decades to prepare the playwright's feast. And the struggle did not end with the performance of the play or the playwright's death.

THE OLD SNARE

In 1624, a year after the publication of the First Folio, John Gee, a staunch Protestant who confesses that he had once himself been tangled in the Jesuits' subtle nets, published a book called *New Shreds of the Old Snare*.[67] Gee relates a series of incidents during the past three years in which Jesuits have tried to convert young women to Catholicism, to induce them to flee to the Continent and join nunneries, and to lure them to give their money to the Catholic Church. To achieve their cynical ends, "the thrice honourable Company of Iesuites, Players to the Popes Holiness" (10), turn "heaven and holy things" into "Theatrical and fabulous tricks" (16). Their principal device is to stage mysterious apparitions: with a burst of light, "a woman all in white, with countenance pale and wan, with long tresses of hair hanging down to her middle" (3) appears before an impressionable young woman and declares that she has come from the torments of Purgatory. The young woman is told that she can avert these same torments after death if she is "Nunnified" (7). In a related trick, the apparition—"a shape like unto a woman all in white: from her face seemed to come little streams of fire, or glittering light" (12)—declares that she is Saint Lucy, urging the wealthy woman to whom she appears to follow her holy example by giving away her worldly wealth to the priests and joining a convent.

Gee takes it upon himself to dispel the illusion, which is not the result, as some think, of witchcraft but, rather, of theater. The mysterious light, he explains, can be produced by "Paper Lanterns or transparent Glasses" enhanced by the "artificial directing of refractions."[68] The acting can be done "by some nimble handed and footed *Novice Jesuitable Boy*, that can as easily put on the person of *St. Lucy* or *The virgin Mary*, as a Play-boy can act winged *Mercury*, or Eagle mounted *Ganymedes*." The key thing is to understand that the Jesuits are a gifted troupe of actors. "I see no reason," Gee writes, "but that they should set up a company for themselves, which surely will put down *The Fortune, Red-Bull, Cock-pit, & Globe*" (17).

But then, as if he has had second thoughts about their chances for success in the competitive world of London theater, Gee considers three problems with their performances. First, he observes, "the plots of their Comedies twang all upon one string" (18). It is as if they own a single costume and can imagine only one character: "[N]one comes in Acting but *A Woman, A Woman, A Woman*, arrayed in *white, white, white.*" In a repertory company performing daily, the device will quickly lose its force. Still, if you are seeing it for the first time, it is, Gee concedes, an impressive show.

The second problem is the more serious one of a failure to observe decorum, the logical and representational contradictions that Foxe had enjoyed observing in More. The Poet, Gee observes, makes an obvious blunder by sending a ghost in a white robe "from the smoky burning Kitchen of *Purgatory*" (19). Surely that robe should have been scorched. But to this and similar incongruities, Gee counters, with mock generosity, that, after all, "the *Poet* kept within his Circle. For he well knew that deep passions, especially affright and astonishing admiration, do for the time bereave and suspend exact inquiring discourse" (19). Once you regard the apparition as performance and not as truth, you can dispense with anxiety on the score of incoherence and admire the calculation of a powerful psychic and somatic effect.

The third problem is the most serious: quite simply, "*they make their spectators pay too dear*" (20). Gee had explained how the Jesuits managed to get the astronomical sum of two hundred pounds from just one of their victims; that is, he soberly observes, a very dear market price for what is actually being purchased:

> Representations and Apparitions from the dead might be seen far cheaper at other Play-houses. As for example, the *Ghost in Hamlet, Don Andrea's Ghost in Hieronimo.* As for flashes of light, we might see very cheap in the *Comedy of Pyramus and Thisbe*, where one comes in with a Lantern and Acts *Mooneshine.* (20)[69]

"As for example, the *Ghost in Hamlet*": this extraordinary remark goes to the heart of the process I have been describing. With the doctrine of Purgatory and the elaborate practices that grew up around it, the church had provided a powerful method of negotiating with the dead, or, rather, with those who were at once dead and yet, since they could still speak, appeal, and appall, not completely dead. The Protestant attack on the "middle state of souls" and the middle place those souls inhabited destroyed this method for most people in England, but it did not destroy the longings and fears that Catholic doctrine had focused and exploited. Instead, as Gee perceives, the space of Purgatory becomes the space of the stage where old Hamlet's Ghost is doomed for a certain term to walk the night. That term has now lasted some four hundred years, and it has brought with it a cult of the dead that I and the readers of this book have been serving.

EPILOGUE

How seriously would Shakespeare have taken the notion of his theater as a cult of the dead?[1] Does he conceive of his characters as something like ghosts, endowed with the power to claim suffrages?[2] Does he share John Gee's perception that the stage offers customers inexpensive "Representations and Apparitions from the dead"? There is very little direct evidence of a self-conscious and calculated theatrical appropriation of the old system in which spirits solicit prayers and indulgences confer liberation from pain. But it is intriguing that the Chorus in *Henry V* asks the audience's pardon for the "flat unraisèd spirits that hath dared / On this unworthy scaffold to bring forth" (Prologue, lines 9–10) the great spectacle of Agincourt. The spirits are not, to be sure, the ghosts of the monarchs themselves; they are spectral aids to the "imaginary forces" (line 18) that must be deployed by the audience. But there is here a trace at least of the strange scene of conjuring in Marlowe's *Faustus* in which, at the request of the German emperor, the magician calls up spirits to present the shapes of the long-dead Alexander and his paramour.

In an odd moment near the end of his career Shakespeare seems once again to be recalling Marlowe's scene, when in *The Tempest* the magician Prospero presents the betrothal masque—"Some vanity of mine art" (4.1.41)—to Ferdinand and Miranda. Faustus had enjoined the emperor in effect to behave like the polite spectator of a play:

> My lord, I must forewarn your Majesty
> That when my spirits present the royal shapes
> Of Alexander and his paramour,

Your Grace demand no questions of the King
But in dumb silence let them come and go.

(4.2.46–50)

So, too, Prospero tells his daughter and her betrothed to watch without speaking: "No tongue, all eyes! Be silent" (4.1.59).

Shakespeare's magician elsewhere confesses that he has practiced necromancy:

[G]raves at my command
Have waked their sleepers, oped, and let 'em forth
By my so potent art.

(5.1.48–50)

With the spectacle of Iris, Ceres, and Juno, however, his prospective son-in-law understands that he is witnessing not the souls of the dead but something less ominous. "This is a most majestic vision, and / Harmonious charmingly," he says, "May I be bold / To think these spirits?" "Spirits," Prospero confirms,

which by mine art
I have from their confines called to enact
My present fancies.

(4.1.118–22)

Shakespeare has taken the form of Marlowe's spectacle—a silent audience watching the magician's spirits "present the royal shapes"—and pushed it more explicitly toward theater. "Our revels now are ended," Prospero explains to the startled Ferdinand, when the wedding pageant suddenly vanishes,

These our actors,
As I foretold you, were all spirits, and
Are melted into air, into thin air.

(4.1.148–50)

The famous lines that follow, linking the evanescence of the spirit-actors to the evanescence of "the great globe itself," are not a demystification of the theater; they are a revelation of something

theatrical, insubstantial, fading, and ultimately ghostlike in life
itself:

> And like the baseless fabric of this vision,
> The cloud-capped towers, the gorgeous palaces,
> The solemn temples, the great globe itself,
> Yea, all which it inherit, shall dissolve;
> And, like this insubstantial pageant faded,
> Leave not a rack behind. We are such stuff
> As dreams are made on, and our little life
> Is rounded with a sleep.
>
> (4.1.151–58)

Here the dreamlike emptiness long associated with the transitory
illusions of the theater is carried over into all that lies beyond the
boundaries of the stage.

For a character in a play what lies beyond these boundaries is a
kind of death, or rather, as Prospero puts it, "a sleep." Sleep gets
at the possibility, crucial in a repertory company, of an awakening,
the theater's equivalent of a resurrection. But it also gets at the
queasy sense, so powerfully expressed by Hamlet, of an ongoing
condition that is potentially nightmarish:

> For in that sleep of death what dreams may come
> When we have shuffled off this mortal coil
> Must give us pause.
>
> (3.1.68–70)

The Tempest comes to an end—the little lives of the characters all
rounded with a sleep—and then, astonishingly, continues beyond
the confines of its plot with the strange spectacle of a theatrical
afterlife. Delicately poised between the imaginary world of the play
and the commercial world of the theater, between the princely
magician and the impoverished actor, Prospero turns directly to
the spectators and pleads for suffrages:

> Now I want
> Spirits to enforce, art to enchant;
> And my ending is despair

Unless I be relieved by prayer,
Which pierces so, that it assaults
Mercy itself, and frees all faults.
As you from crimes would pardoned be,
Let your indulgence set me free.

(Epilogue, lines 13–20)

"Indulgence" need only mean the gratification of a desire—here the desire for applause—but it also had in Shakespeare's time the specific, technical sense that it still possesses in Catholic theology: the church's spiritual power to remit punishment due to sin. This theological sense is here strongly reinforced by the reference to prayer and by the rapid sketch of a scenario that we have repeatedly seen: a tormented soul saved from despair and lifted up to bliss through the piety of loving friends and the good offices of the church. From this perspective the speaker of the epilogue, whether his sin is sorcery or playacting, sounds like a spirit who is pleading for our help. He is not, of course, crying out from Purgatory; he is speaking from the stage. And in place of prayers, we offer the actor's ticket to bliss: applause.

NOTES

I have, in the interests of readability, modernized the spelling and punctuation of all the texts quoted in this book, except in the notes, where I have retained the original.

PROLOGUE

1. "Shakespeare Bewitched," in *New Historical Literary Study: Essays on Reproducing Texts, Representing History,* ed. Jeffrey N. Cox and Larry J. Reynolds (Princeton: Princeton University Press, 1993), pp. 108–35; "The Eating of the Soul," *Representations* 48 (1994): 97–116; "La souris mangeuse d'hostie: les miettes du repas eucharistique," *Traverses* 5 (1993): 42–54, revised as "The Mousetrap," in *Practicing New Historicism* [with Catherine Gallagher] (Chicago: University of Chicago Press, 2000); "Remnants of the Sacred in Early Modern England," in *Subject and Object in Renaissance Culture,* ed. Margreta de Grazia, Maureen Quilligan, and Peter Stallybrass (Cambridge: Cambridge University Press, 1996), pp. 337–45.

2. Joel Fineman, *The Subjectivity Effect in Western Literary Tradition* (Cambridge: MIT Press, 1991).

3. See Saul Lieberman, *Texts and Studies* (New York: Ktav Publishing House, 1974), esp. pp. 29–56, 235–72.

4. *The Sermons of John Donne,* ed. Evelyn M. Simpson and George R. Potter, 10 vols. (Berkeley and Los Angeles: University of California Press, 1954), 7:168–69. Donne's text is 1 Cor. 15:29: "Else, what shall they do which are baptized for the dead? If the dead rise not at all, why are they then baptized for the dead?" His purpose is to disprove the Catholic claim that "this Baptisme for the Dead must necessarily prove Purgatory, and their Purgatory" (165).

5. Leon Wieseltier, *Kaddish* (New York: Knopf, 1998), p. 194.

6. The complex relations between Judaism and Christianity—relations that by no means always display the priority of Israel—have recently been illuminated by, among others, Ivan Marcus, *Rituals of Childhood: Jewish Acculturation in Medieval Europe* (New Haven: Yale University Press, 1996). and Daniel Boyarin, *Dying for God: Martyrdom and the Making of Christianity and Judaism* (Stanford: Stanford University Press, 1999).

7. For a fascinating argument about the small number of Jews who were living in early modern England, see James Shapiro, *Shakespeare and the Jews* (New York: Columbia University Press, 1996).

8. 7:169. Donne traveled abroad on several occasions, including a voyage in 1619, as chaplain with Viscount Doncaster, that took him to Germany and the Netherlands, where he would have had ample opportunity to observe Jewish worship.

CHAPTER ONE: A POET'S FABLE

1. Simon Fish, *A Supplicacyon for the Beggers*, reprinted as Appendix B in vol. 7 of *The Complete Works of St. Thomas More*, ed. Frank Manley, Germain Marc'hadour, Richard Marius, and Clarence Miller (New Haven: Yale University Press, 1990), p. 412. All citations are to this edition.

2. In *Poverty and Policy in Tudor and Stuart England* (London: Longman, 1988), Paul Slack notes that grain was scarce in some localities in 1527–1528, and there may have been cases of starvation, though, like most social historians, he emphasizes that the figures are extremely unreliable.

3. John Foxe, "The Story of M. Symon Fishe," in *Actes and Monumentes*, quoted in Frederick J. Furnivall, ed. *A Supplication for the Beggers*, Early English Text Society, e.s., 13 (London: N. Trübner, 1871), p. vi.

4. On Fish and the early Protestant agitators, see W. A. Clebsch, *England's Earliest Protestants* (New Haven: Yale University Press, 1964); Susan Brigden, *London and the Reformation* (Oxford: Clarendon, 1989); A. G. Dickens, *The English Reformation*, 2d ed. (London: Batsford, 1989).

5. Etienne de la Boétie, *Contre un (Discours de la servitude voluntaire)*, in *Oeuvres Complètes*, ed. Louis Desgraves (Bordeaux: Blake & Co., 1991) [English translation: *The Politics of Obedience: The Discourse of Voluntary Servitude*, ed. Murray N. Rothbard, 2d ed. (Montreal: Blackrose, 1997)]. La Boétie's analysis is secular, but it was quickly adopted by the Huguenots.

6. It may at first seem difficult to understand why so many people would willingly abandon their innate freedoms, but in fact the process is quite simple. A tiny group chooses, for strategic purposes, to declare allegiance to a single person. The qualities of that person—who may, for all anyone knows, be a dolt or a scoundrel—are not particularly relevant; what matters is his (or her) symbolic position at the apex of the system. Nor does it greatly matter if the members of the inner circle have any serious regard for the person to whom they declare their allegiance; what matters is that their immediate dependents feel similarly bound to them and, through them, bound to the person at the pinnacle. Each of those dependents in turn has his dependents, and before long tens of thousands of people are locked into a system that is exploiting rather than protecting or serving them.

7. See Anne Hudson, *The Premature Reformation: Wycliffite Texts and Lollard History* (Oxford: Clarendon, 1988), esp. pp. 309–10. Hudson argues that Fish's *Supplicacyon for the Beggers* "is a polemic entirely couched in Lollard terms" (501).

8. John Bale, *King Johan*, in *Complete Plays*, ed. Peter Happé (Cambridge: D. S. Brewer, 1985), p. 70.

9. William Tyndale, *An Answer to Sir Thomas More's Dialogue, The Supper of the Lord*, ed. Henry Walter (Cambridge: Cambridge University Press for the Parker Society, 1850), pp. 145–56.

10. Cardinal William Allen, *A Defense and Declaration of the Catholike Churches Doctrine, touching Purgatory* (Antwerp, 1566), fol. 215v.

11. "Purgatory did not exist before 1170 at the earliest," in Jacques Le Goff, *The Birth of Purgatory*, trans. Arthur Goldhammer (Chicago: University of Chicago Press, 1981), p. 135. Le Goff is interested in the first use of the term *Purgatorium* to designate a particular place; many of the concepts connected to the doctrine of Purgatory are of great antiquity. As a neuter adjective, *purgatorium* had long been used; as a noun it entered medieval Latin only in the second half of the twelfth century.

12. *The Lay Folks Mass Book*, ed. Thomas Frederick Simmons Early English Text Society, o.s., 71 (London: Oxford University Press, 1879), pp. 42–44. Here and elsewhere in the body of the text, but not in the notes, I have modernized the letters "thorn" to "th" and "yogh" to "gh."

    See likewise the enumeration of the dead in the "Bidding Prayer" Simmons cites from *Manuale secundum usum matris ecclesie Eboracensis*, published by Wynkyn de Worde in 1509: "Ye shall make a speciall prayer for your fadres sowles: for your moders sowles: godfaders sowles and godmothers sowles: broders sowles and sisters sowles: and for all your elders sowles: and for all the sowles that ye or I be bownde to praye for. and specyally for all the sowles whose bones are buryed in this chirche or in this chirche yerde: or in any other holy place. and in especyall for all the sowles that bydes the great mercy of almighty god in the bytter peynes of Purgatory: that god for his great mercy releas them of theyr peyne if it be his blessyd wyll. And that our prayers may sumwhat stande them in stede: Every man and woman of your charite / helpe them with a Pater noster and an Ave maria" (80).

13. On All Souls' Day, see David Cressy, *Birth, Marriage, and Death: Ritual, Religion and the Life-Cycle in Tudor and Stuart England* (New York: Oxford University Press, 1997): "In the eleventh century, probably between 1024 and 1033, Cluny began commemorating the dead on November 2, the day after All Saints' Day. The prestige of the Cluniac order was such that before long the 'Day of the Dead' was being celebrated throughout Christendom" (125). On bell ringing, see "An Epistle Occasioned By The Most Intollerable Jangling Of The Papists' Bells On All Saints' Night, The Eve Of All Soules' Daye, Being Then Vsed To Be Rung All Night (And All As If The Towne Were On Fire) For The Soules Of Those In Purgatorye. Written From Thouars To Saumur, To Mr. Bryan Palmes," in William Browne, *The Whole Works*, ed. W. Carew Hazlitt (London: Whittington and Wilkins, 1869), 2:242–44. On "soul cakes," see John Mirk, *Mirk's Festial: A Collection of Homilies*, ed. Theodor Erbe, Early English Text Society, e.s., 96, Part 1 (London: Kegan Paul, Trench, Trübner & Co, 1905), p. 270, and Cressy, *Birth, Marriage, and Death*, pp. 8–9, 30. Protestant authorities attempted to put an end to these practices, but as late at 1578 the parishioners of one Worcestershire village had to appear before the bishop's court to explain themselves "about ringing on All Halloween day at night" (30).

14. *The Primer in English after the use of Sarum* (Rowen: N. LeRoux, 1538).

15. "Dominus noster Jesus Christus, qui vos et nos redemit suo pretiosissimo sanguine, dignetur vos a poenis liberare." The Latin is from William Maskell, *Monumenta Ritualia Ecclesiae Anglicanae*, 2d ed., 3 vols., (Oxford: Clarendon, 1882),

3:180. I use the translation of Thomas Rogers, *The Catholic Doctrine of the Church of England* (Cambridge: University Press for the Parker Society, 1854), p. 214.

Comparable prayers for the souls of those buried in the churchyard are included in the Sarum Missal and Processionale. See *Missale Ad Usum Insignis et Praeclarae Ecclesiae Sarum [Missale Sarum]*, ed. Francis Dickinson (Oxford: J. Parker, 1861–1883), pp. 877–78. For an English translation, see *The Sarum Missal*, trans. Frederick E. Warren (London: A. R. Mowbray, 1913), 2:192–93. See likewise the prayer "for alle soules whos bonys resteth in this chirche and chirche yard" in *Ceremonies and Processions of the Cathedral Church of Salisbury*, ed. Chr. Wordsworth (Cambridge: Cambridge University Press, 1901)—an edition of the Sarum Processionale, written 1445, with additions—p. 31.

16. See Peter Brown, "Vers la naissance du purgatoire: Amnistie et pénitence dans le christianisme occidental de l'Antiquité tardive au Haut Moyen Age," in *Annales Histoire Science Sociale* 6 (1997): 1247–61.

17. *A Treatise of the Manner and Mede of the Mass*, Vernon MS of the Bodleian, ca. 1375; text from a century earlier.

> Wust I my Fader in flesch and felle
> Weore holliche I-holden in helle,
> ther weore non hope of hele.
> To preye for him I couthe no Red,
> No more then for A Dogge were ded,
> But let hem with him dele.
> Yit I rede we go to chirche
> Godes werkes for-to worche
> Yif we wole wone in wele.
> Sethe hit is vnknowe to vs,
> We schul preye for alle Fidelibus
> To Rewe soules that beth lele.
>
> (Lines 269–80)

(Quoted from Appendix IV of *The Lay Folks Mass Book*, pp. 135–36. The text, called "How to Hear Mass," is also found in *The Minor Poems of the Vernon MS, Part 2*, ed. F. J. Furnivall, Early English Text Society, o.s., 117 [London: Kegan Paul, 1901], p. 500, lines 265–76.)

18. Maskell, *Monumenta Ritualia Ecclesiae Anglicanae*, 3:180n.

19. Cressy, *Birth, Marriage, and Death*, p. 463. See the story told in Noel Taillepied, *A Treatise of Ghosts* [1588], ed. and trans. Montague Summers (London: Fortune, 1933), pp. 75–76, involving a priest who notes of the village church near Meulan-sur-Seine that "I was preaching in this church, and the stench of corruption and odour of death was so overpowering that we all feared some putrid fever might result."

20. "The satisfactions of Christ are so superabundant," writes one mid-seventeenth-century English Catholic, "that they are sufficient to supply any want of

satisfaction, which any man or men can haue" (James Mumford, *A Remembrance for the Living to Pray for the Dead* [St. Omer, 1641], p. 133).

21. John Lydgate, "On *de Profundis*," in *Minor Poems*, ed. Henry N. McCracken, Early English Text Society, e.s., 107 (London: Kegan Paul, 1911), p. 80. Lydgate's poem is in the form of a commentary on the *de Profundis* which aims to show why that Psalm is "[s]eid as folk passe by ther sepulturys."

22. Jacobus de Voragine, *The Golden Legend: Readings on the Saints*, trans. William Granger Ryan, 2 vols. (Princeton: Princeton University Press, 1993), 2:279–80. On the discussion of Purgatory in *The Golden Legend*, see Alain Boureau, *La légende dorée* (Paris: Editions du Cerf, 1984), pp. 49–52; also Le Goff, *The Birth of Purgatory*, pp. 321–24.

23. Jacobus de Voragine, *The Golden Legend*, 2:283.

24. Aquinas, *Supplement*, quoted in Le Goff, *The Birth of Purgatory*, p. 273. Aquinas is following a statement made by Augustine in his *Commentary on Psalm* 37: "Although some will be saved by fire, this fire will be more terrible than anything that a man can suffer in this life" (in Le Goff, p. 68). This view was frequently reiterated. See, for example, this complaint of a soul in Purgatory in a poem by Thomas Hoccleve (1413–1446):

> The leeste torment of this purgatorie
> That we souffren / exceedith in sharpnesse
> Tormentes all of the world transitorie.
> Heere, of torment / more is the bittirnesse
> In an hour / then the worldes wikkidnesse
> May hurte or greeue in an .C. yeer:
> Greet is thaffliccioun that we han heer.

(Thomas Hoccleve, "How to Learn to Die," in *Minor Poems*, ed. Frederick J. Furnivall, Early English Text Society, e.s., 61 [London: Kegan Paul, 1892], lines 729–35.)

25. The next day, the tale goes, Master Silo recited the following couplet to his class—

> Linquo choax ranis, cra corvis, vanaque vanis,
> Ad logicam pergo, quae mortis non timet ergo—

and took refuge in religion. William Caxton, who translated *The Golden Legend* in 1483, omitted the couplet, whose scholastic joke may have baffled or failed to amuse him. Ryan translates: "I leave croaking to the frogs, cawing to the crows, vanities to the vain, / Therefore I stay with logic, which fears not the *ergo* of death" (2:283 n. 2).

26. Chaucer's *Summoner's Tale* refers to the practice: "Trentals,' seyde he, 'deliueren fro penaunce / Hir freendes soules, as well olde as yonge' " (lines 1724–25 of Fragment III, in Geoffrey Chaucer, *The Riverside Chaucer*, ed. Larry Benson [Boston: Houghton Mifflin, 1987]). In *The Resurrection of the Masse* (Strasbourg, 1554), the Protestant Hughe Hilarie parodies the Catholic sales pitch:

> A trentall of masses is very profitable
> For a soule departed at euery season/
> For that vnto glory without any fable
> Wil bring the soule with all expedicion.

(Lines 251–54)

And the *OED* includes a citation that indicates that not everyone found the price moderate: "For which Masses, Diriges, and Trentals, huge summes of money are giuen daily" (from Thomas Bell, *Motives Concerning Romish Faith and Religion*, 2d ed. [Cambridge: Legate, 1605]). Beginning with Gregory XIII (reigned 1572–1585), popes founded special altars privileged for the dead at which one mass said any day of the year would free a particular soul from Purgatory. In principle, these altars should have made the obtaining of suffrages simpler and far less expensive, but, as Pierroberto Scaramella and others have shown, the faithful, as if mistrusting the papal assurance, routinely chose to pay for hundreds or thousands of masses at these privileged altars. See Christine Göttler, *Die Kunst des Fegebeuers nach der Reformation: Kirchliche Schenkungen, Ablass und Almosen in Antwerpen und Bologna um 1600* (Mainz am Rhein: Philipp von Zabern, 1996).

27. As chronicles and account books suggest, the historical Henry did indeed pay lavishly for Richard's Westminster reburial. All citations of Shakespeare, unless otherwise noted, are to *The Norton Shakespeare*, ed. Stephen Greenblatt et al. (New York: W. W. Norton, 1997).

28. Henry goes on to acknowledge the worthlessness of these measures:

> More will I do,
> Though all that I can do is nothing worth,
> Since that my penitence comes after ill
> Imploring pardon.

(4.2.284–87)

Still, he performs his ritual acts, and the English victory may suggest that his plea for a deferral of the divine judgment—"Not today, O Lord, / O not today" (4.2.274–75)—was successful. Henry's remark that he has the poor "in yearly pay" captures nicely the frank medieval commodification of the prayers of the poor, though it may also subtly reflect Reformation irony about this commodification.

29. Howard Colvin, *Architecture and the After-life* (New Haven: Yale University Press, 1991), p. 172. (Presumably, Colvin is thinking only of England here, since there must have been even more expensive—not to mention larger—structures built elsewhere.)

30. "Testamentum Regis Henrici Octavi," in Thomas Rymer, *Foedera*, 2d ed., 20 vols. (London: J. Tonson, 1726–1735), 15:111. Cf. Lacy Baldwin Smith, "The Last Will and Testament of Henry VIII: A Question of Perspective," *Journal of British Studies* 2 (1962): 14–27.

31. Barnaby Googe, *The Popish Kingdome, or reign of Antichrist* (London: Henry Denham, 1570; reprint, New York: Johnson Reprint Corporation, 1972).

Googe (1540?–1594) was translating from the Latin of Thomas Naogeorgus (or Kirchmeyer).

32. Christopher Haigh, *Reformation and Resistance in Tudor Lancashire* (Cambridge: Cambridge University Press, 1975), p. 71.

33. See, for example, Clive Burgess, " 'By Quick and by Dead': Wills and Pious Provision in Late Medieval Bristol," *English Historical Review* 102 (1987): 837–58.

34. In *Living and Dying in England, 1100–1540: The Monastic Experience* (Oxford: Clarendon, 1993), Barbara Harvey notes that in the later Middle Ages, the life of the monks of Westminster Abbey "was still strongly influenced, as it had been since the eleventh century, by the contemporary belief in a Purgatory where the expiation of the consequences of sin could be assisted" by the endowment of post-obit masses and other ritual acts. "Directly or indirectly, the monks of West-minster owed most of their endowments to their place in this penitential system, and other features of their life were affected too. For example, because they said Masses for the royal and noble dead, they were involved in the distribution of alms on a notable scale" (210). Fish complains that the monks rarely disburse the money they have been given to distribute to the poor, and writes wryly that "[i]f the Abbot of Westminster shulde sing euery day as many masses for his founders as he is bounde to do by his fouindacion, .M monkes were to fewe" (*Supplication for the Beggers*, p. 422).

The benefactions were not only from the rich. See Haigh: "The most distinc-tive feature of popular religion was its preoccupation with death and the ensur-ing of salvation. This explains the detailed provisions for prayers found in most wills, for the period to be spent in purgatory depended, in part, on the arrange-ment of masses and prayers" (*Reformation and Resistance in Tudor Lancashire*, p. 68).

35. Cf. Eamon Duffy, *The Stripping of the Altars: Traditional Religion in England, c.1400–c.1580* (New Haven: Yale University Press, 1992): "According to the spirit who revealed the secrets of Purgatory in the 'Revelacyone schewed to ane holy woman' of 1422, prayers offered in ignorance for a soul damned were not wasted, though they could not help the intended beneficiary; instead 'the helpe and the mede turne to the nexte of his kynne in purgatorye and hastelye spede tham owte of thaire pergatorie' " (354).

36. See the discussion of "All Souls" in *The South English Legendary*, ed. Charlotte d'Evelyn and Anna J. Mill, Early English Text Society, o.s., 236 (London: Oxford University Press, 1956), 2:464:

For if þe preost enioigneþ penance / þat ne beo noȝt ful ynouȝ
In purgatorie hit worþ iȝulde / & elles hit were wouȝ
For penance is in [þre] manere / lasse oþer more
[Oþer] euene after a manes sinne / & noȝt after þe preostes lore
If hit is more þan þe sinne / & a man hit do iwis
Al hit schal in heuene turne / to eching of his blis
If he is euene to þe sinne / þe sinne he wole aquenche
Ac noȝt if he is to lute / ech man him þerof þenche

& to a fol [prest] ne triste he no3t / þat to lute penance him set
For siker her oþer elleswhar / eche synne worþ ibet.

(Lines 39–48)

37. Gret loue þer moste nede beo / þat bituene hem were
  Wiþoute loue & deol of hurte / such þing no3t worþ nere.

(*The South English Legendary*, 2:465, lines 67–68.)

38. Quoted in Henry W. Sullivan, *Grotesque Purgatory: A Study of Cervantes's "Don Quixote,"* *Part II* (University Park: Pennsylvania State University Press, 1996), p. 98.

39. *Purgatory Survey'd. Or, A Particular accompt of the happy, and yet thrice unhappy state, of the Souls there.* (Paris, 1663), trans. by Richard Thimelby of Etienne Binet, *De l'estat heureux et malheureux des âmes souffrantes du Purgatoire*, p. 55.

40. Ibid., pp. 244-45.

41. Ibid., p. 156.

42. Quoted in Hudson, *The Premature Reformation*, p. 301n.

43. John Wedderburn, "Of the Fals Fyre of Purgatorie," in *A Compendious Book of Godly and Spiritual Songs* [1578], ed. A. F. Mitchell, Scottish Text Society (Edinburgh: Blackwood, 1897), p. 187 (lines 13–16).

44. Cf. Henry Jones (bishop of Clogher), *Saint Patricks Purgatory, containing the Description, Originall, Progresse, and Demolition of that Superstitious place* (London: Royston, 1647): "[W]hat hope *The poorer sort of people* may have, of being freed from *Purgatory*, in *whose scorching flames* they are likely long to *fry*, they see, who can well tell, that *no penny, no Paternoster*" (60). Cf. too the street cry of the character called Error in Phineas Fletcher's *The Locusts, or Apollyonists*:

  Come, buy crownes, scepters, miters, crosiers,
  Buy thefts, blood, incests, oaths, buy all for gaine:
  With gold buy out all Purgatory feares,
  With gold buy Heaven and Heavens Soveraigne.

(Lines 264–67)

(In *Poetical Works*, ed. Frederick S. Boas [Cambridge: Cambridge University Press, 1908], p. 60.)

45. This is Le Goff's summary of Aquinas's argument, *The Birth of Purgatory*, p. 276.

46. Hudson, *The Premature Reformation*, p. 300.

47. "Jacke Upland" in *Poetical Poems and Songs relating to English History*, ed. Thomas Wright, Rolls Series (London: Longman, 1861), 2:21 (lines 177–86).

48. Ibid., lines 217–19, 231–32.

49. See, especially, Alan Kreider, *English Chantries: The Road to Dissolution* (Cambridge: Harvard University Press, 1979), and Sandra Raban, *Mortmain Legislation and the English Church, 1279–1500* (Cambridge: Cambridge University Press, 1982).

50. The play is in Bale, *Complete Plays*, 1:35.

51. *Goulafres*, as Germain Marc'hadour notes in the Yale Edition of More's *Supplication of Souls*, is linked etymologically to the French *goulafre/gouliafre* from the O.F. *gole* (animal's mouth) and also possibly to *goulf(r)e* (deep hole).

52. *The Obedience of a Christian Man*, in William Tyndale, *Doctrinal Treatises*, ed. Henry Walter (London: Parker Society, 1848), p. 245.

53. R. W., *A Recantation of famous Pasquin of Rome* (London: John Daye, 1570), lines 29–34.

54. Catholics (including Thomas More) argued that Hunne had committed suicide. Protestants argued that he was murdered by thugs in the employ of the bishop of London and his chancellor, William Horsey. In February 1515 a London coroner's jury found that Hunne had been murdered, and named Horsey and the two jailors as the killers. The case figures prominently in Foxe.

55. *Exposition of Tracy's Testament*, in *Doctrinal Treatises*, ed. Henry Walter (London: Parker Society, 1848), p. 281.

56. Heiko A. Oberman, *Luther: Man between God and the Devil* (New Haven: Yale University Press, 1989), p. 147.

57. Martin Luther *Works*, vol. 32, *Career of the Reformer, II*, ed. George W. Forell (Philadelphia: Muhlenberg Press, 1958), pp. 95–98. I am indebted for these references to Luther's works to Debora Shuger.

58. Luther, *Works*, 32:95–98. For the outright denial of Purgatory, see "Ein Widerruf vom Fegfeuer," in *Martin Luthers Werke* (Weimar: H. Bohlau, 1863–), vol. 20 (1893), pt. 2, pp. 360 ff.

59. Thomas Wilcox, *The Vnfouldyng of sundry vntruths and absurde propositions, latelye propounded by one I. B. a great fauourer of the horrible Heresie of the Libertines* (London, 1581), fol. D6v. Wilcox (1549?–1608) was one of the authors of the *Admonition*, a major work of religious Nonconformity.

60. "Articles Untruly, Unjustly, Falsely, Uncharitably Imputed to Me" (probably 1533, reprinted in Foxe), in *Sermons and Remains*, ed. George Elwes Corrie (London: Parker Society, 1845), pp. 236–38.

61. Hugh Latimer, *Works*, ed. George Elwes Corrie (Cambridge: Cambridge University Press, 1844–1845), 1:305, 550.

62. William Tyndale, *Obedience of a Christian Man*, in *Doctrinal Treatises*, ed. Henry Walter (London: Parker Society, 1848), pp. 158–59.

63. *Exposition of the First Epistle of St. John*, in *Expositions and Notes*, ed. Henry Walter (London: Parker Society, 1849), p. 162.

64. William Tyndale, *An Answer to Sir Thomas More's Dialogue* (Cambridge: Parker Society, 1850), p. 143.

65. R[ichard]C[orbett], *The Times' Whistle*, ed. J. C. Cowper, Early English Text Society, o.s., 48 (London: Trübner, 1871), p. 13:

Your holy water, purgatorie, bulles,
Wherwith you make the common people gulles,
Are grosse abuses of phantastique braines
Subtillie devisd'e only for private gaines,
Which you pull from the simple as you list,
Keeping them blinded in black errours mist;
And from the truth doe lead them clean astray,
Whilst of their substance you doe make your prey.
You false impostors of blinde ignorance,
Think you to 'scape eternall vengeance?
'Tis not your Popes fond dispensation,
Your workes of supererrogation,
Your idle crossings, or your wearing haire
Next to your skin, or all your whipping-cheer,
Your praiers & pilgrimage to Saints, your pixes,
Your holy reliques, beads, & crucifixes,
Your masses, Ave Maries, images,
Dirges, & such like idle fantasies
Of superstitiously polluted Rome,
Can save your soules in that great day of doome.

(Lines 319–38)

66. Wilcox, *The Vnfouldyng*, fol. D6v. See, likewise, Edwin Sandys (1574): "[T]o believe in Purgatory is vain, perilous, injurious"; Robert Pricke (in a funeral sermon, 1608): "[T]he soul after death . . . doth not wander up and down from place to place nor yet remaineth in a third place, as papists and pagans have dreamed . . . but . . . it returneth unto God that gave"; the merchant James Cole (1629): "[C]oncerning a mid-way mansion, or fiery prison, which some have endeavoured to settle by the way, there to purge and purify the blessed souls some certain years before their ascension in to Heaven, we find nothing at all in holy writ" (all quoted in Cressy, *Birth, Marriage, and Death*, pp. 386–87).

67. John Veron, *The Hunting of Purgatorye to Death* (1561; STC 24683), fol. 199v. The license has certain constraints, as we later learn in a discussion of pagan literature. "For, as paynters be wont to set foorthe their pictures after ye fasshion, that thei see men to wear their garmentes, and to decke themselves," declares Veron's character Eutrapelus, "so Poetes do ymagine their fictions, and do inuente theyr fables, vpoon the thinges ye be vsed emonge men: or elles vpon those thinges yt they haue some opinion/ of" (fol. 274r–v).

68. *A Cvrry-Combe for a Coxe-combe. Or Pvrgatories Knell. In ansder of a lewd Libell lately foricated by Iabal Rachil against Sir Edw. Hobies Covnter-snarle: Entituled Purgatories triumph ouer Hell*. Digested in forme of a Dialogue by Nick-groome of the Hobie-Stable Reginoburgi [Queenborough] (London: William Stansby, 1615), p. 53. In the work to which Hoby is replying, *Pvrgatories Trivmph Over Hell, Maugre The barking of Cerberus in Syr Edward Hobyes Counter-snarle* (n.p., 1613), the author had responded to an earlier charge against his using metaphors in a theological argument: "Are not the Psalmes of Dauid the chiefest hymnes of God his

Church? and are not those Poemes full of figuratiue speaches . . . ? why then may not a Theologicall inuocation be vttered in a figuratiue speach?

69. William Fulke, *Two Treatises Written against the Papistes, The one being an answere of the Christian Protestant to the Proud challenge of a Popish Catholicke: The other A cofutation of the Popish Churches doctrine touching Purgatory & prayers for the dead* (London, 1577), pp. 175, 62–63.

70. John Milton, *Paradise Lost*, in *The Poems of John Milton*, ed. John Carey and Alastair Fowler (London: Longman, 1968). Quotations from Milton are to this edition.

71. The "now" in this passage must refer to the time depicted at this point in the poem, before Adam and Eve have fallen and hence before the rise of lunatic superstitions Milton mocks. In a sonnet in praise of Henry Lawes, Milton refers to Purgatory, but it is Dante's Purgatory—that is, a poetic conceit:

> Harry whose tuneful and well-measured song
> First taught our English music how to span
> Words with just note and accent, not to scan
> With Midas' ears, committing short and long;
> Thy worth and skill exempts thee from the throng,
> With praise enough for envy to look wan;
> To after age thou shalt be writ the man,
> That with smooth air couldst humour best our tongue.
> Thou honour'st verse, and verse must lend her wing
> To honour thee, the priest of Phoebus' choir
> That tun'st their happiest lines in hymn, or story.
> Dante shall give fame leave to set thee higher
> Than his Casella, whom he wooed to sing
> Met in the milder shades of Purgatory.

(John Milton, "Sonnet XIII: To Mr. H. Lawes, on his Airs," in *Works*, ed. Frank Patterson, et al. [New York: Columbia University Press, 1931], 1:63.)

Unlike Fulke or Wilcox, Milton cannot hold that the imagination is inevitably fictive and empty, since he himself imagines Hell and Heaven in such detail, but he defends his own imaginings by appealing to the inspiration of the Holy Spirit.

72. John Frith, *A Disputation of Purgatory* (answer to Rastell, More, and Rochester). In *The Works of the English Reformers: William Tyndale and John Frith*, ed. Thomas Russell, 3 vols. (London: Ebenezer Palmer, 1831), 3:89–90, 97, 183.

73. William Camden, *Britain, or a Chorographicall Description of . . . England, Scotland, and Ireland*, trans. Philemon Holland (London, 1610), p. 163. The statistics first appear in the 1607 Latin edition. For modern estimates, see especially Kreider, *English Chantries*.

74. J. J. Scarisbrick writes, "Chantries and guilds were suppressed, but on the whole their schools and hospitals survived. The act of 1547 was aimed against their religious functions, not their good works, and the commissioners sent out to implement the statute of suppression acted conscientiously. . . . For example,

the crown separated out and continued to pay the sum of £6.10s.6d. to the poor of Cambridge, in accordance with the founder's wishes, from the income of a former obit; the remainder of the endowment (from shops and booths) was forfeit because it supported prayer for the dead" (in *The Reformation and the English People* [Oxford: Blackwell, 1984], 112–13).

75. John Donne, *Devotions on Emergent Occasions,* together with *Death's Duel* (Ann Arbor: University of Michigan Press, 1959), p. 18.

76. For distinctions among the genres of medieval accounts of apparations—*miracula, mirabilia, exempla, opuscules* coming out of the *discretio spirituum*—each of which serves a somewhat different purpose and addresses a different textual community, see Jean-Claude Schmitt, *Ghosts in the Middle Ages: The Living and the Dead in Medieval Society,* trans. Teresa Lavender Fagan (Chicago: University of Chicago Press, 1998), esp. pp. 123 ff.

77. On the appearance of ghosts at midnight, see Noel Taillepied, *A Treatise of Ghosts* (1588), trans. Montague Summers (London: Fortune Press, 1933), pp. 97–98: "In all ages throughout history has it been recorded that disembodied Spirits have appeared, as well by day as night, but more often about midnight when a man wakes from his first sleep, and the sense are alert, having taken some repose."

78. Elegy VI ("Oh, let me not serve so, as those men serve") in John Donne, *The Complete English Poems,* ed. A. J. Smith (Middlesex: Penguin, 1971), pp. 101–2.

79. Donne, *Devotions,* p. 74.

80. Ibid., pp. 137–38.

81. Ibid., p. 109.

82. James Pilkington, bishop of Durham from 1561 to 1576, wrote rules for funerals (published posthumously in 1585) in which he insisted "that no superstition should be committed in them, wherein the papists infinitely offend; as in masses, dirges, trentals, singing, ringing, holy water, hallowed places, year's days and month-minds, crosses, pardon letters to be buried with them, mourners, *de profundis* by every lad that could say it, dealing of money solemnly for the dead, watching of the corpse, bell and banner, with many more that I could reckon" (quoted in David Cressy, *Birth, Marriage, and Death: Ritual, Religion, and the Life-Cycle in Tudor and Stuart England* [New York: Oxford University Press, 1997], p. 399).

In his Funeral Sermon for the Emperor Ferdinand, Edmund Grindal reflects on whether and how it is appropriate to remember the dead. An honorable memorial, he observes, is quite distinct from prayers for the soul of the dead. Such prayers are not mentioned in the canonical Scriptures and have, since the time of Gregory the Great, been maintained "principally by feigned apparitions, visions of spirits, and other like fables, contrary to the scriptures" (Edmund Grindal, *Remains* [Cambridge: Cambridge University Press, 1843], p. 24). There is no "third place"—only Heaven and Hell, where prayers are strictly irrelevant. (In those places, "it needeth not or booteth not, as the old proverb goeth" [25].) But Grindal has to account for the existence of prayers for the dead in the works of the ancient fathers: "If the ancient fathers therefore, when they pray for the dead, mean of the dead which are already in heaven, and not elsewhere; then must we needs by their prayer understand either thanksgiving, or else take such petitions for the dead, (as they be indeed in some places,) for figures of eloquence and exornation of their style and oration, rather than necessary grounds of reason of any doctrine" (25). This is a clear and extremely revealing expression of the role that rhetoric, and particularly figuration (including personification), is made to play in Protestant discourse. What is at stake here? A shift in categorical understanding, so that what appears to be straightforward (and hence "necessary" in the sense of doctrinal), becomes figurative and ornamental, a piece of art rather than belief. In Grindal's instructions for visitations, he is intensely concerned about the way the bell is tolled.

83. Donne makes the point explicitly in his final sermon, "Death's Duell": "for this whole world is but an universal churchyard, but our common grave, and the life and motion that the greatest persons have in it is but as the shaking of buried bodies in their grave, by an earthquake" (*Devotions*, 171).

84. Donne, *Devotions*, p. 141.

85. Izaak Walton, *The Lives of Dr. John Donne, Sir Henry Wotton, Mr. Richard Hooker, Mr. George Herbert* (1670) (Menston, England: Scolar Press, 1969), p. 71.

86. Donne, *Devotions*, pp. 176, 180.

87. *The Sermons of John Donne*, ed. Evelyn M. Simpson and George R. Potter, 10 vols. (Berkeley and Los Angeles: University of California Press, 1954), 7: 167–68.

88. "For of that which *Virgil* sayes of Purgatory, *Lactantius* sayes, *propemodum vera*, *Virgil* was very neere the truth, *Virgil* was almost a Catholique." In John Donne, "Sermon Preached at S. Pauls, May 21, 1626" (on text: 1 Cor. 15:29: "Else, what shall they doe which are baptized for the dead? If the dead rise not at all, why are they then baptized for the dead?" [Simpson and Potter, *Sermons*, 7:176–77]).

CHAPTER TWO: IMAGINING PURGATORY

1. *The New Science of Giambattista Vico* (3d ed. [1744]), trans. Thomas Goddard Bergin and Max Harold Fisch (Ithaca: Cornell University Press, 1968), p. 21. All citations are to this edition.

2. These are the titles of polemics exchanged between the Jesuit John Floyd and the Protestant Edward Hoby.

3. The panel, by the Meister des Palant-Alters, is reproduced in the useful catalog *Himmel, Hölle, Fegefeuer: Das Jenseits im Mittelalter*, ed. Peter Jezler (Zurich: Schweizerisches Landesmuseum, 1994), p. 284.

4. In the First Quarto, Horatio does not utter this celebrated farewell, but the dying Hamlet's last words are a prayer: "Farewel *Horatio*, heauen receiue my soule." See *The Three-Text Hamlet*, ed. Paul Bertram and Bernice W. Kliman (New York: AMS Press, 1961), Q1: line 2196.

5. Meister des Lebensbrunnes (Messe des Heiligen Gregors, ca. 1510), reproduced in Jezler, *Himmel, Hölle, Fegefeuer,* p. 295 and detail, p. 293.

6. Takami Matsuda, *Death and Purgatory in Middle English Didactic Poetry* (Cambridge: D. S. Brewer, 1997), p. 107. "The general reticence about the details of punishment creates an impression of Purgatory as a place of mercy and hope rather than of punishment" (107). The wealth of evidence assembled by Peter Jezler (*Himmel, Hölle, Fegefeuer*) and by Christine Göttler (*Die Kunst des Fegefeuers nach der Reformation: Kirchliche Schenkungen, Ablass und Almosen in Antwerpen und Bologna um* 1600 [Mainz: Philipp von Zabern, 1996]) partially, but only partially, bears out this claim.

7. "Of þe relefyng of saules in purgatory," British Library MS Additional 37049, fol. 24v, in Matsuda, *Death and Purgatory in Middle English Didactic Poetry,* p. 155.

8. R. W. (fl. 1570), *A recantation of famous Pasquin of Rome* (London: John Daye, 1570), lines 738–39.

9. William Tyndale, *Obedience of a Christian Man,* in *Doctrinal Treatises,* ed. Henry Walter (London: Parker Society, 1848), p. 329.

10. John Veron, *The Hunting of Purgatorye to Death* (1561; STC 24683), fol. 178r.

11. On the role of vision narratives in helping "to create a solid, spatial image of the otherworld which was easy to understand and easy for preachers to represent," see Carl Watkins, "Doctrine, Politics and Purgation: The Vision of Tnúthgal and the Vision of Owein at St Patrick's Purgatory," *Journal of Medical History* 22 (1996): 234.

12. Brother Marcus, *The Vision of Tnugdal,* trans. Jean-Michel Picard (Dublin: Fourt Courts Press, 1989), p. 141.

13. Ibid., p. 142.

14. "Of a vision which was seen by a certain monk, of Purgatory and the places of punishment," in Roger of Wendover (d. 1236), *Flowers of History,* ed. J. A. Giles (London: Bohn, 1849), pp. 154–56. For the source, see Herbert Thurston, "Vision monaci de Eynsham," *Analecta Bollandiana* 22 (1903): 225–319. For the first printed version (William de Machlinia, ca. 1482), see *The Revelation to the Monk of Evesham* (1196), ed. Edward Arber, English Reprints 18 (London: English Reprints, 1869).

15. "The Vision of Thurkill," ed. H.L.D. Ward, *Journal of the British Archaeological Association* 31 (1875): 433. Latin text in *Die Vision des Bauern Thurkill,* ed. Paul Gerhard Schmidt (Leipzig: B. G. Teubner, 1987). The vision dates from ca. 1206, and its preface acknowledges its links to the *Tractatus Sancti Patricii* and to the visions of Tondal and the Monk of Evesham. On the status of the theater image in this text, see Roger S. Loomis and Gustave Cohen, "Were There Theatres in the Twelfth and Thirteenth Centuries?" *Speculum* 20 (1945): 92–98, and the responses by Dino Bigongiari, "Were There Theatres in the Twelfth and Thirteenth Centuries?" *Romanic Review* 37 (1946): 201–4; and Mary H. Marshall, "Theatre in the Middle Ages: Evidence from Dictionaries and Glosses,"

Symposium 4 (1950): 1–39, 366–89. I have profited from an unpublished essay by Henry S. Turner, "*Narrare Seriatim*: Representing Otherworld Space in the *Visio Thurkilli* (1206)."

16. "The Vision of Thurkill," p. 433.

17. Ibid., p. 434.

18. "Ita plane quamuis salui per ignem, gravior tamen erit ille ignis, quam quid-quid potest homo pati in hac vita" (*Enarrationes in Psalmos* 38.3, *Corpus Christian-orum Latinorum*, 38.384; quoted in Jacques Le Goff, *The Birth of Purgatory*, trans. Arthur Goldhammer [Chicago: University of Chicago Press, 1981], p. 384 n. 31). The fire, theologians wrote, is "intelligent." It will, as a seventeenth-century Italian Jesuit wrote, "extend its search even to sins already confessed, already pardoned, in order to remove, expiate, and efface the least vestiges of them, the tiniest remnants, the slightest blemishes" (Paolo Segneri the Elder, quoted in Jean Delumeau, *Sin and Fear: The Emergence of a Western Guilt Culture, Thir-teenth–Eighteenth Centuries* (orig. French ed. 1983), trans. Eric Nicholson (New York: St. Martin's Press, 1990), p. 392.

19. Richard Rolle, "To live well, consider Hell, Purgatory, Heaven, [etc.]," in *York-shire Writers: Richard Rolle and His Followers* (London: Swan Sonnenschein, 1896), lines 163–68.

20. James Mumford, *A Remembrance for the Living to Pray for the Dead* ([St. Omer], 1641), pp. 38–39.

21. Ibid., p. 40. Mumford takes his image of the painted fire, as he acknowledges, from "our worthy Countrey-man Syr Thomas More in the end of his rare worke called, The supplication of the Soule."

22. Alonso de Orozco, *Victoria de la muerte*, cited in Carlos Eire, *From Madrid to Purgatory: The Art and Craft of Dying in Sixteenth-Century Spain* (Cambridge: Cambridge University Press, 1995), p. 174.

23. Fulvio Fontana, cited in Delumeau, *Sin and Fear*, p. 396. On Gregory XIII and the establishment of altars privileged for the dead, see, especially, Göttler, *Die Kunst des Fegefeuers*, esp. pp. 66–88.

24. On the "bodily semblance," see Le Goff, *The Birth of Purgatory*, pp. 6, 98, 266, passim. The idea that mortal suffering anticipates and pays the debt of suffering after death is found outside of the Christian tradition in the Palestinian Talmud, in the story of a pious man from Ashkelon. The story is retold in a midrash from *Darkhei Teshuvah*, "The Ways of Repentance," an appendix to the responsa of Meir of Rothenburg, a thirteenth-century rabbi. "When both an unworthy tax collector and the man of Ashkelon's pious companion in study die on the same day, the man of Ashkelon is troubled by the contrast between the elaborate mourning for the tax collector and the lack of attention to the death of his friend until it is revealed to him in a dream that both the tax collector and his friend have received their just deserts.

His friend had sinned a single sin in his life: he had once put on the phylacter-ies for the head before the phylacteries for the arm. Thus he dies unmourned.

The tax collector in his life had done one good deed, a charitable act of feeding the poor. Thus he receives a splendid funeral. In his dream the man of Ashkelon sees his friend strolling in the midst of 'gardens and orchards and fountains,' while the tax collector, his tongue stretched out over the river, tries unsuccessfully to drink from it."

The principle, as Martha Himmelfarb (whose version of the story I have quoted) explains, is this: in this world the righteous are punished for every sin they commit so that they may enjoy more completely the bliss of the world to come. The wicked, on the other hand, receive any reward due them in this world so that they may be more completely punished in the world to come. Martha Himmelfarb, *Tours of Hell: An Apocalyptic Form in Jewish and Christian Literature* (Philadelphia: University of Pennsylvania Press, 1983), pp. 29–30.

It is difficult to know how seriously to take this story, since if it were treated with some literalness it would imply that anyone we see who is successful and honored in this world is likely to be facing a ghastly end in the afterlife, and anyone we see despised here is likely to be honored later.

25. *Cursor Mundi* [Northumbrian, fourteenth-century], ed. Richard Morris, 3 vols. Early English Text Society, o.s. (London: Kegan Paul, Trench, Trübner & Co., 1877, 1878, 1892), 3:1575:

> Forthi to man it es grete watch,
> And vnto preste that schriues bath;
> For in his boke saint austyn sais,
> That he the prest that penance layes
> Be vnwise in his fiting,
> Or else the synful in his telling,
> Ather of tham for thaire foly
> Sall brin in fire of Purgatory,
> And mak amendes thare for the plight,
> That tham aw here to do right. . . .

26. Thomas Tuke, *A Discovrse of Death, Bodily, Ghostly, and Eternall: Nor Vnfit for Sovldiers Warring, Seamen sayling, Strangers trauelling, Women bearing, nor any other liuing that thinkes of Dying* (London, 1613), fol. A3r.

27. Richard Rolle, *Prose and Verse*, ed. S. J. Ogilvie-Thomson, Early English Text Society, o.s., 293 (Oxford: Oxford University Press, 1988), p. 73. On Purgatory in this world and the "pragmatic prudence" with which the faithful were urged to seek it, see Matsuda, *Death and Purgatory in Middle English Didactic Poetry*, esp. pp. 167 ff. See Henry W. Sullivan, *Grotesque Purgatory: A Study of Cervantes's "Don Quixote,"* Part II (University Park: Pennsylvania State University Press, 1996), who seems to think that the notion of Purgatory on earth was only fully formulated in the seventeenth century, under the influence of Jesuits and the Counter-Reformation.

28. Henry Jones (bishop of Clogher), *Saint Patricks Purgatory: Containing The Description, Originall, Progresse, and Demolition of that superstitious place* (London, 1647), p. 59. Educated at Trinity, Dublin, Jones (1605–1682) was active in pro-

curing evidence as to the existence of a popish plot in Ireland. Two of his three children became Catholics.

29. "Forthi, if we couait to fle the payn of Helle and the payn of purgatorie vs bihoueth restreyne vs perfitly fro the lustes and the lykinges and fro the il delites and the wicked drede of this life, and that worldis sorowe be nat in vs, bot that we hold al oure herte fast on Ihesu Criste, and stand manly agayns temptaciouns" (*Ego Dormio*, in Rolle, *Prose and Verse*, p. 32 (lines 260–64)).

30. Etienne de Bourbon, mid-thirteenth-century *Tractatus de diversis materiis praedicabilibus*, writes in a discussion of Purgatory of "the gift of fear" (*De dono timoris*). Cited, with many other examples, in Delumeau, *Sin and Fear*, p. 385.

31. Jane Owen, *An Antidote Against Purgatory* (1634). Facsimile in *English Recusant Literature*, ed. D. M. Rogers (Menston, Yorkshire: Scolar Press, 1973), vol. 166. Cf. the brief discussion of Owen in Sullivan, *Grotesque Purgatory*, pp. 97–98.

32. Owen, *An Antidote Against Purgatory*, pp. 239–40.

33. Ibid., p. 105. This argument seems to have been current in Jesuit preaching from the period. See, for example, Philippe d'Outreman, *Le Pédagogue chrétien* (Saint Omer, 1622): "Among the legacies that you arrange for your nearest and dearest, do not forget yourself, that is, remember to also leave something so that masses may be said for the eternal rest of your soul. For it is not right that your children, relatives, and friends should have the support and benefit of your wealth, while you would be burning for ten, twenty, thirty, and fifty years in the unspeakably raging fire of Purgatory" (quoted in Delumeau, *Sin and Fear*, p. 398).

34. Owen, *An Antidote Against Purgatory*, pp. 183, 160–61.

35. Anticipating a reward for killing Hotspur, as he fraudulently claims to have done, Falstaff imagines himself repenting: "If I do grow great, I'll grow less, for I'll purge, and leave sack, and live cleanly as a nobleman should do" (5.4.162–65). Perhaps that fantasy of purgation stuck in Jane Owen's mind, or alternatively she recalled that Falstaff likens Bardolph's red nose to a *memento mori*: "I never see thy face but I think about Hell-fire, and Dives that lived in purple: for there he is in his robes, burning, burning" (3.3.29–32).

36. On voyages to the otherworld, see Le Goff, *The Birth of Purgatory*, and Claude Carozzi, *Le Voyage de l'âme dans l'Au-Delà* (Rome: Ecole Française de Rome, 1994). On the reviving of those who had died, see the remark of the Catholic Jane Owen, *An Antidote Against Purgatory*: "And because, there are many men, who can hardly be induced to belieue any thing, which themselues haue not seene, God sometimes therefore hath vouchsafed, to raise certain persons from death to lyfe; commanding them to relate to others liuing, what themselues touching this payne haue seene." These are, Owen writes, "eye-witnesses" (31).

37. Shane Leslie, comp., *Saint Patrick's Purgatory: A Record from History and Literature* (London: Burns Oates & Washbourne, 1932), p. xix.

38. The author gives only his initial, "H," which was expanded in the thirteenth century, by Matthew Paris, to "Henricus."

39. Thus it appears in the Cistercian Caesarius of Heisterbach's *Dialogus miraculorum* (1219–1223), among many purgatorial exempla. "Let him who doubts the existence of Purgatory go to Ireland," Caesarius writes, "and let him enter into Saint Patrick's Purgatory. He will then have no more doubts about the reality of Purgatorial punishments" (quoted in Le Goff, *The Birth of Purgatory*, p. 309).

40. Michael Haren and Yolande de Pontfarcy, eds., *The Medieval Pilgrimage to St. Patrick's Purgatory: Lough Derg and the European Tradition* (Enniskillen: Clogher Historical Society, 1988).

41. See the map in ibid., p. 49.

42. Leslie, *Saint Patrick's Purgatory*, p. xvii; quoted, among other places, in *St. Patrick's Purgatory: Two versions of Owayne Miles and The Vision of William of Stranton, together with the long text of the Tractatus de Purgatorio Sancti Patricii*, ed. Robert Easting, Early English Text Society, o.s., 298 (Oxford: Oxford University Press, 1991), xvii. All citations of *Owayne Miles* are to Easting, *St. Patrick's Purgatory*. *Owayne Miles* survives in two distinct versions, one in six-line tail-rhyme stanzas (*aabccb*) and the other in octosyllabic couplets. The first version is extant in a single copy, the Auchinleck manuscript; the second survives in two copies, Cotton (BL MS Cotton Caligula A ii) and Yale (MS 365). Easting prints Auchinleck, Cotton, and Yale. Quotations, unless otherwise noted, are from the Auchinleck version.

43. This is the central claim of Le Goff, who writes that "this brief work occupies an essential place in the history of Purgatory, in whose success it played an important, if not decisive, role" (*The Birth of Purgatory*, p. 193).

44. Leslie, *Saint Patrick's Purgatory*, p. 45.

45. Pedro Calderón de la Barca, *El Purgatorio de San Patricio* (ca. 1634; originally published 1636), ed. J. M. Ruano de la Raza (Liverpool: Liverpool University Press, 1988). See other Spanish texts, summarized in Sullivan, *Grotesque Purgatory*.

46. Cotton manuscript, lines 37–44. Note the alternative reading of the second line, in the Yale manuscript: "As it is written in the story" (Easting, *St. Patrick's Purgatory*, pp. 38–39).

   In Marie de France's version, the skeptics ask to see the joys as well as the pains:

> Quant seinz Patriz aveit parlé
> a cele gent, e demustré
> de Deu la grant puissance veire,
> n'i aveit nul ki volsist creire
> s'il ne mustrast certeinement
> qu'il veïssent apertement:
> les joies dunt il a mustré
> e les peines dunt a parlé.

(Marie de France, *Saint Patrick's Purgatory: A Poem*, ed. and trans. Michael J. Curley [Binghamton: Medieval and Renaissance Texts and Studies, 1993], lines 265–72).

47. Charlotte d'Evelyn and Anna J. Mill, eds., *The South English Legendary*, Early English Text Society, o.s., 235 (London: Oxford University Press, 1956), lines 45 ff. Jones notes wryly a parallel with Ulysses, who in legend had created a cave by tracing it with his sword (*Saint Patricks Purgatory*, p. 44). Easting notes (*St. Patrick's Purgatory*, p. 196) that the staff was a prized relic—it is mentioned as such in the Auchinleck MS—but was publicly burned in Dublin in 1538.

48. In other accounts Owein was born in Ireland, which he had left in order to follow King Stephen of England to war.

49. Thomas McAlindon, "Comedy and Terror in Middle English Literature: The Diabolical Game," *Modern Language Review* 60 (1965): 323–32.

50. Himmelfarb, *Tours of Hell*.

51. The otherworld is, as Aron Gurevich observes, "an aggregate of disconnected places (hills, valleys, swamps, pits, buildings, etc.); they are divided by unexplained voids unevenly surmounted in the narrative" (Aron Gurevich, *Medieval Popular Culture: Problems of Belief and Perception*, ed. Peter Burke and Ruth Finnegan, trans. Janos M. Bak and Paul A. Hollingsworth, Cambridge Studies in Oral and Literate Culture, vol. 14, [Cambridge: Cambridge University Press, 1988]).

52. In Matthew Paris's account Owein returns to be a monk and interpreter in the Lough Derg abbey.

53. "Quae sunt qui dicunt quod Aulam ingressus in extasin fuerat raptus, & haec omnia in spiritu viderat quod nequaquam contigisse, Miles certissime affirmat, sed corporeis occulis se omnia vidide & corporaliter pertulisse constantissime testatur" (trans. Jones, *Saint Patricks Purgatory*, p. 85). There are equivalent passages in the *Owayne Miles*: the demons tell that knight that he "was comen with flesche and fel / To fechen him the ioie of Helle" (54.4–5), and "He was deliuerd from the fendes turment, / Quic man into that plas" (139.5–6).

54. Roger of Wendover, *Flowers of History*, trans. J. A. Giles, quoted in Robert Easting, "The English Tradition," in Haren and de Pontfarcy, *The Medieval Pilgrimage*, p. 61.

55. In the other extant text, the date, given with equal specificity, is Friday, September 20, 1409. "The Vision of William Stranton," in Easting, *St. Patrick's Purgatory*, pp. 78–79. Easting prints two fifteenth-century texts of this vision, BL MS Royal 17 B xliii and BL MS Additional 34.193. Unless otherwise noted, I cite Additional.

56. The contrast here is with Owein, about whom we are told only that he sees some of his acquaintance.

57. "Telle also for the bet, / Matrymony yet t'1ow haue let" (John Mirk, *Instructions for Parish Priests*, ed. Edward Peacock, 2d ed., Early English Text Society, o.s., 31 [London: Kegan, Paul, Trench, Trübner, 1868, rev. 1902], lines 1381–82).

58. "The Vision of William Stranton," in Easting, *St. Patrick's Purgatory*, p. 101.

59. William repeatedly has the experience of forgetting his prayers, during moments of terror, and then, recalled to the right way to deal with the challenge, he "marks" himself with his prayers. In a fusion of word and sign, "mark" here has the force of making the sign of the cross on one's forehead. See the Italian pilgrim to Saint Patrick's Purgatory, Antonio Mannini, in 1411: "The bearer of this will tell you how I came out marked, for I shewed him that he might tell you; perhaps I shall bear the mark for ever" (Leslie, *Saint Patrick's Purgatory*, p. 39).

60. In *Grotesque Purgatory*, Sullivan claims that the *Tractatus* had at least an indirect influence on a literary work far greater than any of these: Cervantes' *Don Quixote*.

61. According to Le Goff, "Purgatory did not exist before 1170 at the earliest" (*The Birth of Purgatory*, p. 135; cf. also pp. 149, 163).

62. Indeed, as Le Goff remarks, "the success of Purgatory was contemporary with the rise of the narrative" (ibid., p. 291). The historian is speaking here not of such works as *Saint Patrick's Purgatory* but of the principle of narrative itself as it is manifested in a theological doctrine that assumes a succession of individual experiences in time. Purgatory, he argues, "introduced a plot into the story of individual salvation. Most important of all, the plot continued after death" (292). For souls in Heaven and Hell there is no narrative, properly speaking, since they no longer exist in time but have been translated into eternity. By contrast, with its graded process of punishments and cleansing, its story of progress toward salvation, its "temporary fire," Purgatory virtually requires a narrative account of the soul's fate in the afterlife. The phrase "temporary fire" comes from the pontifical definition of 1254, which Le Goff calls "the birth certificate of Purgatory as a doctrinally defined place" (284).

63. Cotton MS in Easting, *St. Patrick's Purgatory*, lines 57–64.

64. See Easting, *St. Patrick's Purgatory*, p. 196n. Cf. J. Healy, *The Life and Writings of St. Patrick* (Dublin, 1905), pp. 633–36.

65. Elaine Scarry, *Dreaming by the Book* (New York: Farrar, Straus, Giroux, 1999), p. 16.

66. On the ways in which space was constituted in the Middle Ages, see Paul Zumthor, *La Mésure du monde: Représentation de l'espace au Moyen Age* (Paris: Seuil, 1993).

67. "Through a mimesis of givenness," writes Elaine Scarry, "the quality of instruction in a poem of prose narrative brings about a radical change from daydreaming to vivid image-making" (*Dreaming by the Book*, p. 31). "Givenness" here is nothing more or less than the ordinary condition of perception: we do not look about us at the world with a sense that we are free to make up what we are perceiving. Writers produce this effect of perception, Scarry argues, by suppressing an awareness of volition, directing the movements of the mind, providing detailed instructions for what you are to imagine that you see. "The 'instructional' character is key, because it allows the image to seem to come into being by an agency not one's own" (244).

68. Kircher's device turns Scarry's example of the magic lantern, meant only to affirm the reality of the underlying wall, inside out: the wall is mere dross, but the reality is the burning soul. Still, Scarry's analysis of perceptual mimesis may help us to grasp the principle here. Why, she asks, "when the lights go out and the storytelling begins, is the most compelling tale (most convincing, most believable) a ghost story?" After all, she continues,

> Since most of us have no experience of ghosts in the material world, this should be the tale we least easily believe. The answer is that the story instructs its hearers to create an image whose own properties are second nature to the imagination; it instructs its hearers to depict in the mind something thin, dry, filmy, two-dimensional, and without solidity. Hence the imaginer's conviction: we at once recognize, perhaps with amazement, that we are picturing, if not with vivacity, then with exquisite correctness, precisely the thing described. (Ibid., pp. 23–24)

From this perspective it may have been easier than we initially supposed to instruct a large number of medieval people on how to imagine the afterlife. They had only to take on faith, as it were, narrative's default mode.

69. The promise, explicit in the *South English Legendary* version (d'Evelyn and Mill, *The South English Legendary*), is repeatedly challenged. On Lough Derg as a pilgrimage site, see Haren and de Pontfarcy, *The Medieval Pilgrimage;* Jones, *Saint Patricks Purgatory;* Victor and Edith Turner, *Image and Pilgrimage in Christian Culture: Anthropological Perspectives* (New York: Columbia University Press, 1978).

70. Quoted by Jones, *Saint Patricks Purgatory,* p. 61.

71. "This place is called St. Patrick his Purgatory of the inhabitors," Holinshed continues (Leslie, *Saint Patrick's Purgatory,* p. 45).

72. Borrowed, as skeptics observed, from legends associated with Trophonius's cave; cf. Erasmus, quoted in Jones, *Saint Patricks Purgatory,* pp. 46 ff.

73. Leslie, *Saint Patrick's Purgatory,* p. 28.

74. Sullivan: "The popularity of Patrick's shrine withered with the Italian Renaissance and, after a high-minded Dutch Augustinian protested the place's blatant traffic in sacred objects in 1494, the pit was broken up by edict of Pope Alexander VI in 1497" (*Grotesque Purgatory,* p. 71).

75. John of Trevisa translates a passage from Ranulph Higden's *Polychronicon*—"He telleth that who so suffereth the paines of that Purgatory, if it be enjoyned him for penance, he shall never suffer the paines of Hell, but he shall die finally without repentance of sinne . . ." (Jones, *Saint Patricks Purgatory,* p. 49)—and then comments tartly, "But truly no man may be saved, but if he be very repentant whatsoever penance he doe. And every man that is very repentant at his lives end shall be sickerly saved, though he never heare of Saint Patricks Purgatory" (cited in Easting, *St. Patrick's Purgatory,* p. 197). The force of the popular idea is explained, at least by Jones, as a response to the inherent unfairness of the doctrine of suffrage, as favoring the rich (Jones, *Saint Patricks Purgatory,* pp. 62–63).

76. Leslie, *Saint Patrick's Purgatory,* p. 40.

77. Jones, *Saint Patricks Purgatory*, pp. 119–20.

78. The uneasiness does not only concern Saint Patrick's Purgatory. In his colloquy *On Exorcism*, More's friend Erasmus provides a deeply skeptical analysis of the way in which eyewitness testimony of spiritual wonders is generated.

79. Leslie, *Saint Patrick's Purgatory*, p. 43

80. Ibid., p. 45.

81. Veron, *The Hunting of Purgatorye to Death*, fols. 174v–175r.

82. Noel Taillepied, *A Treatise of Ghosts*, trans. Montague Summers (London: Fortune Press, 1588), 145.

83. Veron, *The Hunting of Purgatorye to Death*, fol. 175r.

84. Ibid., fols. 175v–176r.

85. Thomas Dekker, *The Honest Whore, Part Two*, in *The Dramatic Works of Thomas Dekker*, ed. Fredson Bowers (Cambridge: Cambridge University Press, 1955), 1.1.40–44. Dekker repeats the same feeble joke in *The Welsh Embassador* and refers to Saint Patrick's Purgatory again in *Old Fortunatus*.

86. Ralph Knevet, "Securitye," in *The Shorter Poems of Ralph Knevet*, ed. Amy C. Charles (Columbus: Ohio State University Press, 1966), lines 7–12.

87. Jones, *Saint Patricks Purgatory*, p. 128.

88. Ibid., p. 129.

89. Ibid., pp. 133–34. For an attempt at remystification, see the account from the Jesuit mission in Ireland, 1651—referring to the Parliamentary depradations: "The Franciscan Brethren were ejected, who had the care of the sacred place, and the crypt itself or Purgatory was defiled with muck that no insult might be missing, and then filled in with earth and stones: all were smitten in their hinder parts and in a few days they had perished of dysentery and the foulest flux" (Leslie, *Saint Patrick's Purgatory*, p. 103).

CHAPTER THREE: THE RIGHTS OF MEMORY

1. On ghosts, see Jean-Claude Schmitt, *Ghosts in the Middle Ages: The Living and the Dead in Medieval Society*, trans. Teresa Lavender Fagan (Chicago: University of Chicago Press, 1998). Jean Delumeau, *Sin and Fear: The Emergence of a Western Guilt Culture, Thirteenth–Eighteenth Centuries*, trans. Eric Nicholson (New York: St. Martin's Press, 1990), p. 37, quotes a sonnet entitled "Des esprits des morts," composed by Ronsard's secretary, Amadis Jamyns (1540–1593):

    The Shadows, the Spirits, the ghastly Images
    Of the Dead, burdened with sins, wander in the night:
    And to show the grief and the evil that afflict them
    They make the silence moan with their long and piteous voices
    For they are deprived of the rapturous delights
    Which attend the soul, after death, in Paradise,
    Banished from the day, they make noise in the shadows,
    Begging for help for their shameful sufferings.

2. See Thomas Hohmann, ed., *Heinrichs von Langenstein "Unterscheidung der Geister": Lateinisch (De discretione spirituum) und deutsch* (Munich: Artemis Verlag, 1977), and Paschal Boland, *The Concept of "Discretio Spirituum" in John Gerson's "De probatione spirituum" and "De distinctione verarum visionum a falsis"* (Washington: Catholic University of America Press, 1959).

3. Schmitt, *Ghosts in the Middle Ages*, p. 158.

4. Ibid., p. 224.

5. Ibid., p. 136.

6. Jacques Chiffoleau, *La Comptabilité de l'Au-Delà: Les hommes, la mort et la réligion dans la région d'Avignon à la fin du Moyen Age (vers* 1320–*vers* 1480), vol. 47, *Collection de l'Ecole Française de Rome* (Rome: Ecole Française de Rome, 1980).

7. Jean Gobi, *Dialogue avec un Fantôme*, ed. and trans. Marie-Anne Polo de Beaulieu (Paris: Les Belles Lettres, 1994), pp. 36, 68. For a detailed analysis of the early transmission and elaboration of the report, see Marie Anne Polo de Beaulieu, "De la Rumeur aux Textes: Echos de l'apparition du revenant d'Alès (après 1323)," in *La Circulation des Nouvelles au Moyen Age*, XXIVe Congres de la S.H.M.E.S., juin 1993 (Avignon, Série Histoire Ancienne et Mediévale—29 / Collection de l'Ecole Française de Rome—190), (Paris: Sorbonne, 1994), pp. 129–56.

8. In Gobi, *Dialogue avec un Fantôme*, Beaulieu observes that the mention of the mayor of Alès, along with other details added to the original first-person deposition, indicates the presence of another, second author of the longer treatise, one who was unfamiliar with the town and the region (for, among other things, Alès had no mayor). The evidence for Italian authorship of the longer treatise is the insertion of two prominent mentions of Bologna in the ghost's responses.

9. Both English texts report that the noises continued for eighteen days, but the Latin versions both of Jean Gobi's deposition and of the treatise specify eight days. Guido of Alet, *The Gast of Gy, Eine englische Dichtung des* 14. Jahrhunderts, ed. Gustav Schleich, in *Palaestra*, ed. Alois Brandl and Erich Schmidt (Berlin: Mayer & Müller, 1898). All quotations from the verse *The Gast of Gy* are to this text. All quotations from the Middle English prose version are to Guido of Alet, *The Gast of Gy: A Middle-English Religious Prose Tract Preserved in Queen's College, Oxford, MS.* 383, ed. R. H. Bowers, in *Beitrage zur Englischen Philologie* (Leipzig: Bernhard Tauchwitz, 1938).

10. In the verse version, the widow *hopes* it is her husband's ghost, since whoever it is is haunting her bed:

> And how scho hoped ryght wyterly,
> It was þe gast of hir lord Gy;
> For in þat chaumbre oft herd was he,
> Whare hir lord was wont to be;
> To spyll þat bed wald he noght blyn,
> Þat Gy, hir lord, and scho lay in.

(Lines 71–76)

11. The verse version uses similar language. The prior obtains armed men to accompany him

> To Gy hows, þat was newly dede,
> To se þa wonders in þat stede.

(Lines 123–24)

The sight of the widow writhing in anguish is terrible,

> Bot neuer þe less all men, þat myght,
> Assembled for to se þat syght
> And persued vnto þat place;
> For þai wald witt þat wonder case.

(Lines 1357–60)

12. "In the yere of his incarnacioun a Ml.CCC.xxx. and iij. wolde shewe siche an vntgaliliche) myracle thurg his ordynaunce. so that we miyt haue gretter certeyn of the lyf that is to come" (18). The reference to Augustine is to the *Liber de fide ad Petrum*; the actual source of the definition is *De credendi utilitate*.

13. Cf. the similar paradox in the verse version:

> "Dame," he said, "ne dred þe noght,
> For out of bale þou sall be broght;
> And haue na meruail in þi mynde
> Of cases, þat falles omang mankynde,
> Forwhi," he said, "als kennes þir clerkes,
> God is wonderfull in his werkes."

(Lines 85–90)

The translations are attempting to render the similar paradox in the Latin: "Non mireris de isto casu, quia dominus mirabilis eset in operibus suis" (*De Spiritu Guidonis*, in Schleich, *The Gast of Gy*, 5n).

14.
> When þe mayre had herd þis thing,
> Twa hundreth men sone gert he bring
> And armed þam fra top to ta
> And bad þam with þe pryor ga:
> "And baynly do, what he will byd!"
> And, als he bad, ryght swa þai dyd.

(Lines 129–34)

15. Schmitt, *Ghosts in the Middle Ages*, pp. 147–48.

16. "The spirit of the young man from Apt of whom Gervase of Tilbury speaks even had the gift of ubiquity: at the same moment he appeared to a priest who was taking a nap on the left bank of the Rhone, and to his young cousin in Beaucaire, on the right bank" (ibid., p. 179).

17. "And all, þat þan wald howsell take / He howsyld sone for godes sake" (lines 143–44).

18. "For cristen saules both more and lesse" (line 140).

19. "And in his mynde þan toke he Gy / And prayd for him full specially" (lines 141–42).

20. "And the priour toke priuely with hym. þat no man wiste; the box wiþ goddis fleisch and his blood. and hongid hit priuely bifofe his breest vndir his scapello-rie als worschipfully as he mygt" (lines 47–50).

21.
      Þe woman was full mased and mad,
      Scho trembyld þan, so was scho rad;
      Vnto þe bed sone scho him tald,
      Þe care was at hir hert full cald;
      Bot in hir wa yhit als scho was,
      Scho said: "Sir pryor, or yhe pas,
      I pray yhow for þe luf of me
      And als in dede of charyte,
      Þat yhe wald byd som haly bede
      And mak prayers in þis stede
      For his saule, þat noble man."

(Lines 183–93)

22.
      A febyll voyce þan might þai ken
      Als of a child sayand: "Amen."

(Lines 209–10)

23. "som gastly thing" (line 232)—"gastly" here probably has its current sense of "horrible," as well as the sense of both "spiritual" (as opposed to material) and spectral.

24. "Whether ertow ane ill gast or a gud?" (line 237).

25. "I am a gud gast" (line 250).

26. "I am euyl for mine euil dede" (line 251).

27. "And y am a wickid goost. as vnto my wickid payne þat y suffre" (line 87).

28.
      All payn es gud (þat proue I þe),
      Þat ordaind es in gud degre

(Lines 259–60)

29.
      Þe saules in hell may I noght se:
      I was neuer þare ne neuer sall be;
      Ne in to heuen may I noght wyn,
      Till I be clensed clene of syn.

(Lines 437–40)

30.
      And I am sett for sertaine space,
      Till god will gyf me better grace,
      Þus for my syns to suffer payne.

(Lines 489–91)

The fact that the ghost is condemned to suffer for a finite and not an eternal term—a point resonant for an understanding of the ghost in *Hamlet*—is repeat-edly stressed in *The Gast of Gy*. Hence, for example, this way of characterizing purgatorial spirits as temporarily "evil":

      And þai er euell for certayne space,
      Þat suffers payne in any place

> For þair syns, þat es to say,
> Till tyme þat þai be wasted oway.
>
> > (Lines 393–96)

31.   Þarfor es no lyknes to tell
>   Betwene me and þe fendes in hell.
>
> > (Lines 523–24)

32.   Þe voyce answerd on þis manere
>   And said: "Þare er purgatoryes sere:
>   Ane es comon to mare and les,
>   And departabill ane other es."
>
> > (Lines 537–40)

The claim is reiterated later in the text, without a challenge, when the ghost tells the prior that after death a soul learns whether he is judged to Heaven, to Hell or

> To comon Purgatory, þat es stabyll,
> Or vnto Purgatory departabyll.
>
> > (Lines 1563–64)

The notion of a double Purgatory is found as well in Richard Rolle's *The Pricke of Conscience*:

> Yhit says þir grete clerkes namly,
> Þat twa stedes er of purgatory;
> Þe tane es comon, als yhe herd me telle,
> Þat with-in erthe es, oboven helle;
> And þe togher es speciele, thurgh grace,
> Þat es oboven erthe, in sere place.
> For in þe comon stede som er noght ay,
> Bot er here punyst, outher nyght or day,
> In sere stedes specialy in gast,
> Whar þai haf synned in body mast.
> And þat may be thurgh helpe and spede
> Of prayer of frendes and almusdede,
> Til wham þai ofte in gast apere,
> Thurgh speciel grace, in sere stedes here,
> For to hast þair deliverance
> Out of þair payne and þair penaunce,
> Þat, als I ar sayde, gretely greves,
> And for warnyng of frendes þat lyefes.
>
> > (Lines 2872–89)

Richard Rolle de Hampole, *The Pricke of Conscience (Stimulus Conscientiae)*, ed. Richard Morris (Berlin: A. Asher & Co., 1863). I am grateful to Professor H. A. Kelly for calling this passage to my attention.

33. Quoted in Jacques Le Goff, *The Birth of Purgatory*, trans. Arthur Goldhammer (Chicago: University of Chicago Press, 1981), p. 92.

34. There was a fundamental tension in the church's position: on the one hand, medieval theologians wished to assert that all souls were purged in the prison house of Purgatory; on the other hand, they wished to acknowledge and to lay claim to at least some of the many reports of ghosts who appeared on earth. Hence the latent contradiction in a conventional summary like that of Noel Taillepied, *A Treatise of Ghosts* (1588), trans. Montague Summers (London: Fortune Press, 1933). The great Schoolmen, Taillepied writes, "are unanimously agreed and plainly write that there are four places or states whereunto the souls of men at death repair": "Heaven, Hell, Limbo (for unbaptized infants), and Purgatory." But a moment later, he adds: "Now besides this realm of Purgatory it sometimes pleases the hidden counsels of God that for certain mysterious reasons disembodied souls endure their Purgatory, either among mountains or in waters, or in valleys, or in houses, and particularly are they attached to those spots where on earth they sinned and offended God" (147–48). Allusions to "hidden counsels" and "mysterious reasons" are almost always the mark of doctrinal incoherence.

35. Chiffoleau characterizes Jean Gobi's deposition as a "domestication" of the haunting: "L'exorcisme récupérateur de Jean Gobi consiste à faire discourir le revenant, à le changer en un esprit bavard et raisonneur" (*La Comptabilité de l'Au-Delà*, p. 405). This taming of the wildness of the folkloric materials is certainly present, and perhaps reinforced, in the longer version of the encounter, but the "domestic" has its own peculiar gravitational force, not entirely swept up in the self-justifying rituals of the church.

36. The Virgin will speak to the demons, the Gast of Gy reports, in the following terms:

> "Mayden and moder both am I
> Of Jesu, my son, god allmyghty,
> And of heuen am I coround quene
> And lady of all þe erth bidene,
> And I am emperys of hell,
> Whare yhe and other deuels dwell.

(Lines 715–20)

37. The ghost supports this claim with Jesus' own words from Matt. 12:34:

> If any man outher ald or yhing
> Of ane other suld ask a thing,
> What thing so lygges his hert most nere,
> Þat in his speche sall fyrst appere
> And first be in his wordes allways;
> For god þus in his gospell says:
> "Ex habundancia cordis os loquitur:
> Of þe fulnes of þe hert
> Spekes þe mowth wordes smert."

(Lines 825–33)

38.
> All if þine office ordaind ware
> For cristen saules, als þou said are,

290 NOTES TO CHAPTER THREE

> Þou toke with gud deuocioune
> Of þe haly gast ane orysoune,
> And þat ilk orysoune, for certayne,
> Alegged me mare of my payne
> Þan all þe other, þat þou sayd
> (For tyll all saules þai war puruayd);
> And, sen þat helped me all ane
> Wele mare þan þe other ilk ane,
> Of þe haly gast, I say, þou sang:
> If þou me wyte, þou has þe wrang.

(Lines 891–902)

39. The latter question was the object of considerable controversy during the papacy of John XXII, and the ghost here is upholding the Dominican position against that taken by the pope. See Bowers, *The Gast of Gy*, p. 26 n. 25, and Schleich, *The Gast of Gy*, p. 165, note to lines 769 ff.

40. It is noteworthy that both the prose and verse texts of *The Gast of Gy* leave out a feature, present in the deposition itself and in the expanded Latin treatise, that restores to the prior some of his tattered moral authority. The prior asks if the indulgences that he has acquired for the relief of his own postmortem sufferings are transferable; that is, can he voluntarily strip them from himself and confer them upon the ghost? The ghost answers in the affirmative, whereupon the prior makes him a generous gift of one entire year's accumulated indulgences. This pious act echoes that attributed to Christina of Saint-Trond in Thomas de Cantimpré's thirteenth-century *Life of Christina the Astonishing*. When Louis, count of Looz, died, Christina (1150–1224) obtained from God the right to suffer in her own body half of the purgatorial torments that were due to him. "Having taken on these burdens," we are told, "for a long time afterwards you might have seen Christina in the middle of the night being tormented with burning smoke and at other times with freezing cold" (Thomas de Cantimpré, *The Life of Christina the Astonishing*, trans. Margot H. King, 2d ed. [Toronto: Peregrina, 1999], p. 69). Cf. Robert S. Sweetman, "Thomas of Cantimpré, Mulieres Religiosae and Purgatorial Piety: Hagiographical Vitae and the 'Beguine Voice,'" in *A Distinct Voice: Medieval Studies in Honor of Leonard E. Boyle O.P.*, ed. Jacqueline Brown and William P. Stoneman (Notre Dame, Ind.: University of Notre Dame Press, 1997), pp. 606–28.

41. Bowers, *The Gast of Gy*, p. 15.

42.   So Ragget, so Rencht, so elyng, so vuel,
> As hidous to bi-holden as helle-deuel;
> Mouth and Moose, Eres and Eyes,
> Fflaume al ful of furi liyes.

(Lines 63–66)

(Carl Horstmann, ed., *The Minor Poems of the Vernon MS.*, Part 1, Early English Text Society, o.s., 98 [London: Kegan Paul, Trench, Trübner, 1892], pp. 260 ff.)

43. "a trewe trentel / Of ten cheef festes of al the yer" (ibid., lines 106–7).

44. The story seems to bear witness not only to the effectiveness of the trental but also to the pope's astounding holiness, since it apparently suffices to keep his mother from the eternal torment she would appear to deserve. For a variant that does not concede so happy an outcome, see a Middle English sermon that tells the story of a priest who devoutly sings masses and does other good deeds for seven years on behalf of the soul of his mother. One day, alone in church and busy with his prayers, he greatly desires to know how his mother is faring, when suddenly a horrible, ugly shadow appears to him and says, "I am thi modere, and I am perpetually dampned." The priest asks, "Where be all the good deeds that thou did in thy life, and where is all the rewards of all the masses that I sung for thee and other good deeds that I have done for thee?" The horrible figure answers, "That thou dud for me, itt shall aveyll the sowles in purgatory, and ther-fore thou shalte haue thin mede." But for her they can do nothing because in her youth she had committed adultery and then for shame had never confessed her sin. (See Woodburn O. Ross, ed., *Middle English Sermons*, Early English Text Society, o.s., 209 [London: Oxford University Press, 1940], p. 183.)

45. Cf. Taillepied, *A Treatise of Ghosts*: "A ghost will naturally, if it is possible, appear to the person whom he has most loved whilst on earth, since this person will be readiest to carry out any behest or fulfill any wish then communicated by the departed" (95).

46. These feelings are resolved into a series of pious actions, culminating in the three hundred masses that the widow arranges to be said on a single day for her husband's soul:

> And, so when that they sungen were,
> The gast of Gy grieved her no more.
>
> (Lines 1883–84)

The efficacy of the church's practice is thus affirmed. Yet in three separate accounts of the ghost's vanishing, *The Gast of Gy* is careful to mark a certain tension or at least a measure of distance between the suffering soul and the institution that is essential to salvation. This distance seems to be a way of highlighting the emotional intimacy that lies at the heart of the experience of mourning, an intimacy that the doctrine wisely does not attempt to efface. In the first account, at the end of the long sequence of questions and answers, the prior is allowed one last expression of skepticism about the ghost's nature. You seem to have been able to hear our speech, he remarks to the voice, and the voice replies, "Yea, for certain" (line 1897). Then you have ears, the prior quickly counters, and are therefore "a bodily thing / And not ghostly, as thou has told" (lines 1900–1901). The voice once again cites Scripture against his interrogator: the spirit inspires where it will and you may hear its voice, but you do not know where it comes from or where it is going. "And right as he these words gan say, / Suddenly he went away" (lines 1909–10).

The second account, on the Feast of the Epiphany, marks the tension between the prior and the ghost still more sharply. When the prior asks how many popes there shall be from this time until the Day of Judgment, the ghost rebuffs the question and dismisses the questioners:

> And therefore may ye now each one,
> Whereso ye will, wend forth your way.
>
> (Lines 2036–37)

He adds an appeal for prayers, both for himself and for all souls that suffer pain, but the appeal turns immediately into a reproach. "Holy Church prays not so fast / For Christian souls" (lines 2041–42) as it once did, and religious men should mend their ways quickly, before evil befalls them. Having said these words, the voice again falls silent, this time forever. For the third account of the ghost's disappearance is only confirmation of its silence. At Easter the pope sends his men "to seek the sooth of this" (line 2056), that is, to investigate further the truth of the haunting, but in "the house of Gy" they find no trace of the ghost. They conclude—as the ghost himself had predicted—that Gy's spirit has ascended to heaven "where comfort is withouten care" (line 2061). The end is a happy one in which the church can claim to have played an important role, but the ghost's parting words remain a reproach and a warning.

47. Cf. William Henry Schofield, *Mythical Bards and the Life of William Wallace*, Harvard Studies in Comparative Literature, 5 (Cambridge: Harvard University Press, 1920), pp. 26–54.

48.   And sumetyme lyke ane feind, transfigurate,
            And sumetyme lyke the greislie gaist of Gye;
            In divers formis oft-tymes disfigurate,
            And sumtyme dissagysit full plesandlye.

(Ibid., pp. 42–43, citing Eyre-Todd, *Scottish Poetry of the Sixteenth Century* [Glasgow: Hodge, 1892], p. 29.)

49. "What is all the legend of fictitious miracles in the lives of the saints; and all the histories of apparitions and ghosts alleged by the doctors of the Roman Church, to make good their doctrines of hell and purgatory, the power of exorcism, and other doctrines which have no warrant, neither in reason nor Scripture; as also all those traditions which they call the unwritten word of God; but old wives' fables?" Thomas Hobbes, *Leviathan*, ed. C. B. Macpherson (London: Penguin, 1968), p. 702. Hobbes concedes that there are stories dispersed in the writings of the church fathers that support a belief in apparitions from the dead, but their prevalence indicates only that the early fathers were too prone to believe false reports: "Gregory the Pope and St. Bernard have somewhat of apparitions of ghosts that said they were in purgatory; and so has our Bede: but nowhere, I believe, but by report from others. But if they, or any other, relate any such stories of their own knowledge, they shall not thereby confirm the more such vain reports, but discover their own infirmity or fraud" (702–3).

50. John Foxe, "The Story of Simon Fish," in *The Complete Works of St. Thomas More*, ed. Frank Manley, Germain Marc'hadour, Richard Marius, and Clarence Miller (New Haven: Yale University Press, 1990), Appendix D, 7:441. Elsewhere Foxe remarks simply that copies of the Beggar's Supplication "were strewed abroad in the streets of London and also before the king" (*Acts and Monuments*, ed. George Townsend, 8 vols. [New York: AMS Press, 1965], 4:666).

51. In the event, the interrogation, according to Foxe, did not take place because Fish's young daughter was ill with plague. Fish himself died of the disease within the year. His wife survived and went on to marry James Bainham, another Protestant who was arrested by More a few years later and burned at the stake.

52. *Utopia*, ed. Edward Surtz, S.J., and J. H. Hexter, in *The Complete Works of St. Thomas More*, vol. 4 (1965), p. 225. "How great and how lazy is the crowd of priests and so-called religious!" (131), More's traveler had earlier exclaimed, in accounting for the grinding poverty in Europe.

53. Ibid., p. 239.

54. *The Supplication of Souls*, in vol. 7 of *The Complete Works of St. Thomas More*, p. 120. All citations are to this edition.

55. More follows Jean Gerson's *Querela defunctorum in igne purgatorio detentorum ad superstites in terra amicos* (1427). See Germain Marc'hadour's introduction to *The Supplication of Souls*, pp. xcvi–ciii.

56. John More's will, signed February 26, 1527, "bestows more money on masses to be said for his soul than on any other purpose: £5 (or more) per year for seven years for two priests studying divinity, one at Oxford the other at Cambridge; an annual obit at St. Lawrence Jewry for ten years; and a trental of masses (in addition to a dirge and requiem) to be said by each of the four orders of friars" (Germain Marc'hadour, "Popular Devotions Concerning Purgatory," in Yale *Supplication of Souls*, Appendix E, pp. 452–53).

57. Jean Molinet (d. 1507), *Complainte des Tresspassés*, has a passage very reminiscent of More's *Supplication*, written only a few years later:

> You rest on silken sheets,
> While we in torment burn and roast;
> The soothing lute lulls you to sleep,
> Most sweetly, while we harshly and most
> Hideously from bed are pressed
> All naked, while you are well dressed;
> We are tortured, and while you laugh, we weep.

(Quoted in Delumeau, *Sin and Fear*, p. 386.)

Cf., similarly, further verses from Molinet, p. 396.

58. Aside from slyly paying tribute to his own clandestine sources of information, More's account carefully sidesteps any claim that the dead might have been able to discover who wrote *A Supplication for the Beggars* by spying on the living. In this caution, More is following Augustine's line of thought in "On Care to Be Had for the Dead" (*De cura pro mortuis*): "So then we must confess that the dead indeed do not know what is doing here . . . : afterwards, however, they hear it from those who from hence go to them at their death; not indeed every thing, but what things those are allowed to make known who are suffering also to remember these things; and which it is meet for those to hear, whom they inform of the same. It may be also, that from the Angels, who are present in the things which are doing here, the dead do hear somewhat, which for each one

of them to hear He judgeth right to Whom all things are subject" (New Advent Catholic Website: http://www.newadvent.org/fathers/1316.html). More imagines, however, that the dead in Purgatory are temporarily in the hands of demons and the devil, not of angels.

59. For More's use of Scripture, see Germain Marc'hadour's introduction to the Yale edition of *The Supplication of Souls*, pp. lxxiv–lxxxvii. An attempt to justify the doctrine of Purgatory only "by natural reason & good phylosophye" (Aiiv) was made by More's brother-in-law, John Rastell, in *A new boke of Purgatory which is a dyaloge & disputacyon betwene one Comyngo an Almayne a Christen man & one Gyngemyn a turke of Machometts law* . . . (London, 1530). The Turk persuades the German, who is rehearsing Protestant objections to Purgatory, that Purgatory must exist.

60. "Purgatory," writes Le Goff, "did not exist before 1170 at the earliest" (*The Birth of Purgatory*, p. 135).

61. Quoted in Yale *Supplication*, p. 368. For "Exorcism," see *The Colloquies of Erasmus*, trans. Craig R. Thompson (Chicago: University of Chicago Press, 1965), pp. 230–37. More himself is thought to be figured in one of the characters in this colloquy.

62. See, similarly, *Speculum Sacerdotale*: a fifteenth-century English collection of "sermones de tempore et de sanctis," of the same type as *Mirk's Festial*. The account of All Souls' Day to help the dead in Purgatory rehearses some of the usual tales of the help that masses, alms, etc. can do for the dead. Such tales function to shore up the doctrine. Edward Weatherly, ed., *Speculum Sacerdotale*, Early English Text Society, o.s., 200 (London: Oxford University Press, 1936).

63. Gobi, *Dialogue avec un Fantôme*, pp. 130–31.

64. Ross, *Middle English Sermons*, pp. 176–77.

65. Schmitt, *Ghosts in the Middle Ages*, p. 219.

66. Quoted in Le Goff, *The Birth of Purgatory*, p. 275.

67. Quoted in ibid., p. 319.

68. Miles Coverdale, *Remains*, ed. George Pearson (Cambridge: Cambridge University Press, 1846), p. 475.

69. *Miscellaneous Writings and Letters of Thomas Cranmer*, ed. John Edmund Cox (Cambridge: Cambridge University Press, 1846), pp. 43–44.

70. The idea, which seems to anticipate Marlowe's Mephostophilis, is quite old. Cf. Hugh Ripelin (thirteenth-century): "[W]e say that demons always carry Hell with them" (quoted in Le Goff, *The Birth of Purgatory*, p. 264).

71. The passage concludes with another conventional misogynistic joke: "Yet hear we sometimes our wives pray for us most warmly. For in chyding with her second husband to spight him withal, God have mercy says she on my first husband's soul, for he was y-wisse an honest man far unlike you. And then marvel we much when we hear they say so well by us. For they were wont to tell us far otherwise" (149).

72. On the close relation between Purgatory and charity, see, for example, Clive Burgess, " 'By Quick and by Dead': Wills and Pious Provision in Late Medieval Bristol," *English Historical Review* 305 (1987): 837–58. Since the prayers of the virtuous poor were thought to be particularly efficacious, the rich in effect purchased them through charitable donations. Doles of bread or money, Burgess points out, invariably accompanied funerals, and the wills of the wealthy often established long-term almsgiving, in the hope and expectation of the beneficiaries's prayers.

73. The ratio deployed here—the worst fire on earth, compared to the fire of otherworld, is as painted fire is to real fire—is traditional. See, for example, Richard Rolle, "To live well":

> For as fire is hatter euerywhore
> Þen is a fire paynted on a wowe:
> right so þo fire is hatter þore
> Þen is þo fire here þat we knowe.

(In *Yorkshire Writers: Richard Rolle and His Followers* [London: Swan Sonnenschein, 1896], lines 97–100.) See, likewise, *The Pricke of Conscience*:

> Wharfor þe payn þat þe saul þar hentes
> Er mare bitter þan alle þe tourmentes
> Þat alle þe marters in erthe tholed,
> Sen God for us boght and sold.
> For þe lest payn of þe payns þar sere
> Es mare þan es þe mast payn here.

Rolle, *The Pricke of Conscience*, lines 2722–27. (Rolle's authorship of this work is now considered doubtful.)

74. *A Disputation of Purgatory*, in *The Works of the English Reformers: William Tyndale and John Frith*, ed. Thomas Russell, 3 vols. (London: Ebenezer Palmer, 1831), 3:183.

75. On poor relief in Tudor England, see Paul Slack, *Poverty and Policy in Tudor and Stuart England* (London: Longman, 1988).

CHAPTER FOUR: STAGING GHOSTS

1. A. L. Rowse, *Tudor Cornwall: Portrait of a Society* (London: Jonathan Cape, 1943), p. 335. Henry Caesar was the brother of Dr. Julius Caesar, an important judge and member of Parliament. At dinner, Rowse writes, Henry Caesar had "maintained the apparition of souls after their departure out of this life, and for proof affirmed that Sir Walter Mildmay was desirous to see Cardinal Pole after his death, and one by conjuration caused the said Cardinal to appear unto Sir Walter. Then the conjurer asked of Sir Walter Mildmay what he did see, and Sir Walter answered him 'a man much like the cardinal' " (335).

2. "Sweet William's Ghost" (appended by Scott to "Clerk Sanders") in *The English and Scottish Popular Ballads*, ed. Francis James Child, pt. 3 (Boston: Houghton Mifflin, 1885), p. 230. In version D of this ballad, the ghost describes various aspects of the afterlife to Margaret.

3. Caesar was suspected of popish leanings when he was still quite young, and he had fled briefly to the Continent. He returned and recanted his errors, but the suspicions persisted for years.

4. Paul Gottschalk, *The Meanings of Hamlet: Modes of Literary Interpretation since Bradley* (Albuquerque: University of New Mexico Press, 1972).

5. Another significant exception, perhaps, is history, not only because they have a place in chronicles influenced by classical precedents but also because in more fanciful narratives, such as *The Mirror for Magistrates*, the ghosts of historical figures relate their own tragic downfalls.

6. *The Tenne Tragedies of Seneca*, pt. 1 (Manchester: The Spenser Society, 1887), p. 212. The appearance of a ghost in this translation may not be an innocent piece of classicizing. Jasper Heywood was a Catholic who lost his fellowship in All Souls' College, Oxford, in the wake of Queen Elizabeth's accession, on the grounds that he refused to conform to the religious changes. Having already been ordained as a priest, he went to Rome and in 1562 became a Jesuit. It is quite possible that he had a charged interest in the existence of ghosts.

7. *The Misfortunes of Arthur*, ed. Brian Joy Corrigan (New York: Garland, 1992), Appendix A, p. 194. The spectators included Queen Elizabeth, before whom the play was performed at Greenwich on February 8, 1587/88. Francis Bacon helped to arrange the dumb shows. Hughes's fellow student, William Fulbecke, tried his hand at alternative speeches by the ghost of Gorlois—evidently, it was a particularly amusing exercise—which Hughes appended to his text.

8. *The Lamentable Tragedy of Locrine*, ed. Jane Lytton Gooch, Garland English Texts 7 (New York: Garland Publishing, 1981), 3.3.34–35.

9. *Antonio's Revenge* (3.1.35–37), in *Selected Plays of John Marston*, ed. Macdonald P. Jackson and Michael Neill (Cambridge: Cambridge University Press, 1986).

10. More precisely, the issue is not specifically *confessional*. See the very full discussion in Eleanor Prosser, *Hamlet and Revenge* (Stanford: Stanford University Press, 1967).

11. Quoted in F. W. Moorman, "The Pre-Shakespearean Ghost," *Modern Literary Review* 1 (1906): 94. A "pilch" is an outer garment. Moorman cites the plays I have discussed in the last paragraph and others, to which may be added many references now easily culled from the Chadwyck-Healey database.

12. The ghost of Sylla, who speaks the prologue of *Catiline*, is directly descended from the Senecan "spright" of Achilles whom Jasper Heywood added to the *Troas*. Heywood's Achilles seems to forget the insubstantiality of ghosts; he claims that "[t]he soil doth shake to bear my heavy foot." Jonson, aware of the absurdity, has Sylla wonder why the soil is *not* shaking: "Do'st thou not feel me, *Rome?* not yet? Is night / So heavy on thee, and my weight so light?" There is a faint suggestion, too, that he is a demon come to possess the soul of the already wicked Catiline: "[I]nto / Thy darker bosom," he declares, "enter Sylla's spirit: / All, that was mine, and bad, thy breast inherit." But Jonson does not succeed in making Sylla's ghost much more than a flat, formal device, a piece of classical machinery: he signals Catiline's passage from merely personal crimes to a more

ambitious project—"The ruin of thy country" (1.1.1 ff.)—and then disappears from the scene, never to return.

In *Poetaster* 3.4 Jonson mocks the whole business of revenge ghosts:

> TVCCA. Nay, thou shalt see that, shall ravish thee anon: prick up thine /
> ears, stinkard: the Ghost, boys. /
> 1. BOY *Vindicta.* /
> 2. BOY *Timoria.* /
> 1. BOY *Vindicta.* /
> 2. BOY *Timoria.* /
> 1. BOY *Veni.* /
> 2. BOY *Veni.* /
> TVCCA. Now, thunder, sirrah, you, the rumbling player.

(In Ben Jonson, *Works*, ed. C. H. Herford and Percy Simpson [1932; Oxford: Clarendon, 1986], 4:252–53.)

13. *The Jew of Malta*, in Christopher Marlowe, *Doctor Faustus and Other Plays*, ed. David Bevington and Eric Rasmussen (Oxford: Clarendon Press, 1995), 2.1.24–30. The haunting of buried treasure is one of the theories that Horatio invokes, when he tries to get the ghost to speak:

> [I]f thou hast uphoarded in thy life
> Extorted treasure in the womb of earth—
> For which, they say, you spirits oft walk in death—
> Speak of it, stay and speak.
>
> (1.1.117–20)

14. *Doctor Faustus* (B-text), in Bevington and Rasmussen, *Doctor Faustus and Other Plays*, 4.1.74–78.

15. *The Historie of the Damnable life and deserved death of John Faustus*, ed. William Rose (Notre Dame: University of Notre Dame Press, 1963), p. 150.

16. Among the very many studies of theatrical ghost lore, two early-twentieth-century essays by F. W. Moorman provide a helpful starting place: "The Pre-Shakespearean Ghost," *Modern Language Review* 1 (1906): 86–95, and "Shakespeare's Ghosts," *Modern Language Review* 1 (1906): 192–201. Marjorie Garber's *Shakespeare's Ghost Writers: Literature as Uncanny Causality* (New York: Methuen, 1987) is particularly rich in insights.

17. Using *Hamlet* as his principal example, Jacques Derrida proposes what he calls a "hauntology," a queasy awareness of a suppressed politics. Derrida's overriding concern is the ghostly presence in contemporary culture of Karl Marx, but his book, *Specters of Marx: The State of the Debt, the Work of Mourning, and the New International*, trans. Peggy Kamuf (New York: Routledge, 1994), has many acute observations about the functioning of the ghost in Shakespeare's play.

18. *The Puritan: or, the Widow of Watling Street* (2.1) in *Disputed Plays of William Shakespeare*, ed. William Kozlenko (New York: Hawthorn Books, 1974), pp. 239–40.

19. See, for examples, the Catholic LeLoyer's extensive rehearsal of all of the ways in which people may be deceived into mistaking the products of their own fear or imagination for ghostly apparitions.

20. See Lodovico Ariosto, *Supposes*, trans. George Gascoigne, ed. Donald Beecher and John Butler, Carleton Renaissance Plays in Translation 33 (Ottawa: Dovehouse Editions, 1999). Cf. Joel Altman, *The Tudor Play of Mind* (Berkeley and Los Angeles: University of California Press, 1978).

21. Shakespeare's interest in this genius or daemon is manifested again in the Soothsayer's advice to Antony that he keep at a distance from Caesar:

> Therefore, O Antony, stay not by his side.
> Thy daemon, that thy spirit which keeps thee, is
> Noble, courageous, high, unmatchable,
> Where Caesar's is not. But, near him, thy angel
> Becomes afeard, as being o'erpowered. Therefore
> Make space enough between you.
>
> (*Antony and Cleopatra*, 2.3.16–21)

22. "Suit" may also have the latent sense of "attendance at court and personal service": Sebastian appears to Viola as someone in the court of Olivia.

23. Charlotte Beradt, *The Third Reich of Dreams*, trans. Adriane Gottwald (Wellingborough, Northamptonshire: Aquarian Press, 1985), pp. 21, 135.

24. A historical account of the Third Reich that strips away the nightmare in order to concentrate on the events themselves risks missing a crucial dimension of the Nazis' peculiar exercise of *Gewaltherrschaft*. The victims' dreams, Reinhart Koselleck argues, "are more than fictional testimony of terror and about terror. . . . They are physical manifestations of terror but without the witnesses having fallen victim to physical violence. In other words, it is precisely as fiction that they are elements of historical reality. . . . Even as apparitions, the dreams are instrumentalizations of terror itself." Reinhart Koselleck, *Futures Past: On the Semantics of Historical Time*, trans. Keith Tribe (Cambridge: MIT Press, 1985), p. 220.

25. There were many means besides terror for obtaining compliant behavior, means that have been amply documented in recent years: cunning lies, clever dangling of false hopes, the exploitation of petty greed, the arousal of a fantasy of special treatment or unusual exemption, the lure of normal assumptions by which certain things could not possibly be envisaged because they made no rational sense. In the company of such strategies, terror had its risks, from the point of view of the perpetrators, since it could trigger desperate acts of resistance. Nonetheless, it came to play an essential role in the organization and execution of the complex scheme of genocide.

26. Terror had the further advantage of inhibiting outright opposition or even simple, modest acts of humanity on the part of those non-Jews—among them congenial colleagues, neighbors, friends of the victims—who were not slated for destruction, and it could attract and excite that part of the population that enjoys the spectacle of terror.

On terror's producing the immobilizing effect of dreams, see the end of *The Aeneid*:

Just as in dreams when the night-swoon of sleep
Weighs on our eyes, it seems we try in vain
To keep on running, try with all our might,
But in the midst of effort faint and fail;
Our tongue is powerless, familiar strength
Will not hold up our body, not a sound
Or word will come: just so with Turnus now. . . .
He trembled now before the poised spear-shaft
And saw no way to escape.

(bk. 12, lines 1232–45; trans. Robert Fitzgerald [New York: Random House, 1983].)

27. Koselleck, *Futures Past*, p. 218. Throughout the 1930s the Nazi regime moved to transform phantasmatic representations—wildly malevolent imaginings recycled in the pages of *Die Stürmer* and the ranting of Hitler and Goebbels—into lived reality. The dreams of the victims work as dreams by reversing this process, transforming lived reality into phantasmatic representation by means of the smallest effects of exaggeration. But this desperate, terrified attempt at reversal was continually outstripped by reality itself. By the time of the extermination camps, exaggeration itself had virtually become impossible, but even in the 1930s reality had taken on a dreamlike horror that frequently edges toward insane comedy, particularly where the dreamers we have quoted find it, in the language of decrees. January 29, 1936: "To avoid giving foreign visitors a negative impression, signs with strong language will be removed. Signs, such as 'Jews are unwanted here,' will suffice." August 17, 1938: "All Jews must adopt the names of 'Israel' for men and 'Sara' for women as additional first names." I recognize that it takes a strong stomach to find the comedy here, but it exists, in the abyss between the formal, normative, and communitarian implications of bureaucratic rationality and a twisted authoritarianism that scarcely bothers to masquerade or justify itself.

28. Shakespeare uses the imagery of vomiting surprisingly often in his work. Still, it is perhaps noteworthy that Clarence's dream of his death agonies is strikingly reminiscent of More's vision of damnation as perpetual seasickness: "But then shall ye sometimes see there some other whose body is so incurably corrupted that they shall walter and totter and wring their hands and gnash the teeth, and their eyes water, their head ache, their body fret, their stomach wamble, and all their body shiver for pain, and yet shall never vomit at all: or if they vomit, yet shall they vomit still and never find ease thereof" (*The Supplication of Souls*, in *The Complete Works of St. Thomas More*, 7:189).

29. It is not my purpose to insist on a close connection between every aspect of Shakespeare's plays, which are not, after all, theological allegories, and the discourse of Purgatory. But there is an obvious parallel here not only to the centrality of fear and guilt but also to the way in which dreams in the religious texts we have examined are said to materialize in bodily suffering.

30. Koselleck, *Futures Past*, p. 219.

31. Edward Hall, *The Union of the Two Noble Famelies of Lancastre and Yorke* (1548), in *Narrative and Dramatic Sources of Shakespeare*, ed. Geoffrey Bullough, 8 vols. (London: Routledge and Kegan Paul, 1975), 3:291. Hall makes a fine distinction here between fear and the imagination, the heart and the head: Richard's terrible dream *almost* "damped" his heart, but its principal effect was to stuff his head and trouble his mind, that is, to poison his imagination. The consequence in the morning was an evident lack of alacrity (a feature that Shakespeare, as we have seen, noticed and borrowed). Richard was sufficiently concerned, in Hall's account, that his appearance might be interpreted as a sign that he was afraid of his enemies that he related to his followers the content of his dream. It was better that the king be thought to be mentally unsettled by shadows than frightened by real soldiers.

32. *The True Tragedy of Richard III*, in Bullough, *Narrative and Dramatic Sources of Shakespeare*, 3:338.

33. Hall, in Bullough, *Narrative and Dramatic Sources of Shakespeare*, 3:291.

34. All citations of *King Lear* are to the Folio text (*The Tragedy of King Lear*) in *The Norton Shakespeare*, ed. Stephen Greenblatt et al. (New York: W. W. Norton, 1997).

35. A few of the effigies may still be seen in Westminster Abbey. See the important discussion in Horst Bredekamp, *Thomas Hobbes, visuelle Strategien der Leviathan: Urbild des modernen Staates* (Berlin: Akademie, 1999).

36. It is perhaps worth noting that Lady Macbeth's term for her husband's terror—the "fit"—is the same term he himself had used when the murderer revealed that Fleance had escaped: "Then comes my fit again." Lady Macbeth had not, of course, overheard Macbeth's soliloquy (we are explicitly told that she is keeping her "state," that is, sitting in her formal place as hostess). The use of the same term could simply be an accident—after all, it is a reasonable word to use for what is going on—but it also serves as a tiny instance of the strange overlapping of consciousness, the presence of one mind within another, that eerily characterizes the relationship between this particular husband and wife.

37. The term "Ghost" is used in the stage directions, which are not, however, reliably attributed to Shakespeare and are not, in any case, part of the audience's information.

38. The following six paragraphs on *Macbeth* are adapted from my essay "Shakespeare Bewitched," in *New Historical Literary Study*, ed. Jeffrey Cox and Larry Reynolds (Princeton: Princeton University Press, 1993), pp. 108–35.

39. The significance of this encounter, principally in *A Midsummer Night's Dream* and *Macbeth*, is discussed in ibid.

40. *The Discoverie of Witchcraft* (London, 1584), p. 258.

41. Ibid., p. 74.

42. To these we can add, by way of *Antony and Cleopatra*, erotic fantasies. In the wake of the report that Cleopatra has killed herself, Antony makes his botched

suicide attempt. As he calls for his aptly named assistant, Eros, to run him through with a sword, Antony imagines his soul rushing to catch up with Cleopatra's in the afterworld.

> Eros!—I come, my queen:—Eros!—Stay for me.
> Where souls do couch on flowers we'll hand in hand,
> And with our sprightly port make the ghosts gaze.
> Dido and her Aeneas shall want troops,
> And all the haunt be ours. Come, Eros, Eros!
>
> (4.15.50–54)

"Dido and her Aeneas": in Antony's erotic imagination, Dido's bitter anger at Aeneas, which continues in Virgil's account into the underworld, has vanished. Instead, there is an ecstatic vision of souls, couched on flowers in an amorous "haunt," bearing witness to a kind of competitive celebrity in love. Characteristically, Shakespeare's play shatters this vision—Cleopatra, who has not in fact killed herself, a few minutes later cravenly refuses to risk her safety in order to give the dying Antony the farewell kiss he craves—and immediately reconstitutes it: "I am again for Cydnus / To meet Mark Antony" (5.2.224–25). At the end of the play, the dead lovers—Cleopatra and "her Antony"—are united by Caesar, in lines that strangely echo the imagery of postmortem celebrity in love, though it is not quite an Elysian couch that Caesar's words invite us to imagine when he tells his followers to "take up" the queen's bed:

> She shall be buried by her Antony.
> No grave upon the earth shall clip in it
> A pair so famous.
>
> (5.2.348–51)

Now that they are safely dead, it suits the coldly calculating Caesar to foster the mythmaking: it confers a certain glamour upon his triumph. But, even as it brilliantly exploits this glamour for its own triumph, Shakespeare's play keeps enough ironic distance to call into question whether such ghosts could exist anywhere but on the stage.

43. "You speak a language that I understand not," Hermione responds to Leontes' accusation; "My life stands in the level of your dreams." "Your actions are my dreams," Leontes replies (3.2.78–80). (The Norton Shakespeare adds scare quotes to Leontes' "dreams," thereby clarifying the dominant sense at the expense of the rich ambiguity of the line.)

44. Paulina continues with a variant of the fantasy:

> Yet if my lord will marry—if you will, sir;
> No remedy but you will—give me the office
> To choose you a queen. She shall not be so young
> As was your former, but she shall be such
> As, walked your first queen's ghost, it should take joy
> To see her in your arms.
>
> (5.1.76–81)

CHAPTER FIVE: REMEMBER ME

1. Thomas Lodge, quoted in *Narrative and Dramatic Sources of Shakespeare*, ed. Geoffrey Bullough, 8 vols. (London: Routledge and Kegan Paul, 1975), 7:24.

2. The passage, from an epistle "To the Gentlemen Students of both Universities" written by Nashe and prefixed to Greene's *Menaphon*, printed in 1589, is worth quoting at length:

> Ile turne backe to my first text, of studies of delight, and talke a little in friendship with a few of our triviall translators. It is a common practice now a daies amongst a sort of shifting companions, that runne through every arte and thrive by none to leave the trade of *Noverint* whereto they were borne, and busie themselves with the indevours of art, that could scarcelie latinize their necke-verse if they should have neede; yet English Seneca read by candle-light yeeldes manie good sentences, as *Blould is a begger*, and so foorth: and if you intreate him faire in a frostie morning, he will affoord you whole *Hamlets*, I should say Handfulls of tragical speaches. But O grief! *Tempus edax rerum;*—what is it that will last always? The sea exhaled by drops will in continuance be drie; and Seneca, let bloud line by line, and page by page, at length must needs die to our stage.

(In *Hamlet: A New Variorum Edition*, ed. Horace Howard Furness, 2 vols. [1877; New York: Dover, 1963], 2:5).

This passage has occasioned mountains of speculation that it refers to Shakespeare, who must have begun, on this evidence alone, as an attorney (*Noverint*) and then turned to the stage, writing an early version of *Hamlet* when he would have been twenty-five years old. In the absence of any corroborating evidence, it seems wiser to conclude only that there was an earlier version of the Hamlet story onstage, that it was a bloody revenge play, and that it clearly struck at least one canny observer, Nashe, as a popular English adaptation of Seneca.

The "neck-verse" to which Nashe alludes is the psalm (in Latin) that prisoners accused of capital crimes would read in an effort to be tried in an ecclesiastical court, where there was no death penalty, rather than in a civil court. See my essay "What Is the History of Literature?" *Critical Inquiry* 23 (1997): 460–81.

3. Saxo Grammaticus, *Historiae Danicae*, trans. Oliver Elton, in Bullough, *Narrative and Dramatic Sources of Shakespeare*, 7:62.

4. Ibid., p. 70.

5. *Fratricide Punished*, translation adapted from H. H. Furness, in Bullough, *Narrative and Dramatic Sources of Shakespeare*, 7:133.

6. Quoted in Furness, *Variorum, Hamlet*, 1:109.

7. Nikolaus Delius makes the interesting observation that Hamlet uses the word "bound" in the sense of *ready addressed*, while the Ghost uses it as the past participle of the verb *to bind* (cited in Furness, *Variorum, Hamlet*, 1:96). The shift, then, is from preparation or expectation to obligation.

8. The Folio text of *Hamlet*, which is the basis for the Oxford edition on which the *Norton Shakespeare* is based, assigns this line to Marcellus, but the hint of skepticism seems to support Q2's assigning it to Horatio.

9. *The Homilies of S. John Chrysostom on the Gospel of St. Matthew* (Oxford: Parker, 1844), pp. 418–19. The image of demonic stage playing is recurrent in earlier church writings. See, for example, Eusebius, *Evangelicae praeparationis (The Preparation for the Gospel)*, ed. and trans. E. H. Gifford (Oxford: Oxford University Press, 1903), bk. 3, chap. 17: "The ministrants of the oracles we must in plain truth declare to be evil daemons, playing both parts to deceive mankind, and at once time agreeing with the more fabulous suppositions concerning themselves, to deceive the common people, and at another time confirming the statements of the philosophers' jugglery in order to instigate them also and puff them up: so that in every way it is proved that they speak no truth at all" (139).

10. The pattern of dual hauntings is described in Jacques Le Goff, *The Birth of Purgatory*, trans. Arthur Goldhammer (Chicago: University of Chicago Press, 1981), p. 294, and in Jean-Claude Schmitt, *Ghosts in the Middle Ages: The Living and the Dead in Medieval Society*, trans. Teresa Lavender Fagan (Chicago: University of Chicago Press, 1998), pp. 201–5.

11. Occasionally, the ghost's "body" or "clothing" upon its return would be only partially white, to indicate how much of the purgatorial sentence had passed and how much still remained to be endured. And there could then be a third apparition—and in theory, at least, others as well—in which more of the clothing would be white, in keeping with the gradual progress of purification.

12. The ghost does not answer; it stalks away, "offended" as Marcellus puts it, by the way Horatio has addressed it. There is scholarly debate about what it is that has offended the ghost. Eleanor Prosser (*Hamlet and Revenge* [Stanford: Stanford University Press, 1967]), who believes that the apparition is demonic, thinks it is offended because Horatio has gone on to invoke Heaven: "By heaven, I charge thee speak." Harold Jenkins thinks that it is because "this interlocutor is not the one it seeks" (*Hamlet*, Arden Shakespeare [London and New York: Metheun, 1982], pp. 168–69), though it is difficult to see why this fact would cause it to feel offended. G. R. Hibbard, glossing the word "usurp'st," writes that "Horatio means that the Ghost has no right to be out at this time of night, and no right to the form it has assumed. It is not, therefore, surprising that this unfortunate victim of usurpation should be *offended*" (*Hamlet*, Oxford Shakespeare, ed. G. R. Hibbard [New York: Oxford University Press, 1994), p. 146). Hibbard's seems to me easily the most plausible explanation, though we have no way of knowing whether Marcellus's assessment is correct.

13. The point is reinforced when we subsequently learn that the king has been dead for more than two months, and still more when we learn that something horrible had happened to the king's skin at the point of his death. The play goes on, of course, to stage a scene of exhumation that vividly depicts various degrees of decay and putrefaction: "My gorge rises at it," Hamlet remarks.

14. *IIII Livres des Spectres ou Apparitions et visions d'Esprits, Anges et Demons se monstrans sensiblement aux hommes*, quoted in John Dover Wilson, *What Happens in "Hamlet"* (1935; Cambridge: Cambridge University Press, 1951), p. 67.

15. In *On Memory*, Aristotle argues that memory, and indeed that all intellectual activity, is impossible without images or phantasms. Aristotle, *On Memory*, in *The*

Complete Works of Aristotle, ed. Jonathan Barnes, 2 vols. (Princeton: Princeton University Press, 1984), 1:714.

16. Furness, *Variorum, Hamlet,* 2:146.

17. Claudius's opening speech, in act 1, scene 2, depicts this preoccupation in direct relation to the accelerated and deliberate dulling of remembrance entailed by his marriage to Gertrude:

> Though yet of Hamlet our dear brother's death
> The memory be green, and that it us befitted
> To bear our hearts in grief and our whole kingdom
> To be contracted in one brow of woe,
> Yet so far hath discretion fought with nature
> That we with wisest sorrow think on him
> Together with remembrance of ourselves.
>
> (1.2.1–7)

Both Horatio and Gertrude confirm Prince Hamlet's own anguished perception that the remarriage was, as Gertrude puts it, "o'er-hasty" (2.2.57).

18. Polonius is willing to stake his head that Hamlet is mad for love, and describes, with the precision of a physician, the progress of the disease:

> And he, repulsèd—a short tale to make—
> Fell into a sadness, then into a fast,
> Thence to a watch, thence into a weakness,
> Thence to a lightness, and, by this declension,
> Into the madness wherein now he raves.
>
> (2.2.146–50)

Ophelia, though with less certainty, concurs:

POLONIUS. Mad for thy love?
OPHELIA. My lord, I do not know,
  But truly I do fear it.

> (2.1.86–87)

Rosencrantz and Guildenstern speculate that Hamlet may be suffering from a kind of political claustrophobia. "To me," Hamlet tells them, Denmark "is a prison." "Why, then your ambition makes it one," Rosencrantz replies; " 'tis too narrow for your mind" (2.2.245–47). Gertrude has a clearer grasp of the sources of her son's distemper:

> I doubt it is no other but the main—
> His father's death and our o'er-hasty marriage.
>
> (2.2.56–57)

19. For brilliant reflections on the path that leads from mourning to anger, see Philip Fisher, "Thinking about Killing: *Hamlet* and the Path among the Passions," *Raritan* 11 (1991): 43–77.

20. Later in the play Laertes similarly embodies the spirit of rash, reckless revenge. In both cases the play suggests the limits of this heroic rashness: Fortinbras's incursion is easily outmaneuvered by Claudius's diplomacy, and Laertes is deftly

turned into Claudius's secret agent. At the same time *Hamlet* does not endorse as an alternative a more sober deliberation: Hamlet praises rashness for saving his life at sea, and his revenge, when it finally does come about, happens as a consequence of unpremeditated actions.

21. Contrast his response to the first haunting: "Angels and ministers of grace defend us!" (1.4.20). It is notable that though the Ghost of old Hamlet, like the ghost of Gy, appears in his widow's closet, he does not appear to his widow or wish to communicate with her. Contrast *The Revelation to the Monk of Evesham Abbey*, ed. Valerian Paget (New York: McBride, 1909): "The same young man witnessed on oath that the third night of his father's appearing, he heard his mother enquiring, and sometimes answering him; and then afterwards she told me the words that he had said to her. The son said he heard no words when his father was speaking to her, but he waited patiently till they had done talking. His mother told him that she had heard from her husband twice before. She acknowledged that her husband was full of wrath, and blamed her because he was forgotten and put out of mind, for, though she was warned by him after his death to do but a little thing for him, yet she had neglected to do even that" (145–46).

22. Furness, *Variorum*, cites *Miscellaneous Observations on "Hamlet"* (1:299).

23. In an eloquent essay that pursues several of the key questions that concern me in this chapter, Anthony Low argues that Hamlet's whole problem is a failure or inability to remember what the Ghost's visit should have prompted him to remember: the obligation to pray for his father's soul in Purgatory. "Hamlet takes his oath to 'remember,' " Low writes, "with reference only to vengeance. He never remarks that to remember the dead in Purgatory means chiefly to pray for them, especially by offering masses for their souls" ("*Hamlet* and the Ghost of Purgatory: Intimations of Killing the Father," *English Literary Renaissance* 29 [1999]: 456). For Low, who unequivocally laments the loss of the Catholic Purgatory, the tragedy is the tragedy of a whole generation's systematic forgetting and hence killing the father. That is, in Low's account, by ceasing to be a Catholic, by forgetting or no longer knowing how to pray for his father's soul, "Hamlet implicates himself, as all the younger generation are unwittingly implicated, in the hidden crime" (465).

24. Francis Bacon, "Of Revenge," in *A Selection of His Works*, ed. Sidney Warhaft (New York: Odyssey, 1965), p. 55.

25. Later in the play Hamlet saves his life by using his father's signet, which he has been carrying in his purse, so that the altered commission, now calling for the deaths of Rosencrantz and Guildenstern, appears to come from the Danish king. Of course, the king in question is now Claudius—and Hamlet explains that the signet was "the model of that Danish seal" (5.2.51) that Claudius had used—but perhaps the fact that Hamlet was carrying the seal is an extension of this will to ventriloquize his father's voice.

26. Johann Wolfgang von Goethe, *Wilhelm Meister's Apprenticeship*, trans. Eric Blackall (Princeton: Princeton University Press, 1989), p. 146.

27. Thomas White, *The Middle State of Souls from the hour of death to the day of judgment* (London, 1659).

28. "Claim" rather than "meaning" because the Ghost may only be lying, luring Hamlet into a belief that Purgatory actually exists and then luring him further toward damnation by inducing him to commit an act of vengeance.

29. See Le Goff, *The Birth of Purgatory*, p. 227.

30. *The Last Judgement* in *The Chester Mystery Cycle* (1475), ed. R. M. Lumiansky and David Mills, Early English Text Society, s.s., 3 (London: Oxford University Press, 1974), p. 441. See, similarly, *A lyttel boke . . . of Purgatorye* (London, [1534?]):

> Betwene the payne of hell / certaynly
> And betwene the payne / of Purgatorye
> Is no dyfference / but certes that one
> Shall haue an ende / and that other none.

(Quoted in Germain Marc'hadour, "Popular Devotions Concerning Purgatory," in the Yale Edition of *The Supplication of Souls*, in *The Complete Works of St. Thomas More*, ed. Frank Manley, Germain Marc'hadour, Richard Marius, and Clarence Miller [New Haven: Yale University Press, 1990], Appendix E, 7: 447.)

31. *Everyman*, in *Medieval Drama*, ed. David Bevington (Boston: Houghton Mifflin, 1975), lines 70–71.

32. Cf. Paget, *The Revelation to the Monk of Evesham Abbey*, p. 141: "I saw numberless people there, who had died suddenly, and who were being punished almost beyond measure." William of Auvergne (regent and master of theology at Paris from 1222 to 1228 and bishop of Paris from 1228 until his death in 1249) argued that Purgatory is a continuation of earthly penance. It is necessary because "those who die suddenly or without warning, for example, 'by the sword, suffocation, or excess of suffering,' those whom death takes unawares before they have had time to complete their penance, must have a place where they may do so" (Le Goff, *The Birth of Purgatory*, p. 242).

33. On the importance of deathbed houseling, for example, see a sermon by John Mirk. A Christian man, dying, sends for the priest to "come to hym wyth Godys body." He receives the sacrament steadfastly believing that it is the real body of Christ, "And so wyth his perfite beleue he armeth hym, and maketh hym strong and myȝty forto aȝenstond þe fendes þat wol assayle hym, when he passeth oute from þe body, in al wyse þat þai con, forto assay, ȝef þei mow bryng hym oute of þe beleue. Then schal þe sacrament þat he receyvet make hym so myghty, þat he schal overcome hem and sett noȝt by hem" (quoted in C. W. Dugmore, *The Mass and the English Reformers* [London: Macmillan, 1958], p. 68). The specificity of the Catholic nature of these last rites is open to debate, since some version of each of them was compatible with Protestantism.

34. Hamlet's "Rest, rest, perturbed spirit" may be compared to the mad Ophelia's prayer for her murdered father: "God 'a' mercy on his soul. / And of all Christian souls, I pray God" (4.5.194–95). What would these prayers have sounded like to Elizabethan ears? "Prayer for the dead was such a deeply engrained practice in mid-Tudor England that it took several decades of preaching and disci-

pline to draw it to a close. Some people believed that the soul still lingered in the vicinity of the body during the first thirty days after burial, a liminal situation requiring great ritual caution. During the Elizabethan period, especially in the early part of the reign, some testators continued to provide for this 'trigintal' period by ordering a black cover for their coffin or grave during this month's mind, or arranging for another service, dole, and funeral feast when it came to an end. Though repudiated by the Reformation, the traditional month-mind and year-mind had a customary half-life in many parts of England as far apart as Lancashire and Essex. Provisions for obits and month-minds and prayers for all Christian souls were not uncommon in wills of the 1550s, 1560s, and 1570s, though heirs and executors were increasingly hard-pressed to carry them out." David Cressy, *Birth, Marriage, and Death: Ritual, Religion and the Life-Cycle in Tudor and Stuart England* (New York: Oxford University Press, 1997), p. 398. Cressy writes, however, that the disciplinary process, though prolonged, was basically completed by the second half of Elizabeth's reign, so Hamlet in 1601 would seem to hark back to a world lost.

35. Quoted in Furness, *Variorum, Hamlet*, 1:111.

36. John Grange, *The Golden Aphroditis* (London, 1577; reprint, New York: Scholars' Facsimiles and Reprints, 1939), fol. Cv.

37. See, however, the speculation in Fr. Christopher Devlin, *Hamlet's Divinity* (London: Rupert Hart-Davis, 1963), pp. 31–32: "One may find another [reference to the Roman Breviary] in Hamlet's first reaction to the Ghost, 'Angels and ministers of grace defend us' (I.iv.39). For the prayer in the Office of St. Michael, 'May we be defended on earth by thy ministers in heaven' is accompanied by an antiphon which invokes the Angelic protection HIC ET UBIQUE (i.V.136). An ironic echoing of the Liturgy may be sufficient explanation of Hamlet's odd irruption in Latinity, 'Hic et ubique!', when the Ghost moans beneath him."

38. "*Pro quiescentibus in cimiterio.*
   Oratio
   Deus, in cujus miseratione animae fidelium requiescunt; animabus famulorum famularumque tuarum omnium, hic et ubique in Christo quiescentium, da propitius veniam peccatorum, ut a cunctis reatibus absoluti, tecum sine fine laetentur. Per Dominum," in *Missale Ad Usum Insignis et Praeclarae Ecclesiae Sarum* [*Missale Sarum*], ed. Francis Dickinson (Oxford: J. Parker, 1861–1883), p. 878. The phrase *hic et ubique* is repeated in the *Secreta* and *Postcommunio* as well.

39. Thomas Rogers, *The Catholic Doctrine of the Church of England* (Cambridge: University Press for the Parker Society, 1882), p. 221.

40. Edgar C. S. Gibson, *The Thirty-Nine Articles of the Church of England*, 2 vols. (London: Methuen & Co., 1897), 2:537.

41. In *The Fate of the Dead: A Study in Folk Eschatology in the West Country after the Reformation* (Ipswich: Rowan and Littlefield, 1979), Theo Brown argues that in repudiating the "Romish doctrine" of Purgatory, the English church had not meant to abolish Purgatory altogether but only the abuses of the doctrine, abuses associated with Rome. The wholesale assault on suffrages for the dead

makes this argument implausible, but, as we have seen, early reformers like Tyndale kept open the imaginative possibility that there might be an unspecifiable process of purgation. It is this imaginative possibility, rather than any practice, that the careful Anglican language seems to preserve—and that Shakespeare, as I have been arguing, realized he could exploit.

42. *Doctor Faustus* (B-text), 3.2.79–81, in Christopher Marlowe, *Doctor Faustus and Other Plays*, ed. David Bevington and Eric Rasmussen (Oxford: Clarendon Press, 1995).

43. Quoted in Bullough, *Narrative and Dramatic Sources*, 7:170–71.

44. The issue has been the subject of extensive scholarly discussion. Arguing for the Catholic position, I. J. Semper has suggested that, under certain circumstances, vengeance could be called for, but there is no evidence that Hamlet's circumstances in any way match those that might possibly justify the assassination of Claudius. See I. J. Semper, *Hamlet without Tears* (Dubuque, Iowa: Loras College Press, 1946). For the dominant counterview, see Prosser, *Hamlet and Revenge*.

45. In the Second Quarto, the spirit that Hamlet has seen may be "a deale [*devil*]." The singular has the effect of individualizing this particular apparition—that is, individual devils, in the service of Satan, could impersonate individuals or inhabit pagan statues.

46. For a sampling, see Dover Wilson, *What Happens in "Hamlet"*; Roy Battenhouse, "The Ghost in *Hamlet*: A Catholic 'Linchpin'?" *Studies in Philology* 68 (1951): 161–92; John Vyvyan, *The Shakespearean Ethic* (London: Chatto and Windus, 1959); Miriam Joseph, "Discerning the Ghost in *Hamlet*," *PMLA* 76 (1961): 302; Christopher Devlin, *Hamlet's Divinity* (Carbondale: Southern Illinois University Press, 1963); Miriam Joseph, "*Hamlet*, a Christian Tragedy," *Studies in Philology* 59 (1962): 119–40; Prosser, *Hamlet and Revenge*; Robert F. Fleissner, "Subjectivity as an Occupational Hazard of 'Hamlet Ghost' Critics," *Hamlet Studies* (New Delhi) 1 (1979): 23–33; Walter N. King, *Hamlet's Search for Meaning* (Athens: University of Georgia Press, 1982), pp. 22–40; Roland Mushat Frye, *The Renaissance "Hamlet": Issues and Responses in* 1600 (Princeton: Princeton University Press, 1984), pp. 11–24.

47. Robert West, among others, has trenchantly argued that "Shakespeare knowingly mixed the evidence and did it for the sake of dramatic impact" (Robert H. West, *Shakespeare and the Outer Mystery* [Lexington: University of Kentucky Press, 1968], p. 63). West notes that quite a few critics have preceded him in this perception.

48. These pages on the Eucharist in *Hamlet* are adapted from the longer and more detailed discussion in my essay "The Mousetrap" in Catherine Gallagher and Stephen Greenblatt, *Practicing New Historicism* (Chicago: University of Chicago Press, 2000).

49. *Hamlet*, The Oxford Shakespeare (Oxford: Oxford University Press, 1987), p. 165.

50. See Alan Kreider, *English Chantries: The Road to Dissolution* (Cambridge: Harvard University Press, 1979).

51. See Robert Whiting, *The Blind Devotion of the People: Popular Religion and the English Reformation* (Cambridge: Cambridge University Press, 1989); Christopher Haigh, *Reformation and Resistance in Tudor Lancashire* (Cambridge: Cambridge University Press, 1975; J.J. Scarisbrick, *The Reformation and the English People* (Oxford: Blackwell, 1984). Many historians agree with Christopher Haigh's summary view that "[f]or much of the reign of Elizabeth, the Church of England was a prescribed, national Church with more-or-less Protestant liturgy and theology but an essentially non-Protestant (and in some respects anti-Protestant) laity" ("The Church of England, the Catholics and the People," in *The Reign of Elizabeth I*, ed. Christopher Haigh [Houndsmill: Macmillan, 1984], p. 196). In the latter part of Elizabeth's reign, however, evangelical campaigns of reform seem to have made considerable headway.

52. *The English Rite*, ed. F. E. Brightman, 2d ed. rev., 2 vols. (London: Rivingtons, 1921), 2:858. See the remarks in Eamon Duffy, *The Stripping of the Altars: Traditional Religion in England, c.1400–c.1580* (New Haven: Yale University Press, 1992):

> The funeral service of 1549 did contain prayers for the dead, and emphasized their community with the living, "they with us and we with them." That sense of the continuing presence of the dead among the living was vividly expressed in the Sarum funeral rite and in the 1549 prayer-book by the fact that at the moment of the committal of the body to the earth the priest turned to the corpse, scattered earth on it and, in Cranmer's translation, said "I commend thy soule to God the father almighty, and thy body to the grounde, earth to earth, asshes to asshes, dust to dust." The dead could still be spoken to directly, even in 1549, because in some sense they still belonged within the human community. But in the world of the 1552 book the dead were no longer with us. They could neither be spoken to nor even about, in any way that affected their well-being. The dead had gone beyond the reach of human contact, even of human prayer. There was nothing which could even be mistaken for a prayer for the dead in the 1552 funeral rite. The service was no longer a rite of intercession on behalf of the dead, but an exhortation to faith on the part of the living. Indeed, it is not too much to say that the oddest feature of the 1552 burial rite is the disappearance of the corpse from it. So, at the moment of committal in 1552, the minister turns not towards the corpse, but away from it, to the living congregation around the grave. "Forasmuche as it hath pleased almightie God of his great mercy to take unto himselfe the soule of our dere brother here departed: we therefore commit his body to the ground, earth to earth, asshes to asshes, dust to dust." Here the dead person is spoken not to, but about, as one no longer here, but precisely as departed: the boundaries of human community have been redrawn. (475)

It should be noted, however, that *The Book of Common Prayer* does offer "charitable prayers" for the dead, and that the Anglican liturgy has prayers for the souls of all the faithful departed (prayers to which, as Hooker notes, the Puritans objected).

53. Horatio's adjuration to the Ghost uses the language that is the very core of the stories of ghosts who return from Purgatory. In *The Renaissance "Hamlet"*, Frye comments on Horatio's words "If there be any good to be done / That may to thee do ease and grace to me" (1.1.111–12): "That question goes to the heart of the sixteenth-century Roman Catholic system of mortuary endowments, indulgences, masses and prayers, all directed to alleviating the pains of souls in purgatory and to lessening the time which they must spend before passing on to the unmixed bliss of heaven" (22).

54. Anglican burials seemed to Nonconformists to be papist in their ceremonies. The largely Presbyterian Westminster Assembly in 1644 had replaced the *Book of Common Prayer* with its *Directory*, where orders required that the dead be buried publicly, "without any Ceremony." The *Directory* said that "the customes of kneeling down, and praying by, or towards the dead Corps, and other such usages, in the place where it lies, before it be carried to Burial, are superstitious: and for that, praying, reading, and singing both in going to, and at the Grave, have been grosly abused, are no way beneficiall to the dead, and have proved many wayes hurtfull to the living, therefore let all such things be laid aside" (*Directory for the Publique Worship of God* [1644], 73–74). James Pilkington, bishop of Durham from 1561 to 1576, wrote rules for funerals (published posthumously in 1585) in which he insisted "that no superstition should be committed in them, wherein the papists infinitely offend; as in masses, dirges, trentals, singing, ringing, holy water, hallowed places, year's days and month-minds, crosses, pardon letters to be buried with them, mourners, *de profundis* by every lad that could say it, dealing of money solemnly for the dead, watching of the corpse, bell and banner, with many more that I could reckon" (*Works*, ed. James Scholefield, Parker Society, vol. 41 [Cambridge: Cambridge University Press, 1842], 1:399). Of course, wealthy and powerful Protestants were often buried with considerable ceremony, though not with Catholic rites of passage. Thus, for example, Sir Philip Sidney's funeral procession carried a full display of the symbols of his chivalry—shield, crest, helm, sword, spurs, and so forth—which would once have been presented at the offertory of a requiem mass. See J.F.R. Day, "Death Be Very Proud: Sidney, Subversion and Elizabethan Heraldic Funerals," in *Tudor Political Culture*, ed. Dale Hoak (Cambridge: Cambridge University Press, 1995), pp. 179–203, esp. p. 185.

55. It is perhaps worth noting that Laertes' words seem to imply a passage of time before Ophelia's soul reaches its destined end as a ministering angel. Of course, the time could simply be the interval before the priest himself dies and goes to Hell, but there remains something odd about Laertes' locution.

56. Thomas Watson, *The Fight of Faith Crowned: or, a Sermon Preached at the funeral of that Eminently Holy man Mr. Henry Stubs* (London: Joseph Coller at the Bible on London Bridge, 1678), p. 18. I owe this reference to Sharon Achinstein, "Death and Dissent in Restoration England" (unpublished MS). Low ("*Hamlet* and the Ghost of Purgatory*,*" p. 462) comparably quotes Matthew Parker at the

funeral of Martin Bucer in 1551: "Moreover, it agreeth not with the rules of faith, for a christian man to bewayle the dead. For, who can deny that to be against faith, which is flatly forbidden by the scriptures? And how can that be sayed to agree with the rule of fayth, which the scriptures most evidentlye proove to be done by those that have no hope?" In his *Book of Discipline* (1560) John Knox opposed even the funeral sermon, arguing as many reformers did that burial was properly a civil rather than an ecclesiastical office (and pointing out that Scripture—Lev. 21:1—prohibited the presence of clergy at funerals). Knox cautions that "albeit things sung and read may admonish some of the living to prepare themselves for death, yet shall some superstitious and ignorant persons ever think that the works, singing, or reading of the living do and may profit the dead" (cited in Frederic B. Tromly, " 'According to sounde religion': The Elizabethan Controversy over the Funeral Sermon," *Journal of Medieval and Renaissance Studies* 13 (1983): 295). Thomas Cartwright's similar attack—"funeral sermons . . . are put in the place of trentals"—is cited in David Stannard, *The Puritan Way of Death* (New York: 1977), p. 104.

57. Cressy notes that "[p]rayer for the dead was such a deeply engrained practice in mid-Tudor England that it took several decades of preaching and discipline to draw it to a close" (*Birth, Marriage, and Death*, p. 398).

58. In *Twelfth Night*, which was probably written in the same year as *Hamlet*, the countess Olivia has embarked on a course of obstinate and extravagant mourning for her deceased brother. Feste—who elsewhere in the play takes on the part of the curate Sir Topas, in an apparent parody of the noted Puritan exorcist John Darrell—undertakes a mock catechism to prove that Olivia is a fool:

> FESTE. Good madonna, why mournest thou?
> OLIVIA. Good fool, for my brother's death.
> FESTE. I think his soul is in hell, madonna.
> OLIVIA. I know his soul is in heaven, fool.
> FESTE. The more fool, madonna, to mourn for your brother's soul, being
> in heaven.
>
> (1.5.57–62)

59. The "Spiritual Testament" (both the English version of the formulary in its entirety and the document transcribed in the eighteenth century) are printed in James G. McManaway, "John Shakespeare's 'Spiritual Testament,' " *Shakespeare Quarterly* 18 (1967): 197–205. Since the original has been lost, it is not clear whether the document was a blank form on which John Shakespeare simply entered his name or a specially prepared local transcript. McManaway observes that "since the poet's father had no parents living in 1581, the earliest date the testament might have been in distribution in England" (205), the mention of parents in article XII may indicate a form. But "parent," especially in the sixteenth century, could simply mean kinsman. See also John Henry de Groot, *The Shakespeares and "The Old Faith"* (New York: King's Crown Press, 1946), pp. 64–110. The testmonial to the character of the workman who found the document is cited in Samuel Schoenbaum, *William Shakespeare: A Compact Documentary Life* (New York: Oxford University Press, 1977), p. 45.

60. This implication has found support in recent biographical studies that have explored the network of interlinked Catholic families in Lancashire with whom one "William Shakeshafte," possibly a young schoolmaster or player, was connected in the late 1570s or early 1580s.

61. On a possible link between *Hamlet* and More's *Supplication of Souls*, see Vittorio Gabrieli's note in *Notes and Queries* 26 (April 1979): 120–21. See also Robert F. Fleissner, "*Hamlet* and *The Supplication of Souls* Reconvened," *Notes and Queries* 32 (March 1985): 49–51.

62. Thomas More, *The Apology*, ed. J. B. Trapp, Yale Edition of *The Complete Works of St. Thomas More*, 9:76.

63. All citations of Foxe's account are to the introduction of Furnivall's edition of Fish's *A Supplication for the Beggars*. Foxe's mock-title is taken from More's dead, who characterize themselves as "we sely poore pewlyng sowles" (136).

64. Hugh Latimer, "Sermon Preached Before the Convocation of the Clergy," in *The Works of Hugh Latimer*, 2 vols. (Cambridge: Cambridge University Press, 1844), 1:50.

65. Quintilian's *Institutes of Oratory, or Education of an Orator*, trans. John Selby Watson, 2 vols. (London: George Bell, 1902), 2:161. See the similar warning in Puttenham's account of "*Hypotiposis*, or the counterfeit representation": "The matter and occasion leadeth vs many times to describe and set foorth many things, in such sort as it should appeare they were truly before our eyes though they were not present, which to do it requireth cunning: for nothing can be kindly counterfait or represented in his absence, but by great discretion in the doer. And if the things we couet to describe be not naturall or not veritable, than yet the same axeth more cunning to do it, because to faine a thing that neuer was nor is like to be, proceedeth of a great wit and sharper inuention than to describe things that be true." Puttenham goes on to distinguish between *Prosopographia*, which includes the feigning of "the visage, speach and countenance of any person absent or dead" and "*Prosopeia*, or the Counterfeit in personation [*sic*]," which includes giving "reason or speech to dombe creatures or other insensible things" (*The Arte of English Poesie*, ed. Glady Doidge Willcock and Alice Walker [Cambridge: Cambridge University Press, 1936], pp. 238–39).

66. John Foxe, "The Story of M. Symon Fish," Appendix D in the Yale Edition of *The Complete Works of St. Thomas More*, 7:442–43.

67. John Gee, *New Shreds of the Old Snare* (London: Robert Mylbourne, 1624).

68. It is not clear what Gee has in mind, but Kircher's later use of the magic lantern, discussed in chapter 3, suggests one possibility.

69. Gee provides a mock justification of the high price: the play is performed for only a single spectator, and therefore the players "must haue as much of that one as if they had an whole Theater full" (21). Moreover, even if there is only one actor onstage, there is a large staff inside the "tyring-house, that take a great

deale of paines to proiect the plot, to instruct the Actor, and to furnish him with habit and ornament. And who can tell how many sharers there are that must take part of that which is paid?" (21).

1. We know that he entertained the idea of posthumous existence in his sonnets. The "living record" of his beloved, he writes in sonnet 55, will outlast marble and the gilded monuments of princes.

> 'Gainst death and all oblivious enmity
> Shall you pace forth.

Through the incantatory power of the poet's verse, the fair young man will defy mortality and walk the earth—pace forth—like a ghost. Though the grave contracts the space of human existence to nothing, though oblivion is the fate of the proudest of mortals, the beloved will continue to inhabit the world:

> [Y]our praise shall still find room
> Even in the eyes of all posterity
> That wear this world out to the ending doom.
> So, till the judgement that yourself arise,
> You live in this, and dwell in lovers' eyes.

The claim could scarcely be more magnificently extravagant: for the beloved, the interval between death and judgment, between the body's dissolution and its resurrection, will not be a story of inexorable vanishing. It will instead be a story of miraculous survival: "[Y]our praise shall still find room / Even in the eyes of all posterity."

But posterity has in fact altogether lost the youth's identity—centuries of feverish effort have failed to give him a convincing local habitation and a name—and perhaps this loss is entirely appropriate. The life, the room, the dwelling that the poet lovingly conferred upon him was always and only "in this"—that is, in the poem. The pacing forth signifies not, it turns out, the creaking footsteps of a ghost but the sweet cadences of a sonnet:

> Not marble nor the gilded monuments
> Of princes shall outlive this powerful rhyme,
> But you shall shine more bright in these contents
> Than unswept stone besmeared with sluttish time.

Swept or unswept, stones have the names of the dead indelibly carved in them—that is the whole point of using stone—but Shakespeare's powerful rhymes name no names. We know next to nothing about the young man—sluttish time has taken care of that—though the lines in which he is praised continue, as the poet hoped, to possess an eerie and intense life.

2. Shakespeare seems to have had little or no interest in the kind of posthumous existence that the cult of Purgatory and prayers for the dead had helped to foster: the continued claims after death of particular named individuals. Long after Purgatory had been officially labeled a fiction and prayers for the dead

had been outlawed, poets could continue to serve these claims. We have only to think of Ben Jonson's exquisite epitaphs for his son Benjamin and his daughter Mary or John Donne's anniversary commemorations of Elizabeth Drury. But Shakespeare's interest lay elsewhere. He seems to have written a small number of epitaphs—for Elias James, John Combe, Edward or Thomas Stanley, and possibly for his own bones—and he may have written the long, largely tedious funeral elegy for William Peter. But none of these modest efforts participates in a meaningful way in any cult of the dead. What shines brightest in the traces Shakespeare left behind are not the memories of the actual people among whom he lived—his parents, his wife, his son Hamnet, his daughters Judith and Susanna, his nameless lovers—and not even his own unchronicled identity but rather his imaginary characters. The question is what claims these unreal men and women can possibly make upon us.